UNDERGROUND WARFARE

Underground Warfare

Daphné Richemond-Barak

UNIVERSITY PRESS

Underground Warfare. Daphné Richemond-Barak.
© Oxford University Press 2018. Published 2018 by Oxford University Press.

UNIVERSITY PRESS

Oxford University Press is a department of the University of Oxford. It furthers the University's objective of excellence in research, scholarship, and education by publishing worldwide. Oxford is a registered trademark of Oxford University Press in the UK and certain other countries.

Published in the United States of America by Oxford University Press
198 Madison Avenue, New York, NY 10016, United States of America.

© Oxford University Press 2018

All rights reserved. No part of this publication may be reproduced, stored in a retrieval system, or transmitted, in any form or by any means, without the prior permission in writing of Oxford University Press, or as expressly permitted by law, by license, or under terms agreed with the appropriate reproduction rights organization. Inquiries concerning reproduction outside the scope of the above should be sent to the Rights Department, Oxford University Press, at the address above.

You must not circulate this work in any other form
and you must impose this same condition on any acquirer.

Library of Congress Cataloging-in-Publication Data
Names: Richemond-Barak, Daphné, author.
Title: Underground warfare / Daphné Richemond-Barak.
Description: New York : Oxford University Press, 2018. | Includes bibliographical references and index.
Identifiers: LCCN 2017021976 | ISBN 9780190457242 ((hardback) : alk. paper) | ISBN 9780190457259 ((pbk.) : alk. paper)
Subjects: LCSH: Tunnel warfare (International law)
Classification: LCC KZ6429 .R53 2017 | DDC 341.6/3—dc23
LC record available at https://lccn.loc.gov/2017021976

9 8 7 6 5 4 3 2 1

Paperback printed by Webcom, Inc., Canada
Hardback printed by Bridgeport National Bindery, Inc., United States of America

Note to Readers
This publication is designed to provide accurate and authoritative information in regard to the subject matter covered. It is based upon sources believed to be accurate and reliable and is intended to be current as of the time it was written. It is sold with the understanding that the publisher is not engaged in rendering legal, accounting, or other professional services. If legal advice or other expert assistance is required, the services of a competent professional person should be sought. Also, to confirm that the information has not been affected or changed by recent developments, traditional legal research techniques should be used, including checking primary sources where appropriate.

(Based on the Declaration of Principles jointly adopted by a Committee of the American Bar Association and a Committee of Publishers and Associations.)

You may order this or any other Oxford University Press publication by visiting the Oxford University Press website at www.oup.com.

Contents

Acknowledgments   ix
Introduction   xi

1. Tunnels in Conflict: Ancient Uses and Contemporary Threats   1
    I.   A Feature of War from Time Immemorial   3
    II.   State-to-State Tunnel Mining during World War I   5
    III. World War II and the Challenge of Entrenched Japanese Forces   8
    IV. Civilians and Combatants in the Vietcong's Tunnels   9
    V.   The Cross-Border Threat: The North Korean Tunnels   12
    VI. The Use of Underground Caves and Tunnels by the Mujahedeen in Afghanistan   13
    VII. More of the Same: The Allied War in Afghanistan   15
    VIII. A Different Type of Tunnel in Libya   17
    IX. Ten Years On: AQIM Entrenches in Mali   19
    X.   From Smuggling to Terror: Hamas's Tunnels at the Gaza-Egypt Border   22
    XI. Hamas's Tunnels at the Israeli Border: Underground Warfare Meets Urban Warfare   24
    XII. The Widespread and Innovative Use of Tunnels in Syria   30
    XIII. ISIS's Tunnels in Iraq   33
    Conclusion   35

2. Underground Warfare: From a Tool of War to a Global Security Threat   37
    I.   A Global Threat: The Diffusion of Underground Warfare across Battlefields   38
    II.   A Typology of Tunnels   44
    III. Tomorrow's Underground Warfare   50
    Conclusion   53

3. Sovereignty over the Underground   55
   I.   Sovereignty over the Underground under Domestic Law   56
   II. Sovereignty over the Underground under International Law   60
   III. Law of the Sea—Compared   65
   IV. Air Law and Space Law—Compared   69
   Conclusion   72

4. Contending with Tunnels: Law, Strategy, and Methods   75
   I.   Applicable Law   76
        A. *Jus ad Bellum*   76
        B. Human Rights Law   76
        C. International Humanitarian Law   78
        D. The Law of Occupation and the *Jus Post Bellum*   79
   II. Strategy and Methods   85
        A. Why a Strategy   86
        B. Components of a Full-Fledged Underground Warfare Strategy   87
           1. Detection and Mapping   88
           2. Neutralization and/or Destruction   104
           3. Prevention and Monitoring   111
           4. Cooperation: Countering the Diffusion of Tactics   114
   Conclusion   116

5. Underground Warfare and the *Jus* ad Bellum   119
   I.   Strategic Factors Affecting the *Jus ad Bellum* Analysis   123
   II. Underground Threats Giving Rise to a Right of Self-Defense   126
        A. Tunnel(s) as Armed Attack   127
        B. Preemptive and Anticipatory Self-Defense   132
   III. Underground Threats *Not* Giving Rise to a Right of Self-Defense   135
        A. Violation of Sovereignty and Territorial Integrity   135
        B. Illegal Intervention in the Affairs of Another State   138
        C. Illegal Threat or Use of Force   139
        D. Possible Responses   143
           1. Countermeasures   143
           2. The Plea of Necessity   147
           3. Involvement of the UN Security Council   154
   Conclusion   157

6. Underground Warfare and the *Jus in Bello: General Considerations*   161
   I.   Legality and Status of Tunnels under IHL   164
        A. The Applicable Legal Framework: Key Principles   164
        B. Defining a Tunnel under IHL   168

C. The Legality of Digging and Using Tunnels in War　172
　　　D. The Legal Status of Tunnels under IHL　177
　　　　　1. Tunnels as Military Objectives　177
　　　　　2. Tunnels as War-Sustaining Objects　182
　II. The Unknown Factor and Its Implications for IHL　184
　III. Weapons Underground　195
　　　A. Unnecessary Suffering and Military Necessity　196
　　　B. Non-lethal Weapons　205
　Conclusion　206

7. Underground Warfare in Urban Areas　209
　I. Underground Warfare Meets Urban Warfare: Tunnels *near* Civilians　210
　　　A. The Spread of Underground Warfare to Civilian Populated Areas　211
　　　B. State Practice and Civilian Protection　215
　　　C. The Legality of Urban Tunnels under IHL　218
　II. The Use of Tunnels *by* Civilians　222
　　　A. The Unknown Factor and Urban Tunnels　223
　　　B. How Civilian Presence Affects Anti-Tunnel Operations　226
　　　　　1. Targetable v. Non-targetable Civilians　227
　　　　　2. Detection and Mapping　231
　　　　　3. Neutralization and/or Destruction　234
　III. The Use of Tunnels *against* Civilians　240
　IV. Urban Tunnels and Reflexive Obligations under IHL　244
　Conclusion　248

Conclusion　251

INDEX　257

Acknowledgments

THIS BOOK IS dedicated to my grandmother, Viviane, of blessed memory, whose calm, inspiration, and support have guided me and provided me with strength for decades. Those who knew her will understand that I cannot mention her without also mentioning my grandfather, Prosper, whose genes—though not genius—I definitely inherited. I owe him for my deep fascination with the workings of international law.

I would also like to dedicate this book to the soldiers who have experienced the fear, darkness, and uncertainty of the subterranean. Despite predicting otherwise in the book, I express here the sincere hope that soldiers will no longer have to engage in the horrors of underground warfare.

Thanks go, first and foremost, to the Interdisciplinary Center (IDC) Herzliya, my home for the past eight years. I admire the institution I belong to and its founder, Professor Uriel Reichman, for the strength, audacity, and hard work involved in its establishment. As a French-born and UK- and US-educated academic, I cherish its international feel and open-mindedness. There are no words to describe the innovation-driven and academically stimulating environment of the Lauder School of Government, Diplomacy and Strategy. Its Dean, Professor Boaz Ganor, has been a mentor and an inspiration for a decade, even before I joined the IDC. This book would not have been possible without his long-standing moral, institutional, and intellectual support.

Professor William C. Banks, whose friendship and collaboration I value immensely, deserves all my gratitude for reading the entire manuscript and doing so much more along the way to this project's completion. I also greatly benefited from eye-opening conversations with Professor Michael Schmitt, who challenged my assumptions and helped me make my way through countermeasures. I am truly lucky to have had Professors Ganor, Banks, and Schmitt by my side throughout this endeavor. Their encouragement, guidance, and (constructive) criticism have had the most meaningful impact. Any mistake remains mine and mine only, of course.

This book would not have been written without the vision and trust of my editor, Blake Ratcliff, who believed in this project before tunnels even made headlines. Trust was also demonstrated by my anonymous reviewers, as well as countless experts—military and state officials, academics, geologists and others—who agreed to meet with me and share their wisdom. Not all of them wish to be named but I am indebted to each of them for helping me understand the subterranean.

I cannot but acknowledge the assistance I received from three outstandingly smart women, who played critical roles at different stages of the process: Danit Gal, Polina Beliakova, and Rebecca Baskin Zafrir. Their analytical skills and creative thinking were invaluable. Special thanks also go to Ran Yosef, Katja Knoechelmann, Nissim Ben Ephraim, Efrat Sznaj, Eden Lapidor, Kelsey Davidson, and Shai Shalgi.

I am grateful for the support of The Minerva Center for the Rule of Law under Extreme Conditions, Faculty of Law and Department of Geography and Environmental Studies, University of Haifa. I also wish to thank the American Society of International Law, the Minerva Center for Human Rights, Faculty of Law, at the Hebrew University of Jerusalem, the International Committee of the Red Cross, the Institute for Policy and Strategy at IDC Herzliya and others for inviting me to present my work on underground warfare. I gained so much from exchanges with colleagues on these and other occasions. I am grateful, in particular, to Laurie Blank, Geoffrey Corn, and Ido Rosenzweig for their suggestions and their friendship.

The most heartfelt thanks go to my colleagues at the Lauder School of Government, Diplomacy and Strategy for their invaluable insights—acknowledged in the book itself—over lunch and other more formal get-togethers.

I do not know if I should thank my husband and my children—or apologize to them for the time and energy I devoted to writing this book. Their understanding, genuine interest, and unparalleled patience made it all possible.

Last but not least, I would like to thank my parents for occupying the children on countless occasions so I could complete this book. Together with my husband, they are probably most relieved to know I'm through.

Thank you.

Introduction

THE DISCOVERY OF the Zhawar Kili tunnel complex in Afghanistan by the United States, only a few months after 9/11, was met with disbelief. The maze of tunnels had been built to fight the Soviets in the 1980s, and used again by Osama bin Laden in the late 1990s. Much more than a series of underground passages, Zhawar Kili included 70 interconnecting tunnels where al-Qaeda kept tanks, artillery, anti-aircraft guns, explosives, and ammunition.[1] The underground complex was much larger than the forces had expected or prepared for.

A decade later, al-Qaeda and its affiliates entrenched again—this time in the mountains of Northern Mali.[2] They stockpiled ammunition, trained recruits, and launched attacks from nearly impregnable underground hideouts.[3] French and Chadian forces were taken by surprise. Having failed to intercept any communications for weeks, they did not anticipate what awaited them in this particularly challenging terrain.

---

[1] Steve Vogel, *Al Qaeda Tunnels, Arms Cache Totaled*, WASH. POST (Feb. 16, 2002), https://www.washingtonpost.com/archive/politics/2002/02/16/al-qaeda-tunnels-arms-cache-totaled/29166b3c-29ce-4252-a95b-51d9b3ebac92/?utm_term=.f98a2256703d.

[2] Associated Press, *Al-Qaeda Stronghold Grows in Mali*, NY DAILY NEWS (Dec. 31, 2012), http://www.nydailynews.com/news/world/al-qaeda-stronghold-grows-mali-article-1.1230181#ixzz2yT8Ql5f2.

[3] Chris Hughes, *Mali Menace: Why We Will End Up Fighting Al-Qaeda's Army in Africa*, MIRROR (Jan. 16, 2013), http://www.mirror.co.uk/news/uk-news/mali-menace-why-we-will-end-up-fighting-1536512; Rukmini Callimachi, *Al Qaeda Fighters Carve Out Own Country in Mali*, WASH. POST (Jan. 16, 2013), http://www.washingtontimes.com/news/2013/jan/16/al-qaeda-fighters-carve-out-their-own-country/.

Fast forward to October 2013 in kibbutz Ein Hashlosha, Israel. The IDF discovers a cross-border tunnel originating in Gaza and exiting in close proximity to the Israeli kibbutz.[4] The tunnel, built by Hamas, was 65 feet deep and over 8,000 feet long. Its construction required 800 tons of concrete.[5]

The mountains of Afghanistan, Northern Mali, and the Israeli kibbutz of Ein Hashlosha all form part of the ever-expanding modern battlefield. The United States, the United Kingdom, France, and Israel may face different enemies in different places, but their enemies' modus operandi is strikingly similar: IEDs, raids on remote bases, suicide bombings, and now tunnels that enable non-conventional forces to hide, plan and carry out attacks and store and smuggle ammunition.

On this battlefield, the appeal of the underground cannot be underestimated. States' intelligence, surveillance, and reconnaissance (ISR) capabilities have significantly improved in the past two decades, widening the gap between tech-savvy belligerents and those with lesser capabilities. Satellite imagery and drones have increased the amount and quality of information available to decision-makers in real time—making those operating aboveground and in open terrain highly vulnerable. In parallel, sophisticated militaries have also improved the processing of such information by enhancing data analysis. They are more able than ever to anticipate impending attacks. Weapon systems equipped with a plethora of sensors can be operated remotely and with greater precision, keeping forces out of harm's way and collateral damage to a minimum (though not always). Information flows much faster and decision-making processes have been streamlined to ensure that targeting decisions can be made in just a few minutes. Technology-enabled ISR has a greater impact than ever before on situational awareness and the conduct of operations. In this context, the underground offers a valuable and virtually impenetrable refuge. Inside tunnels, operatives and soldiers can operate undetected and with minimal exposure to enemy ISR systems. By employing tunnel tactics, the weaker party forces the stronger, more conventional party to enter its terrain (a terrain often unfamiliar to them), thereby decreasing the relative advantage that comes with sophisticated modern armor, surveillance, intelligence, and training. New tunneling technology, including noise reduction capabilities and advanced digging equipment, intensifies this trend.

Like other aspects of modern warfare, the renewed use of the underground by violent nonstate actors presents a challenge to liberal democracies. In my view, this challenge has not only been underexplored in the scholarship, but is also largely underestimated by the community of states, security experts, and public opinion. The lack of a systematic treatment of underground warfare in history, military theory, and law has left states without resources or records of state practice to turn to. Historically, no attempt has been made to analyze

---

[4] *Gaza "Terror Tunnel" Uncovered Inside Israel, Says Army*, BBC News (Oct. 13, 2013), http://www.bbc.com/news/world-middle-east-24512761.

[5] *Tunnel May Signal Shift in Hamas-Israel Conflict*, AL-MONITOR (Oct., 2013), http://www.al-monitor.com/pulse/originals/2013/10/gaza-tunnel-israel-shift-hamas-war.html#ixzz2ySz5MtgH.

the evolution of underground tactics or to compare the various ways in which the tactic has been used. All major works dealing with underground warfare focus on a given conflict. I am certainly no historian, and my historical account is undoubtedly selective. Yet I believe in the value of such a historical account. I have cherry-picked those events in an effort to identify patterns of usage, relevant actors, tunnel features, and innovation in this unique environment.

Military theory, too, has remained quite silent about the underground. Although sporadic acknowledgments of the specificity of the subterranean can be found, it is difficult to gauge how states' military doctrine accounts for underground warfare in general: Is the decision-making process any different when underground threats arise? Are all units trained in underground warfare, or only specialized ones? When it exists, what does such training consist of? Questions abound, but answers are scarce, to say the least. Finally, in the legal realm, the silence is deafening. No treaty, no doctrine, no piece of legal scholarship has ever mentioned the underground. Although air, naval, and cyberwarfare have all received attention, underground warfare has been completely left out of the conversation—despite its recurrent use in war.

This book hopes to fill these gaps. As the first of its kind, it provides a blueprint for conceptualizing the threat, offers suggestions on how to minimize it, and addresses legal questions that arise in the process. This is no simple task given that, as mentioned above, little previous scholarship exists. I overcome these challenges by drawing upon a multitude of fields, using analogies (particularly in the legal analysis), and constantly verifying assumptions (either via interviews or with the help of the data collected through *New York Times* reports, as I explain further below).

The methodological difficulties, however, did not quell my urge to expose the various facets of this form of warfare. Despite the prevailing belief, I was convinced that waging war underground is not "the same thing" as waging war aboveground, from either an operational or a legal standpoint. I also believed that the risks tunnels pose to civilians deserved to be better understood. Finally, I was eager to reconcile the legal constraints with the relatively aggressive anti-tunnel measures adopted by states over the course of history. Accordingly, history, law, and operational constraints constitute indispensable components of this book.

History shows that states have taken extreme measures to prevail in tunnel wars. American forces used tear gas to clear tunnels in Vietnam,[6] and the Soviet army used explosives and chemical agents to destroy tunnel complexes and everything inside them during the Afghan-Soviet War.[7] Such tactics would likely be regarded as unlawful today, raising some concerns about how states ought to contend with contemporary underground warfare. Developments in international law have changed not only how liberal

---

[6] *See* Thomas Dethlefs, *Tear Gas and the Politics of Lethality: Emerging from the Haze*, 2 YALE HIST. REV. 83 (2013).

[7] *See* M. HASSAN KAKAR, AFGHANISTAN: THE SOVIET INVASION AND THE AFGHAN RESPONSE, 1979–1982, at 220 (1995).

democracies perceive challenges, but also how they counter them. Covering more aspects of warfare and more conflicts, international humanitarian law has come to bind states, even against the least law-abiding enemies. The historical review also helps understand why and how belligerents have used tunnels in conflict, and anticipate future trends.

As mentioned above, **international law** does not address the underground or tunnel warfare as such. Some would interpret this silence as suggesting that tunnel warfare does not raise distinct legal issues. This book challenges that view. The legal analysis demonstrates the uniqueness of the challenge at all stages of a tunnel's construction and use. While under construction, tunnels pose a substantial risk to those digging them—often children—and to any civilian structures under which they are dug. Filled with explosives and weapons, tunnels can detonate at any time, risking not only the lives of the diggers and operatives who use them, but also those of civilians living above them. In contrast to Cold War-era tunnels in the mountains of Afghanistan, today's tunnels are increasingly dug and employed in the midst of civilian populated areas. In Aleppo and Mosul, tunnels originate in, lead to, or pass under homes, schools, religious sites, and business premises. Tunnels in Egypt and Israel lead from civilian areas on one state's territory to civilian areas on another's. These cross-border tunnels raise their own set of issues, and I analyze them in depth in the book.

Equally challenging are the conditions in which tunnels may be eliminated—particularly those dug in or near civilian populated areas. The destruction of a tunnel inevitably results in the destruction of civilian structures above the subterranean passage, and in many cases the loss of civilian lives. Destroying a tunnel typically necessitates the exercise of massive force from above or finding its access points and destroying it from within. An explosion in one part of a tunnel may inflict unforeseen damage on different and potentially unknown segments of the tunnel, or even to the land surrounding it—including any schools, civilian homes, and businesses located in the vicinity. In legal terms, this means that a tunnel's interconnected infrastructure impedes the assessment of proportionality prior to its destruction, that is, the determination of whether collateral damage resulting from the destruction of the tunnel might be excessive in relation to the military advantage anticipated from that destruction. Even careful mapping of a tunnel ahead of a strike may not suffice to ascertain collateral damage, as tunnels can be expanded rapidly and relatively discreetly.

Yet there is no other option but to destroy tunnels once they have been detected. Tunnels must be destroyed for the threat to be eliminated. When tunnels are not eliminated they can be "inherited" by other actors—sometimes centuries later. The Cù Chi underground complex was inherited from Viet Minh nationalist guerrillas that used them in the anticolonial struggle with France. Al-Qaeda inherited the underground hideouts dug by the Mujahedeen when fighting the Soviets in the 1980s, and ISIS inherited Saddam Hussein's tunnels. This pattern of inheritance highlights the need to eliminate tunnels: until tunnels are fully eliminated, they continue to pose a security threat and endanger any civilians living near them—and in the case of cross-border tunnels, civilians and protected objects *on both sides* of the conflict.

Underground warfare also intensifies some of the dilemmas encountered more generally on the contemporary battlefield. For example, it pushes the limits of the requirement of advance warning: leaflets, text messages, and social media—commonly used when fighting in highly populated areas—are hardly helpful when the battle is underground. Human shielding, a constant and heavily debated feature of urban warfare, also takes on grave undertones in the underground context. States may be unaware of the presence of civilians in a tunnel. Even when they gain knowledge of such presence, ascertaining with precision *how many* civilians are hiding inside a tunnel can be impossible. The difficulty of gaining access to information magnifies the consequences of human shielding, thereby maximizing its appeal.

The **operational complexity** of underground warfare forms the third axis of this book for at least two reasons. First, without understanding the operational complexity, it is difficult to make sense of the relatively aggressive nature of anti-tunnel measures that states have used against underground threats. Tunnels trigger feelings of helplessness on many levels—psychological, technological, operational, tactical, and more. These feelings shape the nature of the response. Second, the complexity of the terrain has a direct impact on the application of the law. A lack of familiarity with the subterranean can lead to flawed legal assessments, impose unrealistic expectations on states, and impact compliance negatively.

The main complexity, referred to in this book as the "unknown factor," permeates virtually every aspect of anti-tunnel operations from the strategic level down to the tactical level, and even the technical level—and in degrees exponentially higher than in aboveground operations. Once inside a tunnel, a soldier is very much alone. GPS systems do not work underground, and although states have invested in GPS-free localization technology—such as boot sensors that track a person's footsteps underground[8]—it is largely experimental. Finding one's way inside a tunnel can be a challenge. Border patrols working inside the cross-border tunnels between the United States and Mexico report the difficulty in establishing whether a tunnel has crossed the border. Inside a tunnel, a soldier is also disconnected from the rest of the troops, as usual means of communication are not available. This explains how, in the summer of 2014, Hamas's operatives located inside a tunnel may have been unaware that a ceasefire had been brokered with Israel.[9]

The unknown factor also significantly diminishes incoming intelligence. Underground warfare offers none of the "visibility" of aboveground operations. Knowing where the enemy is hiding, assessing the extent of its destructive capabilities, and localizing the threat present a nearly insurmountable challenge in the context of underground warfare.[10]

---

[8] Michael Keller, *GPS-Free Tech Can Track Miners' and Soldiers' Boots Underground*, SCI. AM. (Oct. 23, 2012), http://www.scientificamerican.com/article/gps-free-tech-can-track-miners-and-soldiers-boots-underground/.
[9] Robert Naiman, *Gaza Ceasefire Collapses; What Should We Do Now?*, Huffington Post (Aug. 1, 2014), http://www.huffingtonpost.com/robert-naiman/gaza-ceasefire-collapses-_b_5641634.html.
[10] Kassam rocket launchers are increasingly placed underground to make sure that the precise location of the launcher remains secret. *See* Yasser Okbi, *Islamic Jihad Unveils Underground Rocket Launchers Used to Target*

Choosing which weapons to use and what level of force to exercise can be a difficult call for military commanders when they do not know what is going on underground. Even the consequences of simple operations—blowing up a tunnel entrance, for example—cannot be predicted with any degree of certainty. The difficulty in detecting tunnels and gaining access to enemy communications also complicates the forces' understanding of the enemy's modus operandi (including its organizational structure, available arsenal, and relationship with other groups).

So while underground warfare resembles ordinary urban warfare in many ways, it raises distinct operational and legal issues that should not be underestimated. Tunnels that burrow under civilian populated areas and protected sites such as hospitals or schools—that is, the combination of urban warfare and tunnel warfare, which sets Gaza apart from Afghanistan and Mali—present the greatest challenge both militarily and legally.

To sum up, this book makes three main points: *first*, underground warfare has re-emerged on contemporary battlefields as a global and rapidly diffusing threat favored by violent nonstate actors; *second*, underground warfare raises operational and legal issues—some that are truly unique to the terrain, and others that magnify dilemmas encountered in contemporary warfare more generally; *third*, the growing and concerning proximity between tunnels and civilians will make it more difficult to counter underground threats and apply core legal principles going forward.

The unique features of underground warfare emerge from Chapter 1, which paints a panoramic and multifaceted picture of tunnel warfare across time and geography. As noted above, I do not focus on any single conflict or type of tunnel. Rather, I address underground warfare as a global phenomenon that raises unique challenges under international law, and that is currently benefiting from strategic and technological tailwinds. I begin with World War I, which has marked history with powerful tunnel mining attacks, face-to-face underground combat, and the demonstration of how tunnel users improve their skills on the go (I call this the learning curve).

State-to-state underground warfare continued during World War II, in two main forms. First, bunkers and other underground structures were dug for defensive purposes—either to deter invasions, such as the Maginot Line, or, in the case of those built by Hitler, as safe living quarters and command-and-control structures. The other type of underground use witnessed during World War II was more offensive in nature and took place on the Japanese islands, where Allied forces faced the deceptive use of tunnels by the Japanese Army. Although Japanese forces did not prevail, their use of the underground underscores the versatility of the subterranean. It also shows that tunnels have the potential of

---

Israel, Jerusalem Post (Mar. 13, 2014), http://www.jpost.com/Middle-East/Islamic-Jihad-unviels-underground-rocket-launcher-used-to-target-Israel-345264; *Israel Attacks Two Sites in Gaza Strip*, Al Jazeera (Feb. 13, 2014), http://www.aljazeera.com/news/middleeast/2014/02/israel-attacks-two-sites-gaza-strip-20142117438628461.html.

inflicting high casualties and causing maximum operational and psychological hardship to the enemy—even though they are not usually sufficient to impact the broader war.

The Vietcong knew this well. The underground enabled them to establish a more level playing field with U.S. forces, and momentarily overcome the discrepancy in the belligerents' respective military capabilities. As in the Pacific theater of WWII, this was not sufficient to win the war, but it did pose a painful challenge to the United States, both in terms of harm to American soldiers and the country's image. The Vietcong innovated in that they brought their tunnels close to civilians by digging underneath cities, even allowing women to give birth in underground military hospitals. This changed the nature of underground warfare forever. Two wars in Afghanistan, decades apart, saw a reversion to a more traditional use of caves and underground structures, of a nonurban and exclusively military nature.

The cross-border threat posed by the underground also became apparent when South Korea discovered tunnels dug by North Korea under the Demilitarized Zone. The tactic was picked up by Hamas and implemented on two different fronts: at the border with Egypt and at the border with Israel. Hamas's underground tactics underscore the inadequacy of conceptualizing tunnels based on their purpose. With a cross-border tunnel inevitably comes a security threat. Tunnels dug for smuggling goods can be used for terror—and vice versa. Hamas's cross-border tunnels also embody the modern equivalent of the Vietcong's strategy: by bringing tunnels closer to civilian centers, Hamas has rendered them at times untouchable.

From Gaza, tunnel tactics made their way to Syria and Iraq. Tunnel mining and tunnel combat—both features hardly seen since World War II—made a successful comeback in Syria. In Iraq, ISIS has dug extensive underground networks connecting civilian homes and buildings, providing fighters with long-term hideouts and endless ways to surprise the enemy in places such as Sinjar, Fallujah, and Mosul.

Though the type of actor, tunnel, and use may differ, the resurgence of underground warfare as an element of contemporary conflicts is undeniable. The United States, Canada, Israel, and NATO member states have all contended with tunnel warfare in the past decade—in one form or another.

It is important to point here to a related and widespread significant phenomenon that this book does not directly address, known as "deeply buried facilities."[11] Deeply buried facilities are typically constructed by militarily sophisticated states to ensure leadership

---

[11] NATIONAL SECURITY ARCHIVE, UNDERGROUND FACILITIES: INTELLIGENCE AND TARGETING ISSUES, U.S. INTELLIGENCE: HIDING OF MILITARY ASSETS BY "ROGUE NATIONS" AND OTHER STATES A MAJOR SECURITY CHALLENGE FOR THE 21ST CENTURY (Nat'l Sec. Archive Electronic Briefing Book No. 439, Mar. 12, 2012), http://nsarchive.gwu.edu/NSAEBB/NSAEBB372/ ("In 1999, a Defense Intelligence Agency assessment of the threat for the following twenty years stated that 'The proliferation of underground facilities in recent years has emerged as one of the most difficult challenges facing the U.S. intelligence community and is projected to become even more of a problem over the next two decades.'")

protection, weapon production, and/or the preservation of command, control, and communications capabilities in times of crisis. No one, however, anticipates that soldiers will ever fight inside deeply buried facilities. Israel, China, Iran, and Canada all possess such facilities. Although their proliferation is not in doubt and has been identified in some quarters as a security priority, their existence and features are generally kept highly secret.

Deeply buried facilities are larger, better equipped, more reinforced, and deeper than tunnels (Iran's are reportedly dug 1,600 feet into the ground, whereas most tunnels do not reach beyond 100 or so feet)[12]—and, as a result, typically beyond the reach of even the most powerful weapons. Interestingly, much of the technology now used to detect tunnels was initially developed to locate deeply buried facilities.

Although they are not described or addressed here in detail, deeply buried facilities raise many of the same issues as tunnels and other "lighter" underground structures and complexes. States perceive them as military and strategic assets of the enemy. Like tunnels, deeply buried facilities complicate the assessment of the enemy's destructive capabilities and hinder the anticipation of a first strike. The proliferation of deeply buried facilities and tunnels points to the same fact: the appeal of the underground. Whereas states have penetrated to the depths of the earth to hide their most valuable military arsenal and ensure continuity of command and the safety of leaders in time of emergency, nonstates are using the underground to shield themselves from technology and operate undetected. How a party makes use of the underground therefore depends on its capabilities.[13]

As mentioned above, this book does not directly address deeply buried facilities. It focuses instead on individual tunnels and tunnel complexes (either man-made or naturally formed) whose use can lead to an armed conflict or benefit one of the belligerents in times of war. Although the book does occasionally discuss the discovery of tunnels in peacetime, the emphasis is on the use of tunnels in armed conflict.

Chapter 2 builds on the past to learn about the future: How does today's use of tunnels differ from yesterday's? What will tomorrow's underground warfare look like? In order to answer these questions, I supplement the historical narrative with a database of over 40 years of *New York Times* reports on the use of tunnels in conflict. The data—albeit limited and somewhat imperfect from a purely empirical standpoint—fills some of the holes left by the absence of literature. It also confirms trends and patterns identified in the historical review. Finally, it helps shape a typology of tunnels, providing a conceptual and analytical tool I frequently return to in the book.

---

[12] Agence France-Presse, *Iran Reveals Huge Underground Missile Base with Broadcast on State TV*, GUARDIAN (Oct. 15, 2015), https://www.theguardian.com/world/2015/oct/15/iran-reveals-huge-underground-missile-base-with-broadcast-on-state-tv.

[13] Although this book maintains the dichotomy between deeply buried facilities and tunnels, with a focus on the latter, the dichotomy does lose some of its relevance in the context of large underground complexes such as Zhawar Kili built by al-Qaeda in Afghanistan.

Chapter 2 also encapsulates one of this book's major arguments, namely that underground warfare is likely to intensify and continue its rapid diffusion in the coming years. As noted above, tunnels have proven remarkably versatile and effective, particularly for nonstate actors in asymmetric conflicts. As a result, tunneling tactics that have proved successful on one battlefield have been "exported" to other conflicts. Abu Assad, the celebrated mastermind behind a 2014 tunnel mining operation in Aleppo, claimed to have been inspired by a Palestinian who had visited Syria.[14] It is not surprising that tunnels later spread from Syria to Iraq, and similar attacks can be expected in other theaters of operation as well.[15] Even Europe can no longer consider itself immune to the threat, with jihadi volunteers returning to Western Europe (and to a lesser extent North America) following battlefield experience in Syria and Iraq.[16]

Unless technology renders tunnels obsolete—something which has not happened in thousands of years—underground warfare will continue to spread, following a pattern of diffusion resembling that of suicide terrorism. The practice will be adopted by relatively young and/or flexible nonstate actors who have the organizational capacity to adapt and are not set on specific methods.

In trying to decipher international law's take on the underground, Chapter 3 searches for answers in general principles of the law. Does international law recognize state sovereignty over the underground as it does for air, land, and space, or does sovereignty over the underground fall into an unregulated loophole? This matters, inter alia, for determining the legality of tunnel-digging and anti-tunnel operations, and ascertaining a state's right to respond to cross-border tunnels.

Although international law delineates the contours of sovereignty over land, sea, and space, sovereignty over the underground is only regulated sporadically and unsystematically as part of the law of the sea, the law governing transboundary aquifers, and the right to natural resources. A close analysis of these sources reveals that states have sovereignty over underground resources located in areas under their control or jurisdiction, provided these rights have not been transferred to private entities. I argue that the same principles governing sovereignty over land, air, and water—sovereignty, development, shared resources, cooperation, and peace and security—should apply to the underground. Penetrating the underground space beneath a neighboring state therefore constitutes a violation of the neighboring state's sovereignty. It is unclear, however, whether such

---

[14] Martin Chulov, *Aleppo's Most Wanted Man—the Rebel Leader Behind Tunnel Bombs*, GUARDIAN (May 20, 2014), https://www.theguardian.com/world/2014/may/20/aleppos-most-wanted-man-rebel-leader-tunnel-bombs.

[15] *See* Yaron Friedman, *From Damascus to Gaza: The Under-World War*, YNET (July 21, 2014), http://www.ynet.co.il/articles/0,7340,L-4547290,00.html (in Hebrew; free translation) ("Terror tunnels are likely to inspire other Jihadist groups and threaten the borders of other states in the region. The Islamic State may infiltrate behind the lines of the Jordanian army in the South and into Kurdish territory in the North. Al Nusra in Syria may build tunnels into Lebanon and the Golan Heights. The tunnel war of the Jihadist groups (...) is likely to threaten most state leaders in the region in the future.").

[16] *Brussels Jewish Museum Murders: Nemmouche to be Extradited*, BBC NEWS (June 26, 2014).

sovereignty extends to all layers until the center of the earth and to the entirety of the subsoil under the ocean. Could a very, very deep tunnel circumvent sovereignty altogether? International law provides clear guidance as to where state sovereignty over the underground ends at sea, but no such consensus exists as to where air law ends and space law begins. The underground most resembles the latter: the depth at which state sovereignty over the underground ends is uncertain and will likely evolve with time and technological advances. Deep underground digging for non-peaceful purposes should also be prohibited, as in the legal regimes governing the outer space and the seabed.

This book then moves on to three threshold questions that ought to be answered soon after the discovery of a tunnel, in peace or wartime. Chapter 4 first addresses questions relating to applicable law. When a tunnel was discovered in Toronto in March 2015, authorities could not establish who owned the land on which the tunnel was dug or who was responsible for the investigation and the potential removal of the tunnel.[17] The uncertainty surrounding the legal questions hindered the response and marred its quality. To avoid such problems, I provide an overview of the legal regimes that may apply to tunnels—as well as their implications for states desiring to undertake anti-tunnel measures.

The second threshold matter concerns strategy. States ought to put in place a long-term strategy for underground warfare, incorporating the following components: (1) detecting and mapping tunnels, (2) neutralizing and/or destroying them, (3) prevention and monitoring, and (4) cooperation. Although states have at times attempted to skip some of these steps—mapping and monitoring are the prime candidates—each of them plays an essential role in eliminating the threat. As part of this strategy, states should consider boosting research and development on underground means of warfare and communication, sharing information, and exchanging best practices. Soldiers must be properly vetted, trained, and equipped for subterranean missions. Veterans who have fought in tunnels tell of darkness, claustrophobia, and post-traumatic stress disorder. These aspects can easily be overlooked if they are not integrated into a well-thought-out strategy.

Finally, and this is the third and last threshold matter examined in Chapter 4, states must possess a basic understanding of detection and destruction methods before they embark on anti-tunnel operations. I describe some of the most common methods, highlight their respective strengths and weaknesses, and advocate for a mix-and-match approach as no technology can, on its own, succeed at detecting or mapping tunnels.

In Chapter 5, I envisage situations in which cross-border tunnels may lead to the outbreak of war. The discovery of one or more cross-border tunnels in time of peace could lead to war. This is because such tunnels violate sovereignty and territorial integrity and demonstrate hostile intent on the part of the neighboring entity. Consider, for example,

---

[17] Ian Austen, *Mystery Surrounds a Tunnel in Toronto*, N.Y. TIMES (Feb. 24, 2015), https://www.nytimes.com/2015/02/25/world/americas/mystery-surrounds-a-tunnel-in-toronto.html.

the tunnels dug by North Korea under the Demilitarized Zone, or those dug by Hamas onto Israeli territory. A number of factors affect the decision to go to war in such situations, such as the number of tunnels, their level of completion, their proximity to civilian-populated neighborhoods, and the relationship with the party that dug the tunnel (state or nonstate). The assessment is a qualitative, not quantitative one. Not every cross-border tunnel will trigger the right to self-defense or the strategic urge to go to war. I distinguish between situations in which cross-border tunnels *can* lead to war and those in which they *do* lead to war. Cross-border threats do not significantly differ from other threats in this regard: the same is true with respect to other cross-border tensions. States may possess the right to react using military force but not make use of such right. In situations where war is either unlawful or undesirable, and the threat significant, states can mount a pinpointed incursion into enemy territory to permanently destroy the tunnel(s) (subject to applicable legal requirements).

Once war begins, the use of tunnels is regulated by the laws of war, also known as international humanitarian law or the *jus in bello*, as explained in Chapter 6. This legal framework regulates a broad array of tunnel-related issues, including their legal status (targetable or not), the type of weapons that may be used inside tunnels, and precautions that must be taken vis-à-vis civilians during anti-tunnel operations. A central and completely overlooked question relates to the legality of tunnel-digging in war. Taken together, the recurring use of tunnels in conflict and the silence of international law suggest that tunnel warfare is not, per se, prohibited under the law. This permissive view, however, should not be interpreted too broadly. Although IHL tolerates the digging and use of tunnels in armed conflict *in principle*, certain tunnels ought to be regarded as illegal, such as those dug with the intention of harming civilians, those that spread fear among civilians, and those dug to immunize military targets from attack. IHL should also prohibit the simultaneous use of underground structures for civilian and military purposes. This makes sense at the level of policy, given the law's command to keep civilian and military objectives separated from each other for the sake of civilians.

Though tunnel-digging is not prohibited per se, most tunnels (with the obvious exception of civilian shelters) constitute legitimate targets in war. Tunnels used for tunnel mining and command-and-control structures, even if uncompleted, would qualify as military objectives. Smuggling tunnels may be targetable as war-sustaining objects in situations where they do not meet the stricter and more widely accepted definition of military objective. In most situations, the non-civilian use of underground structures in armed conflict justifies the use of lethal force provided other requirements, such as proportionality and precautions, are met.

Chapter 7 focuses on the application of the law of armed conflict to "urban tunnels", that is, tunnels dug near, by, or against civilians. The intertwining of civilian elements into underground warfare constitutes a growing and considerable challenge. Violent nonstate actors increasingly dig tunnels *near* civilians, sometimes with the specific intent of directing attacks *at* civilians. At a time when nonstate actors purposefully wage war amidst civilians to reap the benefits of facing a law-abiding enemy, this concerning use of the underground is likely to grow. I examine the legal ramifications of urban tunnels for anti-tunnel operations. Is it lawful to use smoke to map a tunnel, or cement to render it unusable? Legal constraints cannot be set aside in such a complex environment. I suggest some answers, with a view to reconciling the rule of law with operational constraints. I also analyze the status of civilians who help dig tunnels or find themselves inside a tunnel at the time of a strike. Although civilians are protected under the law, they can lose this protection if they take "direct part in hostilities." I examine the type of tunnel-related activities that may fall under this definition and justify stripping civilians of their immunity from attack. Finally, I consider the situation in which preexisting underground civilian infrastructure, such as subways or sewage systems, may be used to launch attacks or carry out other types of hostile activity. This can take place in peacetime, as in the 1995 sarin gas attack in the Tokyo subway, or in wartime, as in Hamas's use of the basement of Al-Shifa hospital as a command-and-control center. Each of these scenarios calls for a different response.

Ultimately, the book exposes and examines a tangible and growing security threat—one that complicates intelligence gathering, places civilians and soldiers in unpredictable danger, calls for new strategies and technologies, and further erodes the significance of borders and sovereignty. While the contemporary use of tunnels resembles past use, today's tunnels raise new and under-explored concerns. The use of tunnels across various battlefields, their versatility, the difficulty in eliminating the threat, the risk of tunnels being inherited by new factions, innovative offensive uses in Syria, and changes in the anatomy of and interaction between terrorist groups all point to a long-term threat. Tunnels have gone beyond the battle*field* and now reach cities and civilian populated areas. When they do so, tunnels pose a direct danger to innocent civilians, from their construction to their destruction. As noted above, this danger extends to both sides of the conflict when tunnels are cross-border.

This book provides a framework for contending with subterranean threats within the law. Inevitably, as the first study of underground warfare approaching legal issues in an operational context, it leaves open questions and will spark disagreement. That is its objective. The legal and security communities have remained silent for too long on the ins and outs of this recurring feature of warfare. Now that virtually every contemporary conflict displays underground elements, from Mosul to Sana'a, Rafah, Ein Hashlosha, and Benghazi, it is high time to get the conversation going.

1

TUNNELS IN CONFLICT

Ancient Uses and Contemporary Threats

CALLS OF "ALLAH AKBAR!" resonated as Syrian rebels fighting against Bashar Assad's regime detonated a bomb at the extremity of a 350-foot tunnel on May 8, 2014.[1] The tunnel was used to place explosives under the Carlton Hotel in Aleppo. Unknown to the Syrian authorities who had been using the hotel, the rebels dug for 33 days, which enabled them to bypass security around the governmental compound. Approximately 40 Syrian troops died in the blast, which was felt in a radius as wide as 9 miles from the location of the bomb's blast. The operation was coined the "Aleppo Earthquake"—in reference to the earth-moving effect of the blast captured on video.

The video footage of the visibly successful operation boosted the rebels' morale in unprecedented ways—so much so that the mastermind of the operation did not worry about publicly identifying himself, and rebel groups vowed to dig more tunnels.

Only a few months later, Israel launched Operation Protective Edge with the explicit goal of destroying dozens of tunnels built from Gaza and extending into Israeli territory. The operation brought underground warfare to the forefront of the public discourse for the first time in decades. Strangely, however, the far-reaching consequences such tactics may have on the conduct of warfare in general, and civilian life in particular, still remain misunderstood.[2]

---

[1] Martin Chulov, *Aleppo's Most Wanted Man—the Rebel Leader behind Tunnel Bombs*, GUARDIAN (May 20, 2014), https://www.theguardian.com/world/2014/may/20/aleppos-most-wanted-man-rebel-leader-tunnel-bombs.

[2] See, for example, Al Jazeera English, *Syrian Rebels Use Tunnels to Recapture Strategic Positions*, YOUTUBE (May 25, 2014), https://www.youtube.com/watch?v=tykdi3PmdFw.

Underground Warfare. Daphné Richemond-Barak.
© Oxford University Press 2018. Published 2018 by Oxford University Press.

Though the use of a tunnel for detonating 25 tons of explosives brings back memories of World War I, tunnel mining in Syria embodies a relatively innovative use of tunnels on the contemporary battlefield. The amount of human and financial resources necessary to build a tunnel shows how valuable the tactic is in the eyes of its users.

Recent uses of tunnels also demonstrate the importance and challenge of obtaining intelligence on the construction of potential tunnels. Just as the Syrian authorities had no knowledge of the 350-foot tunnel being built literally under their noses, the Israeli authorities almost missed the tunnel built by Hamas in Gaza and extending to the Israeli town of Ein Hashlosha. The Israeli experience underscores yet another innovative form of underground warfare: the use of tunnels near and against civilians.

Although underground warfare has taken on new shapes and forms on the contemporary battlefield, it has been a feature of war from time immemorial. Yet little has been written about it. Those who have written about tunnel warfare typically focused on a specific conflict—the First World War or the Vietnam War, for example.[3] Others have researched the experience of their country with tunnel warfare.[4] But a study of underground warfare across time and conflicts has yet to be written. This lacuna in the literature leaves many questions unanswered, spanning several disciplines. Before these gaps can be filled, it is necessary to provide a historical overview of the use of tunnels in war.

Providing an exhaustive historical account of underground warfare, however, is not my pretension. Quite the contrary. The examples have been carefully selected because their value is significant for this study. Each example serves to highlight a specific trend or emphasize an operational or legal issue: whereas the Vietnam War illustrates the danger of the cohabitation of civilians and combatants inside tunnels, Gaddafi's tunnels in Libya provide an example of a defensive use of the underground. The objective is to clarify the nature of the threat, its evolution over time, and the various forms it takes. The historical account analyzes the role underground warfare has played and continues to play in armed conflict—and the reasons for its renewed use in the past decade. It provides a window of understanding on who uses tunnels and why. It also helps identify state practice (how states have dealt with the threat), and predict future trends. Finally, it enables the drawing of a typology of tunnels—a useful tool to conceptualize the use of tunnels in conflict, carry out threat assessments, and devise anti-tunnels strategies in compliance with the law. The typology also provides lawyers and advisers a roadmap as they contend with evolving underground threats.

The paucity of the scholarship in history, law, military theory, and military strategy makes it difficult to tell the story of underground warfare. I have used the relatively few

---

[3] *See*, respectively, TOM MANGOLD & JOHN PENYCATE, THE ILLUSTRATED HISTORY OF TUNNEL WARFARE: THE VIETNAM WAR (1987) [hereinafter ILLUSTRATED HISTORY OF TUNNEL WARFARE]; and ALEXANDER BARRIE, WAR UNDERGROUND (1961). Even Patrick Beaver's book (A HISTORY OF TUNNELS (1972)) examines tunneling technology rather than tunnels as such.

[4] *See*, for example, Yiftah S. Shapir & Gal Perel, *Subterranean Warfare: A New-Old Challenge, in* THE LESSONS OF OPERATION PROTECTIVE EDGE 51 (Anat Kurz & Shlomo Brom eds., 2014); Eitan Yitzhak, *Under the Ground*, 422 MAARACHOT 18 (2008); and Joshua S. Bowes, Mark T. Newdigate, Pedro J. Rosario & Davis D. Tindoll,

existing historical accounts, open-source military documents, and media reports to relate the evolution of underground warfare since World War I. In an effort to provide as accurate a picture as possible, I also compiled a database of *New York Times* reports on the use of tunnels in war between 1969 and 2015. Some of the insights included in this chapter build on the analysis of the data thus gathered, which serves as another source of information on tunnels and their use in war.

Taken together, the historical review and the database tell the worrying story of a tool of war turned into a global security threat, used primarily by nonstate actors to smuggle and hide weapons, infiltrate territory, and carry out violent attacks.

I. A Feature of War from Time Immemorial

History shows that human beings have always used tunnels in conflict, either to survive a siege, provide safe passage for citizens and military forces during hostilities, or launch attacks against the enemy. Biblical accounts tell of the use of the underground to store water and defend against military sieges. Hezekiah's Tunnel, for example, was built during the late eighth century B.C. to safeguard water supplies to Jerusalem in anticipation of an Assyrian siege.[5] This was also the case of the tunnel of Eupalinos, built in the sixth century B.C. to safeguard water supplies in the Greek island of Samos, which proved vital in sustaining its inhabitants during the Persian and Peloponnesian Wars.[6]

The use of tunnels as underground hideouts is further documented in archeological explorations, and one of the boldest examples are the subterranean cities of *Derinkuyu* and *Kaymakli* in the Anatolian Peninsula (now part of modern Turkey) that interconnected into an intricate, multilevel complex of tunnels.[7] These underground structures were used as places of residence, work, and social life by more than 20,000 people between the fifth and tenth centuries A.D. After their discovery in the 1960s, the subterranean cities became a popular tourist destination. Most of it remains untouched until today. It is unclear which group first excavated the rock and when. Some believe that it was the Hittites, seeking to protect themselves against the Phrygians' attack in the thirteenth century B.C. Centuries later, Christians used and expanded the underground complex as a shelter against Arab invaders.[8]

Tunnels were used to launch attacks against the enemy around 880 B.C. The Assyrian army dug tunnels under or inside walls and fortifications to allow the passage of troops,

---

The Enemy Below: Preparing Ground Forces for Subterranean Warfare, Dec. 2013 (unpublished AB thesis, Naval Postgraduate School), http://calhoun.nps.edu/handle/10945/38883 [hereinafter *The Enemy Below*].
[5] Philip J. King, *The Eighth, the Greatest of Centuries?*, 108 J. BIBLICAL LIT. 3, 5 (1989).
[6] CHARLES GATES, ANCIENT CITIES: THE ARCHAEOLOGY OF URBAN LIFE IN THE ANCIENT NEAR EAST AND EGYPT 215 (2003).
[7] *See* REGIONAL ARCHITECTURE IN THE MEDITERRANEAN AREA (Alessandro Bucci & Luigi Mollo eds., 2010).
[8] *Id.*

or to collapse the walls by burning down the support for the tunnels.[9] The use of tunnels to weaken walls and fortifications was also witnessed during the battle over the city Dura-Europos (today in Syrian territory) in the middle of the third century A.D., when Sassanid Persian forces dug tunnels in order to undermine the Roman walls protecting the city.[10] According to some reports, the tunnels were used to release chemical agents, providing one of the earliest examples of chemical warfare.[11] Similarly, during the Bar Kokhba revolt (A.D. 132–135), Jews in Galilee, Judea, Samaria, and the Jordan Valley used subterranean complexes to hide from Roman forces and launch surprise attacks, helping them overcome the Romans' numerical and military superiority.[12] The Jews quickly lost their advantage when the Roman forces sealed off the tunnels. After the revolt was suppressed, the tunnels served mostly as shelters.[13] Much later, in the sixteenth century, tunnel mining (the detonation of explosives underground) made one of its earliest appearances. The Russian engineering corps, led by Ivan the Terrible, dug tunnels under the city of Kazan's walls and laced them with explosives to take down Kazan's fortifications.[14] This was around the time that gunpowder made its way to the battlefield, significantly increasing the destructive impact of tunnel warfare.[15]

The American Civil War also featured various types of tunnel mining. Union troops used existing underground structures and dug tunnels from their trenches under enemy lines where they detonated mines—with powerful and deadly results.[16] The Battle of the Crater in 1864 was probably the most devastating. In order to break enemy lines, Union commanders ordered the digging of a shaft under the front lines. The length of the shaft reached more than 511 feet and it was filled with such large amounts of

---

[9] *See* Paul J. Springer, *Fighting Under the Earth: The History of Tunneling in Warfare*, FOREIGN POLICY RESEARCH INSTITUTE (Apr. 23, 2015), http://www.fpri.org/article/2015/04/fighting-under-the-earth-the-history-of-tunneling-in-warfare/.

[10] THE OXFORD HANDBOOK OF WARFARE IN THE CLASSICAL WORLD 722–23 (Brian Campbell & Lawrence A. Tritle eds., 2013).

[11] Simon James, *Stratagems, Combat and "Chemical Warfare" in the Siege Mines of Dura-Europos*, 115 AM. J. ARCHAEOLOGY 69 (2011).

[12] There is also archaeological evidence indicating that the Jews used naturally formed tunnels, which they then expanded, for both defense and offense between 63 B.C. and A.D. 135, during the time of the destruction of the Second Temple, even before the outbreak of the revolt. *See* Yinon Shivtiel, *Underground Hideouts in the Galilee and Their Historical Meaning*, 142 CATHEDRA 3, 7 (2012), http://www.inonscaves.co.il/cave_articles/caves_galil.pdf (in Hebrew).

[13] Yuval Shahar, *The Underground Hideouts in Galilee and Their Historical Meaning*, in THE BAR KOKHBA WAR RECONSIDERED: NEW PERSPECTIVES ON THE SECOND JEWISH REVOLT AGAINST ROME 217 (Peter Schäfer ed., 2003).

[14] Richard Cavendish, *Kazan Falls to Ivan the Terrible*, 52 HISTORY TODAY 54 (2002).

[15] Arthur Herman, *Notes from the Underground*, FOREIGN AFFAIRS (Aug. 26, 2014), https://www.foreignaffairs.com/articles/middle-east/2014-08-26/notes-underground.

[16] RON FIELD, AMERICAN CIVIL WAR FORTIFICATIONS (3)—THE MISSISSIPPI AND RIVER FRONTS 4, 38 (2007).

explosives that its detonation resulted in an enormous crater measuring approximately 170 feet long, 60 feet wide, and 30 feet deep.[17]

Tunnel mining became once again popular in the early twentieth century during the Russo-Japanese War. The Russians tried to counter Japanese mining efforts but failed to do so appropriately for lack of tools and knowledge. Although they succeeded in detecting Japanese mining and prepared explosives to blow up the Japanese tunnelers, the charge was too heavy, and the Russians ended up destroying part of their own positions and losing the advantage to the Japanese.[18]

The versatility of tunnels in time of war was thus apparent to belligerents early on. Tunnel mining, one of the earliest uses of the underground, has re-emerged as a valuable tactic in today's Iraq and Syria.[19] The simultaneous use of tunnels for civilian and military purposes is another feature that has permeated history and is likely to increase as noncompliant nonstate entities make growing use of the underground.

II. State-to-State Tunnel Mining during World War I

Although tunnels had been used before in war, the concept of tunnel warfare evokes the trenches and tunnel mining of World War I. Trenches, perhaps most associated with World War I, are outside the scope of this study as they are partially located aboveground. Less known are the tunnels of World War I, fully buried structures that have inspired some of the most innovative contemporary uses of the underground. The beginning of two years of intensive underground warfare began in late 1914.[20] In 1916 alone, the British made 750 tunnel mining attacks and the Germans detonated 696 mines against the British.[21] In one notable attack, Germany detonated 10 mines in a tunnel in the French village of Givenchy-lès-la-Bassée in order to scare the surviving forces out of their trenches and into shooting range.[22] Tunnel warfare intensified again toward the end of the war in 1917, when the British forces attacked the German forces in Flanders, digging a five-mile-long tunnel complex and lacing it with a million pounds of explosives, killing about 20,000 Germans in one attack. The British also carried out arguably "the largest mining attack in the history of warfare"[23] in Messines in 1917, digging and filling with

---

[17] Bryce C. Suderow, *The Battle of the Crater: The Civil War's Worst Massacre*, 43 CIVIL WAR HISTORY 219, 219 (1997).
[18] SIMON JONES, UNDERGROUND WARFARE 1914–1918, at 16 (2010).
[19] Marcus Weisberger, *ISIS Is Using Tunnel Bombs in Iraq*, DEFENSEONE (June 8, 2015), http://www.defenseone.com/threats/2015/06/isis-using-tunnel-bombs-iraq/114730/.
[20] *Id.* at 30.
[21] *Id.* at 113. *See also* at 168 (noting that by the middle of 1916 the British had 25,000 men employed in underground work).
[22] *See* BARRIE, *supra* note 3; *see also* JONES, *supra* note 18, at 140.
[23] *See also* JONES, *supra* note 18, at 145 ("It was the largest quantity of explosives deliberately detonated at one time and the most effective integration of mines with an attack.")

explosives 21 tunnels under German lines, claiming the lives of 10,000 German soldiers.[24] Following Messines, underground activity slowed down significantly. Both sides had dug so extensively that it was difficult for either of them to gain further advantage:

> When they found themselves baulked on the surface, both sides began to burrow beneath each other's lines to lay and fire heavy explosive charges. A separate, almost private war between the rival sappers started. It was a three-year, bloody, claustrophobic, uncomfortable, primitive, exhausting war-within-a-war. Military experts predict that nothing like it will ever again be seen.[25]

The tunnelers, as these soldiers became known, suffered from severe hardship and dire conditions. Much of what they experienced then remains true today. In spite of technological advances, the reality of underground warfare at the human level has not changed much. German Lieutenant Colonel Otto Füsslein described the daily realities of tunnel warfare as follows:

> The deeper one went, the greater the struggle on the wet, narrow steps, the worse the air, the greater also the danger, from direct hits from above, from enemy mines, from inrush of mud and water to be cut off and suffocated. Endlessly the miners vied with one another, officers and men in long lines in smashed galleries lying one behind the other to save trapped mates.[26]

As part of their work in these difficult conditions, WWI soldiers carefully listened to the other side's tunneling activity to counter enemy advances, or at least gain intelligence on it. Soldiers would lie at the end of the shaft and listen carefully to the digging activities nearby.[27] By the time a soldier identified a noise as digging, enemy tunnel miners would be only feet away from him. He would then report back this activity, making it possible to map approximate locations of enemy tunnels. In addition to recognizing the distinct noise of digging, soldiers were trained to detect when explosives were being brought into the tunnel and unloaded,[28] and to distinguish the noise made by their own side from

---

[24] Ailbhe Goodbody, *Tunneling in the Deep*, MINING MAGAZINE (Sept. 13, 2016), http://www.miningmagazine.com/top-articles/tunnelling-in-the-deep/.
[25] BARRIE, *supra* note 3, at 10. *See also* JONES, *supra* note 18, at 164.
[26] *See* JONES, *supra* note 18, at 137.
[27] *See also id.* at 160 (picture of a French officer using a geophone to detect the sounds of German mining) and at 176 (describing this as "the most nerve-wracking activity of underground warfare, requiring a man to crouch in a tunnel for long periods, often alone, and in close proximity to the enemy").
[28] Evan Hadingham, *The Hidden World of the Great War: The Lost Underground of World War I*, NAT'L GEOGRAPHIC (Aug. 2014), http://ngm.nationalgeographic.com/2014/08/wwi-underground/hadingham-text.

that of their opponents.[29] Listening records were kept and patterns analyzed.[30] Given the importance of noise detection, soldiers were instructed to dig in clay only.[31]

The Allied forces used heavy artillery to destroy German tunnels. They assigned soldiers the task of clearing out the tunnels with explosives, incendiary munitions, and gas grenades.[32] The use of flamethrowers was also reported.[33] Although their deep dugouts and sophisticated underground accommodations did help,[34] the Germans largely failed to counter the Allies' underground tactics. German military leader Füsslein criticized "the disregard and lack of awareness of this ancient and yet modern weapon" and the "lack of historical knowledge, expertise and experience" in the realm of underground warfare.[35] His judgment was harsh and sounds almost like a warning to future commanders: "Divisional commanders rejected mine warfare because they did not understand it; others made it the scapegoat, although they knew secretly that they had insufficiently valued this weapon."[36] It is interesting to note that he referred to underground warfare as a weapon, rather than a tactic or a domain.[37]

To conclude, underground warfare during 1914–18 was used by states, and exclusively against combatants. The tunnelers,[38] as they were known, benefited significantly from the input of civilian experts who were able to share their know-how and practices for the good of their country.[39] In this regard, the experience of WWI underscores the importance of gaining knowledge and seeking expertise when it comes to underground warfare.

---

[29] *See* JONES, *supra* note 18, at 176.
[30] *Id.*
[31] *Id.* at 136.
[32] *Id.* at 222 (for more details on the use of gas in tunnels during WWI, *id.* at 161, 127–28).
[33] *Id.* at 188.
[34] *Id.* at 254. *See also* at 160 (picture of men of the German 148th Infantry Regiment in a tunnel 15m below ground, which included accommodation, electricity, and a light railway truck).
[35] *See* JONES, *supra* note 18, at 163.
[36] *Id.*
[37] For a discussion of underground warfare as a domain, *see infra* Chapter 6.
[38] EDWARD SYNTON, TUNNELLERS ALL 143–44 (1918) ("Everybody damns the tunneller: [General Headquarters] because he invariably has his job finished months before the rest of the Army are ready for the "great push"; army troops because he invariably upsets all their preconceived notions as to the safety of trenches and dug-outs; divisional troops damn him because he is outside their sphere of influence; brigade troops because he refuses to move when they do, and because he knows by heart that part of the line to which they come as strangers; brass hats because they dislike his underground habits; regimental officers because he refuses to allow them to use his deep and snug dug-outs; subalterns because of his superior knowledge; Tommy because he is the direct cause of numerous extra fatigues and—alas that it should be so!—because of his extra pay; and last and loudest, the Boches damn him because of his earnest and unceasing attempts at uplifting and converting them into surprised angels. It is also owing to his success in this noble work of the missionary that the tunneller is highly respected by all branches of the forces.")
[39] JONES, *supra* note 18, at 165.

It also demonstrates the need to adapt to underground tactics (both offensive and defensive) as the war unfolds.[40]

III. World War II and the Challenge of Entrenched Japanese Forces

Whereas World War I was marked primarily by tunnel mining, World War II saw a more diversified use of tunnels. Concerned with the rise of Hitler, the French hoped to counter a German invasion by digging an extensive complex of bunkers connecting dozens of kilometers of tunnels. In spite of all of France's efforts, however, Hitler invaded France through Belgium and never encountered the Maginot defense line. Hitler, too, made use of bunkers and tunnels for defensive purposes, primarily toward the end of the war.[41]

In contrast, the Japanese used intricate naturally-made underground structures to undermine U.S. forces by catching them by surprise and causing significant casualties. In Palau, in the Western Pacific Ocean, Japanese forces allowed American troops to land on the island before launching a massive attack against them.[42] The Japanese had been fortified for almost two weeks, and had laced the island with mines. They hit U.S. forces with small firearms and grenades from hidden positions. The U.S. Marines fought to break the resistance of the stronghold with tanks, flamethrowers, and rifles. The operation claimed the lives of an estimated 1,749 U.S. Marines as well as thousands of casualties on the Japanese side.[43] It took several months to seal the tunnels, as the United States waited for the resisters to come out of hiding; when they refused to surrender, the Americans sealed the tunnels by blasting their entrances.[44] In February 1945, about five months after the attacks, five Japanese survivors dug their way out of the tunnels. On April 22, 1947, 35 additional Japanese soldiers came out of the tunnel complex, marking the last official WWII surrender.[45]

The Japanese used similar tactics on Iwo Jima, an eight-square-mile island strategically located south of Japan. During the war, the Japanese used the small island as a base to launch attacks against American forces, and as an intelligence frontline to gain information on incoming Allied forces' attacks. On February 19, 1945, the United States launched Operation Detachment to take over the island. Twenty-one thousand Japanese

---

[40] *Id.* at 131–32.
[41] Scott Shuger & Donald Berger, *Hitler Slept Here*, SLATE (June 21, 2006), http://www.slate.com/articles/news_and_politics/slates_10th_anniversary/2006/06/hitler_slept_here.html.
[42] GORDON D. GAYLE, BLOODY BEACHES: THE MARINES AT PELELIU 3 (1996), http://www.marines.mil/Portals/59/Publications/Bloody%20Beaches%20The%20Marines%20At%20Peleliu%20%20PCN%2019000313700_1.pdf?ver=2012-10-11-163203-753 ("Umurbrogol was in fact a complex system of sharply uplifted coral ridges, knobs, valleys, and sinkholes.").
[43] ROBERT ROSS SMITH, THE APPROACH TO THE PHILIPPINES (UNITED STATES ARMY IN WORLD WAR II: THE WAR IN THE PACIFIC) 561 (1953).
[44] *Id.*
[45] *Id.*

entrenched themselves in Suribachi Mountain, at the southwest end of the island, building a 7.5-mile-long tunnel complex with nearly 1,000 exits and over 700 sheltered caverns to store ammunition and serve as living quarters and medical facilities for the Japanese troops. The complex had fortified rooms, steel doors, and a ventilation system.[46] Aerial attacks meant to destroy extensive Japanese underground arms caches and infrastructure had little effect. The Japanese troops remained largely unharmed deep inside their tunnels. The U.S. forces therefore landed on the island. An hour after they had arrived on the beach, the Japanese launched a full-scale, heavy artillery attack that claimed the lives of nearly 2,400 Americans in half a day. The battle was described as one of the most violent in American history, with troops withstanding harsh weather, unforgiving ground, and nonstop Japanese attacks.[47] The U.S. Marines used flamethrowers and grenades to clear and destroy Japanese bunkers. However, this tactic, too, proved unsuccessful: the Japanese used tunnel shafts to go underground and attack American forces from behind.[48]

On the second day of the battle, American tanks and aircraft arrived on the island as reinforcement, allowing the Marines to advance toward the mountain and seize it. Out of the 21,000 Japanese fighters, only several hundred were taken as prisoners. The battle inflicted heavy losses on the Allied forces, with nearly 7,000 dead and over 25,000 wounded, making it the only battle in the Pacific War to have caused more Allied casualties than Japanese.[49] It demonstrates the scope and nature of the violence that underground warfare can generate. The Japanese used the underground to trick the enemy, leading it to believe that no forces were in the vicinity or that the danger had been eliminated—only to strike with greater strength a short time thereafter.

Overall, the features of underground warfare during World War II resemble those of World War I: tunnels were used by one state against another, and by combatants against other combatants. Importantly, however, tunnels were not used by the Japanese for tunnel mining, but rather as long-term hideouts in a mountainous terrain.

IV. Civilians and Combatants in the Vietcong's Tunnels

Overall, the Vietnam War took contemporary underground warfare to another level. The Vietcong combined offensive and defensive uses of the underground, turning tunnels into both death traps for U.S. soldiers and safe nursery wards for Vietnamese women.

---

[46] C. Peter Chen, *Battle of Iwo Jima*, WORLD WAR II DATABASE (Feb. 20, 2017), http://ww2db.com/battle_spec.php?battle_id=12.
[47] *Battle for Iwo Jima, 1945*, NAVAL HISTORY AND HERITAGE COMMAND (Mar. 25, 2015), https://www.history.navy.mil/research/library/online-reading-room/title-list-alphabetically/b/battle-for-iwo-jima.html.
[48] Hadingham, *supra* note 28.
[49] Cyril J. O'Brien, *Iwo Jima Retrospective*, MILITARY, http://www.military.com/NewContent/0,13190,NI_Iwo_Jima2,00.html.

The Vietcong's tunnels displayed distinctive features: they were built at a depth of 5 feet to ensure safety from bombardment and were about 3 feet wide, with a height of between 2.7 feet and 6 feet. The tunnels were built in "zigzag" formation with many turns and segments in order to make demolition and detection harder for the enemy.[50] Entrances to tunnels were carefully camouflaged and laced with mines and traps (such as buckets with poisonous animals and improvised torture machines).[51] Tunnel structures often consisted of several levels connected through secret passageways or trap doors. The passageways were made to barely fit the body type of a Vietnamese adult, but were too small for most American soldiers.[52]

Vietcong fighters used the tunnels to carry out surprise attacks: they would emerge onto the battlefield, attack U.S. forces, steal their supplies, and disappear back into the earth. These surprise attacks were often launched simultaneously from several directions to keep the enemy surprised, confused, and ineffective despite its military superiority.[53]

The tunnels allowed the Vietnamese to contend with U.S. technological superiority by using the underground defensively (hiding from aerial bombings) and gaining an offensive advantage over U.S. forces. In response, American forces deployed "tunnel rats," whose main task was to map the complexes, gather intelligence, and lace tunnels with explosives. Tunnel Rats were operational teams of compact-sized soldiers equipped with flashlights and 0.45 caliber pistols who entered the tunnels after clearing them and explored them for prolonged periods of time.[54]

One of the hardest tasks was to locate tunnel entrances and exits in the Vietnamese jungle terrain. Tunnel entrances were so well camouflaged that they were invisible to the naked eye, and even when it was known that a tunnel trap door was in close proximity, its location was often not discovered. The most sophisticated underground structures used by the Vietcong were located in the Cù Chi district, which was part of Saigon (the capital of the Republic of Vietnam at the time). Due to the Cù Chi district's close proximity to the Saigon River, its soil is mostly composed of clay, an ideal environment for digging.[55]

Interestingly, the Vietcong did not dig all the tunnels themselves: many tunnels were inherited from Viet Minh nationalist guerrillas that used them in the anticolonial struggle with France.[56] The Vietcong expanded them into a network of complexes in the

---

[50] *See* Tom Mangold & John Penycate, The Tunnels of Cù Chi: A Remarkable Story of War 67 (2005) [hereinafter: "Mangold"].

[51] *Id.* at 119 and 129.

[52] *See Historical Vignette 062—How Army Engineers Cleared VietCong Tunnels*, US Army Corps of Engineers (Jan. 2003), http://www.usace.army.mil/About/History/HistoricalVignettes/Military ConstructionCombat/062VietCongTunnels.aspx.

[53] Smith, *supra* note 43.

[54] Lester W. Grau & Ali Ahmad Jalali, *Underground Combat: Stereophonic Blasting, Tunnel Rats and the Soviet-Afghan War*, 28 Engineer 20, 20 (1998).

[55] *See* Mangold, *supra* note 50, at 29.

[56] Tom Mangold & John Penycate, The Tunnels of Cù Chi: A Harrowing Account of America's 'Tunnel Rats' in the Underground Battlefields of Vietnam (2005), at 32. *See also*

1960s, some of them extending to nearly 40 miles long, and dug approximately 130 miles of passageways connecting the entire intricate network.[57] The tunnels encompassed residential facilities such as hospitals, storage spaces, cinemas, and living compounds, as well as bunkers, ammunition caches, imaginative traps, tunnel mines, and military headquarters.[58] Some military commanders spent more than five years in the tunnels.[59] Civilians, too, spent prolonged periods of time in the tunnels. Dr. Vo Hoang Le, the chief of the medical section of the Cù Chi tunnels, performed "hundreds of operations inside the Cù Chi tunnels," among them countless amputations and even brain surgery with "household" drills.[60]

The deployment of the B-52 bombers by the American Armed Forces rendered life in the tunnels difficult, as the bombs dropped from these planes were able to penetrate the earth (up to 40 feet deep) and detonate moments after penetration. But even the B-52s did not fully succeed in neutralizing the threat:

> Extensive booby-trapping made it nearly impossible for American troops to extricate the enemy from their impregnable safe-havens that allowed them to withstand intense aerial bombardment—even by crater-making B-52 bombs.[61]

The United States also battled the underground threat with chemical agents.[62] These were injected inside the tunnels to force the combatants out of hiding and prevent their return.[63] The Vietcong tried to counter the American use of chemical agents, in some instances successfully, by sealing off sections of the tunnels with any material at their disposal and then waiting for ventilation systems in the passageways to do their work. Still, the use of these agents was devastating for both combatants and civilians on the Vietnamese side. Many people lost their lives through suffocation or poisoning in the immediate aftermath of the deployment of chemical agents into the tunnel shafts.[64] In addition, the soil was contaminated for years to come, crops were destroyed, and livestock poisoned.

The Vietnam experience teaches valuable insights. *First*, it demonstrates the horrific consequences of using tunnels in urban areas, where civilians and combatants are located

---

Max Boot, Invisible Armies: An Epic History of Guerilla Warfare from Ancient Times to the Present 357s (2013).

[57] *See* US Army Corps of Engineers, *supra* note 52.
[58] *See* Illustrated History of Tunnel Warfare, *supra* note 3, at 43.
[59] *See id.* at 29.
[60] *See id.* at 52.
[61] *See* US Army Corps of Engineers, *supra* note 52.
[62] *See* Thomas Dethlefs, *Tear Gas and the Politics of Lethality: Emerging from the Haze*, 2 Yale History Rev. 83 (2013).
[63] *See* Richard A. Muller, *The Weapons Paradox*, MIT Technology Review (May 21, 2003), http://www.technologyreview.com/news/401923/the-weapons-paradox/.
[64] *See* Smith, *supra* note 43.

inside and in the vicinity of tunnels. *Second*, it underscores the complexity of the threat when sophisticated tunnels are used by the enemy as living and military quarters for prolonged periods of time, immune from surveillance and attack. *Third*, it provides a striking example of the use of tunnels by violent nonstate actors in order to compensate for the inferiority of their military capabilities. *Fourth*, it highlights the threat posed by inherited underground structures—particularly when these are later supplemented with man-made construction. *Fifth*, it is noteworthy that despite the brutality of the conflict, the use of the underground remained directed exclusively at military targets.

V. The Cross-Border Threat: The North Korean Tunnels

The Korean arena exposes a very different type of underground threat—cross-border, initiated by states, extremely sophisticated, and designed more for deterrence rather than active use. The tunnels were all dug by North Korea under the North Korea/South Korea border in violation of the 1953 Armistice Agreement, which prohibits the presence of weapons and other military installations in the Demilitarized Zone.[65]

The first tunnel was detected in 1974 by a South Korean army patrol that noticed changes in vegetation and steam coming from the ground.[66] After investigating further, it was discovered that the tunnel was only a few feet underground and the presence of fresh food suggested that the tunnel was still under construction. A second tunnel was discovered in 1975, after troops deployed in the area felt ground tremors. This information, combined with photographic and defector intelligence, gave a general idea of the tunnel's location. Scientists and geologists then located the tunnel with greater precision with the help of seismic monitoring. The third tunnel, known as the "Third Tunnel of Aggression," which was discovered in 1978 thanks to a defector who had worked on the tunnel,[67] has been turned into a tourist site as a warning to younger generations about the "danger

---

[65] According to some experts, as many as 20 tunnels could be in existence, only four of which have been discovered. *See* Michael O'Hanlon, *Stopping a North Korean Invasion: Why Defending South Korea Is Easier than the Pentagon Thinks*, 22 INT'L SECURITY 135, 142 n.18 (1998); *see also Seoul Uncovers a Border Tunnel*, N.Y. TIMES (Mar. 4, 1990), http://www.nytimes.com/1990/03/04/world/seoul-uncovers-a-border-tunnel.html; and Nicholas D. Kristof, *Tunneling toward Disaster*, N.Y. TIMES (Jan. 21, 2003), http://www.nytimes.com/2003/01/21/opinion/21KRIS.html. It is interesting to note that the South Korean government discredited claims that 84 tunnels had been dug under the border with North Korea (*see* Julian Ryall, *South Korea Investigates Reports of "Invasion Tunnels" from North*, TELEGRAPH (Oct. 28, 2014), http://www.telegraph.co.uk/news/worldnews/asia/northkorea/11192736/South-Korea-investigates-reports-of-invasion-tunnels-from-North.html).

[66] *See* KOREAN OVERSEAS INFORMATION SERVICE, SECRET TUNNEL UNDER PANMUNJOM: NORTH KOREA'S THIRD INVASION PASSAGE DISCOVERED 24 (1978), http://www.imjinscout.com/images/North_Korean_Tunnels.pdf.

[67] *See id.* at 11.

North Korea still poses six decades after the Korean War ended in a truce."[68] Tourists can enter the seven-by-seven foot tunnel, which lies 240 feet deep, and walk all the way to the military demarcation line where the Demilitarized Zone begins aboveground. A fourth tunnel was discovered in 1990 by South Korean and U.S. troops. It was over 1.2 miles long, reaching over 0.7 miles into South Korean territory.[69] Importantly, the tunnels' size, depth, and sophistication improved over time, suggesting that the North Koreans continued digging even as the first tunnels were discovered.[70]

The North Korean cross-border tunnels are highly advanced: wide, and equipped with electricity and highly fortified support structures. The fourth tunnel can transport as many as 10,000 North Korean soldiers per hour behind the South Korean defense lines, with some of the shafts reportedly wide enough to transport jeeps and artillery.[71]

More than two decades after the discovery of the fourth tunnel, the threat of North Korea's invasion tunnels still lingers.[72] The cross-border, high-tech tunnels have made an invasion that much more likely and easy. They continue to be regarded by South Korea as an existential threat[73]—raising the question of why it chose not to destroy them, as I explain in Chapter 5.

VI. The Use of Underground Caves and Tunnels by the Mujahedeen in Afghanistan

The Afghan-Soviet war witnessed the next major and active use of tunnels in war. In their fight against the Soviets, the Mujahedeen used extensive irrigation systems known as Karez, which had already been used as early as A.D. 1221 by locals who sought shelter from the Mongol invasion of Genghis Khan.[74] The irrigation tunnels were key in facilitating the Mujahedeen fighters' ambush tactics and overcoming their inferior weaponry, logistical capabilities, and infrastructure. They used them as hiding places to store ammunition, launch surprise attacks, and allow undetected passage between different battlefield positions.[75] The Mujahedeen also used bunkers and underground shelters near Kandahar

---

[68] See *Dorasan Observatory*, Visit Korea, http://english.visitkorea.or.kr/enu/ATR/SI_EN_3_1_1_1.jsp?cid=264488.
[69] See *Seoul Uncovers a Border Tunnel*, supra note 65.
[70] See SECRET TUNNEL UNDER PANMUNJOM, supra note 66, at 8 and 15 (which includes a comparison of the features of the first three tunnels).
[71] See Kristof, supra note 65.
[72] Choe Sang-Hun, *Hunting for Tunnels to Prove a Threat*, N.Y. TIMES (July 2, 2012), http://www.nytimes.com/2012/07/04/world/asia/for-south-korean-tunnel-hunters-a-quixotic-quest-to-prove-a-threat.html?_r=0.
[73] *Id.* (reporting that, according to the South Korean Defense Ministry, "these tunnels could determine the outcome of a war and our country's survival").
[74] See Grau & Jalali, supra note 54, at 2.
[75] See ALI AHMAD JALALI & LESTER W. GRAU, THE OTHER SIDE OF THE MOUNTAIN: MUJAHIDEEN TACTICS IN THE SOVIET-AFGHAN WAR (2012), http://www.tribalanalysiscenter.com/TAUDOC/Other%20Side%20of%20Mountain.pdf.

and underground headquarters and weapons caches near Kabul.[76] Some of these underground hideouts were naturally formed, others were designed for civilian use but taken over by the Mujahideen for military purposes, and yet others were man-made. Their use of the underground was highly diversified. In some cases, the use of tunnels and caves by the Mujahedeen was spearheaded by the United States in an attempt to bring about the defeat of the Soviets.[77]

The Soviets' response to the Mujahedeen's underground tactics evolved with time. At first they would wait for the Mujahedeen to get out of the tunnels before killing or detaining them—a tactic similar to that used by the Mongolian army hundreds of years before.[78] However, by the mid-1980s, the Soviets started training Afghan and Soviet special forces in "tunnel neutralization courses."[79] They were taught to clear out the tunnels in four stages: *first*, soldiers shouted into the tunnel, demanding that those taking shelter in it come out. Civilians who might have been hiding in the tunnel could then leave. *Second*, if there was no answer, they launched two RGD-5 concussion grenades into the tunnel to force anyone out. It was then advised to shout into the tunnel again and declare that it was about to be destroyed. *Third*, assuming the tunnel was cleared, the soldiers used mirrors to reflect sunlight into the shafts dug alongside the tunnel to better examine their surroundings. *Fourth*, they lowered explosives with cords and, taking shelter, detonated them with hand grenades.[80] This created a "deadly overpressure between the two charges," which the Soviets called a "stereophonic blast."[81] Then the soldiers launched nontoxic smoke pots to test for the existence of adjunct tunnels. If the smoke vanished it meant that the ventilation system was still intact and exploration teams could safely descend into the tunnels to conduct a search. The search team was composed of three to four men armed with knives, grenades, digging tools, pistols, and rifles with attached flashlights.[82]

The Soviets also developed special weapons for tunnel warfare. Among them was the signal mine, a type of firework that would emit pyrotechnic stars in different colors and broadcast a loud siren sound to stun potential Mujahedeen forces and subdue them without much effort.[83] The Soviets also employed improved range PRO-A flamethrowers reaching effectively up to 650 yards ahead. The soldiers would lower the flamethrower into shafts with cords and activate it while facing a tunnel opening to burn it out.[84]

---

[76] Ali Ahmed Jalali & Lester W. Grau, Afghan Guerrilla Warfare: In the Words of the Mujahideen Fighters 46, 393 (2002).

[77] Mary Anne Weaver, *Lost at Tora Bora*, N.Y. Times (Sept. 11, 2005), http://www.nytimes.com/2005/09/11/magazine/11TORABORA.html?pagewanted=1&_r=1.

[78] *See* Grau & Jalali, *supra* note 54, at 2–3.

[79] *Id.* at 3.

[80] *Id.* at 4.

[81] *Id.*

[82] *Id.* at 5.

[83] *Id.*

[84] *Id.* at 6.

The experience of the Soviets in contending with the Mujahedeen's tunnels highlights the extreme measures that states are willing to take in order to eliminate underground threats. The Soviets understood the need to develop new tactics, methods, and weapons to overcome the advantage gained by the Mujahedeen through their use of the underground. With the Afghan-Soviet war, and with a likely influence of the Vietnam War just a few years prior, states begun to understand that underground warfare calls for its own strategy and skills.

VII. More of the Same: The Allied War in Afghanistan

The United States and its allies invaded Afghanistan on October 7, 2001—less than a month after the 9/11 attacks. In their effort to hide from enemy forces, the Taliban and al-Qaeda made use of the tunnel and cave networks built decades before by the Mujahedeen. The tunnels, inherited and expanded, were deemed valuable as a way of contending with America's aerial superiority and its desire to avoid ground combat. Taliban and al-Qaeda forces used the underground to launch missiles and mount attacks that were nearly impossible to predict and counter. Even for the most sophisticated army, overcoming forces entrenched in caves and tunnels posed a great challenge.

In the public consciousness, the name Tora Bora evokes this challenge better than any other.[85] Osama bin Laden is believed to have made his way to this "series of mountain caves near the Pakistani border" shortly after 9/11.[86] The complex had hydroelectric power generators, a ventilation system, and numerous rooms in finely carved granite. It is estimated that 1,000 to 2,000 fighters were barricaded inside.[87] Bin Laden knew the area well: back in 1987, he had used bulldozers to build an escape road through the mountains in an (unsuccessful yet impressive) effort to prevail against the Soviets in Jaji, near the Pakistani border.[88] This time he chose Tora Bora to protect himself from the United States.

Having received intelligence regarding his presence in the area, the United States began intensive air strikes, using B-52s and ground-penetrating weapons. The United States

---

[85] It is important to note that other reports describe Tora Bora as a natural structure of a few tunnels without any special amenities such as power generators and fine granite carving. According to these reports, Tora Bora could not have held more than 200 fighters, but did have small passages into the mountains. *See* Matthew Forney, *Inside the Tora Bora Caves*, TIME (Dec. 11, 2011), http://content.time.com/time/world/article/0,8599,188029,00.html.

[86] Peter Bergen, *The Account of How We Nearly Caught Osama Bin Laden in 2001*, THE NEW REPUBLIC (Dec. 30, 2009), https://newrepublic.com/article/72086/the-battle-tora-bora; *see also* MIR BAHMANYAR, AFGHANISTAN CAVE COMPLEXES 1979–2004: MOUNTAIN STRONGHOLDS OF MUJAHIDEEN, TALIBAN AND AL QAEDA (2004).

[87] *See* Weaver, *supra* note 77.

[88] *See* Bergen, *supra* note 86.

also dropped the Daisy-Cutter, a 15,000-pound bomb that had been used during the Gulf War to clear minefields,[89] killing many al-Qaeda operatives, but not Osama bin Laden.

As is often the case with underground warfare, a ground offensive followed a month of intensive aerial bombardments: approximately 2,500 Afghan opposition forces and 40 Coalition Special Forces struck the east, west, and north fronts of the complex. The southern front, facing the Pakistani border, was the highest and thus the hardest to reach.[90] The Tora Bora battle lasted five days: the Coalition and Afghan forces succeeded in taking over the complex but Osama bin Laden managed to escape along with over 800 fighters, who subsequently entrenched deeper in the Afghani mountains.[91]

Less known than Tora Bora, the tunnels of Zhawar Kili offer another compelling example of the challenging nature of underground warfare. The underground complex was located in the Paktia province of Afghanistan, near the Pakistani border. It served as a command-and-control center and hosted a hotel, a mosque, repair shops, a garage, a medical facility, and a communications center.[92]

The American Navy SEALs who secured the premises in early 2002 uncovered a much larger underground complex than intelligence estimates had initially suspected: 70 tunnels reinforced with steel and construction beams.[93] As they cleared tunnel exits and caves, they recorded all information to account for the attack's progress and for future use. Snipers were stationed around the mountain in order to provide backup and share intelligence with the ground forces. Intelligence gathered in the process was significant; so was the immense weapons cache confiscated and destroyed (millions of pounds of explosives, biological and chemical suits, tanks, rifles and machine guns, and other heavy weaponry).

The forces had planned to clear the complex in one day but had to stay for nine in order to complete the task. They also requested vehicles in order to fully account for the vast tunnel network—reportedly the biggest and most important al-Qaeda underground complex discovered in Afghanistan. According to military reports, the SEALs demolished over 60 ordinary structures and over 50 tunnels. Importantly, the complex remains under watch to prevent its reoccupation by al-Qaeda or other hostile forces.[94]

---

[89] *Id.*

[90] The proximity of the complex to the Pakistani border created significant challenges: al-Qaeda fighters fled to Pakistani territory where Coalition forces could not pursue them. Air strikes were also limited as the perimeter needed in order to effectively attack the facility from multiple fronts overlapped with Pakistani air space.

[91] *See* Weaver, *supra* note 77.

[92] *See* BAHMANYAR, *supra* note 86, at 54.

[93] Steve Vogel, *Al Qaeda Tunnels, Arms Cache Totaled*, WASH. POST (Feb. 16, 2002), https://www.washingtonpost.com/archive/politics/2002/02/16/al-qaeda-tunnels-arms-cache-totaled/29166b3c-29ce-4252-a95b-51d9b3ebac92/?utm_term=.a9215c1350fe.

[94] *Id.*

A similar operation took place later that year, after the fall of the Taliban regime, at a time when Coalition forces increased their ground presence and decreased their reliance on aerial superiority. Operation Anaconda was staged in the Shahi-kot Valley, also part of the Paktia Province, in March 2002. Afghan forces, led and directed by Coalition Special Forces, posted snipers around the mountains to strike at al-Qaeda's hidden cave posts. It quickly became evident that al-Qaeda forces were entrenched in the mountains with large food and ammunition stocks. They moved swiftly between tunnel exits and hidden launching spots, camouflaging their locations, and only seemed vulnerable to direct contact fighting. They also held strategic observational intelligence posts that allowed them to strike, undetected, at Afghan/Coalition forces with great precision, limiting these forces' ability to strike back. On the first day of the operation, more than half of the ground troops and all but one helicopter carrying reinforcements were severely hit by al-Qaeda fire.[95]

This time, Afghan/Coalition forces used thermobaric weapons to overcome the underground challenge. Thermobaric bombs act as "vacuum bombs" by sucking out the air, yielding a strong detonation and very high temperatures that can cause significant damage to fortified structures. After a 2,000-pound thermobaric bomb was used on one of the fighting caves in the Shahi-kot Valley, military authorities determined that if the bomb was to detonate in a cave, tunnel, or other closed area nearly all the people inside would be incinerated or suffer from fatal internal injuries.[96]

The U.S experience in Tora Bora, Zhawar Killi, and other places where al-Qaeda used underground structures is extremely relevant at a time when underground warfare is used by more actors in more theaters of operation. It embodies a distinct type of underground warfare: non-urban, used exclusively for the benefit of combating forces, mixing old and new tunnels, often equipped with state-of-the-art facilities, and offering a major advantage to militarily-inferior forces over tech-savvy ones. Ten years later, al-Qaeda elements would rely on almost identical tactics in their fight against Malian and French forces.

VIII. A Different Type of Tunnel in Libya

Libya illustrates the use and appeal of yet another type of tunnel—dug on the basis of existing underground infrastructure, and primarily intended to serve as shelter in

---

[95] Richard Kugler, *Operation Anaconda in Afghanistan: A Case Study of Adaptation in Battle*, CASE STUDIES IN DEFENSE TRANSFORMATION 5 (2007), https://www.seongbae.com/wp-content/uploads/2015/07/Operation-Anaconda.pdf.
[96] THE ENCYCLOPEDIA OF MIDDLE EAST WARS: THE UNITED STATES IN THE PERSIAN GULF, AFGHANISTAN, AND IRAQ CONFLICTS 1237 (Spencer C. Tucker ed., 2010); The United States used thermobaric weapons again in Falluja in 2004 but not as part of Operation Anaconda (*see* Gordon Duff, *VT Nuclear Education: Fission Based Thermobaric Weapons*, VETERANS TODAY (July 8, 2014), http://www.veteranstoday.com/2014/07/08/vt-nuclear-education-fission-based-thermobaric-weapons/).

difficult times. In the mid-1980s, Libyan leader Colonel Muammar Gaddafi decided to invest 33 billion dollars into the construction of irrigation canals, a project known as the Great Man Made River.[97] These irrigation canals were meant to transport water from the Sub-Saharan aquifer to the Tripoli and Benghazi region.

The immense depth and length of the canals, combined with the amounts of concrete used for reinforcement, however, quickly raised questions about their true purpose.[98] The irrigation canals, built with the help of European and South Korean engineers, were deep (up to 2,500 feet) and wide (13 feet).[99] They were constructed with pipes made of reinforced concrete, each one weighing 75 tons, and ran for approximately 2,000 miles from Tunisia to Egypt, reaching almost to Sudan and Chad in the south.[100]

It was suggested that they were built to provide protection for Gaddafi and his military, including his suspected chemical weapons arsenal, in case of invasion or bombardment.[101] Gaddafi reportedly hid Libyan gas bombs in the underground tunnels during the Gulf War of 1991 to avoid the fate of the Iraqi chemical arsenal.[102] However, it remains unclear whether the tunnels used for this purpose were the same irrigation tunnels discussed above or a separate underground facility.

Some of these suspicions were confirmed during the 2011 NATO campaign:[103]

> In and around Garyan, about 80 kilometers south of Tripoli, NATO's air operations have hit 18 military targets, including a tunnelled military complex in Wadi, southeast of Tripoli. This complex has been built into the mountains and was used to resupply pro-Qadhafi forces, tanks and other military vehicles.[104]

Colonel Gaddafi hid near Tripoli in tunnels built with high ceilings, solid walls, and heavy steel doors, which contained bombproof bunkers and were equipped with phones,

---

[97] Ian Black, *Have Gaddafi's Tanks Gone Underground?*, GUARDIAN (Apr. 18, 2011), http://www.theguardian.com/world/2011/apr/18/have-gaddafis-tanks-gone-underground.

[98] Raymond Bonner, *Libya's Vast Desert Pipeline Could Be Conduit for Troops*, N.Y. TIMES (Dec. 2, 1997), http://www.nytimes.com/1997/12/02/world/libya-s-vast-desert-pipeline-could-be-conduit-for-troops.html.

[99] See Black, *supra* note 97.

[100] See Raymond, *supra* note 98; ROBIN BIDWELL, DICTIONARY OF MODERN ARAB HISTORY: AN A TO Z OF OVER 2,000 ENTRIES FROM 1798 TO THE PRESENT DAY 162 (1998).

[101] See Raymond, *supra* note 98.

[102] Michael Wines, *U.S. Hints at Chemical Arms Bunker in Libya*, N.Y. TIMES (Mar. 7, 1991), http://www.nytimes.com/1991/03/07/world/us-hints-at-chemical-arms-bunker-in-libya.html.

[103] Martin Evans, *Libya: Vast Tunnel Network Could Make Col Gaddafi Harder to Find*, TELEGRAPH (Aug. 22, 2011), http://www.telegraph.co.uk/news/worldnews/africaandindianocean/libya/8716721/Libya-vast-tunnel-network-could-make-Col-Gaddafi-harder-to-find.html.

[104] See Press Briefing on Libya, NATO (July 7, 2011), http://www.nato.int/cps/en/natolive/opinions_76163.htm; *see also* Press Briefing on Libya, NATO (Sept. 13, 2011), http://www.nato.int/cps/en/natolive/opinions_77984.htm; and John F. Burns & C.J. Chivers, *After Rebel Success in Misurata, NATO Strikes Tripoli*,

food, water supplies, ammunition, golf carts, and gas masks.[105] Tunnels were also found under Gaddafi's summer home in al-Bayda, northeast of Benghazi. These tunnels were equally well-stocked with "bedrooms, bathrooms, kitchens, and even a sauna."[106]

Although speculation continues about the precise route and use of Gaddafi's tunnels,[107] there is little doubt that they created a challenge for NATO forces in 2011. These tunnels were unique as they were built by a political leader, on the territory of Libya alone, and for seemingly an exclusively defensive, long-term purpose. As such, Gaddafi's use of the underground departs from other post-9/11 uses of the underground. It is, however, reminiscent of Hitler's use of tunnels in World War II. As noted above, Hitler hid in an underground bunker complex, which served as a living space and headquarters during the last months of the war.[108]

IX. Ten Years On: AQIM Entrenches in Mali

The 2012 war in Mali replicated a pattern established during the two Afghanistan wars: violent nonstate actors using a mountainous and cavernous terrain as a long-term hideout, line of communication, and base from which to launch surprise attacks against the enemy. As in Afghanistan, the northern Malian terrain is very suitable for tunneling.

The first Tuareg rebellion began soon after Mali became independent in 1960. A second rebellion broke out in the 1990s between state authorities and the ethnic Tuareg populations residing in northern Mali.[109] In the midst of these tensions, a group of rebels joined the fight against Malian authorities, using guerilla tactics. The group became known as the Popular Movement for the Liberation of Azawad (MPLA). Its aspiration: an independent Tuareg state. The group was offered some autonomy but tensions increased again immediately following the signing of the Tamanrasset Accord in 1991.

N.Y. TIMES (May 12, 2011), http://www.nytimes.com/2011/05/13/world/africa/13libya.html ("the NATO bombing might have been aimed at a maze of subterranean tunnels and bunkers, and had done extensive damage. Bomb fragments indicated that bunker-busting bombs—meant to destroy underground sites—had been used, according to a Western security adviser to a TV crew who was on the tour. Close to the playground, a concrete stairway flanked by green-painted steel railings descended to a steel door set about 15 feet below ground level.").

[105] Richard Galpin, *The Web of Secret Tunnels under Gaddafi's Tripoli Compound*, BBC (Sept. 13, 2011), http://www.bbc.com/news/world-africa-14902645.

[106] Andrew Gilligan, *Libya: Col Gaddafi Moving around Tripoli in Secret Tunnels*, TELEGRAPH (May 13, 2011), http://www.telegraph.co.uk/news/worldnews/africaandindianocean/libya/8512986/Libya-Col-Gaddafi-moving-around-Tripoli-in-secret-tunnels.html.

[107] David Williams, Rick Dewsburg, Emily Allen & Rob Cooper, *Inside Gaddafi's Secret Tunnels: Rebels Break into Labyrinth for the First Time as They Claim to Have Cornered Leader and Sons*, DAILY MAIL (Aug. 26, 2011), http://www.dailymail.co.uk/news/article-2030012/Libyan-rebels-break-Gaddafis-secret-underground-tunnels.html.

[108] *See* Shuger & Berger, *supra* note 41.

[109] Baz Lecocq & Georg Klute, *Tuareg Separatism in Mali*, 68 INT'L J. 424, 426 (2013).

The situation in Mali deteriorated anew in 2011 in the wake of the Libyan conflict. The Tuaregs aligned with the Islamists, and the nationalist movement radicalized with the influx of jihadists from Libya.[110] The Malian government, concerned by this turn of events, and believing that the Tuareg had smuggled weapons from Libya into Mali, reinforced its presence in the north of the country. Following a coup d'état organized by a group of Malian soldiers who opposed the government's handling of the Tuareg issue, the newly-formed "National Movement for Liberation of Azawad" (MNLA) launched a series of attacks. Similar to the MPLA, the new MNLA called for an independent homeland for the Tuareg people but, this time, worked closely with Ansar Dine—a front group for al-Qaeda in the country, led by a former leader of the Tuareg revolts. Together, the groups established control over Northern Mali.[111] This takeover and more attacks by Ansar Dine led the Malian government to turn to the French for assistance.[112]

French forces had a difficult time re-establishing governmental control over the region as the nationalists-turned-jihadists had entrenched themselves in mountains and caves.[113] Using abandoned equipment such as bulldozers and Caterpillar machinery, they expanded existing natural structures, digging quickly and more efficiently than in most other theaters of war.[114] A young man was reportedly offered 10,000 francs a day by an al-Qaeda local commander (around $20)—a rate several times the normal wage—to dig tunnels.[115]

The mountainous landscape, already a rough terrain, became virtually impassable.[116] The caves provided excellent cover for the rebels, making surveillance difficult:[117] The only way to find a tunnel was "to observe militants entering and exiting the cave."[118] According to Col. Benoit Desmeulles, Commanding Officer of the Foreign Legion:

> We first used heavy artillery, jets and helicopters to downsize the enemy from a reasonable distance... We then started to clear all the caves in the valleys, which

---

[110] Peter Rutland, *Nationalists or Islamists?*, N.Y. TIMES (Jan. 15, 2013), http://www.nytimes.com/2013/01/16/opinion/global/nationalists-or-islamists.html.

[111] *Id.* at 430.

[112] Hussein Solomon, *Mali: West Africa's Afghanistan*, 158 RUSI J. 12 (2013).

[113] *African Troops to Join French Soldiers in Fight against Islamist Rebels in Mali*, NAT'L POST (Jan. 13, 2013), http://news.nationalpost.com/news/african-troops-to-join-french-soldiers-in-fight-against-islamist-rebels-in-mali.

[114] *Al Qaeda's Own "Country" for 2013: Northern Mali*, CBS NEWS (Dec. 31, 2012), http://www.cbsnews.com/news/al-qaedas-own-country-for-2013-northern-mali/.

[115] *Id.*

[116] *Al Qaeda Finds New Stronghold in Rugged Mountains of Mali as It Regroups in Africa*, FOX NEWS (Mar. 3, 2013), http://www.foxnews.com/world/2013/03/03/malian-mountains-provide-perfect-anctuary-for-al-qaeda-report-finds/.

[117] *Id.*

[118] *Id.*

was down to man-to-man fighting... We clear caves with grenades before entering them.[119]

The tunnels were used to transport and store food, fuel, and ammunition.[120] They were large enough for cars and the storage of barrels of gasoline.[121] Even solar panels were found, suggesting that human life in the tunnels of Northern Mali was largely self-sufficient.[122] In the Valley of the Ametetai, where underground combat mostly took place,[123] French soldiers "uncovered construction trucks that Jihadi fighters used to dig trenches and underground caches," as well as vegetable gardens, bags of rice, and drums of oil.[124]

Tunnels also connected the bases of Ansar Dine and al-Qaeda at the Mali-Algeria border.[125] The Islamist groups not only lived there,[126] but also controlled operations from these underground hideouts.[127] At the operational level, this exacerbated the challenge of locating enemy positions from the ground or from the air. French forces also feared underground, one-on-one combat.[128]

With the war in Mali, underground warfare certainly maintained its decades-long appeal and versatility—while expanding its reach to another battlefield.[129] It is unfortunate, however, that the methods used to defeat the tunnels and the type of opposition faced by French forces remain largely undocumented.

---

[119] Thomas Fessy, *French Fight in Mali's Hostile Desert*, BBC News (Mar. 25, 2013), http://www.bbc.com/news/world-africa-21919769.

[120] Chris Hughes, *Mali Menace: Why We Will End Up Fighting Al-Qaeda's Army in Africa*, Mirror (Jan. 16, 2013), http://www.mirror.co.uk/news/uk-news/mali-menace-why-we-will-end-up-fighting-1536512.

[121] Rukimini Callimachi, *Al Qaeda Fighters Carve Out Own Country in Mali*, Wash. Times (Jan. 16, 2013), http://www.washingtontimes.com/news/2013/jan/16/al-qaeda-fighters-carve-out-their-own-country/?page=all.

[122] *See* Hughes, *supra* note 120.

[123] Michael Shurkin, *France's War in Mali: Lessons from an Expeditionary Army*, RAND (2014), https://www.rand.org/content/dam/rand/pubs/research_reports/RR700/RR770/RAND_RR770.pdf ("[t]he fighting lasted through mid-March and was often hard going, particularly in the Amettetaï valley, where, because of the terrain and because the enemy had taken cover among boulders and in caves, French forces had to dismount and flush out enemy fighters, climbing from rock to rock, often engaging at close quarters, all in extreme heat (50-degrees Celsius).")

[124] Fessy, *supra* note 119.

[125] *See* Callimachi, *supra* note 121.

[126] *Id.*

[127] Stephen A. Harmon, Terror and Insurgency in the Sahara-Sahel Region: Corruption, Contraband, Jihad and the Mali War of 2012–2013 at 196 (2014).

[128] Jean-Philippe Rémy, *Mali: On a Cassé le Donjon d' AQMI*, Le Monde (Mar. 7, 2013), http://www.lemonde.fr/afrique/article/2013/03/08/voila-on-a-casse-le-donjon-d-aqmi_1844350_3212.html (in French).

[129] As noted in Jean-Philippe Rémy, *Dans les Roches de l'Adrar de Tigharghâr, une Bataille Cruciale est Engagée*, Le Monde (Feb. 28, 2013), http://www.lemonde.fr/afrique/article/2013/02/28/dans-les-roches-de-l-adrar-de-tigharghar-une-bataille-cruciale-est-engagee_1840262_3212.html ("No witness has approached [Tigharghâr] to testify. This battle is taking place far from the public's eyes.") (in French; translation by author).

X. From Smuggling to Terror: Hamas's Tunnels at the Gaza-Egypt Border

It is not known exactly when Hamas began digging tunnels.[130] One of the first recorded instances in the international press dates from 1996 when, according to the *New York Times*, "[g]uns by the tens of thousands were smuggled into Gaza from Egypt overland, by sea and by tunnels."[131] What is certain is that the use of tunnels between the Gaza Strip and the Sinai Peninsula began soon after the peace accords were signed between Israel and Egypt in 1979, and long before the digging of cross-border tunnels between Gaza and Israel. Tunnel-digging originally started as an economic activity, posing only a limited challenge to Israel's sovereignty and border control.

Since the mid-1990s, the tunnel infrastructure between the Sinai Peninsula and the Gaza Strip had been extensively used for smuggling basic goods, construction materials, fuel and weapons—and to move freely between Egypt and Gaza.[132] With Israel's unilateral withdrawal from the Gaza Strip in 2005, the purpose of the tunnels began to shift away from the smuggling of goods to the transfer of weapons and people.[133] Despite the fact that cross-border tunnels between Egypt and the Gaza Strip have been used by various Palestinian actors, today their utilization is mainly associated with Hamas.

After the Hamas takeover of Gaza in 2007, tunnels became one of Hamas's largest sources of income, making the border city of Rafah the economic capital of the Gaza Strip and, at the same time, the main target of Israeli anti-smuggling operations. According to data published by the Shin Bet before Operation Cast Lead, over $120 million were smuggled into the Gaza Strip in support of terrorist activities in 2007.[134] Goods smuggled through the tunnels into Gaza accounted for 60 percent of imports into Gaza (which total $1.5 billion), and roughly a fifth of Hamas's income in Gaza came from taxes paid for use of the tunnels.[135]

As a response to the economic and security threat, Egypt's then-president Hosni Mubarak took significant measures to put an end to tunneling activities on Egypt's

---

[130] According to some accounts, smuggling tunnels began to play a role in Gaza as early as the 1980s. Ben Piven, *Gaza's Underground: A Vast Tunnel Network That Empowers Hamas*, AL JAZEERA (July 23, 2014), http://america.aljazeera.com/articles/2014/7/23/gaza-undergroundhamastunnels.html.

[131] A.M. Rosenthal, *On My Mind; Would We Do It Again?*, N.Y. TIMES (Mar. 8, 1996), http://www.nytimes.com/1996/03/08/opinion/on-my-mind-would-we-do-it-again.html.

[132] Stephanie Latte Abdallah and Cedric Parizot, *Israelis and Palestinians in the Shadows of the Wall: Spaces of Separation and Occupation* 132 (2015).

[133] *See* Sarah El-Rashidi, *The Egypt-Gaza Tunnel Network: Humanitarian Necessity or Security Risk?*, AHRAM ONLINE (Sept. 5, 2012), http://english.ahram.org.eg/NewsContent/1/64/51839/Egypt/Politics-/The-EgyptGaza-tunnel-network-Humanitarian-necessit.aspx.

[134] *See* Nadav Zeevi, *The Tunnel Industry: Smuggling in Gaza*, NRG (Jan. 16, 2009), http://www.nrg.co.il/online/1/ART1/840/850.html (in Hebrew).

[135] *See* Eli Tzipori, *Tunnels, Big Money, and the Making of Millionaires in Gaza*, GLOBES (July 25, 2014), http://www.globes.co.il/news/article.aspx?did=1000957886 (in Hebrew).

northeastern border. The first measure, undertaken jointly by Israel and Egypt, was to close their borders with Gaza following Hamas's takeover of the Gaza Strip in 2007. The movement of goods and people became subject to strict limitations. Heavy taxation was levied on all products making their way in from Egypt. These measures only made underground smuggling more attractive.

Two years later, Egypt reportedly began the construction of a steel barrier along its border with Gaza with the technical support of the U.S. and French Armed Forces.[136] The barrier would be constructed 60 feet into the ground in order to prevent the passage of Palestinians into Egypt through the tunnels. The construction was neither announced nor officially confirmed by the Egyptian government, but rather became known through local testimonies reporting unusual military activity along the border.[137] According to the BBC, the barrier was bombproof and made of heavy-duty steel.[138] With a depth of only 60 feet, the barrier could not stop all tunnel smuggling but limited Hamas by destroying existing routes at depths of 60 feet or less. In other words, Egypt's barrier merely made digging (deeper) tunnels more costly and time-consuming.

The barrier was penetrated by Palestinian smugglers within a year. Some Palestinian smugglers reportedly breached the barrier by using a blowtorch to melt a hole in it. Others cut through the barrier with an oxygen-fueled cutter—a task that can take a few weeks.[139] As the barrier proved ineffective, the Egyptian government chose other strategies to contend with the tunnels. Mubarak was replaced as head of state by Mohamad Morsi, then-leader of the Egyptian Muslim Brotherhood, who claimed to be determined "to block the destabilizing flow of weapons and militants into Sinai from Gaza."[140] Measures intensified following an attack on Egyptian troops in the Sinai Peninsula in the summer of 2012 that took the lives of 16 soldiers.[141] Egypt claimed to have intelligence that pointed to the fact that the attackers were Palestinians who had entered Egypt through one of the many cross-border tunnels. Egypt begun using water and even sewage water to flood the cross-border tunnels.[142]

---

[136] *Construction of Egypt's Security Wall Causes Collapse of Smuggling Tunnels*, WORLD TRIB. (Jan. 13, 2010), http://www.worldtribune.com/worldtribune/WTARC/2010/me_palestinians0020_01_13.asp.

[137] Christian Fraser, *Egypt Starts Building Steel Wall on Gaza Strip Border*, BBC (Dec. 9, 2009), http://news.bbc.co.uk/2/hi/8405020.stm.

[138] *Id.*

[139] Jon Donnison, *Gazans Cut Through Egypt's Border Barrier*, BBC (May 6, 2010), http://news.bbc.co.uk/2/hi/8664316.stm.

[140] Fares Akram & David D. Kirkpatrick, *To Block Gaza Tunnels, Egypt Lets Sewage Flow*, N.Y. TIMES (Feb. 20, 2013), http://www.nytimes.com/2013/02/21/world/middleeast/egypts-floods-smuggling-tunnels-to-gaza-with-sewage.html?_r=0.

[141] *Egypt Starts Digging Along Gaza Border in Bid to Flood Tunnels*, Aug. 31, 2015, http://www.haaretz.com/israel-news/1.673801.

[142] *See The Enemy Below, supra* note 4.

When Abdel Fattah el-Sisi, an Egyptian army general, replaced Morsi, he imposed a life sentence on anyone who "digs, prepares or uses a road, a passage or an underground tunnel at border areas to communicate with a foreign body, a state or one of its subjects."[143] In addition, the Egyptian regime enforced a 3,000-foot-long buffer zone in the border area between the Sinai Peninsula and the Gaza Strip, clearing out residential areas in order to limit the reach of the tunnels into Egyptian territory.[144] Overall, Egypt claims to have destroyed about 1,370 tunnels linking Gaza to Egypt.[145]

Egypt's experience fits within a trend identified in the *New York Times* data, namely the rise of cross-border threats emanating from nonstate actors primarily for smuggling weapons and basic goods. Anti-tunnel Egyptian measures also underscore the deep sense of insecurity tunnels create—in this case both in terms of economic stability and human security. Egypt, like many other states, employed a panoply of measures in the hope of eliminating the threat, some of them highly controversial. Egyptian measures, albeit not uncommon as such, stand in stark contrast with the United States' reaction to the digging of hundreds of cross-border smuggling tunnels in Mexico. Unlike Egypt, the United States chose to invest in detection, monitoring, and neutralization. I return to the methods used by states to contend with tunnels in later parts of the book, with a focus on the methods' efficiency and legality.

XI. Hamas's Tunnels at the Israeli Border: Underground Warfare Meets Urban Warfare

Israel's involvement with tunnels dug at the Gaza-Egypt border was relatively limited until the start of the Second Intifada in 2000, when Gaza-based terrorist organizations began using tunnels to bring in weapons from Egypt. At the time, the Israel Defense Forces (IDF) had a presence in the Gaza Strip, and booby-trapped tunnels were often used against IDF forces. The IDF created "tunnel teams" whose job was to identify tunnel exit points, empty the tunnels of their occupants, and then plug or demolish them.[146]

---

[143] *Cabinet Approves Legislation Maximizing Penalty for Digging Border Tunnels*, ASWAT MASRIYA (Apr. 1, 2015), http://en.aswatmasriya.com/news/view.aspx?id=0866eff4-73ef-4fc1-845e-a21c34e3bee1.

[144] Jack Moore, *Egypt to Punish Tunnel Diggers with Life in Jail*, NEWSWEEK (Apr. 13, 2015), http://europe.newsweek.com/egypts-sisi-passes-life-sentence-law-tunnel-smugglers-sinai-321871?rm=eu.

[145] AFP & Times of Israel, *Egypt Destroys 1,370 Gaza Smuggling Tunnels*, TIMES OF ISRAEL (Mar. 12, 2014), http://www.timesofisrael.com/egypt-destroys-1370-gaza-smuggling-tunnels/; and AFP & Times of Israel, *Egyptian Army Destroys 13 More Gaza Tunnels*, TIMES OF ISRAEL (July 27, 2014), http://www.timesofisrael.com/egyptian-army-destroys-13-more-gaza-tunnels/.

[146] In 2004, as the use of tunnels to carry out attacks increased, the teams and the tunnel mandate were transferred to a new unit within the IDF Engineering Corps' Special Forces subdivision (Samur, established under Yahalom, an Engineering division in charge of special operations).

With the growing tension between the Palestinians and Israelis and Israel's unilateral withdrawal from the Gaza Strip in 2005, the nature of the tunnels began to change. Tunnels turned into a useful route for weaponry, explosives, and even human trafficking.[147] With time, tunnels also came in closer contact with the civilian population.

By digging tunnels under the Gaza/Egypt and Gaza/Israel borders, Hamas took the underground threat to another level.[148] The use of underground structures in twenty-first century warfare had until then generally been confined to rural areas such as the mountains of Afghanistan and Mali.

The tunnels leading from the Gaza Strip into Israel have assumed prominence because they were dug in close proximity to civilian populated areas and for different purposes than those between Gaza and Egypt—namely, kidnapping, tunnel mining, and/or infiltrating Israeli territory to carry out attacks. In addition, and despite Egypt's long-standing struggle with Hamas's tunnels, it was not until the confrontation between Hamas and Israel during the summer of 2014 that tunnels led to a full-fledged war for the first time in the region.

One of the earliest instances of the use of tunnels by Hamas against Israel dates from September 26, 2001, when Hamas operatives detonated explosives under an IDF post close to the Israeli-Egyptian border, injuring three IDF soldiers.[149] Although many incidents involving tunnels continued to occur regularly in the following years,[150] tunnels did not come to be regarded as a strategic threat on par with more conventional air, sea, and land warfare until Operation Protective Edge in 2014.[151] In fact, after its unilateral withdrawal from Gaza in 2005, Israel believed that tunnels dug underneath the Philadelphi corridor no longer constituted a threat (aside from the issue of smuggling weapons into Gaza from Sinai). But a period of intensive drilling began, and Israel's assumption proved wrong.

On June 25, 2006, IDF soldier Gilad Shalit was kidnapped. At approximately 5 a.m., Hamas operatives emerged on Israeli territory behind the army's defensive lines at the Israel-Gaza border. They used anti-tank weaponry against an IDF tank. Two of the three soldiers in the tank were shot on the spot by Hamas operatives.[152] The

---

[147] See El-Rashidi, *supra* note 133.
[148] See *infra* Chapter 7 for examples of tunnels dug in proximity to civilian dwellings in other conflicts.
[149] *Hamas Use of Gaza Strip-Based Subterranean Route*, ISRAELI SECURITY AGENCY, http://www.shabak.gov.il/English/EnTerrorData/Reviews/Pages/hamas-tunnel.aspx.
[150] *Id.*; see also *Summarizing Four Years of Conflict—Statistics and Trends of Terrorism*, ISRAELI SECURITY AGENCY (2004), http://www.shabak.gov.il/SiteCollectionImages/ופרסומים%20סקירות/terror-summary-4years-new.pdf (in Hebrew); and Noam Sharvit, *5 Soldiers Killed in the Detonation of an Explosives Tunnel Under the Rafah Border Crossing*, NEWS1 (Dec. 12, 2004), http://www.news1.co.il/Archive/001-D-59806-00.html (in Hebrew).
[151] Shapir & Perel, *supra* note 4.
[152] Amos Harel, *How Were Palestinian Militants Able to Abduct Gilad Shalit?*, HAARETZ (Oct. 18, 2011), http://www.haaretz.com/print-edition/news/how-were-palestinian-militants-able-to-abduct-gilad-shalit-1.390573.

third soldier—Gilad Shalit—was wounded during the assault on the tank and kidnapped shortly thereafter; within six minutes he was out of reach of IDF forces. Hamas operatives had used a tunnel—hundreds of feet long and dug over the course of months—to reach their target undetected and escape with the hostage quickly and safely.[153] Whereas in the past tunnels serving noneconomic purposes had often been dug under enemy forces' camps to detonate explosives, the Shalit incident introduced another use of tunnels in the region: kidnapping and direct engagement with enemy forces. Hamas established a special unit for this purpose, known as "Nuhba."[154] This innovative and successful use of the underground, combined with the strategic impact of kidnapping a soldier, was significant for Hamas.

Notwithstanding the set back, Israel's policy regarding the tunnels did not change fundamentally. The unfortunate outcome of the attack was blamed on improper operational preparation. The perception remained that cross-border tunnels were a means to carry out sporadic terror attacks, rather than a strategic threat requiring unique expertise and solutions.[155] Hamas's tunnel network was primarily thought of as an internal asset designed to help the group operate without being detected or targeted from the air.

The Second Lebanon War in 2006 against Hezbollah further demonstrated the scope of the underground threat, albeit confined to Lebanon and not crossing over to Israel:

> Before the conflict Hezbollah had constructed an elaborate system of bunkers, tunnels, and safe houses linked together by a private communications system and stocked with ample food, water, and ammunition. Once the battle started, its fighters were able to resupply themselves and to maneuver effectively under fire ... [T]hey were able to attack Israeli troops from unexpected directions, knocking out tanks and troop concentrations with missiles ranging from the older Sagger to the more modern Kornet.[156]

Following the war, Israel stepped up its effort to combat the growing threat by building a special underground training facility in which all combat units operating along Israel's

---

[153] *Id.*

[154] THE STATE OF ISRAEL, THE 2014 GAZA CONFLICT (7 JULY–26 AUGUST 2014)—FACTUAL AND LEGAL ASPECTS, (May 2015), at 45, http://mfa.gov.il/ProtectiveEdge/Documents/2014GazaConflictFullReport.pdf [hereinafter ISRAEL REPORT].

[155] *See* Ben Caspit, *The True Story: What Shalit Told the IDF After His Release*, MAARIV (Mar. 25, 2013), http://www.maariv.co.il/news/new.aspx?pn6Vq=EE&or9VQ=HMHL (in Hebrew); *see also* Yariv Peleg, *Operation Cast Lead: Step by Step*, MAKO (Sept. 12, 2013), http://www.mako.co.il/pzm-israel-wars/operation-cast-lead/Article-6377d1b8743e041006.htm (in Hebrew).

[156] *See* Boot, *supra* note 56, at 511. *See also* Steven Erlanger & Richard A. Oppel, Jr., *A Disciplined Hezbollah Surprises Israel with its Training, Tactics and Weapons*, N.Y. TIMES (Aug. 7, 2006), http://www.nytimes.com/2006/08/07/world/middleeast/07hezbollah.html?_r=0.

southern border undergo training.[157] The unique facility prepared troops for what was to come next. Just two year later, a confrontation broke out with Hamas. The escalation was triggered to some extent by a small operation, known as "Double Challenge," during which the Israeli army made an incursion over 800 feet into Gaza to destroy a cross-border tunnel.[158] A month and a half later, on December 27, 2008, following intensive rocket fire from Gaza into Israeli territory, the IDF launched Operation Cast Lead. On the second day of the operation, 40 smuggling tunnels along the Gaza-Egypt border were targeted, as were the homes of senior Hamas operatives known to be storing weapons caches or housing tunnel entrances.[159] For the first time, cross-border tunnels were used in the midst of a conflict in the Gaza-Israel theater.

IDF officials soon realized that air strikes would not be sufficient; Hamas retreated inside the tunnels as soon as they began. Only a ground operation would destroy the network of tunnels dug beneath Gaza. Although a ground operation would be needed for the IDF to physically reach the tunnels, particularly those located in the midst of civilian populated areas, it was well understood that it would lead to more direct confrontations between IDF soldiers and Hamas operatives and probably to more casualties on both sides. On January 3, 2009, IDF ground troops entered the Gaza Strip. As they had anticipated, they encountered enemy forces emerging from tunnels, many of them booby-trapped.[160]

Tunnels played a more subdued role in the next confrontation, four years later. Operation Pillar of Defense began with air strikes, one of which killed Hamas's military commander, Ahmad Jabbari, and seriously damaged Hamas's caches of Fajr-5 missiles.[161] In contrast to Cast Lead, Operation Pillar of Defense lasted only a short time (eight days), and thousands of targets within Gaza were hit from the air, including hundreds of tunnel-related targets, most of which were smuggling tunnels along the Gaza-Egypt border, rather than beneath the Israel-Gaza border. Due to the success of the aerial campaign, the damage done to Hamas's operational capabilities, and the concern for the cost, in resources and lives, of a possible ground operation, the Israeli government decided to end the operation after eight days.

Yet barely a year later, tunnels were back in the spotlight. In October 2013, the IDF discovered a cross-border tunnel between Khan Younis in Gaza and the civilian-populated

---

[157] Smadar Krampf, *Deep Underground*, 21 BAYABASHA (2012), http://mazi.idf.il/6939-10870-he/IGF.aspx (in Hebrew).

[158] *See* Hanan Greenberg & Ali Wakad, *Gaza: IDF Tries to Destroy Tunnel; 6 Terrorists Dead*, YNET (Nov. 4, 2008), http://www.ynet.co.il/articles/0,7340,L-3617788,00.html (in Hebrew).

[159] *See* Amir Buchbut & Ori Binder, *Air Force Strikes in Rafah; Palestinians Illegally Cross to Egypt*, NRG (Dec. 28, 2008), http://www.nrg.co.il/online/1/ART1/831/884.html (in Hebrew).

[160] Hanan Greenberg, *Senior Army Officer Describes Recently Discovered Gaza Tunnels*, YNET (Jan. 6, 2009), http://www.ynet.co.il/articles/0,7340,L-3651617,00.html (in Hebrew).

[161] Shahar Hai & Gilad Morag, *Defense Minister: We Hit Most of Hamas' "Fagerim"*, YNET (Nov. 14, 2012), http://www.ynet.co.il/articles/0,7340,L-4305503,00.html (in Hebrew).

area of Kibbutz Ein Hashlosha in Israel.[162] The tunnel was spacious enough to allow an adult to stand upright and to transport several people at the same time; it also had multiple openings in different locations and was a little more than a mile long and 65 feet deep. The tunnel was fortified with concrete, and equipped with railways, electrical wires, numerous branches, and exit shafts inside the kibbutz.[163] According to the IDF, this was the third and most sophisticated tunnel uncovered that year. Intelligence officials believed the tunnel was meant for a future round of fighting between Israel and Hamas. Estimates claim that it took over a year and about 24,000 Israeli concrete slabs to construct, costing millions of dollars in construction materials and labor. The IDF destroyed the tunnel in a joint operation with the Israeli Air Force by injecting liquid explosives into the ground. Following the discovery of the Ein Hashlosha tunnel, Israel became more vocal about the threat to its civilians and soldiers.[164]

Only a few months later, another round of hostilities broke out between Hamas and Israel—with the tunnels taking center stage. Operation Protective Edge was the outcome of escalating tension between Israel and the Hamas government in the Gaza Strip, and the kidnapping and murder of three Israeli teenage boys in the West Bank. The IDF bombed a tunnel in the Kerem Shalom area close to the Israeli-Egyptian border on July 6th, amidst fears it might be used for kidnapping. The IDF strike killed seven Hamas Special Forces personnel. Hamas responded with massive rocket fire on southern Israel, and Israel ramped up air strikes on Hamas targets in Gaza, including many tunnels.[165] With Operation Protective Edge, cross-border tunnels built by Hamas in Gaza and exiting onto Israeli territory came to be regarded for the first time by the public as a significant threat—and by the security and military establishment as one of the main reasons for the confrontation. Despite their sporadic use over more than a decade, Hamas's tunnels had not yet received such attention.

Importantly, the escalation that began the second phase of Operation Protective Edge was also caused by a tunnel-related incident. Israel decided to launch a comprehensive ground operation into the Gaza Strip following an attempt by 13 Hamas fighters to cross the border with Israel using a tunnel near Kibbutz Sufa on July 17th.[166] As soon as the

---

[162] Yoav Zeitun & Ilana Kuriel, *Inside Israel: Discovery of a Terror Tunnel*, YNET (Oct. 13, 2013), http://www.ynet.co.il/articles/0,7340,L-4439702,00.html (in Hebrew); Sinai Libel, *What to Know Before the Fight*, 458 MAARACHOT 64 (2014), http://maarachot.idf.il/PDF/FILES/8/113578.pdf (in Hebrew).

[163] *See* Zeitun & Kuriel, *supra* note 162.

[164] *See, e.g.,* Yaakov Lappin, *IDF Uncovers Palestinian Terrorist Tunnel Leading from Gaza to Kibbutz in Israel*, JERUSALEM POST (Oct. 13, 2013), http://www.jpost.com/National-News/IDF-discovers-Palestinian-terrorist-tunnel-leading-from-Gaza-to-Kibbutz-in-Israel-328584; and Gili Cohen & Shirli Saydler, *IDF Uncovers a Tunnel Leading from Gaza to Israel*, HAARETZ (Oct. 13, 2013), http://www.haaretz.co.il/news/politics/1.2138631 (in Hebrew).

[165] Amos Harel, *Intelligence War: Gaps in Preparedness at "Aman" and "Shabak"*, HAARETZ (Sept. 5, 2014), http://www.haaretz.co.il/news/politics/.premium-1.2425438 (in Hebrew).

[166] Yochai Ofer, *IDF Averted Large-Scale Attack via Terror Tunnel*, NRG (July 17, 2014), http://www.nrg.co.il/online/1/ART2/597/355.html (in Hebrew).

IDF spotted the infiltration, it attacked the tunnel shaft, killing five Hamas operatives. Though no Israeli civilians or army personnel were injured during this attempted infiltration,[167] subsequent Israeli scans of the tunnel uncovered ammunition, grenades, grenade launchers, and military-grade vests.

The decision to launch a ground operation in Gaza led to additional encounters with tunnel warfare, including the infiltration of Hamas operatives in civilian populated areas through cross-border tunnels. On July 19th, nine operatives used a cross-border tunnel to infiltrate a residential area between Kibbutz Be'eri and Kibbutz Ein Hashlosha. They engaged in frontal combat with IDF soldiers, causing two casualties on the Israeli side and one on the Palestinian side.[168] Hamas operatives emerged from the tunnels wearing IDF uniforms and were thus not immediately identified as a threat. Upon reaching Israeli territory, they entered a deserted IDF post and fired RPG rockets at two IDF jeeps. The Israeli forces fired back, forcing the operatives to retreat back to Gaza though the tunnel. After the incident, the Air Force attacked the tunnel shaft and destroyed it.[169]

Less than a week later, four Hamas operatives infiltrated the Israeli residential area of Kibbutz Nachal-Oz, 500 feet from the Gaza border, and killed five IDF soldiers in their post with an antitank missile.[170] Other IDF soldiers in a nearby post noticed the attack and fired back, killing one Hamas fighter and preventing the others from kidnapping the bodies of the dead soldiers back into Gaza. The fighters left their weapons behind (four AK-47 rifles and two RPG launchers) and retreated back into the tunnel. In yet another incident involving the underground, Lt. Hadar Goldin was kidnapped into a tunnel and killed. The incident, which revived the Gilad Shalit trauma of 2006, played on one of the IDF's greatest vulnerabilities.[171]

The amount and diversity of tunnel-related attacks make clear that underground warfare permeated the 2014 war in Gaza like never before in contemporary warfare. The belligerents' strategies were mostly improvised as the conflict unfolded. As Israel learned to contend with the threat, Hamas, too, improved its tactical use of tunnels. For instance, Hamas understood that it could use the tunnels to launch surprise attacks against IDF soldiers, kidnap soldiers (dead or alive), bury rocket launchers, and hide ammunition—thereby

---

[167] Mitch Ginsburg, *Tunnel Infiltration Thwarted near Kibbutz Sufa*, TIMES OF ISRAEL (July 17, 2014), http://www.timesofisrael.com/tunnel-infiltration-thwarted-near-kibbutz-sufa/.

[168] See *Protective Edge—Day by Day, Hour by Hour*, HAARETZ (Aug. 8, 2014), http://www.haaretz.co.il/news/politics/.premium-1.2395400 (in Hebrew).

[169] A similar incident took place on July 21, 2014, in the residential area of Kibbutz Nir-Am, over 800 feet deep into Israel. Again, the terrorists wore IDF uniforms, allowing them to penetrate Israeli territory undetected.

[170] See *Operation Protective Edge—Update No. 15*, THE MEIR AMIT INTELLIGENCE AND TERRORISM INFORMATION CENTER (July 29, 2014), http://www.terrorism-info.org.il/he/articleprint.aspx?id=20689 (in Hebrew); and Gili Cohen, *The Nachal-Oz Infiltration: Four Armed Men Fired an Anti-tank Missile at an IDF Post and Attempted to Abduct a Dead Body*, HAARETZ (July 29, 2014), http://www.haaretz.co.il/news/politics/.premium-1.2390672 (in Hebrew).

[171] See Gal Perl Finkel, *Analysis: The IDF vs Subterranean Warfare*, JERUSALEM POST (Aug. 16, 2016), http://www.jpost.com/Opinion/Analysis-The-IDF-vs-subterranean-warfare-464229.

complicating the IDF's response against rocket fire and Israel's assessment of Hamas's destructive capabilities. To protect its tunnels from attack, Hamas hid tunnel shafts under schools, hospitals, mosques, and private civilian dwellings.[172]

In sum, tunnels dug by Hamas between Gaza and Israel embody a shift towards the use of cross-border tunnels by nonstate actors, as part of a long-term strategy designed to overcome the technological superiority of their opponents. These tunnels are man-made, sophisticated for the most part, and, importantly, dug in the midst of civilian populated areas. In addition to posing a significant security threat, this type of tunnel has deep psychological effects on civilians and combatants, as will be explained in Chapter 7. As time goes by and Hamas takes full measure of the versatility of the underground, its tunnels will better serve their wide variety of purposes—from lines of communication to kidnapping and attacking civilians and combatants alike.

XII. The Widespread and Innovative Use of Tunnels in Syria

Along with Operation Protective Edge, the ongoing conflict in Syria provides some of the most compelling evidence of the growing threat posed by underground warfare. The war in Syria exposes innovative and far-reaching uses of tunnels, which has led both sides to go underground to an extent not witnessed since World War I.

Interestingly, the use of the underground in Syria began as an attempt to shield civilians from the devastating effects of the civil war. Shortly after the start of the war in 2012, civilians sought shelter from aerial bombardments in underground caves and tunnels. Students and teachers were relocated in order to allow classes to continue despite the conflict.[173] Soon entire Syrian families were taking refuge in newly excavated ancient Roman caves.[174] Today these ancient caves have been transformed into intricate tunnel complexes, used by both pro-government and rebel forces in the fight for the control of Syria.[175]

The use of the underground for civilian, defensive purposes quickly evolved as fighters took measure of its appeal. In August 2013, in one of the earliest recorded instances of

---

[172] Israel Report, *supra* note 154, para. 130 (noting that a tunnel, rigged with a massive explosive, was hidden under a health clinic in Khan Yunis) and para. 142 (another tunnel ran under the Jema'at a-Salah school in the refugee camps of the central Gaza Strip). *See also Watch: IDF Finds Mosque with Weapons and Tunnel Openings*, HAARETZ (July 31, 2014), http://www.haaretz.com/israel-news/videos/1.608165; and Judah Ari Gross, *In Gaza, Hamas Tunnels Run Under Mosques, Homes—Shin Bet*, TIMES OF ISRAEL (July 5, 2016), http://www.timesofisrael.com/in-gaza-hamas-tunnels-run-under-mosques-homes-shin-bet/.

[173] Ben Brumfield & Saad Abedine, *Cave Becomes Classroom for Syrian Kids*, CNN (Oct. 12, 2012), http://edition.cnn.com/2012/10/05/world/meast/syria-underground-school/index.html.

[174] C.J. Chivers, *Jammed in Roman Caves, Ducking Syria's War*, N.Y. TIMES (Mar. 23, 2013), http://www.nytimes.com/2013/03/24/world/middleeast/syrians-fleeing-home-crowd-in-roman-caves.html.

[175] Christian Storm, *Tens of Thousands of People Are Hiding in These Immense Syrian Tunnels and Caves*, BUS. INSIDER (Mar. 10, 2015), http://uk.businessinsider.com/syrian-secret-cave-hideouts-2015-3?op=1?r=US.

use of the underground for offensive purposes in Syria, rebels used a tunnel to infiltrate a Syrian army building, killing 12 soldiers.[176] The surviving Syrian soldiers later discovered a tunnel 7 feet high and 10 feet wide, running a 1,000 feet long and 33 feet deep. The tunnel was reinforced with metal pillars, wide enough to allow a steady flow of fighters and weapons, and equipped with electricity, lighting, and ventilation systems for long-term stays.[177]

It was, however, Operation Aleppo Earthquake that marked the real turning point in the conduct of underground warfare in Syria. On May 8, 2014, rebels filled a 350-foot-long tunnel with explosives and remotely detonated them under the Carlton Hotel in Aleppo, which served as a command center for Assad's forces.[178] It took 33 days to dig the tunnel using pickaxes and other cheap digging tools (they worried that advanced digging machines would make noise and give away the attack).[179] Approximately 40 Syrian soldiers died in the attack. The ground shook as if an earthquake had occurred—contributing to the dramatic effect of the explosion and, ultimately, its name. The blast, which was felt within a radius of 9 miles, left nothing but piles of dust and rubble. The Islamic Front claimed responsibility,[180] adding that tunnels formed part of a new strategy and vowing to carry out similar attacks in the near future.[181] Operation Aleppo Earthquake was perceived as a significant success and left an important imprint on the conflict from the perspective of underground warfare.[182]

Both the manual digging and the specific designation of the tunnel for mining in Operation Aleppo Earthquake are reminiscent of World War I tunnel warfare.[183] Part of the inspiration, however, seems to have come from Gaza. When asked how he got the

---

[176] Sammy Ketz, *Syria Rebel "Moles" Wage Battle from Underground Tunnels*, FOX NEWS (Aug. 5, 2013), http://www.foxnews.com/world/2013/08/05/syria-rebel-moles-wage-battle-from-underground-tunnels/.

[177] *Id.*

[178] Chulov, *supra* note 1.

[179] Ruth Sherlock, *Syrian Rebels Tunnel Under Aleppo Front Line to Bomb Government Hotel*, TELEGRAPH (May 8, 2014), http://www.telegraph.co.uk/news/worldnews/middleeast/syria/10817967/Syrian-rebels-tunnel-under-Aleppo-front-line-to-bomb-government-hotel.html.

[180] Rob Williams, *Syria Conflict: Rebels Claim Responsibility for "Huge" Aleppo Blast That Destroyed Hotel*, INDEPENDENT (May 8, 2014), http://www.independent.co.uk/news/world/middle-east/syria-rebels-claim-responsibility-for-huge-blast-that-leveled-hotel-in-aleppo-9337826.html.

[181] *See* Sherlock, *supra* note 179.

[182] The delayed detonation of the bomb allowed the rebels to film the attack, and the footage soon went viral (for a video of the detonation, see https://www.liveleak.com/view?i=308_1399551931 (on file with author)). On the role of social media in diffusing the tactic, see *ISIS Is Using Tunnel Bombs in Iraq*, *supra* note 19 ("As part of an information operations campaign, these attacks are documented and widely proliferated via social media which increases the likelihood of migration to other conflict areas or adoption by other extremist organizations on a worldwide basis.").

[183] *See* JONES, *supra* note 18, at 117, citing Lieutenant Geoffrey Malins who was filming a mining attack during World War I ("Then it happened. The ground where I stood gave a mighty convulsion. It rocked and swayed. I gripped hold of my tripod to steady myself. Then, for all the world like a gigantic sponge, the earth rose in the air to the height of hundreds of feet. Higher and higher it rose, and with a horrible, grinding roar the earth fell back upon itself, leaving in its place a mountain of smoke.").

idea for the Aleppo Earthquake operation, the operation's mastermind explained that it came to him from a friend from Gaza who came to visit Syria and shared his experience with tunnels in the Gaza/Israel theater: "They said they had some success in Palestine, so I decided to try it."[184] That the know-how is passing from Gaza to Syria has been confirmed by other reports.[185] The diffusion of the tactic from Gaza to Syria highlights the process through which the tactic is imported to and adapted on new battlefields, as I explain further in Chapter 2.

Empowered by the success and broad coverage of the Aleppo Earthquake operation, the rebels conducted repeated tunnel mining operations in the week that followed. Another massive tunnel attack took place on May 14, 2014, under the Tallet al-Swadi Syrian military checkpoint in the Wadi Deif Base.[186] A tunnel packed with as much as 60 tons of explosives was detonated, sending the ground on the hillside several meters into the air. At least 20 soldiers were killed in the attack. The Islamic Front once again claimed responsibility.[187] Two weeks later the organization claimed yet another deadly tunnel attack, killing approximately 40 Syrian Army soldiers in the northern part of Aleppo.[188]

With time, the rebels developed new skills in tunnel warfare. They used the tunnels to infiltrate hostile territory and launch surprise attacks by "rebel moles" inside military strongholds.[189] Faced with the growing threat, Assad's forces turned to geologists in order to improve their ability to detect tunnels.[190] They also began digging their own tunnels in the hope of finding the rebels before they could strike. Although Syrian Army and rebel forces dig their tunnels on different levels, they commonly launch underground surprise attacks against each other. When such an encounter takes place, Assad's forces and the rebels engage in direct underground confrontation.

Frontal underground combat, combined with tunnel mining, sets the Syrian experience apart in contemporary underground warfare. Assad not only destroyed and neutralized tunnels, he also sent his troops inside the tunnels to engage in underground

---

[184] Chulov, *supra* note 1.
[185] *See, e.g., Hamas Is Training the Rebels in Syria on Building Tunnels*, YNET (Apr. 5, 2013), http://www.ynet.co.il/articles/0,7340,L-4364324,00.html (in Hebrew).
[186] Mariam Karouny, *Massive Tunnel Bomb Hits Syrian Army Base*, REUTERS (May 15, 2014), http://www.reuters.com/article/2014/05/15/us-syria-crisis-airstrikes-idUSBREA4E09520140515.
[187] *Id.*
[188] *See Aleppo Tunnel Blast Kills 20–40 Syrian Army Security Forces*, I24NEWS, (Jan. 6, 2014), http://www.i24news.tv/en/news/international/middle-east/140601-aleppo-tunnel-blast-kills-20-40-syrian-army-security-forces; and *Syrian Troops Hit in Aleppo Tunnel Bombing*, AL JAZEERA (July 31, 2014), http://www.aljazeera.com/news/middleeast/2014/05/syrian-troops-hit-aleppo-tunnel-bombing-201453113263576410 2. html. The Islamic Front claimed responsibility for a third tunnel attack on July 29, 2014, killing at least 13 Syrian military personnel (see *Syrian Soldiers Killed by Rebel Tunnel-Bombs*, AL JAZEERA (July 29, 2014), http://www.aljazeera.com/news/middleeast/2014/07/syrian-soldiers-killed-rebel-tunnel-bombs-20147291993231487.html).
[189] *See* Ketz, *supra* note 176.
[190] *Id.*

combat—something most states have avoided since WWI. Syria also provides an example of the "stronger" party in the conflict adopting the tactics of the "weaker" party.[191] The Syria War therefore stands out as a conflict in which tunnels have been used by both state *and* nonstate actors, and by both combatants (to launch surprise attacks *and* protect military personnel and ammunition) *and* civilians (as shelter). Syrian actors have maximized the use of man-made *and* existing underground structures, rudimentary *and* sophisticated tunnels, for short-term *and* long-term purposes—thereby demonstrating their mastery of underground warfare and the breadth of its strategic appeal.

XIII. ISIS's Tunnels in Iraq

Tunnel warfare in contemporary Iraq can be traced back to Saddam Hussein's expensive and expansive underground project—some say it was initially meant to host a subway.[192] Decades later tunnels became part and parcel of the Islamic State's attempts at establishing control over Iraqi territory.[193]

ISIS reliance on the underground in Iraq borrows heavily from the war in Syria. The group has used the subterranean to host detention facilities and living quarters, carry out tunnel mining and cross-border attacks, and engage in underground combat.[194] Most ISIS tunnels are man-made. The more sophisticated ones are used to hide from aerial air strikes and attack anti-ISIS forces by surprise. Tunnels of this type have been found under civilian dwellings in the city of Sinjar, equipped with sleeping quarters and electricity, and fortified with sandbags.[195] Kurdish forces who discovered the tunnels found "mattresses, blankets, fans, food, electrical cables and light bulbs, curtains for privacy,

---

[191] I am indebted to Adv. Ido Rosenzweig for this point.
[192] *See U.S. Forces Venture into Saddam's Vast Tunnels*, Fox News (Apr. 9, 2003), http://www.foxnews.com/story/2003/04/09/us-forces-venture-into-saddam-vast-tunnels.html; Richard Muller, *Baghdad Express*, MIT Tech. Rev. (March 14, 2003), https://www.technologyreview.com/s/401855/baghdad-express/; Robert Tanner, *Underground Operations*, Guardian (April 9, 2003), https://www.theguardian.com/world/2003/apr/09/iraq5.
[193] *See ISIS Is Using Tunnel Bombs in Iraq*, *supra* note 19.
[194] ISIS has also used the underground for detention facilities. *See Report: 1500 Prisoners Released from ISIS Underground Prison*, Mako (Apr. 3, 2016), http://www.mako.co.il/news-world/arab-q2_2016/Article-c06ea014dd8d351004.htm (in Hebrew); *ISIS Shows Off Tunnels That It Claims Let Fighters Survive U.S. Airstrikes*, NBC News (Nov. 12, 2014), http://www.nbcnews.com/storyline/isis-terror/isis-shows-tunnels-it-claims-let-fighters-survive-u-s-n247361.
[195] *ISIS Dug Networks of Tunnels Under Conquered Iraqi City of Sinjar*, NBC News (Nov. 25, 2015), http://www.nbcnews.com/storyline/isis-terror/isis-dug-network-tunnels-under-conquered-iraqi-city-sinjar-n469366; Loveday Morris, *Iraqi Troops Face Booby Traps, Tunnels Packed with Explosives as They Advance on Fallujah*, Wash. Post (June 11, 2016), https://www.washingtonpost.com/world/middle_east/iraqi-troops-face-booby-traps-tunnels-packed-with-explosives-as-they-advance-on-fallujah/2016/06/11/97dd7314-2f19-11e6-b9d5-3c3063f8332c_story.html.

shelves with books on them, prescription drugs" as well as military material and ammunition.[196] ISIS also used a tunnel network near the city of Fallujah to hide from aerial strikes, move fighters and weapons around safely, and launch ambushes against Iraqi and coalition forces. A U.S. national fighting ISIS in Iraq alongside Kurdish forces reported that ISIS fighters hide in these tunnels during the day and wait for darkness to come out and attack.[197] ISIS tunnels stretch for about a half mile, says Brig. Gen. Ali Jamil of Iraq's counterterrorism forces, adding that "[t]he Iraqi forces do not know how far others they have found extend, because they blow up the entrances so the tunnels can't be used."[198]

Tunnels dug for short-term purposes tend to be more rudimentary; their objective is to serve for tunnel mining and they are sometimes referred to as "tunnel bombs". ISIS relied in part on this type of tunnels to gain control over the Iraqi city of Ramadi:[199]

On March 11, 2015, ISIS forces detonated a tunnel bomb under an Iraqi army headquarters, killing an estimated 22 people. The blast consumed seven tons of explosives in an 800-foot long tunnel that took months to dig (…) On March 15, a second tunnel bomb was used to attack Iraqi Security Forces. The city fell two months later.[200]

The underground also played a major role in the fight over Mosul. ISIS rigged the city and surrounding areas with extensive tunnels used to improve mobility across the battlefield, stage surprise attacks, and quickly retreat.[201] Inside the tunnels, ISIS fighters were almost self-sufficient: food and electricity equipment were discovered by coalition forces after taking over the area.[202] The presence of the tunnels in an urban setting created a challenge for Iraqi forces wanting to retake the city. In particular, the existence of underground

---

[196] Eddy Van Wessel, *Video Shows ISIL's Underground War Tunnels and "Mass Grave" in Sinjar*, Telegraph (Nov. 25, 2015), http://www.telegraph.co.uk/news/worldnews/islamic-state/12015819/Video-shows-Isils-underground-war-tunnels-and-mass-grave-in-Sinjar.html.
[197] Matt Blake, *What It's Like to Fight ISIS in Iraq as a Westerner*, Vice (June 29, 2016), http://www.vice.com/read/two-years-islamic-state-caliphate-british-fighter.
[198] See Morris, *supra* note 195.
[199] See ISIS Is Using Tunnel Bombs in Iraq, *supra* note 19.
[200] Id.
[201] Andrew Tilghman, *Tunnel Warfare: In Mosul, the ISIS Fight Is Likely to Go Underground*, Military Times (Oct. 1, 2016) http://www.militarytimes.com/articles/tunnel-warfare-in-mosul-the-isis-fight-is-likely-to-go-underground; Matt Hunter, *Inside the Tunnels Where Jihadis Fought to the Death*, Daily Mail (June 1, 2016), http://www.dailymail.co.uk/news/article-3626120/Hidden-network-ISIS-tunnels-jihadis-live-weeks-underground-avoid-caught-Peshmerga-forces.html.
[202] Harriet Agerholm, *Isis' Labyrinth of Underground Tunnels That Could Await the US-Led Forces Attempting to Take Raqqa*, Independent (Nov. 8, 2016), http://www.independent.co.uk/news/world/middle-east/isis-labyrinth-underground-tunnels-could-await-us-led-forces-attempting-take-raqqa-syria-kurdish-a7402971.html; Jeremy Berke, *Take a Look Inside ISIS' Newly-Discovered Escape Tunnels Outside of Its Iraqi Stronghold*, Bus. Insider (Oct. 28, 2016), http://www.businessinsider.com/isis-escape-tunnels-in-iraq-2016-10/#some-tunnels-are-big-enough-for-a-motorbike-and-some-tunnel-entrances-were-to-be-connected-by-a-newly-built-road-3.

passages and bunkers prevented areas won over by Iraqi forces from being truly secured, as the threat of ISIS fighters emerging from the ground lingered.[203]

Even cross-border tunnels have been found in the region.[204] In late 2013, Iraqi authorities uncovered three smuggling tunnels between the Iraqi al-Anbar region and the Syrian al-Kamal region.[205] The discovery of another cross-border underground complex reaching almost four miles into Iraqi territory was also reported in March 2014. Iraqi forces detonated the complex after confiscating carts filled with ammunition.[206] As in Syria, the use of the underground by ISIS seems to be pushing Iraqi forces below ground. Some reports indicate that tunnels helped Iraqi forces push ISIS out of the Anbar province, for example.[207]

The advanced and varied use of the underground in Iraq and Syria suggests that underground warfare, in one form or another, is likely to spread to more theaters of operations in the future. This prediction finds support in theories advanced to explain the diffusion of military tactics. I show in Chapter 2 that the evolution of underground warfare resembles that of suicide terrorism. A comparison of the two tactics suggests that underground warfare is likely to further diffuse in the future among relatively young and/or flexible nonstate actors, using the Internet and the relationships between the various actors as vectors.

Conclusion

Tunnels are a common feature of war. Across regions and centuries, they have taken various shapes and forms—and been used for a wide variety of purposes. At times, the underground enabled the population to save water or other resources. At others, it facilitated the undetected movements of fighters. It has helped weaken fortifications, surprise the enemy, and survive conflicts raging aboveground. The underground has maintained

---

[203] William Booth & Aaso Ameen Shwan, *Islamic State Tunnels Below Mosul Are a Hidden and Deadly Danger*, WASH. POST (Nov. 5, 2016), https://www.washingtonpost.com/world/middle_east/islamic-state-tunnels-below-mosul-are-a-hidden-and-deadly-danger/2016/11/05/5199afcc-a2c7-11e6-8864-6f892cad0865_story.html?utm_term=.fa04ffaee5a2; Jared Malsin, *Qurans and Solar Cells—Inside the ISIS Tunnels Around Mosul*, TIME (Oct. 22, 2016), http://time.com/4541647/isis-defensive-tunnels-mosul-iraq/.

[204] ISIS fighters have also been reported to make use of irrigation canals in order to avoid detection and attack by Iraqi forces. *See* Michael Georgy & Ahmed Rasheed, *Tunneling Through "Triangle of Death", Islamic State Aims at Baghdad from South*, REUTERS (Aug. 4, 2014), http://www.reuters.com/article/2014/08/04/us-iraq-security-south-insight-idUSKBN0G41CO20140804.

[205] *Iraq Discovers Smuggling Tunnels at Syria Border*, AL-ALAM NEWS NETWORK (Dec. 7, 2013), http://en.alalam.ir/news/1542238. It is unclear what happened to the tunnels since then.

[206] Mohammed Al-Qaisi, *Iraqi Army Destroys Al-Qaeda's Illicit Tunnels at Syria Border*, MAWTANI (Mar. 13, 2014) (on file with author).

[207] Erin Bianco, *Sunni Tribes and Iraqi Military Score Victories Against ISIS with "Tunnel Warfare"*, INT'L BUS. TIMES (Oct. 3, 2015), http://www.ibtimes.com/sunni-tribes-iraqi-military-score-victories-against-isis-anbar-tunnel-warfare-1842838.

its appeal and versatility since at least the third century A.D., when Sassanid Persian forces dug tunnels to undermine the Roman walls protecting the city, through the American Civil War, and up until the conflict raging in modern Mali. Belligerents who successfully used the underground understood that tunnels require expertise, knowledge, and unique methods. The use of tunnels by the British during World War I and, albeit to a lesser extent, the tailor-made tactics developed by the Mujahedeen during the Afghan-Soviet war illustrate this well.

From a tactic used by states against other states' military forces, the underground gradually gained the favors of nonstate actors. They, too, have primarily directed underground attacks at military forces. However, they introduced a novelty by shifting the epicenter of underground warfare from mountainous and rural areas to cities. The growing proximity between tunnels and civilians, reminiscent of the Vietnam War, has created operational and legal complexities I explore in later chapters.

Part of the difficulty lies in that varied uses of the underground cause a broad array of challenges. Tunnels can be more or less sophisticated, dug for short- or long-term purposes, used only for military purposes or simultaneously for civilian purposes, and destined for offensive or defensive use. Cross-border tunnels, such as the ones dug in South Korea, Gaza, or Mexico raise their own distinct issues. The war in Syria incarnates, better than any other conflict, this kaleidoscope of underground uses. It displays, on a single battlefield, many of the themes encountered over this selective history of underground warfare. I return to these themes later on, with an explanation of how tunnel warfare diffused among actors and battlefields, and how it will evolve in future conflicts.

2

UNDERGROUND WARFARE

From a Tool of War to a Global Security Threat

STATES ACROSS THE globe have faced underground threats, armed with little guidance beyond their own understanding and typically rather limited experience of the subterranean. Air, sea, and land warfare have generated military theory, historical studies, and legal inquiries. Underground warfare has generated close to no literature or long-term studies. The result: states' perception of the threat follows no systematic or consistent patterns. Each state develops procedures through the prism of its own reality. Consider the difference between the U.S. classification of tunnels into sophisticated, rudimentary, interconnecting, and mechanically bored tunnels[1] and that of Israel, where the prevailing view distinguishes among smuggling, defensive (used mainly as hideouts), and offensive tunnels (used to launch attacks).[2] Both countries would benefit from a broader view of the threat, informed by an understanding of the shape it takes and the purposes it fulfills elsewhere. Although admittedly sufficient to contend with the threat at a given moment, domestic approaches fail to capture all potential scenarios. Ultimately, they hinder states' ability to prepare for the next thing. In the hope of creating a shared lexicon and perspective, I offer a typology of tunnels—the first attempt at creating a comprehensive framework for thinking about and dealing with tunnels.

---

[1] U.S. DEPARTMENT OF HOMELAND SECURITY, CROSS-BORDER TUNNELS AND BORDER TUNNEL PREVENTION 9 (2015), https://assets.documentcloud.org/documents/3038045/DHS-Report-to-Congress-on-Cross-Broder-Tunnels.pdf.

[2] Israel Defense Editorial Team, *Maneuver in the Underground*, ISRAEL DEFENSE (July 15, 2014), http://www.israeldefense.co.il/he/content/%D7%AA%D7%9E%D7%A8%D7%95%D7%9F-%D7%91%D7%AA%D7%AA-%D7%94%D7%A7%D7%A8%D7%A7%D7%A2 (in Hebrew).

Underground Warfare. Daphné Richemond-Barak.
© Oxford University Press 2018. Published 2018 by Oxford University Press.

38 | Underground Warfare

The resurgence of tunnels on the contemporary battlefield also calls for an analysis of past and current practices and patterns of diffusion. The emerging picture is one where underground warfare, once an acceptable tactic of war, has become used primarily by violent nonstate actors with inferior technological capabilities. In the years to come, theaters of operation will display more sophisticated and widespread uses of the underground, an extension of underground tactics to the civilian world, the morphing of sporadic underground tactics into long-term strategies, and an almost exclusively nonstate use of the underground in conflict. This chapter explains why.

I. A Global Threat: The Diffusion of Underground Warfare across Battlefields

Tunnels have been used in conflict in places as varied as the Balkans, North Korea, Somalia, Nicaragua, Gaza, and Northern Ireland. As Figure 2.1 below shows, 77.5 percent of reported instances of underground warfare by the *New York Times* since 1969 relate to events that took place in the Middle East or Asia. These two regions have also seen the most significant increase in underground warfare in the past decades: over the years 2006 to 2010, *NYT* reports on tunnel warfare were *all* related to the Middle East and Asia.

Since 9/11, the tactic has spread to more battlefields—a diffusion that has spearheaded some of the innovative uses of the underground witnessed in Gaza, Syria, and Iraq. In his book *The Diffusion of Innovations*, Everett Rogers defines diffusion as "the process by which (1) an innovation (2) is communicated through certain channels (3) over time (4) among

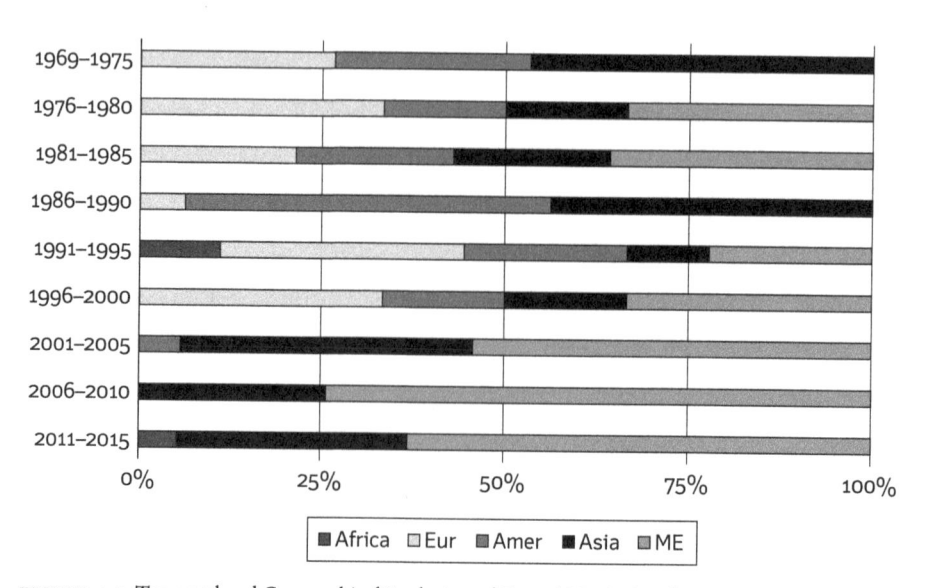

FIGURE 2.1 Temporal and Geographical Evolution of Tunnel Use in Conflict

the members of a social system."[3] The concept explains the spread of new ideas, tactics, and technology through direct or indirect channels across a social system. The basic premise is that living beings, and among them human beings, tend to emulate successful actions and behavioral patterns in order to carry out tasks, while avoiding the pitfalls encountered by their predecessors. It applies to any form of social practice.[4] Scientific attempts to identify the factors leading to such emulation or, on the contrary, to innovation, shed some light on the phenomenon of diffusion much beyond the social context.

According to the theory, tactics may "diffuse" in three main ways. *First*, and this is known as direct diffusion, an idea or tactic can spread through interpersonal relationships and known social contacts.[5] This type of diffusion explains the spread of tunnel warfare from Gaza to Syria. *Second*, tactics may diffuse indirectly through a process called "attribution of similarity." Groups or "activists who define themselves as similar to other activists may imitate the actions of others."[6] This is how the Shantytown protest advocating divestment from South Africa spread on U.S. campuses in the 1980s.[7] And, *third*, indirect diffusion can occur through a third, mutual party.[8] For example, terrorist groups that have ties to a mutual organization can share tactics through that organization.

This may clarify *how* diffusion occurs, but it does not explain *why* it occurs. What leads a group—a social movement or a terrorist organization—to try something different? Trying something different, in the context of tunnel warfare, means the adoption of underground tactics by a group that has never used them before or adopts them after an extended period of nonuse; or the weaving in of underground tactics as part of a broader strategy (the novel pairings of existing tactics).[9] In the social context, new movements are generally more likely to resort to new tactics.[10] The inclination of such movements to innovate is important, as those who innovate are typically more effective.[11]

These findings help shape the profile of the groups and organizations most likely to embrace underground tactics and, accordingly, anticipate the diffusion of the tactic in future years. Further insights can be gained from the diffusion of military power. Michael Horowitz's "adoption-capacity theory" posits that military innovations occur as a result

---

[3] EVERETT M. ROGERS, DIFFUSION OF INNOVATIONS 11 (5th ed. 2003).

[4] Sarah A. Soule, *The Student Divestment Movement in the United States and Tactical Diffusion: The Shantytown Protest*, 75 SOC. FORCES 855, 860 (1997). ("The use of the term social practices, refers to anything from child-rearing to agricultural practices, religious symbols to welfare policies, urban riots to aircraft hijacking.")

[5] REBECCA KOLINS GIVAN, KENNETH M. ROBERTS & SARAH A. SOULE, THE DIFFUSION OF SOCIAL MOVEMENTS: ACTORS, MECHANISMS, AND POLITICAL EFFECTS 10 (2006).

[6] *Id.* at 11.

[7] *See* Soule, *supra* note 4.

[8] *Id.* at 12.

[9] Dan J. Wang & Sarah A. Soule, *Tactical Innovation in Social Movement: The Effects of Peripheral and Multi-issue Protest*, 81(3) AM. SOC. REV. 517, 520 (2016).

[10] *Id.* at 533.

[11] *Id.* at 519, 540 (citing a number of scholars [HOLLY J. MCCAMMON, THE U.S. WOMEN'S JURY MOVEMENTS AND STRATEGIC ADAPTATION: A MORE JUST VERDICT (2012); SIDNEY TARROW, POWER IN MOVEMENT (3rd ed. 2011)] and noting that those who fail to innovate experience defeat).

of two elements: financial intensity and organizational capital.[12] It applies to the diffusion of military innovations among both states and nonstate actors.[13]

Financial intensity refers to the resources needed to adopt a military innovation:[14] the cost of an innovation will affect experimentation and, ultimately, the likelihood that the innovation will be adopted.[15] For example, the production of the B-2 bomber, which costs between one and two billion dollars per plane on average, does not allow for experimentation—making its diffusion more difficult.

Organizational capital, the second requirement, "represents the intangible capacity of organizations to adapt to a changing strategic environment."[16] Submarine warfare was difficult to implement because it required forces to adapt at the institutional and tactical levels.[17] The greater the organizational capital needed to implement an innovation the slower it is likely to diffuse.[18]

The diffusion of suicide terrorism is particularly interesting,[19] as suicide terrorism and underground warfare share several important characteristics. *First*, they both require extensive preparatory clandestine activities. *Second*, they both require cooperation within and, sometimes, between groups of violent nonstate actors. *Third*, both tactics turn the inherent asymmetry in military capabilities between states and violent nonstate actors to the benefit of the latter, by exploiting the weaknesses and vulnerabilities of the former. Both suicide terrorism and tunnel warfare can easily proceed undetected, creating challenges for intelligence agencies of even the most powerful nations. Like suicide terrorism, underground tactics act as an "equalizer" between militarily unequal enemies.[20] Fourth, both tactics are widely used by violent nonstate actors. Fifth, they are both tainted with a stigma and perceived by states as immoral and dangerous, albeit for different reasons (suicide terrorism because it is typically directed at civilians, and underground warfare because it tends to be used by violent, non-law-abiding actors). Finally, in both cases the Internet has acted as a catalyst in the diffusion of the tactic.

The resemblance between the two tactics further grows when examined through the lens of Horowitz's theory. As regards financial intensity, underground warfare is not uniform. Rudimentary tunnels can be dug using hands and shovels, or even using preexisting structures. Sophisticated tunnels, however, demand more expensive tools such as

---

[12] Michael C. Horowitz, The Diffusion of Military Power: Causes and Consequences for International Politics 170 (2010).

[13] *Id.* at 9, 30, and 209.

[14] *Id.* at 31.

[15] *Id.*

[16] *Id.* at 209.

[17] *Id.* at 33.

[18] *Id.* at 39.

[19] *Id.* at 170.

[20] *Id.* at 180.

excavators and cement mixers. Although testing the former may be easy, determining the feasibility of the latter is more complicated. Different types of tunnels thus appeal to different actors, who use them for different purposes. These variations also exist in suicide terrorism:

> The financial intensity of a suicide terror campaign is quite low ... [T]he often cited statistic for the "cost" of a suicide bomb, from A to Z, is $150. While that figure can vary depending on the cost of the explosive, whether it is a car bomb or not, and other factors, the point is simply that the monetary cost per unit of the hardware for a suicide attack is extremely low.[21]

The low cost of implementing the tactic and the possible variations in the cost also apply to tunnels whose pricetag will vary depending on the digging equipment, the type of materials used, and the level of sophistication of the tunnel.

The same is true with regard to Horowitz's second requirement, namely organizational capital. Underground warfare requires a unique set of skills: diggers must be carefully selected and trained, they must be able to withstand the hardship of digging and operating in confined spaces for long periods of time, and remain extremely discreet about their activity and the location of the tunnels. Similar organizational obstacles face organizations wishing to adopt suicide terrorism:

> [A]doption requires a high level of organizational capital, especially for older groups. Recruiting suicide bombers is a social as much as a physical process; the extreme nature of the act, since it guarantees death for the actor, requires a large investment in training to convince someone to sign on.[22]

Additionally, organizations recruiting for suicide terrorism suffer an organizational loss every time a member dies in a suicide mission. A group lacking a high level of organizational capital is therefore unlikely to adopt the innovation.[23] Table 2.1 summarizes

TABLE 2.1

A COMPARISON OF SUICIDE TERRORISM AND UNDERGROUND WARFARE USING HOROWITZ'S ADOPTION-CAPACITY THEORY

"Adoption Capacity" theory	Financial intensity	Organizational Capital
Suicide Terrorism	Low (with some variations)	High
Underground Warfare	Low (with some variations)	High

---

[21] *Id.* at 177 (references omitted).
[22] *Id* at 118.
[23] *Id.* at 179.

the resemblance between suicide terrorism and underground warfare through the prism of Horowitz's adoption-capacity theory.

The resemblance between the two tactics makes it possible to predict the evolution of underground warfare based on the factors that influenced the spread of suicide terrorism. Like suicide terrorism, underground tactics will likely spread to groups who possess the organizational capacity to adopt the innovation.[24] These groups typically do not strongly identify with specific methods (such as kidnapping or hijacking), are relatively young (organizations with well-established command-and-control structures find it more difficult to shift focus and innovate), and are highly connected to other groups.[25] Group connections facilitate both direct and indirect diffusion. In the military context, direct diffusion occurs when groups physically coordinate and train together, and knowledge is transferred from one group to another (for example, when Hezbollah operatives trained Hamas operatives after the latter's expulsion to Lebanon in 1992).[26]

Indirect diffusion occurs when one group reads or otherwise learns about the exploits of another group, and then attempts to mimic those exploits (for example, when reports of the suicide vest created by the Liberation Tigers of the Tamil Eelam (LTTE) in Sri Lanka inspired similar tactics by Hamas).[27] Nowadays, the Internet and social media act as vectors of indirect diffusion. Message boards and training and recruiting websites have replaced face-to-face meetings between members of various organizations.[28] Access to know-how has changed: technical information on how to build a bomb or carry out an attack is within everyone's reach. The filming of the aftermath of the tunnel mining attack against the Carlton Hotel in Aleppo (the Aleppo Earthquake Operation) illustrates the impact of social media in diffusing and promoting military innovation. However, the know-how needed to build complex tunnel systems is not yet readily available online, suggesting that direct diffusion still plays an important role in underground warfare—not only in terms of speed[29] but also in terms of the quality of the information.[30]

Direct and indirect methods drive a learning process called "emulation."[31] Emulation is triggered when actors perceive a given tactic as successful. The LTTE perceived Hezbollah as having successfully used suicide terrorism to drive Israel out of Lebanon—and used it in turn to bring Sri Lanka to the negotiating table.[32] Hamas similarly viewed Hezbollah's use of tunnels in the 2006 Lebanon War as a success. Hamas saw that Hezbollah's tactics

---

[24] *Id.* at 180.
[25] *Id.* at 181.
[26] *Id.* at 170.
[27] *Id.*
[28] *Id.* at 223.
[29] *Id.* at 181.
[30] *Id.*
[31] *Id.* at 176 (references omitted).
[32] *Id.* at 174.

worked, learned from Hezbollah, and mimicked those tactics in Gaza.[33] According to Matti Friedman, "if the technical details of tunnel digging may have moved from Gaza to Beirut, the inspiration for the type of guerrilla warfare currently undertaken by Hamas has certainly traveled in the opposite direction."[34] As a matter of fact, a Hezbollah newspaper reported that in Qusayr, Syria, tunnels "had been dug using small Iranian devices that Hezbollah had transferred to Hamas."[35] Syrians, for their part, received assistance from the Izz ad-Din al Qassam Brigades, the military wing of Hamas,[36] and the group Ahrar al-Sham.[37]

To conclude, absent a major technological breakthrough, the spread of underground warfare will likely continue in future years. Patterns of diffusion among social movements and military groups suggest that subterranean tactics will diffuse among relatively young and/or flexible nonstate actors who have the organizational capacity to adapt, and whose modus operandi is not set on specific methods. The diffusion of underground warfare will benefit from direct and indirect channels, particularly the Internet, social media, and formal and informal links between terrorist groups. In many ways, the diffusion of underground warfare will follow the trajectory of suicide terrorism. Like suicide terrorism, which helped nonstate actors counter states' technological superiority, the underground meets the needs of less sophisticated armed groups. Its appeal will only grow with time.

---

[33] The involvement of Lebanon in spreading tunnel warfare tactics has been stressed by the press, IDF sources, and scholars alike (see, for example, Tia Goldenberg, *Hamas' Massive Network of Underground Tunnels Is a Military Game-Changer*, ASSOCIATED PRESS (July 25, 2014), http://www.businessinsider.com/hamas-underground-tunnels-2014-7); *After Gaza, New Security Challenges on the Northern Front*, ISRAEL DEFENSE FORCES (Sept. 18, 2014), https://www.idfblog.com/blog/2014/09/18/gaza-new-security-challenges-northern-front/ (a senior IDF officer was reported as saying that "Hezbollah thought of building an underground terror network well before Hamas started its own, and it taught Hamas how to construct these tunnels." He added that the tunnels destroyed by Operation Protective Edge were based on the model built by Hezbollah in Lebanon); and Mark E. Manyin, *North Korea: Back on the Terrorism List?*, CONGRESSIONAL RESEARCH SERVICE 22 (June 29, 2010), http://fas.org/sgp/crs/row/RL30613.pdf (noting that in 2004 Syrian president Bashar Al-Assad requested the help of North Korean officials in helping Hezbollah design and construct underground military installations).

[34] Elhanan Miller, *Hamas, Hezbollah and the Tunnels: Who Is Inspiring Whom?*, TIMES OF ISRAEL (Aug. 4, 2014), http://www.timesofisrael.com/hamas-hezbollah-and-the-tunnels-whos-inspiring-whom/.

[35] Mamoon Alabbasi, *How Did Hamas' Military Expertise End Up with Syria's Rebels?*, MIDDLE EAST EYE (May 22, 2015), http://www.middleeasteye.net/news/how-did-hamass-military-expertise-end-syrias-rebels-1129524334. Interestingly, however, Hamas denies claims that it has assisted Syrian rebels (*see* Shaul Shay, *Syria and Sub Terrain Warfare—The Hamas Connection*, Policy Paper, Institute for Policy and Strategy (Aug. 2014), http://herzliyaconference.org/eng/_Uploads/dbsAttachedFiles/SyriaHamasConnection(1).pdf). This could be true if Hamas members gave individual advice to friends in Syria or if members of Hamas defected to join Syrian rebel groups. According to Ibrahim Khader, a Palestinian journalist covering the conflict in Syria, "[t]here are Palestinians from Gaza, who have split from Hamas or from smaller militant groups [but not from Islamic Jihad] and are fighting in Syria. They have special expertise in tunnel digging or rocket making." *See* Alabbasi, *supra*.

[36] Shay, *supra* note 35.

[37] Gedalyah Reback, *Syria Rebels Get Hamas Assistance Building Tunnels*, TIMES OF ISRAEL (May 25, 2015), http://www.timesofisrael.com/syria-rebels-get-hamas-assistance-building-tunnels/.

II. A Typology of Tunnels

The historical analysis and the database reveal that there are several types of tunnels, which serve multiple, at times simultaneous, users and purposes. These various types of tunnels raise distinct operational and legal challenges—subtleties that policymakers, legal advisers, and (at least some) military experts are unlikely to recognize without guidance or prior experience. As a framework is lacking for thinking about tunnels and assessing the threat they pose, I have developed a list of parameters to assist in identifying the threat, assessing the risks, and devising operational and legal tools to contend with tunnels. Although the parameters do not answer all the questions or provide ready-made solutions to underground warfare, they will be useful in the early stages of detection and intelligence gathering. They can be updated as more information becomes available.

WHERE. The first query has to do with location: Is the tunnel located in the territory of a single state, or does it cross over to the territory of a neighboring state?

If the tunnel is dug on the territory of a single state, it matters whether an armed conflict is currently ongoing in that state. The discovery of a tunnel in the midst of a non-international armed conflict (essentially the legal equivalent of a civil war) will likely affect the balance of power and the course of the conflict in profound and long-lasting ways. In such a situation, it would be fair to assume that the tunnel was dug by one of the nonstate groups involved in the conflict. If the government is fighting rebels, for example, security forces should proceed under the assumption that the tunnel was dug by the rebels (as in Yemen where a tunnel was discovered under the former president's palace).[38] The introduction of underground warfare into a preexisting conflict should trigger internal processes within the military apparatus—as I explain further in Chapter 4. If the practice is perceived as successful by the rebels, the state party to the conflict should prepare for more tunnel warfare, envisage all types of scenarios and uses, and quickly implement anti-tunnel strategies.

The discovery of tunnels as part of an armed conflict makes it relatively easy to identify the perpetrator or the purpose for which the tunnel was built. In peacetime, the possibilities for both of these (who dug the tunnel and why) are countless. Intelligence services must work quickly and systematically in an effort to narrow down the options to only a handful. The likelihood of a terrorist threat, which would have to be dealt with using law

---

[38] *See* Reuters, *Yemen: Assassination Plot Foiled*, N.Y. TIMES (Aug. 15, 2014), https://www.nytimes.com/2014/08/15/world/middleeast/yemen-assassination-plot-foiled.html. *See also* Nasser Arrabyee, *War Looms in Yemen*, AL-AHRAM WEEKLY (Sept. 18, 2014), http://weekly.ahram.org.eg/News/7299.aspx (reporting that, on August 11, 2014, Saleh discovered a 250-foot-long tunnel dug from a nearby hangar to his palace).

enforcement, must be envisaged. I return to the differences between peacetime and war-time below.

When the tunnel is dug in proximity to a recognized border, authorities must consider a potential violation of sovereignty. Factually, they must determine whether the tunnel does indeed physically cross the border—an exercise that requires unique tools and expertise in and of itself.[39] Although the discovery of a single cross-border tunnel is unlikely to trigger a war, as explained in Chapter 6, a state will likely consider all options—including military ones—in response to the violation. Legal advisers should be consulted on the availability of the right to self-defense under international law. As part of this process, the question will likely arise as to *why* the tunnel was built at the border. The pattern of relationship with the neighboring state (and potentially with nonstate actors active in the area) can provide valuable cues in this regard. However, I argue in Chapter 5 that the purpose of the tunnel should remain a secondary consideration: its very existence poses a security threat and should be addressed as such.

The second most important parameter to consider in early assessments of underground threats is the proximity of tunnels to civilian populated areas. Such proximity significantly increases the risks posed by tunnels. I explain in Chapter 6 why it may also affect the tools available to neutralize them. If a tunnel is discovered near populated areas, authorities should operate on the assumption that the diggers intend to harm civilians. This would apply both in peacetime and wartime.

WHEN. As mentioned above, the discovery of a tunnel will be treated very differently in time of war and in time of peace. In time of war, states have a broader arsenal of tools at their disposal to combat threats, regardless of their nature, including the use of lethal force, provided principles of humanitarian law are complied with. In time of peace, by contrast, states may use lethal force only in response to an imminent threat and in application of human rights law. I elaborate further on these important concepts in the first part of Chapter 4.

Tunnels dug in time of peace will raise suspicions and uncertainty—leaving authorities puzzled and many questions unanswered. Much confusion reigned when tunnels were discovered in Rome and in Toronto in 2002[40] and 2015, respectively.[41]

---

[39] Jason McCammack, *What Lies Beneath*, U.S. CUSTOMS AND BORDER PROTECTION (Feb. 20, 2017), https://www.cbp.gov/frontline/what-lies-beneath.

[40] Melinda Henneberger, *A Nation Challenged: Rome; Investigators Show That U.S. Embassy Is Vulnerable*, N.Y. TIMES (Feb. 27, 2002), http://www.nytimes.com/2002/02/27/world/a-nation-challenged-rome-investigators-show-that-us-embassy-is-vulnerable.html.

[41] Ian Austen, *Mystery Surrounds a Tunnel in Toronto*, N.Y. TIMES (Feb. 24, 2015), http://www.nytimes.com/2015/02/25/world/americas/mystery-surrounds-a-tunnel-in-toronto.html.

Tunnels dug in time of war will likely be treated less as an anomaly, yet they are likely to affect the conflict in long-lasting ways. History and current practice show that the appearance of tunnels in a conflict affects the balance of power between the parties by, inter alia, limiting the availability of intelligence and hindering the assessment of the enemy's destructive capabilities. These changes should not be underestimated by political and military leaders upon the discovery of a tunnel.

WHAT. The features of a tunnel, and what may be found inside the tunnel (food, beds, weapons, etc.), provide some insight on *why* the tunnel was dug. Tunnels can be made from scratch or expanded based on a preexisting structure. Then, depending on their use, tunnels can be wired with electricity, equipped with sleeping quarters, detention facilities, and even hospitals or schools. These tend to be found in tunnels destined for long-term use, which serve as bunkers, headquarters, shelters, or routes of communication (as seen in North Korea, Lebanon, and Iraq).

If the tunnel was dug (usually man-made in this case) to carry out a tunnel mining operation of the type witnessed during World War I or in Syria, the tunnel need not display any sophisticated features. This type of tunnel is typically rudimentary, as it exists only for a short period of time and for a single, limited purpose: the remote detonation of explosives against a premeditated target.

Man-made tunnels are the most difficult and dangerous to excavate, as the rock has not been naturally eroded. It is both harder to dig and more prone to collapses and sinkholes. Experts consider that when groundwater is present just below the surface, or when a rocky subgrade composes the surface, tunnels are unlikely to be dug artificially.[42] Generally speaking, if and when tunnels are dug from scratch, a solution will have to be found for the removal of the soil, potentially jeopardizing the secrecy of the underground effort. However, because man-made tunnels usually take longer to dig, they offer intelligence services more opportunity to discover the identity of the diggers and the route of the tunnel. As explained in Chapter 3, this can be done using human and visual intelligence (for example by detecting changes in the topography or noticing the transport of excavated soil).

Man-made tunnels can later be used for tunnel mining or inherited and expanded by different actors if they have not been eliminated. Because of time, financial, and discretion concerns, "inheriting" tunnels is much more advantageous than digging them. Inherited tunnels may be of three types. *First*, tunnels used in previous wars that have not been fully neutralized or eliminated can be inherited by new groups, sometimes years later.

---

[42] P. Beyr, *Military Prediction of Incursion from Underground*, 6 ADVANCES MIL. TECH. 39, 44 (2011), http://aimt.unob.cz/articles/11_02/11_02%20(4).pdf.

Examples include the Cù Chi underground complex inherited by the Vietcong from the Indochina War;[43] tunnels and cave networks built by the Mujahedeen, used against the Soviets in Afghanistan, and later inherited by al-Qaeda and the Taliban; and Saddam Hussein's tunnels used by Islamic State fighters as means to acquire territory, move around freely, and hide from aerial attacks.[44]

Second, natural caves and tunnels can be expanded and connected into vast underground complexes. Naturally occurring caves or tunnels are the results of rock erosion from precipitation that creates crevices of different diameters and depth within the solid material. Different rocks can be eroded by different amounts and components of precipitation sources. This naturally occurring phenomenon can also be the product of natural disasters or animal presence, which may expand the crevices and form new ones. Naturally-formed underground structures were used during World War II in Japan. In Iwo Jima in particular natural caves were turned into complex underground structures that played a crucial role in the battle over the island.[45]

Third, existing underground civilian infrastructure (such as subways, sewage systems, and various types of maintenance tunnels) should be monitored as they can be used or inherited by hostile elements. The Afghani Karez tunnel complex, formed naturally, was then expanded for irrigation purposes, and ultimately used both as a shelter by civilians and as a bunker by the Mujahedeen forces.[46] Similarly, ISIS used an abandoned train tunnel as a training site near Mosul, Iraq.[47]

To summarize, the ultimate purpose of a tunnel drives much of its construction process and features. If the tunnel is meant to be used within a couple of days or weeks, keeping its location secret will be easier than if it is being built for a massive attack months away. Besides location, the ultimate purpose of the tunnel will also affect its structure (number of rooms, doors, and arteries), the construction materials used (cement or wood), and the type of structural reinforcement needed. Finally, the designation of the tunnel for short-term or long-term use will affect its depth, width, and the availability of amenities

---

[43] Tom Mangold & John Penycate, The Tunnels of Cù Chi: A Harrowing Account of America's 'Tunnel Rats' in the Underground Battlefields of Vietnam (2005), at 32; and Arthur Herman, *Notes from the Underground: The Long History of Tunnel Warfare*, Foreign Affairs (Aug. 26, 2014), https://www.foreignaffairs.com/articles/middle-east/2014-08-26/notes-underground.

[44] Michael Georgy & Ahmed Rasheed, *Tunneling Through Triangle of Death, Islamic State Aims at Baghdad from South*, Reuters (Aug. 4, 2014), http://www.reuters.com/article/us-iraq-security-south-insight-idUSKBN0G41CO20140804.

[45] Evan Andrews, *The Battle of Iwo Jima Begins, Over 70 Years Ago*, History (Feb. 18, 2015), http://www.history.com/news/the-battle-of-iwo-jima-begins-70-years-ago.

[46] Paul Kelso, *Taliban Secret Weapon: Ancient Irrigation Trenches*, Nat'l Geographic News, (Nov. 5, 2001), http://news.nationalgeographic.com/news/2001/11/1105_wirekarez.html.

[47] Isabel Coles & Jamie Bullen, *Abandoned Train Tunnel in Mosul Used by ISIS as Underground Training Camp for Its Elite Fighters*, The Mirror (Mar. 6, 2017), http://www.mirror.co.uk/news/world-news/abandoned-train-tunnel-mosul-used-9975543.

(food, water, electricity, and fuel). For example, short-term tunnels typically do not possess supporting beams or ventilation shafts.

WHY. Although tunnels have been used in war for various purposes, the rationale behind underground warfare has remained constant: tunnels, in their various iterations, have been perceived as affording a military advantage to their users. The appeal of the underground is undeniable.

It is not clear whether one use of the underground has prevailed, over time, over others. Tunnels have been and continue to be used for a wide array of purposes. In fact, in any given conflict displaying elements of underground warfare, tunnels will likely fulfill multiple functions. Such functions range from kidnapping to smuggling, launching surprise attacks, storing ammunition, serving as command-and-control centers, lines of communications, hideouts for combatants, and shelter for civilians. According to the data I have compiled (based on *NYT* reports), the use of tunnels for weapons smuggling and storage is the most widely reported phenomenon over time. The use of tunnels to penetrate into an enemy's territory to undertake violent activities is the second most popular. While the use of tunnels to shelter civilians has decreased over time, the use of tunnels for the transportation of basic goods has grown in recent years.

Though the intended purpose of a tunnel is not always readily apparent, it can be deduced from its characteristics. As explained above, authorities should try and ascertain the purpose for which the tunnel was dug immediately upon its discovery. Chances are that it will not be determined with precision at that stage; however, attempts should at least be made to narrow the range of possibilities.

WHO. The discovery of a tunnel will almost immediately lead the public to wonder who is involved in its construction and use. Two questions arise: (1) who dug the tunnel (this includes both the entity behind it, if any, and the specific individuals who dug), and (2) who is using it.

If the tunnel-diggers are not affiliated with any entity—in other words if they are not working on behalf of a state or members of a terrorist organization—the identity of the individuals will suffice. However, this must be established as part of the investigation.

It also matters whether the tunnel was dug by a hostile (or non-hostile) party. In the case of a cross-border tunnel, the question will arise whether the construction can be attributed to the neighboring *state* itself—or to a group within that state, with or without the state's involvement.[48] If, however, the tunnel was dug in the territory of a single state,

---

[48] The data I have gathered suggests that, in conflict, approximately 73 percent of tunnels are dug by nonstate actors (who are also the main actors in contemporary conflicts).

authorities will have to examine the background of the individual digger(s) and their potential link to an armed group. Answering these questions is essential to a prompt and accurate assessment of the threat.

In addition, efforts must be made to ascertain who is using the tunnel: Are they civilians or combatants? This very much depends on the circumstances. Unlike in Gaza and Mali where tunnels were used almost exclusively by militants, in Vietnam both civilians and the Vietcong fighters made use of the underground. The leverage of those seeking to counter the underground threat will be seriously affected if, as in Vietnam, civilians and combatants cohabit inside the tunnels. For this reason, policymakers should quickly identify both the tunnel-diggers and the tunnel-users. Whether in peacetime or wartime, far-reaching implications—operational and legal—flow from these factual determinations as I explain below.

AGAINST WHOM. Tunnels have mostly been used in war to weaken the adversary's armed forces—from World War I to Afghanistan and Mali. Even in Vietnam, where civilians made use of tunnels alongside combatants, civilians did not become the intentional target of attacks. This, incidentally, could explain why international law never regulated underground warfare. It might have been regarded as a legitimate practice insofar as it was only used away from cities and against enemy forces.

Though the trend will likely continue, recent conflicts suggest that civilians could increasingly become the targets of tunnel-based attacks. Decision-makers and military leaders should contemplate this possibility when confronted with underground warfare. As I explain in Chapter 7, the interface between civilians and tunnels has grown in the past decade. Tunnels have been dug in civilian populated areas, some of them (particularly Hamas's) with the intent of harming civilians. These developments could signal a dangerous shift toward a greater use of the underground near and/or against civilians.

In some cases, the intended target cannot be determined with certainty. This could happen even when the perpetrator and the tunnel's purpose have been established. If the tunnel was dug in close proximity to civilian infrastructure, authorities should proceed under the assumption that civilians are the intended target—until proven otherwise—to ensure maximum preparedness. Regardless of the diggers' true intention, the very likelihood of underground attacks suffices to spread terror and cause fear among the population. It must be dealt with accordingly.

To conclude, the typology of tunnels presented in this chapter provides a framework for thinking about tunnels and contending with the threat—both in theory and in practice. Military, historical, and legal scholars can use this framework to distinguish between various types of tunnels. Practitioners can use it to assess the threat and deal with its consequences, as a checklist whenever an underground threat emerges, both in time of war and in time of peace. The typology is unique in that it transcends the offense-defense dichotomy and paints a detailed and informed picture, relying on history and data, of the multifaceted nature of underground threats.

III. Tomorrow's Underground Warfare

The trends and patterns identified in this chapter make it possible to reflect on the future of underground warfare without indulging in speculation. In my view, and assuming no revolutionary technology becomes available, tomorrow's underground warfare will feature the following: more sophisticated and widespread uses of the underground in conflict, an extension to the civilian world, the morphing of sporadic underground tactics into long-term strategies, and an almost exclusively nonstate use of the underground in conflict.

First, the use of the underground will become **more sophisticated and widespread**. As parties become more knowledgeable about underground warfare, they will use multiple types of tunnels to entertain a wider variety of tactics. Once a party to a conflict begins to use the underground, it typically discovers new ways in which to maximize the investment of time and energy put into the tunnels. Both the party using the tunnels and the one contending with them go through a learning curve—making the challenge grow as the threat evolves.

From the point of view of the party using the tunnels, it makes operational sense to develop a strategy combining various uses of tunnels and underground spaces. At that point, the party might be borrowing ideas from history (such as tunnel mining) and adapting them to its individual operational needs and technological capabilities. Hamas offers an interesting example as it has developed (and continues to develop) a holistic approach to tunnel warfare, combining various types and uses of tunnels. Hamas uses smuggling tunnels, offensive cross-border tunnels, underground shelters, and bunkers for the higher ranks of its military wing, as well as shallow underground structures to conceal its rocket launchers. A second example is the use of tunnels by rebel forces in Syria, where tunnel mining is used alongside long-term combat tunnels. The Syrian and Iraqi theaters demonstrate how cross-border tunnels are used to transfer combatants, weapons, and other supplies; and the Islamic State's use of tunnels shows that tunnels can be instrumental in gaining control over territory. Each conflict embodies a unique and tailor-made mix of uses of the subterranean. Operational and construction schemes vary depending on the availability of naturally-formed structures and the quality of the soil. The role of innovation in the process should not be underestimated: future conflicts will display more innovative uses of the underground as well as the deployment of more technology to counter it.

As explained in Chapter 4, even the most sophisticated armies still lack technological solutions to contend simultaneously with the threat of tunnel mining, underground smuggling, and nearly undetectable transportation and invasion routes. States must work together to develop an interdisciplinary approach to underground warfare that addresses the full scope of methods available and the risks posed by the diffusion of tactics to new conflicts.[49] There is a real need to develop a flexible, long-term, and hands-on approach.[50]

Underground warfare will also witness a geographic expansion. It will spread beyond a cluster of Middle Eastern conflicts and merge into an unconventional threat posed to varying degrees across the globe. Considering the many ways in which terrorist actors cooperate, and the spread of knowledge and ideas that inevitably comes with such cooperation, this trend raises concerns.[51] If anything, tunnels could offer an alternative for evading tight border controls and immigration policies. The discovery of a tunnel close to the Turkish border in Syrian territory by Kurdish forces in June 2015 has led some to speculate that cross-border tunnels could be used by foreign fighters to enter Syria and Iraq.[52] The return of foreign fighters to their home countries, combined with the lessons learned from the diffusion of tactics, raises the possibility that more states might have to contend with the proliferation of such tactics on their own soil.

Second, although contemporary underground warfare remains primarily combatant-based, an **extension to the civilian world** is likely to further and sadly magnify the challenge. Groups such as the Islamic State, Hamas, and Hezbollah have demonstrated their willingness to place civilians in harm's way. An extension of this modus operandi to the underground hardly seems farfetched. Consider tunnel mining, for example. It has so far been carried out with man-made tunnels. There is no reason, however, that it could not be conducted using preexisting structures—including existing underground civilian infrastructure such as subways, sewage systems, or underground commercial buildings. Similarly, tunnel mining would have dramatic effects were it to be used in cross-border smuggling tunnels, such as the ones between Mexico and the United States or between Egypt and Gaza.[53]

---

[49] *See, e.g., Joint IDF, US Marines Exercise Focuses on War against Islamic State,* ALGEMEINER (July 28, 2016), https://www.algemeiner.com/2016/07/28/joint-idf-us-marines-exercise-focuses-on-war-against-islamic-state/ (noting that, "as part of the exercise, troops performed urban and tunnel warfare tasks, drilled helicopter landings behind enemy lines and simulated extractions under fire").

[50] *See infra,* Chapter 4.

[51] *See* ASSAF MOGHADAM, NEXUS OF GLOBAL JIHAD: UNDERSTANDING COOPERATION AMONG TERRORIST ACTORS (2017).

[52] *Kurdish Forces Discover 400-Meter-Long Tunnel Dug by Islamic State Group near Turkish Border,* U.S. NEWS (June 22, 2015), http://www.usnews.com/news/world/articles/2015/06/22/turks-open-border-hundreds-of-syrian-refugees-return-home.

[53] Consider, for example, the attack launched by Aum Shinrikyo in 1995, where the group released sarin gas in the Tokyo subway killing 13 commuters (*see Aum Shirinkyo,* COUNCIL ON FOREIGN RELATIONS (2012), http://www.cfr.org/japan/aum-shinrikyo/p9238).

Third, the morphing of underground warfare from a war tactic into a **long-term strategy** creates its own set of challenges. This strategic shift has emerged in the past century with the construction and fortification of long-term invasion tunnels by North Korea. Unlike improvised smuggling and mining tunnels, or even preexisting tunnels that have been inherited and expanded, underground complexes such as those dug in Lebanon or the Gaza Strip are man-made and purposely built as combative strongholds for the future. A vast amount of resources is invested in cement-fortified tunnels meant to conceal weapons, mobilize troops beyond enemy lines, and serve as shelter for armed forces. These complexes are reminiscent of those built by the Vietcong in Cù Chi and al-Qaeda in Afghanistan, but they are unique in that they are part of a well-thought out, long-term strategy. Like suicide terrorism, the adoption of underground tactics embodies a strategic choice. It is not necessarily a "weapon of last resort."[54]

Fourth, underground warfare will be used almost exclusively by **nonstate actors**. The *New York Times* data shows that approximately 73 percent of tunnel uses in war are by nonstate actors (for both cross-border tunnels and non-cross-border tunnels). However, it does not provide any indication on the cause of such an increase. The increase in the use of tunnels by nonstate actors may result from an attachment to underground tactics. It can also, quite naturally, be a function of the growing involvement of nonstate actors in conflicts. The historical account in Chapter 1 suggests that nonstate actors have embraced the tactic in order to defeat militarily superior enemies on the contemporary battlefield. Yet it also identified two notable state users of the underground: Syria and North Korea. This means that nonstate actors, although they increasingly make use of the underground, do not yet have exclusivity over this terrain.

The construction of deeply buried facilities further points to states' continued attraction to the underground—albeit for different reasons.[55] Deeply buried facilities allow states to conceal personnel, munitions, and command and control functions such that they are difficult to find—and even more so to destroy.[56] Like tunnels, they protect the military and strategic interests of their owner and are perceived as a threat by others. State use of such facilities raises its own set of challenges, however they are beyond the scope of this book.

The use of the underground by states and nonstate actors shows that how an entity makes use of this terrain is, in large part, a function of its capabilities and how those compare to its opponents'. States that possess the technological and military upper hand opt for a long-term, mostly defensive use of the underground in the form of secure and highly

---

[54] *See* HOROWITZ, *supra* note 12, at 180.
[55] *See supra*, Introduction.
[56] Eric M. Sepp, *Deeply Buried Facilities: Implications for Military Operations*, OCCASIONAL PAPER NO. 14, CENTER FOR STRATEGY AND TECHNOLOGY 1 (2000), http://www.au.af.mil/au/awc/awcgate/cst/csat14.pdf.

sophisticated facilities rather than tunnels. The decrease in state's use of underground complexes and tunnels—which World War I best exemplifies—will likely continue as underground warfare increasingly becomes associated with violent actors such as Hamas, Hezbollah, and ISIS. These actors' use of the underground has tainted a tactic that was once used by nation-states against each other's forces. Because of this stigma, whether quantitatively measurable or not, states will become increasingly reluctant to dig and use tunnels.

In sum, tomorrow's underground warfare will be relatively ubiquitous, dangerous for armed forces and civilians, and integrated into long-term strategies combining multiple uses of the subterranean for maximum impact. Tunnel warfare will take on new shapes in the hands of actors who blatantly violate the laws of war and have demonstrated a willingness to use their opponent's compliance with the law to their advantage—only intensifying the challenge for those who face it.

Conclusion

Predicting the future of underground warfare is less speculative than it seems. Underground warfare has not actually changed much over time. What has changed is the environment armed groups operate in. Their growing familiarity with the law and the strategic advantage offered by urban warfare, the interaction between groups acting in different theaters, their perception of belonging to one community sharing common goals and common enemies, and the very structure of these groups—have all contributed to the evolution of underground warfare into a global security threat.

There is little doubt that more conflicts will "go underground" or at least incorporate underground warfare elements. Asymmetric conflicts, where the aerial and technical superiority of one party stands out, are particularly vulnerable to the spread of underground warfare. In Syria, for example, one party decided to import underground tactics into an already complex and bloody conflict—affecting the war in profound ways and leading both sides to increase their use of the underground (each for its own strategic and operational reasons). This is also the case in Iraq, where the Islamic State has inherited Saddam Hussein's tunnels and dug its own. Hamas' and Hezbollah's large-scale investment in tunnel development in the Gaza Strip and Lebanon respectively underscores the diffusion of tactics, strategy, and know-how. More groups will take possession of underground caves and complexes, particularly in conflict-prone areas, as a part of their underground strategy. These complexes may be inherited, expanded, purposely built for either offensive or defensive purposes—or not. As explained above, it is likely that they will eventually serve all of these functions to varying degrees. There is every reason to believe that the development of long-term strategies relying on the underground will weave in civilian elements, either by placing civilians in tunnels or through the use of existing civilian infrastructure such as subways and sewage systems. These potential developments will put the civilian population in direct danger and, in turn, will considerably complicate the neutralization of underground threats.[57]

Militaries around the world have taken measure of this challenge. Both the Israeli and the U.S. armies have built underground training facilities and are working together toward the development of a technology allowing the early detection of tunnels. In the past, sporadic (yet recurring) instances of underground warfare were answered with largely ad hoc military tactics. Today's armies should aspire instead to a developed, informed, and comprehensive counterstrategy to underground warfare, cognizant of the military, political, and legal ramifications.

---

[57] *See infra*, Chapter 7.

3

SOVEREIGNTY OVER THE UNDERGROUND

THE DISCOVERY OF a 30-foot tunnel near York University in 2015 left Toronto authorities puzzled and the public frazzled.[1] Who had dug the tunnel, and for what purpose? Did the tunnel digger violate any law? No one could tell whether digging a hole amounted to a criminal offense. Perhaps because the incident took place outside of an armed conflict, the tunnel was not regarded as a security threat. Yet the Toronto tunnel underscores the unsettling nature of the underground threat, the uncertainty surrounding applicable legal regimes, and the lack of clarity as to the legality of tunnel-digging.

Tunnel-digging, or tunneling, hardly features in international legal instruments. Unlike land, space, and sea, the underground remains largely unregulated. In a rare occurrence, tunneling is mentioned in the United Nations Convention on the Law of the Sea (UNCLOS), which provides that states have the right to "exploit the subsoil by means of tunneling, irrespective of the depth of water above the subsoil."[2] However, the treaty does not elaborate further on the meaning or modalities of tunneling.

---

[1] Ian Austen, *Mystery Surrounds a Tunnel in Toronto*, N.Y. TIMES (Feb. 24, 2015), https://www.nytimes.com/2015/02/25/world/americas/mystery-surrounds-a-tunnel-in-toronto.html?_r=0.

[2] *Id.*; United Nations Convention on the Law of the Sea, art. 85, Dec. 10, 1982, 1833 U.N.T.S. 397. Article 85 was inserted into UNCLOS verbatim from the Convention on the Continental Shelf, Article 7 [Convention on the Continental Shelf, art. 7, Apr. 29, 1958, 15 U.S.T. 471, 499 U.N.T.S. 311]; *see* 2 THE UNITED NATIONS CONVENTION ON THE LAW OF THE SEA 1982: A COMMENTARY 992 (Satya N. Nandan, Shabtai Rosenne & Neal R. Grandy eds, 1993).

Underground Warfare. Daphné Richemond-Barak.
© Oxford University Press 2018. Published 2018 by Oxford University Press.

The underground is also touched upon very sporadically and unsystematically as part of the law governing transboundary aquifers and the right to natural resources. A close analysis of these sources reveals that a state does have sovereignty over underground resources located in areas under its control or jurisdiction—assuming it has not transferred these rights to private entities. It is unclear, however, whether such sovereignty extends to all layers until the center of the earth and to the entirety of the subsoil under the ocean. Depth matters—and it involves normative frameworks as diverse as domestic law, international law, and the law of the sea. Even in situations where international law acknowledges state sovereignty over the underground, domestic law can decide otherwise based on statutory law or public/private agreements. It is necessary to understand how these bodies of law interact and delineate their respective scope of application in order to determine whether tunnel-digging is lawful or not in any given situation.

I. Sovereignty over the Underground under Domestic Law

The discovery of the tunnel in Toronto tunnel in 2015 underscores the relevance of domestic law in delineating the scope of a right to the underground, and the need to develop tools to assess and deal with the threat—even in times of peace. When the tunnel was discovered, law enforcement authorities were ill-prepared to handle the situation. It took days, if not weeks, before the investigation began. Had the case been connected to terrorism, this delay could have had serious repercussions for security.

The sheer disbelief at the discovery of the tunnel confused investigators who had never been confronted with such a threat. Turning to lawyers did not help: the situation was unprecedented, and answers were not readily available. They could not agree on who owned the land, determine the motives of the digger, or make up their mind on whether the digging of the tunnel amounted to an offense.

First, the land on which the tunnel had been dug belonged to the Toronto and Region Conservation Authority, a private entity.[3] But it took time before this could be ascertained with certainty. Determining ownership over the land was significant for at least two reasons: it affected which law was applicable, and only the owner of the land could press charges against the digger. Second, the possible motive behind the digging added to the confusion. The incident pointed to the challenge of unveiling the raison d'être of a tunnel: Why is it here? What would it be used for? Although a tunnel, in and of itself, may not violate the law—it could amount to a crime depending on its purpose. That question, like so many others, remained both untouched and unresolved. Third, it was not clear whether digging a hole, in and of itself, amounted to an offense:

> [Q]uestions remain about whether the city or the Toronto Region Conservation Authority (TRCA), which owns and manages the land, should pursue trespassing

---

[3] For more information about the Toronto and Region Conservation Authority, *see* https://trca.ca/about/.

charges to deter other would-be tunnellers. Police typically don't lay charges in property cases. "It would definitely be up to the property owner to pursue trespassing charges," said municipal lawyer Ron Kantor, who noted that anyone who wants to dig a large hole or build a structure needs a city permit. Ever since the tunnel was revealed last week, triggering global media attention and widespread speculation about its purpose, police have insisted that it's not illegal to dig a hole. But, as Victor Kwong, a Toronto police spokesperson, told CP24, "[Y]ou can't just go into a park and dig a hole."[4]

Eventually a consensus emerged that there is no criminal offense for digging a hole.[5] Given the legal uncertainties, the absence of criminal intent, and the prevailing belief that nothing would be gained from prosecution, no criminal charges were filed.[6]

Still, an overwhelming sense of confusion and "unknown" cloaked the entire story. It was not clear to anyone involved which law applied or what the law actually said. Neither the Toronto and Region Conservation Authority for the Living City (which was responsible for security of the area ahead of the Pan Am games in the summer of 2015) nor the Toronto police knew how to approach this case. The authorities also failed to grasp the security risk posed by the tunnel, waiting days before investigating the matter.[7]

Ownership over the underground is typically regulated by domestic property laws. In common law countries, the doctrine of *cuju est solum ejus est usque ad coelum et ad inferos* has had a very strong impact on the scope of a state's right to the underground and its resources. The doctrine, first applied in England by the Court of King's Bench in 1586,[8] posits that the "sky and depths" above and beneath a landowner's property belong to that landowner. This general rule was reaffirmed by the House of Lords[9] and the courts

---

[4] John Lorinc, *Police Find Toronto Tunnel Builders, Say They Meant No Harm*, GLOBE & MAIL (Mar. 2, 2015), http://www.theglobeandmail.com/news/toronto/toronto-tunnel-builders-identified-police-say/article23241282/.

[5] John Barber, *Toronto Mystery Tunnel: #terrortunnel, Drug Lab or Something Else Entirely?*, GUARDIAN (Feb. 24, 2015), https://www.theguardian.com/world/2015/feb/24/toronto-mystery-tunnel-theories-terror-drug-lab-police-baffled. One scholar addresses the question of whether the surface owner could dig a mile-deep hole on her land and construct a small dwelling at the bottom, and concludes that this would raise many legal questions (including whether or not a permit had been granted, and compliance with environmental regulations). However, he does not address the arguably more complicated question of the digging of a hole by a third party (i.e., not by the surface owner). *See* John Sprankling, *Owning the Center of the Earth*, 55 UCLA L. Rev. 979, 1015 (2008).

[6] Manisha Krishnan, *Conservation Authority Does "Not Want to be Punitive" About Tunnel*, STAR (Mar. 6, 2015), https://www.thestar.com/news/gta/2015/03/06/conservation-authority-does-not-want-to-be-punitive-about-tunnel.html.

[7] Marco Chown Oved, *Cops Weren't Told About York Tunnel for a Month*, TORONTO STAR, June 17, 2015, at A1.

[8] Bury v. Pope, (1586) Cro. Eliz. 118, 78 E.R. 375.

[9] Rowbotham v. Wilson, (1860) 8 H.L.C. 348, 11 E.R. 463.

of Canada, New Zealand, and Australia.[10] According to Barry Barton, who has written extensively on the issue,

> [L]ittle in the law of property and natural resources can be as familiar and as apparently well established as the principle that the rights of the owner of the subsurface of land extend upwards and downwards. The rights deriving from the ownership or possession of an estate in land are presumed to be capable of exercise on all parts of the land, including upwards and downwards, indefinitely.[11]

The doctrine affords three-dimensional property rights to all landowners—so much so that any underground structure passing under private property likely violates the law. This was the outcome of cases brought before Canadian courts (construction companies that inserted anchor rods under a third party's property paid damages to the property's owner)[12] and New Zealand courts (the Navy had to pay damages to private owners for having built a tunnel under their property).[13] This was also reaffirmed by the United Kingdom Supreme Court in the case of *Bocardo SA v. Star Energy* in which Bocardo, the landowner, successfully sued Star Energy for damages for trespass.[14] Star Energy had bored three pipelines between 800 and 2800 feet beneath Bocardo's property without informing him or obtaining his consent. The court held that the title to the land extended down to the strata through which the pipelines passed. The rights of Bocardo to the surface and below were uncontested. However, "[p]recisely how much further into the earth's crust that ownership might go" formed the heart of the dispute.[15] According to the court, the rule that "the owner of the surface is the owner of the strata beneath" was "still good law" in spite of technological advances:[16]

> There must obviously be some stopping point, as one reaches the point at which physical features such a pressure and temperature render the concept of the strata belonging to anybody so absurd as to be not worth arguing about. But the wells that are at issue in this case, extending from about 800 feet to 2800 feet below the surface, are far from being so deep as to reach the point of absurdity. Indeed the fact that the strata can be worked upon at those depths points to the opposite conclusion.[17]

---

[10] Barry Barton, *The Common Law of Subsurface Activity: General Principle and Current Problems*, in THE LAW OF ENERGY UNDERGROUND: UNDERSTANDING NEW DEVELOPMENTS IN SUBSURFACE PRODUCTION, TRANSMISSION AND STORAGE 21, 23 (Donald N. Zillman, Aileen McHarg, Adrian Bradbrook & Lila Barrera-Hernandez eds., 2014).
[11] *Id.* at 22.
[12] *Id.* at 23, citing Austin v. Rescon Constr. Ltd. (1989) 57 D.L.R. 4th 591 (Can. B.C. C.A.); and Epstein v. Cressey Dev. Corp. (1992) 89 D.L.R. 4th 32 (Can. B.C. C.A.).
[13] Waugh v. Attorney General [2006] 2 NZLR 812.
[14] Bocardo SA v Star Energy UK Onshore Ltd., [2010] UKSC 35, [2011] 1 A.C. 380.
[15] *Id.* ¶ 13.
[16] *Id.* ¶ 27.
[17] *Id.*

The New York Supreme Court took a similar stance on the extent of a landowner's right to the underground. It held that rights extend underground as far as the owner of the soil might reasonably make use of it.[18] Under this interpretation, private and public rights may coexist: private rights would afford the owner of the land ownership over the underground as deep as he can reasonably make use of it (keeping in mind that how deep this actually is would evolve with time and technology) unless the state has reserved rights to underground minerals (in which case the legislation would have to specify to what depth the reservation applies).[19] More utilitarian approaches would confer rights to the underground as necessary to accommodate the owner of the subsurface[20] or as deep as the landowner expects to hold such rights.[21] The state would retain sovereignty of the underground "beneath the depths needed by landowners for full use and enjoyment of the land surface."[22]

Civil law countries, for their part, have borrowed from the Napoleonic Code which provides in its article 552 that ownership of the land includes ownership of what is above and beneath it. However, this version of the *cuju est solum* doctrine has been curtailed with exceptions allowing the state to exploit resources. The French Mining Code of 1810 states that all mining resources belong to the state. If a private owner discovers oil under its backyard, in other words, the oil in question belongs to the state—not to the private owner. The state would then have to pay the land owner adequate compensation. However, French courts have held that a private owner does have ownership over groundwater so long as he does not abuse his right.[23] Napoleon's take on the underground made its way into the codes of Belgium, Austria, Italy, Japan, the Netherlands, Portugal, Spain, Switzerland, Germany, Turkey, and the Province of Quebec, Canada.[24] In Switzerland, for example, article 667(1) of the civil code provides that private ownership includes ownership of the sky and the underground "in the height and depth necessary for its enjoyment."[25] In general, the influence of the *cuju est solum* doctrine can be felt in

---

[18] *See* Boehringer v. Montalto, 142 Misc. 560, 254 N.Y.S. 276 (Sup. Ct. 1931) (holding that a sewer laid 150 feet below the surface "is beyond the point to which the owner can conceivably make use of the property" (at 562). The judge held that "the old theory that the title of an owner of real property extends indefinitely upwards and downward is no longer an accepted principle of law in its entirety. Title above the surface of the ground is now limited to the extent to which the owner of the soil may reasonably make use thereof. By analogy, the title of an owner of the soil will not be extended to a depth below ground beyond which the owner may not reasonably make use thereof" (at 561–62). *See also* Sprankling, *supra* note 5, at 1037–38.

[19] The UK, for example, has reserved the Crown's rights to underground minerals. *See* Barton, *supra* note 10, at 23–24.

[20] In this sense, see Sprankling, *supra* note 5, at 983.

[21] *Id.* at 983 and 1033.

[22] William A. Thomas, *Ownership of the Subterranean Space*, 3 UNDERGROUND SPACE 155, 160 (1979). Yet another approach would set a clear limit at which private rights end (see Sprankling, *supra* note 5, at 1036).

[23] Cour de Cassation, Civ. 3e, 26 nov. 1974.

[24] José Juan Gonzáles, *Civil Law Treatment of the Subsurface in Latin American Countries* in THE LAW OF ENERGY, *supra* note 10, at 59, 65 (Donald N. Zillman, Aileen McHarg, Adrian Bradbrook & Lila Barrera-Hernandez eds., 2014).

[25] Free translation.

civil law systems—albeit subject to more limitations and caveats than in common law systems. When it comes to contemporary uses of the underground—including tunnel-digging–the *cuju est solum* doctrine has become increasingly inadequate.[26] This is because, interpreted literally, the doctrine places the state in a rather precarious situation: it has no right to the underground or any underground resource (except, presumably, under state-owned land), and must pay damages to private owners if it wishes to make any use of the subsurface. The digging of a tunnel in the midst of a city would likely violate the rights of private individuals—though not those of the state. In any case, both the role and the rights of the state end up significantly restricted. One could even argue that private ownership of the underground absolves the state of (at least some of) its responsibility for any misuse of the underground by a private party.

II. Sovereignty over the Underground under International Law

Sovereignty over territory constitutes a fundamental right of the state under international law, yet it is by no means absolute. International law acknowledges certain limits to states' territorial sovereignty, both at sea and in the air. As sovereignty ceases at a certain distance "horizontally" at sea and "vertically" in the air, one would have expected sovereignty to cease at a certain distance underground as well. However, it does not—at least not explicitly.

The absence of a straightforward treatment of sovereignty over the underground can be overcome by an analysis of international law's treatment of sovereignty over national resources: national resources are found underground, therefore by extension states that possess natural resources can be said to "own" the underground. Delineating the rights of states over the underground thus draws on various subfields of international law—from environmental law to the law of the sea, the law of transboundary aquifers, the law of energy underground, and human rights. A comparison with sovereignty over air, space, and water is also helpful, as I explain in Subsections III and IV.

The recognition of state sovereignty over natural resources evolved after World War II as part of the right of states and peoples to dispose freely of their natural resources. At the time, sovereignty over national resources was perceived both as the natural extension of territorial sovereignty and territorial integrity, and a necessary condition for the realization of the right to self-determination. The process through which this law developed was marked by its highly political nature—particularly given the strong involvement of

---

[26] The doctrine was heavily criticized by Lord Wilberforce as early as 1974 (*see* Commissioner for Railways v. Valuer-General [1974] A.C. 328 (P.C.), at 351–52 ("In none of these cases [taken into consideration by the Court in this particular case] is there an authoritative pronouncement that 'land' means the whole of the space from the center of the earth to the heavens: so sweeping, unscientific and unpractical a doctrine is unlikely to appeal to the common law mind.")).

the United Nations General Assembly and the reluctance of states to regulate an area that so directly affected their interests.

The process of decolonization and the creation of newly independent states precipitated the more formal recognition of states' prerogatives to freely dispose of their natural resources. Sovereignty over national resources would guarantee the economic independence for the new entities. In 1952, the UN General Assembly affirmed the right of underdeveloped countries to "determine freely the use of their natural resources and (...) utilize such resources in order to be in a better position to further the realization of their plans of economic development in accordance with their national interests, and to further the expansion of the world economy."[27]

Six years later, the United Nations General Assembly established a commission in order to analyze "the status of permanent sovereignty over natural wealth and resources as a basic constituent of the right to self-determination."[28] The link between the right to natural resources and self-determination could not have been spelled out more clearly. The General Assembly also noted that due regard should be paid to the "importance of encouraging international co-operation in the economic development of underdeveloped countries." Soon thereafter, the General Assembly adopted the landmark resolution entitled *Permanent Sovereignty over Natural Resources*, further tightening the "inalienable right of all States to freely dispose of their natural wealth and resources in accordance with their national interests".[29] Finally in 1966, Article 1 of the International Covenant on Civil and Political Rights and the International Covenant on Economic, Social and Cultural Rights consecrated the right of peoples to "freely dispose of their natural wealth and resources without prejudice to any obligations arising out of international economic cooperation."[30]

The right of states over natural resources was later reaffirmed by international courts and tribunals. The arbitral tribunal set up to resolve the dispute over Libyan nationalization procedures between the government of the Libyan Arab Republic and two oil companies affirmed the customary nature of sovereign rights over natural resources as set forth in United Nations Resolution 1803.[31] So did the International Court of Justice in *Congo v. Uganda*. Although the Court rejected the Democratic Republic of Congo's argument that the looting, pillage, and exploitation of the DRC's natural resources

---

[27] G.A. Res. 523 (VI), U.N. GAOR, 6th Sess., U.N. Doc. A/RES/523(VI) (Jan. 12, 1952).
[28] G.A. Res. 1314 (XIII), U.N. GAOR, 13th Sess., U.N. Doc. A/4025 (Dec. 12, 1958).
[29] G.A. Res. 1803 (XVII), U.N. GAOR, 17th Sess., U.N. Doc. A/RES/1720(XVI) (Dec. 14, 1962), Preamble; *see also* G.A. Res. 3201 (S-VI), U.N. Doc. A/RES/S-6/3201 (May 1, 1974); and G.A. Res. 3281 (XXIX), U.N. GAOR, 29th Sess., U.N. Doc. A/9946 (Dec. 12, 1974).
[30] International Covenant on Civil and Political Rights, Dec. 12, 1966, 999 U.N.T.S. 171; and International Covenant on Economic, Social and Cultural Rights, Dec. 16, 1966, 993 U.N.T.S. 3.
[31] Texaco Overseas Petroleum Co. v. Libya, Int'l Arbitral Award, 104 J. DROIT INT'L 350, 17 I.L.M. 1 (1978), at ¶ 87. Both oil companies had contracts with the Libyan government, which were discontinued when Libya decided to nationalize its oil sector.

constituted violations by Uganda of "the sovereignty and territorial integrity of the DRC, more specifically of the DRC's sovereignty over its natural resources,"[32] it affirmed the customary nature of the principle of permanent sovereignty over natural resources.[33]

Subsequent legal instruments reiterated the principle and introduced the notion of state responsibility in the management of natural resources and the duty of states to cooperate. The 1972 Declaration of the United Nations Conference on the Human Environment[34] and the 1992 Declaration on Environment and Development[35] both reiterated the sovereignty principle—but added important caveats to its exercise. The former established the responsibility of states "to ensure that activities within their jurisdiction or control do not cause damage to the environment of other states or of areas beyond the limits of national jurisdiction."[36] The 1992 Declaration added that state sovereignty over natural resources "must be fulfilled so as to equitably meet developmental and environmental needs of present and future generations" and in such a way as to give priority to the needs of developing countries.[37] Sovereign rights over natural resources (or, for purposes of this book, over the underground) are thus by no means unlimited.

The International Law Commission's *Draft Principles of Conduct in the Field of the Environment for the Guidance of States in the Conservation and Harmonious Utilization of Natural Resources Shared by Two or More States* advanced the notion of shared responsibility by encouraging states to share natural resources located on the territory of two or more states.[38] The Draft principles also crystallized the concept of equitable utilization of shared natural resources, according to which states must cooperate to limit adverse environmental effects that result from the utilization of such resources.[39] Today, most of the discourse has indeed shifted from the recognition of a right to natural resources toward a duty to cooperate in the management and exploitation of shared natural resources.[40]

---

[32] Armed Activities on the Territory of the Congo (Dem. Rep. Congo v. Uganda), 2005 I.C.J. 168, ¶ 226 (Dec. 19).

[33] *Id.* ¶ 244.

[34] U.N. Conference on the Human Environment, Stockholm, Sweden, June 16, 1972, *Declaration of the United Nations on the Human Environment*, U.N. Doc. A/CONF.48/14/Rev.1 (June 16, 1972).

[35] United Nations Conference on Environment and Development, Rio de Janeiro, Braz., June 3–14, 1992, *Rio Declaration on Environment and Development*, U.N. Doc. A/CONF.151/26/Rev.1 (Vol. I), Annex I, Principle 2 (Aug. 12, 1992).

[36] *Declaration of the United Nations on the Human Environment, supra* note 34, Principle 21. *See also id.*, Principles 7 (on preventing pollution) and 22 (on cooperation).

[37] *Rio Declaration on Environment and Development, supra* note 35, at Principles 3 and 6.

[38] United Nations Environment Program: Governing Council Approval of the Report of the Intergovernmental Working Group of Experts on Natural Resources Shared by Two or More States, Co-operation in the Field of the Environment Concerning Natural Resources Shared by Two or More States, GC.6/CRP.2 (19 May 1978), 17 ILM 1091 (1978).

[39] U.N. Environment Programme Governing Council, May 19, 1978, *Draft Principles of Conduct in the Field of the Environment for the Guidance of States in the Conservation and Harmonious Utilization of Natural Resources Shared by Two or More States*, UN Doc. UNEP/IG12/2, Principle 1 (1978).

[40] *See, e.g.*, Franz Xaver Perrez, Cooperative Sovereignty: From Independence to Interdependence in the Structure of International Environmental Law (2000).

International law governing the rights of states to natural resources—and, by extension, to the underground—continued to take form in the 1980s with the adoption of the United Nations Convention on the Law of the Sea. Interestingly, the absence of a clear international legal regime governing underground resources served as an impetus for the adoption of the convention. In 1967, 15 years before the adoption of UNCLOS, the UN General Assembly convened a *Committee to Study the Peaceful Uses of the Sea-Bed and the Ocean Floor beyond the Limits of National Jurisdiction*. Following the publication of the committee's report,[41] the General Assembly recommended that an international conference be convened to, inter alia, "arrive at a clear, precise and internationally accepted definition of the area of the sea-bed and ocean floor which lies beyond the limits of national jurisdiction."[42] The General Assembly expressed concern that "the definition of the continental shelf contained in the Convention on the Continental Shelf of 29 April 1958 does not define with sufficient precision the limits of the area over which a coastal State exercises sovereign rights for the purpose of exploration and exploitation of natural resources, and that customary international law on the subject is inconclusive."[43]

More recently, underground activities such as hydrocarbon extraction, the long-term storage of nuclear waste, and shared oil and gas reservoirs have created renewed legal difficulties—few of which find immediate answers in existing law.[44] These activities raise important and previously untouched questions, including whether some of them might be expressly prohibited, and the role of international law in determining ownership over underground resources.[45] Legal scholars generally agree that "underground activities that take place within the sovereign territory of the state give rise to fewer international implications."[46] Notwithstanding, states are bound by the "customary law duty to prevent, or to mitigate, transboundary impacts arising from activities which may cause significant harm to the environment of other states or to areas beyond national jurisdiction."[47] This means that any activity carried out by a state (including tunnel-digging) must take into consideration such activity's environmental and developmental impact beyond the state's borders. Additional duties may apply when states have become

---

[41] *Report of the Committee on the Peaceful Uses of the Sea-Bed and the Ocean Floor Beyond the Limits of National Jurisdiction*, U.N. Doc. A/7622, U.N. GAOR, 24th Sess., Supp. 22 (1969).
[42] G.A. Res. 2574 (XXIV), ¶ 1 U.N. GAOR, 24th Sess., U.N. Doc. A/Res/2574 (Dec. 15, 1969).
[43] *Id.* at Preamble.
[44] *See* Catherine Redgwell, *Energy Underground: What's International Law Got to Do with It?*, *in* THE LAW OF ENERGY UNDERGROUND, *supra* note 10, at 101–02.
[45] *Id.*
[46] *Id.* at 104.
[47] *Id.*

party to one or more of the treaties regulating the exploitation of underground energy resources.[48] Ratification of any of these instruments would affect the legality of a tunnel.

State sovereignty over the underground *within the boundary of a state's territorial jurisdiction* also transpires from the emerging legal framework governing aquifers. This complex and still unsettled regulatory regime applies to permeable water-bearing geological formations underlain by a less permeable layer and the water—groundwater—contained in the saturated zone of the formation.[49] Aquifers can be located on the territory of a single state or on the territory of several states:

> If the subject matter being regulated is an immovable part of the territory of states, it is only natural to conceive of states as having 'sovereignty' over it."[50]

When located on the territory of a single state, the aquifer is thus presumed to belong to that state, thereby confirming that state sovereignty extends to the underground.

Trickier questions arise when an aquifer or the exploitation of natural resources extends to the territory of a third state. International law is still undecided as to the regime applicable to these underground, cross-border resources. The UN General Assembly has encouraged states to enter into bilateral or regional arrangements to regulate the management of transboundary aquifers.[51] Such bilateral and regional arrangements have sought to fill the gap in the absence of international regulation.[52] Yet the need to squarely delineate the rights of aquifer states cannot be underestimated, as demand for groundwater rises, pumping technologies develop, and the risk of groundwater pollution and abstraction grows.

To conclude, I have sought to overcome international law's odd treatment of the underground by drawing on a variety of subfields, ranging from human rights law to energy law and environmental law. The combined analysis reveals that states have sovereignty over the underground—yet such sovereignty is neither unlimited nor absolute. Its scope will continue to evolve, particularly with regard to the depth at which sovereignty over the underground extends.[53] It is surprising that international law has not given expression

---

[48] *Id.* (Redgwell lists the following: treaties that oblige state parties to protect and preserve the marine environment, conserve biological diversity, maintain the ecological character of wetlands of international importance, conserve drylands, conserve sites of natural and/or cultural heritage, and stabilize climate change).

[49] Rep. of the Int'l Law Comm'n, 60th Sess., May 5–June 6, July 7–Aug. 8, 2008, *Draft Articles on the Law of Transboundary Aquifers*, U.N. Doc. A/63/10; GAOR 63rd Sess., Supp., No. 10, at art. 2(a) (2008).

[50] Stephen C. McCaffrey, *The International Law Commission Adopts Draft Articles on Transboundary Aquifers*, 103 AM. J. INT'L L. 272, 286 (2009).

[51] G.A. Res. 63/124, ¶ 5, U.N. Doc. A/RES/63/124 (Jan. 15, 2009).

[52] Regional instruments should also be mentioned with regard to the regulation of transboundary aquifers (*see, e.g.*, Revised Protocol on Shared Watercourse in the Southern African Development Community, Aug. 7, 2000, 40 I.L.M. 321; and the Convention on the Protection and Use of Transboundary Watercourses and International Lakes, Mar. 17, 1992, 1936 U.N.T.S. 269 (also known as the Water Convention)).

[53] NICO SHRIJVER, SOVEREIGNTY OVER NATURAL RESOURCES: BALANCING RIGHTS AND DUTIES 377 (1997) ("It can be concluded therefore, that despite its complicated genesis the principle of permanent

to—or discussed—the extension of sovereignty "downwards vertically,"[54] particularly given that the question has been addressed in domestic law.[55] None of the bodies of law analyzed above address the question of the downward limit of state sovereignty over the underground.[56] The question has important consequences for the legality of tunnel-digging. If sovereignty over the underground ends at a certain distance from the surface of the earth—as in the case of sovereignty over water or airspace—tunnels dug beyond such a distance would not infringe on anyone's sovereignty. The question, in other words, is whether the underground becomes res communis at a certain depth.

On this and other issues (such as militarization or exploration), underground law should follow general international law trends rather than the doctrine of *cuju est solum*. This is because, although international law has gradually and authoritatively developed norms consecrating state sovereignty, it has clearly delineated its scope. Neither the consecration of state sovereignty over the underground nor the idea of "mitigating" rights to the underground should raise any substantial objections. To the contrary, this would align underground law with other areas of international law.

III. Law of the Sea—Compared

Though it has remained largely silent on the underground, international law has actively regulated state sovereignty over water (alongside land and space). The most significant instrument governing state sovereignty over water is UNCLOS, which lays out the important principle that the

> [S]overeignty of a coastal State extends, beyond its land territory and internal waters and, in the case of an archipelagic State, its archipelagic waters, to an adjacent

---

sovereignty over natural resources has achieved a firm status in international law and is now a widely accepted and recognized principle of international law. However, it cannot be accorded the status of *jus cogens*. This implies that permanent sovereignty does not override other principles of international law and moreover can evolve in the light of new rules and new practices accepted as law, thereby allowing it, for example, also to encompass new duties.")

[54] *See* Barton, *supra* note 10, at 21.
[55] *See supra* Section I.
[56] It could be assumed that whenever international legal instruments refer to sovereignty over territory or over land, they include both the surface and the subsurface. Yet some instruments do mention the subsurface explicitly, casting doubt over an interpretation that would include the subsurface even when it is not specifically mentioned (*see, e.g.*, the Energy Charter Treaty, Dec. 17, 1994, 2080 U.N.T.S. 95, which provides in its Article 1 that a state has sovereignty over the "Area" defined as "(a) the territory under its sovereignty, it being understood that territory includes land, internal waters and the territorial sea; and (b) subject to and in accordance with the international law of the sea: the sea, sea-bed and its subsoil with regard to which that Contracting Party exercises sovereign rights and jurisdiction.")

belt of sea, described as the territorial sea. This sovereignty extends to the air space over the territorial sea as well as to its bed and subsoil.[57]

The recognition of land, water, subsoil, and airspace as components of a four-dimensional concept of sovereignty permeates the entire treaty. Even in areas under their jurisdiction or control, however, states must take all measures so as not to cause environmental damage to other states.[58] In this respect, UNCLOS reaffirms general principles applicable to natural resources.

State sovereignty extends to the continental shelf, defined as comprising the seabed (also known as the seafloor, i.e., the bottom of the ocean) and the subsoil (the soil lying immediately beneath the surface) throughout the natural prolongation of the state's land territory to the outer edge of the continental margin.[59] States have the exclusive right to exploit natural resources on their continental shelf and in their exclusive economic zone, including in the water, the seabed, and the subsoil (up to 200 miles from the baseline).[60]

Sovereign rights over the seabed and subsoil cease to exist when the continental shelf and the Exclusive Economic Zone end. Beyond "the limits of national jurisdiction," that is, beyond 200 miles at most from the baseline, no single state may claim or exercise sovereignty over any part of the seabed, ocean floor, and subsoil thereof. This regime of the subsoil echoes that of the high seas, in the sense that neither the "Area"—as the seabed, ocean floor, and subsoil thereof are known—nor the high seas are susceptible of appropriation.[61]

The right to explore and exploit resources on the continental shelf includes drilling and tunneling.[62] Article 85 of UNCLOS recognizes "the right of the coastal State to exploit the subsoil by means of tunnelling, irrespective of the depth of water above the subsoil." Article 85 preserves the right of the coastal state as it was set forth in the 1958 Convention on the Continental Shelf and reaffirms that right in the context of the new provisions of UNCLOS regarding the continental shelf.[63] However, UNCLOS neither defines "tunneling" nor elaborates on the difference between drilling and tunneling.[64] According to

---

[57] UNCLOS, *supra* note 2, at art. 2.
[58] *Id.* at art. 194.
[59] *Id.* at arts. 76 and 77.
[60] *Id.* at art. 77. It should be noted, however, that "All States are entitled to lay submarine cables and pipelines on the continental shelf" (art. 79).
[61] *Id.* at art. 89 ("No State may validly purport to subject any part of the high seas to its sovereignty."); and art. 1 (for the definition of "the Area").
[62] *Id.* at art. 85.
[63] Commentary to UNCLOS, *supra* note 2, at 992.
[64] *See* Richard Young, *The Geneva Convention on the Continental Shelf: A First Impression*, 52 AM. J. INT'L L. 733, 738 (1958) (noting that "it is not clear whether 'tunneling' includes such techniques as directional drilling").

Ian Brownlie, the provision implies that the right of the coastal state to exploit the subsoil by means of tunneling is governed by customary law.[65]

In spite of these ambiguities, the Convention's provisions on tunneling and the regime governing the subsoil (including the establishment of the International Seabed Authority in charge of organizing and controlling activities in the Area and administering resources)[66] embody the most extensive treatment of the underground in international law to date. It is unfortunate that UNCLOS does not specify whether or where, in areas under state jurisdiction, sovereignty ceases at the deep levels of the earth.

At sea, therefore, state sovereignty decreases progressively from a state's territorial waters (over which the coastal state has exclusive sovereignty) to the high seas (where no state can assert sovereign rights). The same should apply underground: state sovereignty should decrease progressively from the land to the inner layers of the earth.

One could even contemplate that the deep underground would be regulated by a regime akin to that of the high seas, the seabed, and the ocean floor. The high seas and the ocean floor are similar to the underground in the sense that they comprise the farthest and deepest areas of the sea (horizontally and vertically). The deep underground (beneath the land mass) should borrow from the regime applicable to the high seas and the deepest areas of the sea.

In particular, military activity should be restricted in the deep underground as it is on the high seas.[67] States have similarly purported to reserve the use of the seabed and ocean floor for peaceful purposes.[68] In 1969, the UN General Assembly introduced the idea that areas of the seabed and ocean floor and the subsoil lying beyond the limits of national jurisdiction should be used exclusively for peaceful purposes.[69] The *Treaty on the Prohibition of the Emplacement of Nuclear Weapons and other Weapons of Mass Destruction on the Sea-bed and the Ocean Floor and in the Subsoil Thereof*, adopted in 1971, proclaims "the interest of mankind in the progress of the exploration and use of the sea-bed and the ocean floor for peaceful purposes."[70] Limiting the use of the seabed and the ocean floor for military purposes was regarded as serving international peace and security[71]—particularly

---

[65] JAMES CRAWFORD, BROWNLIE'S PRINCIPLES OF PUBLIC INTERNATIONAL LAW 273 (8th ed. 2012) (adding that "[t]here is a notable distinction; if exploitation is by tunnel from the mainland, a different regime applies; if exploitation of the subsoil occurs from above the shelf, the UNCLOS regime applies").

[66] *See* UNCLOS, *supra* note 2, at arts. 156 and 157.

[67] UNCLOS, *supra* note 2, at art. 88. *See* Rüdiger Wolfrum, *Military Activities on the High Seas: What Are the Impacts of the U.N. Convention on the Law of the Sea?*, 71 INT'L L. STUDIES 501, 505 (1998) (noting that Article 88 "does not impose any obligations upon States exceeding those of Article 2, paragraph 4, of the UN Charter"); and Isaak I. Dore, *International Law and the Preservation of the Ocean Space and Outer Space as Zones of Peace: Progress and Problems*, 15 CORNELL INT'L L.J. 1, 18 (1982).

[68] *See* Louis Henkin, *The Sea-Bed Arms Treaty—One Small Step More*, 10 COLUM. J. TRANSNAT'L L. 61 (1971).

[69] UNGA Res. 2574, *supra* note 42, at Preamble.

[70] Treaty on the Prohibition of the Emplacement of Nuclear Weapons and other Weapons of Mass Destruction on the Sea-Bed and the Ocean Floor and in the Subsoil Thereof, Feb. 11, 1971, 955 U.N.T.S. 115 [hereinafter "Sea-Bed Treaty"].

[71] *Id.* at Preamble.

given the area's growing potential for military use.[72] The appeal of the seabed and the ocean floor as a safe location to hide missiles, install submarine detection and monitoring stations, and establish manned underwater installations or colonies was apparent since the late 1960s.[73] As noted by one author, "an undersea system is nontargetable at any given time."[74] In this respect, the strategic appeal of the seabed and the ocean floor very much resembles that of the underground.

Ninety-four states, following the lead of the United States and the Soviet Union,[75] have undertaken "not to emplant or emplace on the sea-bed and the ocean floor and in the subsoil thereof beyond the outer limit of a sea-bed zone [...] any nuclear weapons or any other types of weapons of mass destruction as well as structures, launching installations or any other facilities specifically designed for storing, testing or using such weapons."[76] These constraints, importantly, do not apply to the seabed and ocean floor located beneath a state's territorial waters—which a state presumably might be able to use for all-around military purposes.[77] In addition, weapons other than nuclear weapons, weapons of mass destruction, and "structures, installations or any other facilities designed for storing, testing or using such weapons" arguably do not fall within the scope of the prohibition. These two important carveouts make it difficult to speak of a proper "reservation" of the seabed and the ocean floor for peaceful purposes, and more accurate to speak of an aspiration toward nonmilitary use.[78]

The same aspiration transpires from the Antarctic Treaty of 1961[79] and the Outer Space Treaty of 1967 (as explained further in Subsection III).[80] The Antartic Treaty prohibits "any measures of a military nature."[81] The Outer Space Treaty, like the Sea Bed Treaty,

---

[72] *See* Dore, *supra* note 67, at 7 ("It is clear that contemporary oceanological research relating to the economic exploitation of the seabed cannot take place without the preservation of the oceans as a zone of peace. The need to reserve the oceans for peaceful uses is even more urgent in light of their potential for military use.")

[73] *See* Robert A. Creamer, *Title to the Deep Seabed: Prospects for the Future*, 9 HARV. INT'L L. J. 205, 209–10 (1968).

[74] *See* Dore, *supra* note 67, at 6.

[75] For a detailed account of the events leading to the adoption of the treaty, see *id.* at 7–10.

[76] Sea-Bed Treaty, *supra* note 70, at art. I(1).

[77] *Id.* at arts. I(2) and II; *see also* Dore, *supra* note 67, at 10.

[78] *See* Dore, *supra* note 67, at 58 (noting that neither the Outer Space Treaty nor the Sea-Bed Treaty purports "to achieve complete demilitarization, and in some instances they prohibit that which is under no immediate need of prohibition.") For a discussion of the limitations to the militarization of the continental shelf and within the Exclusive Economic Zone, see James Kraska, *Military Activities on the Continental Shelf*, LAWFARE (Aug. 22, 2016), https://www.lawfareblog.com/military-activities-continental-shelf (arguing that the "emplacement of military devices or construction of military installations or structures in the EEZ and on the continental shelf of a coastal State must be judged by reasonableness, and not be of such scale or cross a threshold of effect that it interferes in a tangible or meaningful way with the coastal State's resource rights.")

[79] The Antarctic Treaty, Dec. 1, 1959, 12 U.S.T. 794, 402 U.N.T.S. 71, at Preamble and art. 1 [hereinafter "the Antarctic Treaty"].

[80] Treaty on the Principles Governing the Activities of States in the Exploration and Use of Outer Space Including the Moon and Other Celestial Bodies, Jan. 27, 1967, 18 U.S.T. 2410, 610 U.N.T.S. 205 [hereinafter: "the Outer Space Treaty"].

[81] The Antarctic Treaty, *supra* note 79, at art. 1.

limits military uses of space—without prohibiting them completely.[82] These limitations should also inform the law applicable to the underground.

To conclude, the principles and rationales underlying the law of the sea should guide state sovereignty over the underground. *First*, the law of the sea corroborates the analysis of the law regulating national resources and aquifers conducted in Subsection I: state sovereignty over the underground exists. *Second*, the law of the sea suggests there should be limitations to military uses of the underground, at the very least in areas beyond a state's national jurisdiction (i.e., in the deep layers of the earth).

IV. Air Law and Space Law—Compared

Sovereignty over the airspace is contemplated in UNCLOS as a complement to sovereignty over the territorial seas, the seabed, and the subsoil.[83] It is further regulated by a body of law known as air law, which governs "the use of airspace and its benefits for aviation, the general public and the nations of the world."[84] Since the early nineteenth century, this corpus of law has recognized that state sovereignty extends to the air situated over its territorial waters.[85] It suggests, by analogy, that a state also has sovereignty over the air located above its territory.

This view crystallized with the initial steps taken toward air travel—particularly an August 1904 aerial incident in which Russian guards shot down the German balloon *Tschudi* when it was flying outside Russian territory,[86] and two similar incidents in 1908 (German balloons carrying German officers landed in France)[87] and 1910 (again Russia shooting down German military balloons).[88] These events led France to convene an international conference whose aim was to clarify the law applicable to air navigation over a third state's territory.[89] The work of the conference was interrupted by the outbreak of War World I, yet the practice of states became increasingly consistent in the years

---

[82] The Outer Space Treaty, *supra* note 80, at art. IV.
[83] UNCLOS, *supra* note 2, at art. 2.
[84] I.H.Ph. Diederiks-Verschoor, Introduction to Air Law 1 (Pablo Mendes de Leon rev. 9th ed. 2012).
[85] *Id.* at 2–3.
[86] Peter H. Sand, Jorge de Sousa Freitas & Geoffrey N. Pratt, *An Historical Survey of International Air Law Before the Second World War*, 7 McGill L.J. 24, 32 (1960).
[87] *See* Michael Milde, International Air Law and ICAO 8 (2008) (citing to John C. Cooper, *The International Air Navigation Conference Paris 1910*, *in* Exploration in Aerospace Law, Selected Essays 105–06 (John C. Cooper & Ivan A. Vlasic eds., 1968)).
[88] *See* Milde, *supra* note 87, at 7 (citing to Joseph Kroell, Traité de Droit International Aérien, Tome I, 36 (Les Editions Internationales, 1934)).
[89] Milde, *supra* note 87, at 8. The conference was attended by Austria-Hungary, Belgium, Bulgaria, Denmark, France, Germany, Great Britain, Italy, Luxembourg, Monaco, Netherlands, Portugal, Rumania, Russia, Serbia, Spain, Sweden, Switzerland, and Turkey. The United States was not invited "since their geographic distance made the operation of their aircraft in European air space unrealistic."

following the conference: states protected their airspace, protested against incursions, and used force to assert their rights over it.[90]

The next step was marked by the signing of the 1919 Paris Convention Relating to the Regulation of Aerial Navigation, which recognizes that a state has "complete and exclusive sovereignty over the air space above its territory," and that "the territory of a State shall be understood as including the national territory (. . .) and the territorial waters adjacent thereto."[91] Although it is no longer in force, the Paris Convention consecrated a state's sovereignty over the airspace above its territory as an established right in international law.[92] It put an end, momentarily, to the rift between states advocating a "free" airspace (by analogy to the high seas) and those preferring to establish state sovereignty.[93]

With World War II and significant advances in aviation technology, states took steps to regulate air transport. Even before the end of the war, they met in Chicago in the hope of adopting a new treaty. The Chicago conference was a success: the Chicago Convention on International Civil Aviation (also known as the "Chicago Convention"), adopted in December 1944, embodies international air law to this day.[94] Its preamble emphasizes the dangers inherent to civil aviation and the need to channel its development toward peace and cooperation.[95] Most importantly, Article 1 of the Chicago Convention affirms that a state "has complete and exclusive sovereignty over the airspace above its territory."[96] Territory is understood as "the land areas and territorial waters adjacent thereto under the sovereignty, suzerainty, protection or mandate of each State."[97] Though the formulation is slightly different from that of the Paris Convention of 1919,[98] the governing principle of state sovereignty over the airspace above a state's territory remains.[99]

---

[90] *Id.* at 9.

[91] Convention Relating to the Regulation of Aerial Navigation, art. 1, Oct. 13, 1919, 11 L.N.T.S. 173 [hereinafter: "Paris Convention"].

[92] *See* RUWANTISSA ABEYRATNE, CONVENTION ON INTERNATIONAL CIVIL AVIATION: A COMMENTARY (2014), at ch. 1 (noting that the use of the word "recognize" suggested that the principle was already well-entrenched in air law at the time). *See also* DIEDERIKS-VERSCHOOR, *supra* note 84, at 3 (noting that "[c]omplete and exclusive sovereignty of states over the airspace above their territory was recognized, in conformity with the Roman adage: 'Cujus est solum, ejus est usque ad coelum et ad inferos.'").

[93] *See* MILDE, *supra* note 87, at 11.

[94] Other instruments adopted in Chicago include the International Air Services Transit Agreement, the International Air Transport Agreement, and a standard form of bilateral agreements for the exchange of air routes. *See* MILDE, *supra* note 87, at 16.

[95] *See* Convention on International Civil Aviation, art. 4, Dec. 7, 1944, 61 Stat. 1180, 15 U.N.T.S. 295 [hereinafter "Chicago Convention"].

[96] *Id.*

[97] *Id.* at art. 2.

[98] *See* Paris Convention, *supra* note 91, at art. 1 (defining the territory of a state as "including the national territory, both that of the mother country and of the colonies, and the territorial waters adjacent thereto.")

[99] Later instruments, such as the multitude of bilateral Open Skies Agreements currently in force (see, for example, Open Skies Agreements to which the United States is a party (with over 100 other states), https://www.state.gov/e/eb/tra/ata/), and the Multilateral Agreement on the Liberalization of International Air Transportation adopted in 2003 (May 1, 2001, 2215 U.N.T.S. 33), do not challenge this fundamental, and by now well-established, principle.

In its various early twentieth century formulations, international air law thus affirms a state's sovereignty over the airspace above its territory and above its territorial waters—but not over the high seas.[100] Air law, like the law of the sea, consecrates *and* limits state sovereignty at the same time.

Importantly, air law should not be confused with space law. Space law applies beyond the limits of states' national jurisdiction, to outer space (which includes the moon and celestial bodies). The existence of two bodies of law to regulate sovereignty over land suggests that sovereign rights do not extend indefinitely: at some point—and the difficulty is to determine when—the exclusive rights of states make way for a more flexible and communal regime:[101]

> In fine, there is nothing inherently impossible in law or in geophysics which prevents States agreeing to an upper limit of national sovereignty beyond the atmosphere of the earth. In the United States a distance of 10,000 miles has been mentioned, and, if States so agree, they are free to choose, with effects limited to those which consent to or recognize it, either this or any other figure, whether above below [sic] the natural limit of the terrestrial atmosphere.[102]

State sovereignty over the air ends at some undefined point, even above and within the limits of its own territory. This, of course, mirrors the regime applicable to water—although the limit of national jurisdiction has been established with more clarity under the law of the sea. The Outer Space Treaty does not specify where outer space begins, yet the treaty's very existence suggests that it begins where exclusive state sovereignty ends.[103] At that undefined point, another legal regime becomes applicable. The Outer Space Treaty stresses the importance of international cooperation in the exploration of outer space: the term "cooperation" is mentioned no less than seven times in the treaty. As mentioned above, the treaty also forbids state parties "to place in orbit around the Earth any objects carrying nuclear weapons or any other kinds of weapons of mass destruction, install such weapons on celestial bodies, or station weapons in outer space in any other manner."[104] In addition, "[t]he Moon and other celestial bodies shall be used by all States Parties to the Treaty exclusively for peaceful purposes."[105] These provisions resemble those applicable to the high seas, the seabed, and the subsoil thereof.[106] Regardless

---

[100] *See* DIEDERIKS-VERSCHOOR, *supra* note 84, at 14 (noting that "there is an important qualification to this basic rule, however, in respect of the airspace above the territorial waters, where no right of innocent passage for aircraft exists like there is for ships in the territorial waters.")

[101] *See* Bin Cheng, *From Air Law to Space Law*, in STUDIES IN INTERNATIONAL SPACE LAW 31, 33–35 (Bin Cheng ed., 1997).

[102] *Id*. at 34 (footnotes omitted).

[103] The Outer Space Treaty, *supra* note 80.

[104] *Id*. at art. IV.

[105] *Id*.

[106] See *supra* Subsection III.

of whether the Outer Space Treaty and UNCLOS achieve a complete demilitarization of outer space and the seabed,[107] respectively, they embody at a minimum an aspiration toward a nonmilitary use of areas beyond national jurisdiction.

In conclusion, the analysis of air law and space law corroborates insights gained from the analysis of the law of the sea and the right to natural resources. *First*, state sovereignty over the underground exists. *Second*, it must end at a certain depth. This depth has yet to be determined. *Third*, considerations of international cooperation, peaceful (or, at the very least, nonaggressive) exploration, and equality must guide emerging international law governing the underground.

Conclusion

Given the relatively developed corpi of law applicable to air and sea, it is odd that international law has not paid more attention to sovereignty over the underground. In this chapter, I have shown that such law can be inferred from legal regimes as varied as the right to natural resources, air law, the law of outer space, and the law of the sea. The emergence of international law in these areas has been guided by key concerns and principles: on one hand, the recognition of state sovereignty over the airspace above a state's territory and above its territorial waters, as well as sovereignty over the seabed thereof; and, on the other hand, the imposition of clear limitations to such sovereignty. The latter have been imposed over time to create a balance between developed and developing countries in the exploration and exploitation of resources. The notion of shared resources and shared responsibility embodies this aim. The freedom of the high seas and the limits to the use of the seabed for military purposes, for their part, capture concerns regarding military uses of resources "beyond national jurisdiction." Ultimately, the regulation of land, air, and water reveals international law's objective: to preserve state sovereignty, while (1) allowing equal opportunities for science and research, and (2) limiting the use of these resources for non-peaceful purposes.

The governing principles—sovereignty, development, shared resources, cooperation, and peace and security—should apply equally to the fourth dimension of state sovereignty: the underground. The layers of the earth located beneath a state's land territory form part of that state's sovereignty; sovereignty over the underground ends where the state's territory ends. Penetrating the underground space beneath a neighboring state therefore, and logically, constitutes a violation of the neighboring state's sovereignty. Taking the analogy one step further, sovereignty over the underground would also end at a certain distance from the surface. Here air law offers an important insight: it is difficult to determine with precision where this takes place, particularly given the constant

---

[107] *See* Dore, *supra* note 67, at 41–46.

evolution of technology. The depth at which state sovereignty over the underground ends, like the scope of air law, will likely evolve with time and technological advances. Major developments could make it possible to dig in previously untouched layers of the earth. Hydraulic fracturing (also known as fracking) might, for example, trigger more international regulation in relation to state sovereignty over the underground and the resources it contains.[108] In any case, international law most certainly recognizes a state's right to the underground—subject to limitations akin to those applying at sea, on land, and in space.

---

[108] Fracking triggered a debate in the United States over who is the appropriate "regulator" (see, for example, Jody Freeman, *Should the Federal Government Regulate Fracking?*, WALL ST. J. (Apr. 14, 2013), http://www.wsj.com/articles/SB10001424127887323495104578314302738867078. Rules governing fracking remain underdeveloped in international law, in part due to the opposition of states (states did not want the International Law Commission to address the question of oil and natural gas—for this reason the Draft Articles on Transboundary Aquifers (*supra* note 49) only address groundwater). As noted by one author, this topic is very political and touches on states' essential interests (see Redgwell, *supra* note 44, at 107).

4

CONTENDING WITH TUNNELS

Law, Strategy, and Methods

WHEREAS ASSAD CHOSE to counter underground threats by sending his men underground, Israel dealt with Hamas's cross-border tunnels by destroying them aboveground and minimizing direct engagement inside the tunnels. In law enforcement situations—Toronto, Seoul, or Nogales—reactions to tunnels have been more muted, focusing instead on detection and monitoring. Regardless of how states choose to deal with tunnels, their decision-making processes and policies must be informed by a solid understanding of subterranean threats. Unfortunately, states do not always share their know-how and experience in this field. Underground warfare often finds them unprepared, adding to the confusion. If not the presence of the tunnels per se, their use, type, and scope can take states by surprise. Tunnels can catch states in the midst of a full-fledged war or in peacetime. The security ramifications of tunnels, as well as the methods to contend with them, differ depending on the circumstances specific to each tunnel and to each setting—war or peacetime, armed conflict or law enforcement, densely populated or remote areas.

This chapter tackles questions that, I argue, states should consider immediately upon the emergence of an underground threat: What law applies? What strategy works? Can and should a tunnel be eliminated? Although states have struggled with various forms of underground warfare across centuries, little has been written on how to address these challenges. The objective in this chapter is to provide a starting kit for approaching tunnels or suspected tunnels.

Underground Warfare. Daphné Richemond-Barak.
© Oxford University Press 2018. Published 2018 by Oxford University Press.

I. Applicable Law

Underground warfare, for the purpose of this book, refers to the use of tunnels and other underground structures in the context of an armed conflict, understood broadly as including the use of tunnels *leading to* an armed conflict (as a cause of war) or *during* an armed conflict (in war). Given this scope, the analysis concentrates on the application of the *jus ad bellum* (the law governing the entry into war) and the *jus in bello* (the law governing war). The applicability of the *jus post bellum* is also envisaged below, as it can become relevant to anti-tunnel operations undertaken *after* the conflict has ended, alongside general principles of international law applicable to inter-state relations. Indeed, when underground threats emerge in situations disconnected from armed conflict or unlikely to lead to an armed conflict, norms such as sovereignty, non-interference, and due diligence (states' obligation to ensure that their territory is not used for hostile activities by nonstate groups) apply. I examine the legal framework applicable outside war-like situations in Chapter 5.

Depending on the circumstances, underground warfare may therefore fall within the scope of several international norms and regimes—in addition to domestic law, as I explained in Chapter 3. When a tunnel threat emerges, states must be prepared and willing to identify the applicable legal framework, as it affects the type of measures they can employ against the tunnel(s).

A. JUS AD BELLUM

Questions of *ad bellum* arise, by definition, outside an armed conflict. Consider the following scenario: a sovereign entity digs cross-border tunnels onto the territory of another. This may—or may not—trigger a full-fledged armed conflict. Determining the precise contour of the victim state's right to self-defense in the underground context presents a challenge, which Chapter 5 seeks to untangle. For now, suffice it to say that the *jus ad bellum* applies to a relatively narrow set of circumstances—namely the digging of cross-border tunnels absent active ongoing hostilities.

B. HUMAN RIGHTS LAW

Human rights law, like international humanitarian law, refers to a subset of international law. It comprises its own set of norms and principles, but does not displace general international norms such as sovereignty and non-interference. Human rights law places strict restrictions on government activities, particularly with regard to the use of lethal force. In peacetime, any violation of the right to life must be non-arbitrary, and justified by strict rules of necessity and proportionality.[1] Life can only be taken as a last resort, if it is the

---

[1] U.N. Human Rights Comm., Draft General Comment 36, Article 6: Right to Life, U.N. Doc. CCPR/C/GC/R.36/Rev.2 (2015), ¶18 [hereinafter: Draft General Comment 36].

least harmful means available to achieve the goal of saving life or limb, and this is subject to strict ex-ante and ex-post review requirements.[2] Under a human rights framework, the right to life continues to be relevant even in the midst of an attack—both the right to life of the perpetrator and that of any innocent bystanders. Capture should always be preferred to killing.[3]

In peacetime, human rights law would apply, for instance, to the above-mentioned 30-feet-long and 20-feet-deep tunnel discovered near York University in Toronto in 2015.[4] The tunnel was dug on Canadian territory and did not cross any internationally recognized boundary. As a result, both Canadian law—albeit with a great measure of uncertainty—and human rights law applied to measures undertaken in connection with the tunnel.

Part of human rights law also continues to apply in wartime alongside the law of armed conflict. Whereas humanitarian law applies exclusively in times of war, human rights law does not apply exclusively in times of peace. Unfortunately, however, consensus has yet to emerge on the precise scope of application of these two bodies of law.[5] The confusion as to the level of co-application of human rights law in armed conflict affects the application of human rights law and IHL across the board—including of course in the context of underground warfare.

---

[2] Michael Ramsden, *Targeted Killings and International Human Rights Law: The Case of Anwar Al-Awlaki*, 16 J. INT'L CONFLICT & SEC. L. 385, 397 (2011); David Kretzmer, *Targeted Killings of Suspected Terrorists: Extra-Judicial Executions or Legitimate Means of Defense?*, 16 EUR. J. INT'L L. 171, 178 (2005); European Convention for the Protection of Human Rights and Fundamental Freedoms, 213 U.N.T.S. 221 (1950) art. 2; *McCann et al v. UK*, Eur. Ct. H.R. 18984/91 (1995) ¶ 148, 194; *McKerr v. UK*, Eur. Ct. H.R. 28883/95 (2001) ¶ 10; *Isayeva, Yusupova and Basayeva v. Russia*, Eur. Ct. H.R. 57947/00 (2005) ¶ 169, 171.

[3] For a discussion on whether a similar requirement exists under IHL, see: Nils Melzer, *Interpretative Guidance on the Notion of Direct Participation in Hostilities Under International Humanitarian Law*, INTERNATIONAL COMMITTEE OF THE RED CROSS 80–81 (2009); HCJ 769/02, Public Committee Against Torture in Israel v. Gov't of Israel 62(1) PD 507 ¶ 40 [2006] (Isr.) (both advocating the existence of such a requirement); Geoffrey S. Corn, Laurie R. Blank, Chris Jenks & Eric Talbot Jensen, *Belligerent Targeting and the Invalidity of a Least Harmful Means Rule*, 89 INT'L L. STUD. 536 (2013); and Michael Schmitt, *Wound, Capture, or Kill: A Reply to Ryan Goodman's "The Power to Kill or Capture Enemy Combatants,"* 24 EUR. J. INT'L L. 855 (2013) (claiming that there is no such requirement under IHL).

[4] *See supra* Chapter 3.

[5] For example, such lack of consensus exists as to the applicability of human rights law in time of war or when states exercise control extraterritorially. *See inter alia*: Legality of the Threat or Use of Nuclear Weapons, Advisory Opinion, 1996 I.C.J. 226, ¶ 25 (July 8) [hereinafter Nuclear Weapons]; Legal Consequences of the Construction of a Wall in the Occupied Palestinian Territory, Advisory Opinion, 2004 I.C.J. 136, ¶ 106 (July 9) [hereinafter Wall Advisory Opinion]; Armed Activities on the Territory of the Congo (DRC v. Uganda) 2005 I.C.J. 168, ¶ 216 (Dec. 19); Al-Skeini v. U.K., 2011-IV Eur. E.Ct. H.R. 99, ¶ 133–137; Loizidou v. Turk., 310 Eur. E.Ct. H.R. (ser. A), at ¶ 56, (1996); U.N. Human Rights Comm., General Comment 31, Nature of the General Legal Obligation on States Parties to the Covenant, 18th Sess., Mar. 29, 2004, U.N. Doc. CCPR/C/21/Rev.1/Add.13 ¶ 10 (May 26, 2004); Special Rapporteur on Extrajudicial, Summary or Arbitrary Executions, *Rep. on Extrajudicial, Summary or Arbitrary Executions: Study on Targeted Killings*, 2004), U.N. Doc. A/HRC/14/24/Add.6 ¶ 29 (May 28, (2010) (by Philip Alston). *See, in general*: MARKO MILANOVIC, EXTRATERRITORIAL APPLICATION OF HUMAN RIGHTS TREATIES (2011).

A Human Rights Watch report on the measures taken by Egypt against Hamas's tunnels aptly illustrates this. Human Rights Watch takes the view that, "[r]egardless of whether the fighting in North Sinai has amounted to an armed conflict, the eviction of the population and the destruction of homes is also subject to international human rights law."[6] Under human rights law, the report continues, "[t]hose evicted outside active hostilities are entitled to various protections, including: genuine consultation with the authorities; adequate and reasonable notice; information on the eviction and future use of the land; adequate compensation or alternative housing; legal remedies; and legal aid."[7] Interestingly, the organization does not take a position on the existence of an armed conflict or the scope of application of human rights law if such a conflict exists. Avoiding the question altogether, it assumes that the relevant norms of human rights law apply both in peacetime and in wartime and proceeds to apply them.

This book does not provide a comprehensive account of human rights law's application to underground warfare. It does, however, envisage the role of human rights law in regulating state behavior when tunnels are suspected or discovered in peacetime; and in delineating obligations owed by states to their *own* nationals during an armed conflict. The latter includes the duty to evacuate nationals along the border when tunnels are suspected, and the duty owed to one's own civilians when measures are undertaken against cross-border tunnels. These aspects have, for the most part, been sidelined by IHL, which primarily regulates the duties owed by a belligerent to the other side at the expense of those owed by a belligerent to its *own* people.[8] In the absence of guidance from IHL, human rights law could fill the gap—as explained further in Chapter 7.

C. INTERNATIONAL HUMANITARIAN LAW

The laws of war—also known as international humanitarian law (IHL)—apply and regulate the activities of belligerents *in armed conflict*.

Despite the centrality of the concept of "armed conflict" to the application of IHL, the law surprisingly does not define the term. The International Criminal Tribunal for the Former Yugoslavia importantly and famously clarified this concept: there is an armed conflict "whenever there is a resort to armed force between States or protracted armed violence between governmental authorities and organized armed groups or between such

---

[6] HUMAN RIGHTS WATCH, "LOOK FOR ANOTHER HOMELAND": FORCED EVICTIONS IN EGYPT'S RAFAH 10, 81 (2015), https://www.hrw.org/sites/default/files/report_pdf/egypt0915_4up.pdf [hereinafter ANOTHER HOMELAND].

[7] *Id.* at 82.

[8] For more on the difference between causative and reflexive duties, see Daphné Richemond-Barak & Ayal Feinberg, *The Irony of the Iron Dome: Intelligence Defense Systems, Law, and Security*, 7 HARV. NAT'L SEC. J. 469 (2016).

groups within a State."[9] The first scenario—when a state fights another state—is known as creating an "international armed conflict." The second and third scenarios—when a state fights a nonstate armed group or when two nonstate armed groups fight each other—are known as giving rise to "non-international armed conflicts." The core of international humanitarian law applies to all actors involved in each of these three scenarios.

This means that IHL applies to all tunnel-related activities undertaken in armed conflict, including the digging, detection, use, and elimination of tunnels. I examine the application of IHL in the context of underground warfare in greater detail in Chapters 6 and 7. I explain that tunnels not only magnify well-known IHL dilemmas (such as human shields or advance warning) but also raise novel issues of IHL (such as whether weapons lawful aboveground may become unlawful when used underground).

D. THE LAW OF OCCUPATION AND THE *JUS POST BELLUM*

IHL, complemented at times by human rights law, regulates most aspects of underground warfare. Any anti-tunnel operation undertaken in the midst of an armed conflict is governed by these two bodies of law. That said, states are advised to carry out counter-tunnel operations while the armed conflict is ongoing and the application of IHL is uncontested. In-conflict, anti-tunnel operations not only benefit from legal clarity, they also afford the state the greater level of leverage to contend with the security threat, as IHL is more permissive in allowing recourse to lethal force than human rights law (which subjects lethal force to stricter standards of necessity and proportionality). The question is what happens when a state carries out anti-tunnel operations on the territory of a foreign state *after* the conflict has ended.

It is inevitable that, even as the war comes to an end, certain objectives have not been attained. Ammunition caches and command and control centers may remain, and certainly animosity. But peace is ushered in and nations make promises. Rifles, tanks, and even tunnels can be removed, confiscated, or set aside. This is particularly true with respect to cross-border tunnels which embody a long-term, durable threat—one that offers direct access to the enemy, invites violations of sovereignty, and makes the prospect of another war that much more likely. For this reason, states that have not successfully destroyed all cross-border tunnels by the time the conflict ends might want to take action against these tunnels after the conflict has ended.

At that point, IHL ceases to apply, except in cases of occupation. A territory is considered occupied when it is placed under the authority and control of a foreign entity, even if such occupation does not encounter armed resistance. The 1907 Hague Regulations and the Fourth Geneva Convention (GCIV), which are considered customary and make up

---

[9] Prosecutor v. Tadić, Case No. IT-94-1-I, Decision on Defense Motion for Interlocutory Appeal on Jurisdiction, ¶ 70 (Int'l Crim. Trib. for the Former Yugoslavia Oct. 2, 1995).

the core of the laws of belligerent occupation, grant the occupier a power of administration within the occupied territory. The legal framework applicable to occupation seeks to balance the protection of the civilian population and the maintenance of public order, on one hand, with the military needs of the occupying power on the other:[10]

> The authority of the legitimate power having in fact passed into the hands of the occupant, the latter shall take all the measures in his power to restore, and ensure, as far as possible, public order and safety, while respecting, unless absolutely prevented, the laws in force in the country.[11]

Insofar as tunnels pose a risk to public order or the safety of the occupied population, the occupier is therefore under an obligation to eliminate the threat. This means that the occupying power can carry out anti-tunnel operations, provided it abides by the relevant norms. Article 64 of GCIV further allows the occupier to adopt legislation "essential to enable the Occupying Power to fulfil its obligations under the present Convention, to maintain the orderly government of the territory, and to ensure the security of the Occupying Power."[12] This would include criminal legislation for the protection of the occupier (for instance, making tunnel-digging a criminal offense).[13] In fulfilling its basic obligations, the occupier can, under certain circumstances, derogate from the rights promised to the occupied population. Finally, in application of Article 27(4) of GCIV, the occupier is entitled to take such "measures of control and security" necessary to deal with the consequences of war.[14] This could include, for example, restricting access to areas surrounding tunnel entrances.[15]

The neutralization or destruction of tunnels will likely cause some damage to nearby property, or require that the occupier take control thereof, even if temporarily. The extent to which public or private property can be destroyed, requisitioned, or confiscated, particularly for the benefit of the *occupier's* security, is a complex question. For purposes of requisition and confiscation, The Hague Regulations distinguish between public and

---

[10] Regulations Respecting the Laws and Customs of War on Land, annexed to Convention Respecting the Laws and Customs of War on Land, art. 42–43 (Oct. 18, 1907), 36 Stat. 2277, 205 Consol. T. S. 277 [hereinafter Hague Regulations]; Geneva Convention Relative to the Protection of Civilian Persons in Time of War, Aug. 12, 1949, 6 U.S.T. 3516, 75 U.N.T.S. 287 [hereinafter "the Fourth Geneva Convention" or "GCIV"]; and Philip Spoerri, *The Law of Occupation, in* THE OXFORD HANDBOOK OF INTERNATIONAL LAW IN ARMED CONFLICT 186 (Andrew Clapham & Paola Gaeta eds., 2014).

[11] Hague Regulations, *supra* note 10, at art. 43.

[12] GCIV, *supra* note 10, at art. 64.

[13] COMMENTARY ON THE GENEVA CONVENTIONS OF 12 AUGUST 1949, VOL. 4: RELATIVE TO THE PROTECTION OF CIVILIAN PERSONS IN TIMES OF WAR 337 (Jean S. Pictet ed., 1952) [hereinafter ICRC Commentary to GCIV].

[14] GCIV, *supra* note 10, at art. 27(4).

[15] ICRC Commentary to GCIV, *supra* note 13, at 207.

private, movable and immovable property. Rules governing immovable public and private property are most relevant to tunnels and other underground structures.[16]

A tunnel qualifies as private property when it is built on private property, or when access to private property is required in order to destroy it. In such situations, the property can be requisitioned by the occupier in accordance with Article 52 of The Hague Regulations:

> Requisitions in kind and services shall not be demanded from municipalities or inhabitants except for *the needs of the army of occupation*. They shall be *in proportion* to the resources of the country, and of such a nature *as not to involve the inhabitants in the obligation of taking part in military operations against their own country*. [. . .] Contributions in kind shall as far as possible be paid for in cash; if not, a receipt shall be given and the payment of the amount due shall be made as soon as possible.[17]

The requisition of private property, temporary in nature, must be distinguished from permanent confiscation. Whereas Article 46 of the Hague Regulations prohibits permanent confiscation,[18] requisition is lawful subject to three conditions: it must be limited to the "needs of the army of occupation," it cannot involve the occupied population in military operations against their own country, and it must include the payment of compensation.[19] This rule was affirmed in several cases before the Nuremberg Tribunal following the Second World War,[20] and finds expression in many states' military manuals.[21] The first requirement—that requisition be limited to the "needs of the army of occupation"—is narrower than "military necessity."[22] IHL does not define with precision the meaning of these terms, but the Israeli Supreme Court has held that the "needs of the

---

[16] Provisions governing movable public property are relevant to munitions or other military equipment found inside a tunnel. These could be requisitioned under Article 53 of the Hague Regulations, which allows an occupier to confiscate movable state property that could be used for military operations, including munitions, even if they belong to private individuals (Hague Regulations, *supra* note 10, at art. 53; ICRC Commentary to GCIV, *supra* note 13, at 301).

[17] Hague Regulations, *supra* note 10, at art. 52 (emphases added); and David Kretzmer, *The Advisory Opinion: The Light Treatment of International Humanitarian Law*, 99 AM. J. INT'L L. 88, 97 (2005).

[18] YUTAKA ARAI-TAKAHASHI, THE LAW OF OCCUPATION: CONTINUITY AND CHANGE OF INTERNATIONAL HUMANITARIAN LAW, AND ITS INTERACTION WITH INTERNATIONAL HUMAN RIGHTS LAW 223 (2009).

[19] Hague Regulations, *supra* note 10, at art. 46, 52.

[20] U.S. v. Flick, U.S. Mil Trib. at Nuremberg (Dec. 22, 1947) IX L. REP. OF TRIALS OF WAR CRIM. 21 (1949); U.S. v. Krauch, U.S. Mil. Trib. at Nuremberg (July 30, 1948) V L. REP OF TRIALS OF WAR CRIM. 44 (1949).

[21] JEAN-MARIE HENCKAERTS & LOUISE DOSWALD-BECK, CUSTOMARY INTERNATIONAL HUMANITARIAN LAW, VOL. I: RULES, Rule 51 (2005) [hereinafter: CUSTOMARY LAW STUDY]; as indicated therein, the prohibition is included in the military manuals of Argentina, Australia, Benin, Canada, Colombia, Germany, Hungary, Indonesia, Israel, Italy, New Zealand, Nigeria, Peru, Philippines, Romania, South Africa, Switzerland, Togo, Uganda, the United Kingdom, and the United States.

[22] Kretzmer, *supra* note 17, at 97.

army of occupation" do not include the national, economic, or social interests of the occupying power, or national security needs in a broad sense.[23]

When the tunnel is located on public land, and thus qualifies as immovable public property, the options of the occupier are more limited:[24]

> The occupying State shall be regarded only as administrator and usufructuary of public buildings, real estate, forests, and agricultural estates belonging to the hostile State, and situated in the occupied country. It must safeguard the capital of these properties, and administer them in accordance with the rules of usufruct.

Unfortunately, the clause does not specifically address property of a military nature, a category into which a tunnel, including the property on which its entrance is located, would almost certainly fall.

In any case, these and all measures undertaken during occupation must comply with the principles of necessity and proportionality.[25] Under Article 53 of the GCIV, the occupier cannot destroy property unless this is rendered "absolutely necessary by military operations."[26] Besides the condition of absolute military necessity, the damage to property must be proportionate to the military advantage anticipated. The ICRC Commentary to Article 53 calls on the occupier to judge, in good faith, the military requirements leading to the destruction of property, and to "keep a sense of proportion in comparing the military advantage to be gained with the damage done."[27] In its Advisory Opinion on the *Legal Consequences of the Construction of a Wall in the Occupied Palestinian Territories*, the International Court of Justice opined that the military exigencies referred to in Article 53 could be invoked even following the end of the hostilities that led to the occupation. However, it did not provide guidance as to what constitutes sufficient military necessity, or how proportionality ought to be assessed.[28] Judge Owada addressed the issue of proportionality in his separate opinion, adopting an overall assessment of the balance between military necessity and damage: that is, considering a specific act in its broader context.[29]

---

[23] HCJ 390/79 Duweikat, v. Gov't of Israel 34(1) PD 1 [1979], at 19 (Isr.).
[24] Hague Regulations, *supra* note 10, at art. 55.
[25] ICRC Commentary to GCIV, *supra* note 13, at 302.
[26] GCIV, *supra* note 10, at art. 53.
[27] *Id.* at 302.
[28] Wall Advisory Opinion, *supra* note 5, ¶ 135.
[29] *Id.* Separate Opinion of Judge Owada, ¶ 26. The approaches of the Court and of Judge Owada have been criticized on this point (see Wall Advisory Opinion, *supra* note 5, Separate Opinion of Judge Buergenthal, ¶ 3, indicating that the Court did not have sufficient facts to make an assessment of military necessity; *see also* Kretzmer, *supra* note 17, at 99–100. In contrast, some scholars have justified the departure from a more specific assessment in the particular situations examined by the Court (*see* ARAI-TAKAHASHI, *supra* note 18, at 190–91).

The Israeli Supreme Court, for its part, developed a three-pronged test of proportionality to the destruction of property during occupation. As applied to tunnels, the test would require (1) a rational connection between the anti-tunnel measure and the legitimate purpose (security), (2) that the said anti-tunnel measure constitutes the least intrusive way of achieving the goal, and (3) that the benefits brought about by the anti-tunnel operation outweigh the harm inherent in leaving the tunnel(s) as is.[30]

Outside of occupation, what legal framework would apply to anti-tunnel operations launched on the territory of a foreign state in the immediate aftermath of a conflict? By then it might be too late to rely on IHL, and too early to revert to the exclusive application of human rights law. The *jus post bellum* could offer a valuable alternative in such circumstances.

Though the prospect of this middle-of-the-road body of law seems attractive when contending with underground warfare, there is no consensus on its existence or its normative content.[31] The *jus post bellum* has been described as "a framework to deal with the challenges of state-building and transformation of States in a post-conflict phase."[32] It borrows from IHL, international human rights law, international criminal law, and domestic criminal, administrative, constitutional, and military law.[33] As a legal framework seeking to ensure a just settlement of the conflict and the security of the victim state,[34] the *jus post bellum* could provide a path for the destruction of tunnels post-conflict. It places the emphasis on the punishment of international crimes,[35] political[36] and economic reconstruction,[37] reconciliation, and rebuilding—including political reconstruction and disarmament.[38]

Disarmament is particularly relevant in the context of subterranean warfare. International law does not impose postwar disarmament on former warring parties. Such an obligation would need to be based on a specific treaty or other agreement between the parties to the conflict. In the *Nicaragua* case, the International Court of Justice ruled that "in international law there are no rules, other than such rules as may be accepted by the

---

[30] David Kretzmer, *The Law of Belligerent Occupation in the Supreme Court of Israel*, 94 INT'L REV. RED CROSS 207, 229 (2012); HCJ 2056/04, Beit Sourik Village Council v. Gov't of Israel 48(5) PD 807, ¶ 41 [2004] (Isr.).

[31] Dieter Fleck, Jus Post Bellum *as a Partly Independent Legal Framework*, in JUS POST BELLUM: MAPPING THE NORMATIVE FRAMEWORK 43 (Carsten Stahn, Jennifer S. Easterday & Jens Iverson eds., 2014).

[32] Carsten Stahn, Jus Post Bellum: *Mapping the Discipline(s)*, 23 AM. U. INT'L L. REV. 311, 321 (2007); and Inger Österdahl & Esther van Zadel, *What Will* Jus Post Bellum *Mean? Of New Wine and Old Bottles*, 14 J. CONFLICT & SEC. L 175, 176 (2009).

[33] Österdahl & van Zadel, *supra* note 32, at 182.

[34] MICHAEL WALZER, JUST AND UNJUST WARS: A HISTORICAL ARGUMENT WITH HISTORICAL ILLUSTRATIONS 121 (4th ed. 2006).

[35] Brian Orend, Jus Post Bellum, 31 J. SOC. PHIL. 117, 124 (2000).

[36] Gary J. Bass, Jus Post Bellum, 32 PHIL. & PUB. AFF. 384, 396 (2004).

[37] Larry May, Just Post Bellum, *Grotius and Meionexia*, in JUS POST BELLUM: MAPPING THE NORMATIVE FRAMEWORK, *supra* note 31, at 15.

[38] Orend, *supra* note 35, at 125.

State concerned, by treaty or otherwise, whereby the level of armaments of a sovereign State can be limited."[39] Postwar tunnel destruction would therefore have to be mandated expressly by treaty or by a ceasefire agreement between the parties to the conflict.

The United Nations has at times included disarmament as part of post-conflict peacemaking with the consent of the host state.[40] The UN has implemented so-called "DDR" policies—disarmament, demobilization and reintegration—in places such as Côte d'Ivoire, the Democratic Republic of Congo, Liberia, and Sierra Leone.[41] The policy, which includes "the collection, documentation, control and disposal of small arms, ammunition, explosives and light and heavy weapons of combatants and often also of the civilian population,"[42] seeks to facilitate long-term peace, stability, and recovery efforts.[43] There is little doubt that the mapping, neutralization, and elimination of tunnels would have to be carried out as part of a DDR policy.

The regime applicable to landmines and other explosive remnants of war offers additional insights on what post-conflict obligations could entail in the context of underground warfare. The 1996 Amended Protocol II and the 2003 Protocol V to the 1980 Convention on Certain Conventional Weapons (CCW) require state parties to clear, remove, and destroy mines, booby traps and other devices, and explosive remnants of war following the conflict, respectively.[44] Though neither instrument provides justification for unilateral third-party interference, they both include fairly robust cooperation requirements. They obligate states to remove explosive remnants located on their territory, including via cooperation "where appropriate."[45] When a state no longer holds

---

[39] Military and Paramilitary Activities in and Against Nicaragua (Nicar. v. U.S.), 1986 I.C.J. 14, ¶ 269.

[40] See U.N. Secretary-General, *An Agenda for Peace: Preventive Diplomacy, Peacemaking and Peace-Keeping: Rep. of the Secretary-General*, ¶¶ 55, 58, U.N. Doc. A/47/277-S/24111 (June 17, 1992); and U.N. Secretary-General, *Supplement to an Agenda for Peace: Position Paper of the Secretary-General on the Occasion of the Fiftieth Anniversary of the United Nations*, ¶¶ 57–65, U.N. Doc. A/50/60-S/1995/1 (Jan. 3, 1995).

[41] See U.N. Secretary-General, *Disarmament, Demobilization and Reintegration: Rep. of the Secretary-General*, ¶¶ 43–44, U.N. Doc. A/60/705 (Mar. 2, 2006) [hereinafter DDR Report]; and U.N. Dep't. of Peacekeeping Operations, Office of Rule of Law and Security Institutions Disarmament, Demobilization and Reintegration Section, DDR in Peacekeeping Operations: A Retrospective (2010), http://www.un.org/en/peacekeeping/documents/DDR_retrospective.pdf. See also UN DDR in an Era of Violent Extremism: Is It Fit for Its Purpose? 47 n.74 (James Cockayne & Siobhan O'Neil eds., 2015), https://collections.unu.edu/eserv/UNU:5532/UNDDR.pdf.

[42] DDR Report, *supra* note 41, ¶ 24.

[43] *Id.* ¶ 43.

[44] Protocol on Prohibitions or Restrictions on the Use of Mines, Booby-Traps and Other Devices (as amended on 3 May 1996) to the Convention on Prohibitions or Restrictions on the Use of Certain Conventional Weapons Which May Be Deemed to Be Excessively Injurious or to Have Indiscriminate Effects, art. 10, May 3, 1996, 2048 U.N.T.S. 93 [hereinafter: Amended Protocol II]; Protocol on Explosive Remnants of War to the Convention on Prohibitions or Restrictions on the Use of Certain Conventional Weapons Which May Be Deemed to Be Excessively Injurious or to Have Indiscriminate Effects, art. 3, Nov. 28, 2003, 2399 U.N.T.S. 100 [hereinafter Protocol V to the CCW on Explosive Remnants of War].

[45] Amended Protocol II, *supra* note 44, at art. 10(4); Protocol V to the CCW on Explosive Remnants of War, *supra* note 44, at art. 3(5).

control of the territory on which explosive remnants are located, such as landmines and booby traps, it must assist the entity in control of the territory to remove them.[46] A post-conflict regime applicable to tunnels could similarly obligate states to neutralize or eliminate tunnels located on their territory and/or seek assistance from a third party.[47]

As noted above, however, none of these regimes envisions unilateral action by one state on the territory of another.[48] The state in which the tunnels are located would have to consent to the operations following a request by the neighboring state. In sum, although the *jus post bellum* does not allow for unilateral anti-tunnel operations, it offers various options for the continuation of the destruction of tunnels after the fighting ends, including through the cooperation of the parties or post-conflict monitoring by a third party.

The latter—post-conflict monitoring at the hands of a third party—seems less relevant to underground warfare. It is difficult to imagine an international body sufficiently well versed in underground warfare to monitor tunnel-digging and tunnel use, and to assist countries facing underground threats. This option seems hardly realistic in the short-term, but it remains a possibility in the future.

No matter the context, the identification of the normative corpus applicable to subterranean warfare must take place early as it impacts the type and level of force that may be exercised in order to eliminate the threat. States should incorporate this step into their strategy (even in situations where anti-tunnel operations affect only their nationals), and ensure that most anti-tunnel operations are undertaken in conflict rather than post-conflict (where the legal framework becomes a lot blurrier).

II. Strategy and Methods

Even before discovering a tunnel, states must take the underground threat seriously and devise a strategy to counter it. Past practice shows that spur-of-the-moment decisions cannot adequately account for the complexity of the threat. Relying exclusively on technology is also ill-advised. Technology cannot provide a foolproof solution to underground warfare in the absence of prior knowledge and expertise. Misconceptions about

---

[46] Amended Protocol II, *supra* note 44, at art. 10(3); Protocol V to the CCW on Explosive Remnants of War, *supra* note 44, at art. 3(1). *See* S/RES/1062 (1996) 28 June 1996, para. 6(c); and S/RES/1092 (1996) (23 Dec. 1996), paras. 6(a) and 9.

[47] *See* Louis Maresca, *A New Protocol on Explosive Remnants of War: The History and Negotiation of Protocol V to the 1980 Convention on Certain Conventional Weapons*, 86 INT'L REV. RED CROSS 816 (2004).

[48] U.N. DEP'T. OF PEACEKEEPING OPERATIONS, DEP'T OF FIELD SUPPORT, UNITED NATIONS PEACEKEEPING OPERATIONS: PRINCIPLES AND GUIDELINES 26–28 (2008), http://www.un.org/en/peacekeeping/documents/capstone_eng.pdf.

underground warfare are all too common, and states must put in place mechanisms to overcome them.[49] This section explains why states should set up a strategy on underground warfare—even if they do so merely preventively—and lays out some of the methods commonly used to map, neutralize, and destroy tunnels.

A. WHY A STRATEGY

All states, especially but not only those that have experienced underground warfare, should elaborate a strategy to contend with subterranean threats. The reasons are manifold. A well-thought-out, pre-planned strategy will help states better channel resources, enhance the effectiveness of their response while minimizing the harm to soldiers and civilians alike, ensure that resources are invested in *both* intelligence and technology, afford soldiers adequate training, and improve response time in the midst of a crisis.

Having a strategy will save states time and resources. Anti-tunnel warfare can be frustrating, lengthy, and costly. Shaping a strategy will enable states to use their resources more efficiently and guarantee that all aspects of anti-tunnel operations are accounted for. Caught by surprise, states that have no strategy for dealing with the underground threat tend to resort to second-best tactics (such as random drillings or searches by infantry soldiers). Efforts at countering the threat end up short-lived at best, and harmful to civilians and military personnel at worst. Only a full-fledged strategy offers lasting security.

Contending with underground warfare also requires states to develop or acquire advanced technology—an aspect that should be incorporated into the strategy. This should not, however, detract from the importance of relying on intelligence gathering (particularly human intelligence). The need to simultaneously develop new intelligence *and* technological capabilities can easily be underestimated by states, particularly when the threat emerges somewhat unexpectedly. Only when intelligence and technological expertise are developed in tandem can states successfully contend with underground warfare. The winning combination of tailor-made technology and intelligence techniques requires an underlying institutional structure and a pre-planned strategy.

Other reasons for devising a strategy on underground warfare include the tactic's rapid spread, of course, as well as the need for expertise not easily acquired "on the go." Troops must be trained for subterranean warfare, including fighting in confined and dark places.[50] Not every soldier is fit for this type of combat. The army must select and train

---

[49] By way of example, a Human Rights Watch report wrongly claims that "tunnels are easier to defeat than they are to construct." See *Razing Rafah: Mass Demolitions in the Gaza Strip*, HUMAN RIGHTS WATCH (Oct. 17, 2004), https://www.hrw.org/report/2004/10/17/razing-rafah/mass-home-demolitions-gaza-strip.

[50] In Israel, for example, soldiers train in purpose-built tunnel simulators: Yuval Azulai, *New Simulators to Train IDF Soldiers for Tunnel Warfare*, GLOBES (Apr. 5, 2015), http://www.globes.co.il/en/article-simulators-training-idf-soldiers-for-tunnel-warfare-1001026216; and Avigail Bukobza, *Tunnels by the IDF*, IDF GROUND FORCES COMMAND (Feb. 18, 2015), http://m.mazi.idf.il/7343-11870-he/Mazi.aspx (in Hebrew).

those who will be contending first hand with tunnels. Ideally, all soldiers should know basic facts and tactics in subterranean warfare, and special units should be established to deal exclusively with tunnels.[51] As part of their training in underground warfare, soldiers must learn how to recognize and distinguish among various types of tunnels. As I explained in Chapter 2, a well-trained soldier can often identify the purpose of a tunnel and its owner based on how the tunnel looks. The typology of tunnels I developed in this book will also help soldiers anticipate new trends and prepare for upcoming challenges. In addition, subterranean warfare requires that rules of engagement be adapted, new means of warfare and communication identified, and procedures for the rescue and evacuation of the wounded updated. Finally, armies should assist their soldiers and veterans in handling the psychological hardship of underground warfare.[52] The dire conditions of this type of war can lead to various forms of post-traumatic stress disorder. Deputy Patrol Agent Kevin Hecht who works at the U.S.-Mexico border speaks of "the claustrophobia and darkness and all the unknowns involved. We try to adopt as many people as we can onto the team but there are some people that freeze. It's just not for them."[53] If tunnels leave such a mark on law enforcement officials, one can only imagine how they affect soldiers on the battlefield.

All of this demands thinking and planning—hence the need to devise the strategy in quiet times to make the know-how readily available and improve the quality of the response in times of crisis. Whether it includes all of the above elements or only some of them, the process of devising a strategy generates an important discussion among the state's various relevant authorities. Notwithstanding the outcome, it enhances a state's readiness in subterranean warfare.

B. COMPONENTS OF A FULL-FLEDGED UNDERGROUND WARFARE STRATEGY

A full-fledged underground warfare strategy includes the following four steps: (1) detection and mapping, (2) neutralization and/or destruction, (3) prevention and monitoring,

---

[51] U.S. Army, *Technologies to Enhance Warfighter Capabilities in Subterranean Environments*, FED. BUS. OPPORTUNITIES (Dec. 11, 2013), https://www.fbo.gov/index?s=opportunity&mode=form&tab=core&id=50279b14e6e0978f0ab544e4b6feffc4 ("Besides specialized tools and equipment, US Forces need to have specialized personnel available for subterranean (SbT) combat operations, or at least incorporate a rigorous and realistic SbT warfare curriculum into the US Force's education system. With proper training and equipment, US Forces can achieve greater success and lower the risk of death or injury occurring during operations within SbT environments"); and Dan Lamothe, *Hamas Tactics Highlight U.S. Military's Preparation for Tunnel Warfare*, WASH. POST (July 21, 2014), https://www.washingtonpost.com/news/checkpoint/wp/2014/07/21/hamas-tactics-highlight-u-s-militarys-preparation-for-tunnel-warfare/?utm_term=.0f0562f30dd2.
[52] U.S. MARINE CORPS, MILITARY OPERATIONS ON URBANIZED TERRAIN (MOUT) E-5 299 (1998), http://www.marines.mil/Portals/59/MCWP%203-35.3.pdf.
[53] Jason McCammack, *What Lies Beneath*, U.S. CUSTOMS AND BORDER PROTECTION (Feb. 20, 2017), https://www.cbp.gov/frontline/what-lies-beneath. [hereinafter *What Lies Beneath*].

and (4) cooperation. The analysis of these various steps includes an overview of the methods available to accomplish each task. It does not purport to present an exhaustive account of anti-tunnel technology—let alone an endorsement of any of the technologies on the market. Ranking the methods is not only beyond the scope of this book, it would also be a mistake: each method's rate of success depends on the context in which it is used (environment, nature of soil, type of tunnels, etc.) and cannot be assessed *in abstracto*.

1. Detection and Mapping

Detecting a tunnel consists in identifying a segment or entry point of a tunnel. It essentially provides evidence that a tunnel exists. Mapping refers to the act of identifying and recording the route of a tunnel once the presence of a tunnel is suspected. Tunnel mapping provides invaluable information about the physical characteristics of an underground structure such as its length and depth, and the location, number, and type of its entrance and exit points. Tunnels can have several entrance and exit points, multiple arteries, and levels. Take, for example, the complex underground structures built by the Vietcong, Hamas, and ISIS. Each entrance, exit, room, and artery poses an imminent threat of its own, particularly when tunnels burrow under civilian populated areas. Both detection and mapping come with their share of complexities. States end up confronted with many different options, none of which guarantees success. The task is daunting, often leading states to rely on dubious techniques or skip the detection stage altogether.

The importance of technology should not overshadow the fact that no single technology is efficient and accurate enough to achieve successful results on its own. The key to handling tunnels consists in understanding the panoply of available options and choosing the most promising methods. Certain methods are more suitable for certain situations than for others. Technology is of limited use if not combined with successful intelligence gathering (particularly human intelligence).

INTELLIGENCE GATHERING. Intelligence can be gathered using a wide variety of methods, including HUMINT (human intelligence, gathered from a human origin); SIGINT (signals intelligence, based on listening to electromagnetic waves and other communication means); OSINT (open source intelligence, gathered by overt sources such as newspapers, television, and the Internet); VISINT (visual intelligence, gathered from ground photography and soldiers' observations); and MASINT (measurement and signature intelligence, gathered via radar, radio frequency, and other methods).[54]

---

[54] *Intelligence Branch*, FBI (Feb. 20, 2017), https://www.fbi.gov/about/leadership-and-structure/intelligence-branch.

In the realm of underground warfare, intelligence gathering should focus on the location of tunnels and their entrance and exit points. Human intelligence gathered by soldiers surveying a given area or by informants behind enemy lines is highly valuable.[55] Each terrain, however, is different. Detecting tunnels in a city or in the jungle calls for different skills. A United States Army field manual teaching soldiers how to detect tunnels in jungle-like terrain lists nine terrain-specific indicators for soldiers to watch for: worn places on trees that the guerrilla uses as handholds; a small trail through the brush into a clump of small trees; cut trees (although the manual notes that this is not a sure sign); limbs tied near tree tops to conceal the use of a tunnel from aircraft; a slight depression in or around a group of small trees; air holes; a lone individual, especially a female, in the area, fresh cooked food with no one attending the site; and human feces.[56] Although it focuses on the jungle, these indicators underscore the role of human intelligence in detecting tunnels in general. At the U.S.-Mexico border, U.S. authorities keep in close touch with the local population and train them to report suspicious behavior and noises.[57] Such methods could be used at the Israel-Gaza, Israel-Lebanon,[58] or Syria-Turkey borders[59] where locals regularly report hearing noises at night.

Intelligence personnel should also learn to detect and map tunnels by monitoring topographical changes.[60] Here is how an escape tunnel dug at the Camp Bucca prison in Iraq came to be suspected:

> The 105th Military Police Battalion, charged with running Camp Bucca in the scorching desert of southernmost Iraq, knew something was amiss: Undetectable to the naked eye, the field's changing color was picked up by satellite imagery. The excavated dirt was also clogging the showers and two dozen portable toilets. The dirt was showing up under the floorboards of tents; some guards sensed that

---

[55] For example, the arrest and interrogation of Hamas operative Mahmoud Atawneh allowed the IDF to obtain information leading to the discovery of a cross-border tunnel emanating from Gaza and reaching into Israeli territory (*see* Isabel Kershner, *Israelis Find Second Tunnel from Gaza and May Know of Others*, N.Y. TIMES (May 5, 2016), https://www.nytimes.com/2016/05/06/world/middleeast/israelis-find-second-tunnel-from-gaza-and-may-know-of-others.html?_r=0).

[56] U.S. ARMY FIELD MANUAL NO. 90-8: COUNTERGUERILLA OPERATIONS, Appendix A: Subsurface Operations (1986).

[57] *See What Lies Beneath*, *supra* note 53.

[58] Adam Ciralsky, *Did Israel Avert a Hamas Massacre?*, VANITY FAIR (Oct. 21, 2014), http://www.vanityfair.com/news/politics/2014/10/gaza-tunnel-plot-israeli-intelligence.

[59] Erin Cunningham, *The Flow of Jihadists into Syria Dries up as Turkey Cracks Down on the Border*, WASH. POST (Aug. 1, 2015), https://www.washingtonpost.com/world/middle_east/the-flow-of-jihadists-into-syria-dries-up-as-turkey-cracks-down-on-the-border/2015/07/31/d95f4234-34ad-11e5-b835-61ddaa99c73e_story.html?utm_term=.9a1a598b9496.

[60] Joshua S. Bowes, Mark T. Newdigate, Pedro J. Rosario & Davis D. Tindoll, *The Enemy Below: Preparing Ground Forces for Subterranean Warfare*, Dec. 2013 (unpublished AB thesis, Naval Postgraduate School), http://calhoun.nps.edu/handle/10945/38883 [hereinafter *The Enemy Below*].

the floor itself seemed to be rising. Mysteriously, water use in the compound had spiked.[61]

The color and general appearance of suspected areas should therefore be carefully monitored, as well as the construction of hangars built to conceal digging equipment and excavated earth. Monitoring construction and human movement in sensitive areas plays a significant role in the detection of tunnels[62] provided authorities corroborate the visual intelligence thus obtained to avoid manipulations by the enemy.[63] As Lt. Col Arnold Streland of the United States Air Force pointed out in 2003, "[t]here is no "silver bullet" intelligence solution to the problem of detecting deeply buried facilities. The solution comes from combining several sources of intelligence".[64]

ANIMALS. The use of animals in the realm of underground warfare is quite frequent. Bedbugs, rabbits, canaries, and dogs have all been used to detect tunnels and help forces determine what lies beneath the ground—with varying degrees of success. Even red foxes have been suggested as a method for tunnel detection, in light of their unique hearing capabilities (they are able to catch their prey under a meter of snow, without even seeing them).[65]

During World War I, the British used animals to detect the presence of gas inside tunnels:

> In 1915 rabbits were most readily available and one would be lowered down a shaft to test the air before descending. Later the British used mice and canaries and each tunnelling company bred its own stock, under the charge of an older miner... Men were fond of the mice and canaries, but a story was often told of the escaped canary whose presence in no man's land threatened to warn the Germans of the presence of miners in the sector.[66]

---

[61] *See* Steve Fainaru & Anthony Shadid, *In Iraq Jail, Resistance Goes Underground*, WASH. POST (Aug. 24, 2005), http://www.washingtonpost.com/wp-dyn/content/article/2005/08/23/AR2005082301525.html.

[62] *See* Jeffrey T. Richelson, *Underground Facilities: Intelligence and Targeting Issues*, NAT'L SEC. ARCHIVE (Mar. 23, 2012), http://nsarchive.gwu.edu/NSAEBB/NSAEBB372/ (listing successful uses of this method in Russia, Libya, Cuba, and China).

[63] Interview with Yaakov Amidror, Maj. Gen. (res.), former National Security Advisor to the Prime Minister of Israel (June 2016).

[64] Arnold H. Streland, *Going Deep: A System Concept for Detecting Deeply Buried Facilities from Space* 2 (Feb. 23, 2003) (Research Paper, Air War College, Air University), http://www2.gwu.edu/~nsarchiv/NSAEBB/NSAEBB372/docs/Underground-GoingDeep.pdf [hereinafter *Going Deep*] (emphasis added).

[65] *Detection of Underground Activity by Red Foxes*, (July 30, 2014), http://www.hayadan.org.il/locating-underground-activity-by-the-red-fox-3007149 (in Hebrew).

[66] SIMON JONES, UNDERGROUND WARFARE 1914–1918, at 182–183 (2010).

U.S. forces faced similar problems when they used bedbugs to detect human presence inside tunnels in Vietnam. Troops would walk around with a bedbug carrier equipped with a sound amplification device. The problem, however, was that the enemy would hear the bedbugs as they came closer.[67]

Dogs seem best equipped to conduct this type of operation. Their distinct ability to smell humans,[68] explosives,[69] drugs,[70] mines,[71] and any other object they have been trained to detect can be extremely valuable in the realm of underground warfare. They can also detect tunnels and then enter them, carrying video cameras that deliver live feed to the armed forces.[72] Dogs detected explosives and tunnels during the Vietnam War.[73] The canine unit of the Israel Defense Forces (IDF), known as "Oketz," was tasked with tunnel detection during Operation Protective Edge in 2014.[74] The unit sent sniffer dogs instead of soldiers inside the tunnels due to fear of explosives and casualties.[75]

SMOKE. Smoke is arguably the most efficient method for detecting and mapping tunnels. When smoke is injected inside a suspected tunnel entrance, watching the smoke come out of the ground makes it possible to detect additional entrances while mapping the route of the tunnel at the same time. During the Soviet-Afghan War, the Soviets used non-lethal smoke grenades to test tunnels for further exits, check ventilation systems, and surprise Mujahedeen hiding inside the tunnels.[76]

Legally speaking, smoke raises fewer concerns than gas. Its legality is largely context-dependent. When smoke ammunition is used primarily on account of its toxic properties, it is prohibited by international law. For example, white phosphorus cannot be used

---

[67] Tom Mangold & John Penycate, The Tunnels of Cù Chi: A Harrowing Account of America's Tunnel Rats in the Underground Battlefields of Vietnam 207 (2005).

[68] U.S. United States Search and Rescue Task Force, Dogs in Search and Rescue (Feb. 20, 2017), http://www.ussartf.org/dogs_search_rescue.htm.

[69] Irit Gazit & Joseph Terkel, *Explosives Detection by Sniffer Dogs Following Strenuous Physical Activity*, 81 Applied Animal Behavior Sci. 149 (2003).

[70] *See Police Use of Drug Detection Dogs in Texas*, Law Offices of David Sloane (Oct. 8, 2014), http://www.sloanelaw.com/Criminal-Defense-Blog/2014/October/Police-Use-of-Drug-Detection-Dogs-in-Texas.aspx.

[71] Sarah Vos, *Sniffing Landmines*, ChemMatters (Apr. 7, 2008), http://www.acs.org/content/dam/acsorg/education/resources/highschool/chemmatters/gc-sniffing-landmines.pdf.

[72] Dan Williams, *Israeli Troops, with Dogs and Robots, Track Gaza Tunnels*, Reuters (July 30, 2014), http://www.reuters.com/article/us-mideast-gaza-tunnels-idUSKBN0FZ20Y20140730.

[73] *Vietnam*, U.S. War Dogs Association, Inc. (Feb. 20, 2017), http://www.uswardogs.org/war-dog-history/vietnam/.

[74] Ohad Hemo, *Operation Protective Edge Through the Eyes of the Combat Dogs*, Mako (Oct. 9, 2014), http://www.mako.co.il/news-military/security-q4_2014/Article-cf59ce32906f841004.htm (in Hebrew).

[75] Williams, *supra* note 72.

[76] *See* Lester W. Grau & Ali Ahmad Jalali, *Underground Combat: Stereophonic Blasting, Tunnel Rats and the Soviet-Afghan War*, 28 Engineer 20 (1998).

when its toxic properties are "deliberately exploited."[77] However, it is generally considered lawful when used in order to produce a smoke screen that provides cover for forces, insofar as the use complies with relevant rules of IHL. In other words, objections to its use focus on the way in which it is employed and not on smoke ammunition itself.[78]

Many states have adopted this view. The Canadian Law of Armed Conflict Manual, for example, specifically distinguishes between illegal chemical weapons and smoke ammunition, such as "smoke grenades, smoke ammunition from indirect fire weapons and tank smoke ammunition". According to the manual, smoke ammunition is not prohibited so long as it is used to conceal position or movement or to mask a target."[79] In the UK as well, guidelines regarding the use of white phosphorus emphasize that it should be used "for the purpose of producing a smoke screen to provide cover" and not against personnel.[80] So long as the toxic or incendiary properties are merely incidental (as is the case with illuminants, tracers, smoke or signaling systems), smoke is not prohibited.

Although this interpretation finds support in the law—smoke does not formally qualify as a toxic chemical under Article 2(2) of the Chemical Weapons Convention (CWC)—one might object that injecting smoke into closed areas where a human presence has been reported (civilian or military) would negate the object and purpose of the CWC. For this reason, I would distinguish between the use of smoke for the limited purpose of mapping tunnels and the use of smoke for clearing or neutralizing tunnels. Whereas the former should be allowed (the toxic properties, if any, are merely incidental), the latter should be prohibited. When used for mapping, the projectile is not intended "to slay or disable by rending and tearing or by choking and poisoning."[81] I analyze further in Chapter 6 the undue harm smoke might inflict on combatants, and in Chapter 7 the harm it can cause to civilians.

TECHNOLOGY. Interestingly, much of the technology used for tunnel detection was originally developed by the civilian sector. Scientists and geographers working on

---

[77] WALTER KRUTZSCH, ERIC MYJER & RALF TRAPP, THE CHEMICAL WEAPONS CONVENTION: A COMMENTARY 79 (2014). I return to the legality of white phosphorus in the context of underground warfare in Chapter 6.

[78] See HUMAN RIGHTS WATCH, RAIN OF FIRE: ISRAEL'S UNLAWFUL USE OF WHITE PHOSPHORUS IN GAZA 60 (Mar. 25, 2009), https://www.hrw.org/sites/default/files/reports/iopt0309web.pdf.

[79] OFFICE OF THE JUDGE ADVOCATE GENERAL, CAN., THE LAW OF ARMED CONFLICT AT OPERATIONAL AND TACTICAL LEVELS 5–4 para. 515(2) (Aug. 13, 2001), https://www.fichl.org/fileadmin/_migrated/content_uploads/Canadian_LOAC_Manual_2001_English.pdf.

[80] 18 Jan. 2006, PARL. DEB., H.C. (2006) 1326W (U.K.). See also Abella v. Argentina, Inter-Am. Ct. I.A.C.H.R. OEA/Ser.L/V/II.98, ¶ 187 (1998); and STATE OF ISRAEL, THE 2014 GAZA CONFLICT: FACTUAL AND LEGAL ASPECTS ¶ 252 (2015). Alongside general principles of IHL, restrictions on use stem from the prohibition on the use of incendiary weapons. For further discussion, see Chapters 6 and 7.

[81] WILLIAM H. BOOTHBY, WEAPONS AND THE LAW OF ARMED CONFLICT 110 (2d ed., 2016) (citing to J.M. SPAIGHT, AIR POWER AND WAR RIGHTS 190 (3d ed., 1947)).

cave and tunnel detection started developing adequate technology as early as 100 years ago.[82] In these early stages, they worked mainly with gravity field measurements to discover underground structures and the general makeup of the ground beneath them. It was already possible at the time to establish the types of minerals that lay beneath the ground.[83] The detection of tunnels has also benefited from technology developed to find people among rubble in the aftermath of earthquakes and discover underground oil fields.[84]

Naturally, considerable progress has been made since then. Today, mapping tunnels with technology consists of using the initial source point detected and expanding the field of search for underground activity in geometrical circles to find the location and route of a given tunnel. Even though some of the technology has made its way to the defense and military establishment, a foolproof solution has yet to be found. As noted above, it is still the combination of intelligence and various technologies that offers the most promising course of action. It has even been suggested that simple technology will prove more beneficial than advanced technology given the complexity and limits of the underground environment.[85] In any case, experts agree that combining various technologies is key to achieving optimal results.[86]

Below is an overview of the various methods employed or under development today in the realm of tunnel detection and mapping. They generally fall within the following broad categories: robotics, seismic and acoustic sensors, magnetometers, electromagnetic induction, gravity measurement technology, thermal imagery, radars, and electrical resistivity. As noted above, this overview should not be conceived as an exhaustive list or a set of recommendations. It has no such ambitions. Rather, it provides a survey of options, highlighting some of their strength and weaknesses.

Robots are primarily used for mapping of tunnels and gathering intelligence about the tunnels' purpose and equipment (such as ammunition caches, mattresses and food for long-term stays, or booby traps). They are the modern equivalent of the tunnel rats, and offer the advantage of keeping soldiers out of harm's way. Whereas in the past soldiers had to risk their lives by entering tunnels with little intelligence on what dangers lingered inside, robots are now able to deliver live feed to military command centers while they are mapping the tunnels and searching for explosives.

---

[82] *Going Deep, supra* note 64, at 2.
[83] *Id.*
[84] *What Lies Beneath, supra* note 53.
[85] Walter Haydock, *Levantine Labyrinth: Preparing for Subterranean Warfare in Iraq and Syria*, WAR ON THE ROCKS (May 19, 2016), http://warontherocks.com/2016/05/levantine-labyrinth-preparing-for-subterranean-warfare-in-iraq-and-syria/.
[86] *See* ROBERT F. BALLARD, GEOTECHNICAL LABORATORY, U.S. ARMY ENGINEER WATERWAYS EXPERIMENT STATION, TUNNEL DETECTION ¶ 132 (1982), http://acwc.sdp.sirsi.net/client/search/asset/1020120 (as the United States Corps of Engineers understood in the early 1980s, "[t]he highest probability of tunnel detection will be achieved by using as many of the methods as possible").

The development of the field began in the early 1990s. In 1993 Foster Miller partnered with DARPA (the American Defense Advances Research Projects Agency) in the United States to develop a robot usable by the U.S. Army for the detection of explosives and mines. The Foster Miller Talon (bought in 2004 by QinetiQ North America), developed for this purpose, is one of the most widely used robots worldwide.[87] The Talon has been used by police and military forces in conflict and law enforcement operations, including following the 9/11 attacks, and in Iraq and Afghanistan.[88]

A version of the Foster Miller Talon, known as Foster-Talon 4, was used by the IDF in a cross-border tunnel exiting near the Israeli Kibbutz of Ein Hashlosha in 2013 and, later, during Operation Protective Edge in the summer of 2014. This powerful tool can climb stairs, and travel through snow, water, and sand. Most important, it can operate as deep as 330 feet underground, self-destruct, and come equipped with nuclear, biological, or chemical sensors.[89] It can also gather intelligence thanks to its four cameras and 24 hours of autonomy. Last but not least, it can neutralize explosives with the help of its gripper arms and whatever additional tools are installed on them.[90]

Other alternatives include the i-Robot, which can be carried in a bag and is operational in any terrain, even underground.[91] It has lights, live stream video, night vision capabilities, encrypted wireless communication, and can be equipped with weapons.[92] The "PackBot" is used by American forces (as of 2011, more than 2,000 robots were deployed in Iraq and Afghanistan),[93] including to clear caves.[94] The Individual Robotic Intelligence System, developed by Roboteam, is a hand-carried, ultra-lightweight unmanned robot. It can maneuver in confined spaces and is equipped with vision and audio technology.[95]

---

[87] Dean Anderson, Thomas M. Howard, David Apfelbaum, Herman Herman & Alonzo Kelly, *Coordinated Control and Range Imaging for Mobile Manipulation*, in EXPERIMENTAL ROBOTICS: THE ELEVENTH ANNUAL SYMPOSIUM 547 (Oussama Khatib, Vijay Kumar & George Pappas eds., 2009); TALON, QINETI-Q, https://www.qinetiq-na.com/products/unmanned-systems/talon/.

[88] TALON, *supra* note 87.

[89] Yoav Zitun, *Newest IDF Weapon: The Little Robot That Could*, YNET (Feb. 17, 2014), http://www.ynetnews.com/articles/0,7340,L-4489254,00.html.

[90] *Army of Robots: 5 Greatest Combat Engineering Tools*, IDF BLOG (Feb. 8, 2012), https://www.idfblog.com/blog/2012/02/08/army-robots-tools-idfs-combat-engineering-corps/.

[91] Yaakov Lappin, *IDF Mobility and Robotics Dept. Seeking Robot for Tunnel Warfare*, JERUSALEM POST (May 8, 2014), http://www.jpost.com/Defense/IDF-Mobility-and-Robotics-Dept-seeking-robot-for-tunnel-warfare-351608.

[92] *Meet i-Robot: The First Soldier to Enter Terror Tunnels*, IDF BLOG (May 1, 2014), https://www.idfblog.com/blog/2014/05/01/meet-robot-first-soldier-enter-terror-tunnels/.

[93] Nicholas Jackson, *The Tech That Could Help Save Fukushima: iRobot's PackBot*, ATLANTIC (Apr. 20, 2011), https://www.theatlantic.com/technology/archive/2011/04/the-tech-that-could-help-save-fukushima-irobots-packbot/237617/.

[94] Nic Robertson, *Meet Packbot: The Newest Recruit*, CNN, Aug. 1, 2002.

[95] *IRIS—Yours Eyes and Ears on the Ground and Under It*, ROBOTEAM, http://www.robo-team.com/products/systems/iris.

Robots (such as the Pointman Tactical Robot)[96] are now also widely deployed along the U.S.-Mexico border to scan tunnels used for cross-border drug trafficking and the crossing of illegal aliens into U.S. territory.[97]

There is little doubt that robots can significantly improve states' performance in the subterranean environment. Highly mobile robots capable of gathering intelligence can play critical roles in mapping and clearing tunnels, assessing the enemy's destructive capabilities, and anticipating threats.

Seismic and acoustic sensors are also very widely used—both to detect existing tunnels and prevent the construction of new ones. They embody one of the most significant contributions of the private sector to tunnel warfare. Seismic sensors were developed to enhance safety in the mining industry and assist in search-and-rescue operations. They can locate a trapper miner or detect sound frequencies in the ruins of destroyed buildings. They can also help in tunnel detection by recognizing a variety of activities such as digging, drilling, scraping, and jackhammering, and measure their intensity and duration.[98] Ground sensors can, for example, detect the movement of a person crawling at 32-feet deep.[99] The challenge with acoustic and seismic sensors is to filter out non-threatening vibrations, such as those from traffic on nearby roads and underground subways, in order to minimize false alarms. This makes them less suitable in urban areas.

Generally speaking, sensors can be divided into two types: active seismic sensors (which send a signal into the ground and analyze the type and level of the reaction),[100] and passive seismic sensors (which can be installed on or in the ground to detect anomalies caused by sounds or vibrations).[101] Both types of sensors have been used in the underground context. It has been suggested that the combination of both types of sensors is most promising:

> [T]he location of clandestine tunneling activity can be detected using a passive technique consisting of a permanent seismic surveillance system supplemented by

---

[96] Lourdes Medrano, *Tiny Robots to Prowl US-Mexico Border's Dark Drug Tunnels*, CHRISTIAN SCI. MONITOR (Jan. 16, 2014), http://www.csmonitor.com/USA/2014/0116/Tiny-robots-to-prowl-US-Mexico-border-s-dark-drug-tunnels.

[97] *Id.*

[98] *See, e.g.*, *Tunnel Detection*, ELPAM ELECTRONICS LTD., http://www.elpam.com/products/tunnels-disclosure/; Ben Sales, *Using Seismic Vibrations, Israeli Firm Aims to Detect Gaza Tunnels*, TIMES OF ISRAEL (Aug. 27, 2014), http://www.timesofisrael.com/using-seismic-vibrations-israeli-firm-aims-to-detect-gaza-tunnels/; and Inna Lazareva, *Israel Tests Hi-tech Tunnel Detection System to Fight Threat from Underground*, TELEGRAPH (July 23, 2014), http://www.telegraph.co.uk/news/worldnews/middleeast/israel/10985663/Israel-tests-hi-tech-tunnel-detection-system-to-fight-threat-from-underground.html.

[99] *See* Sales, *supra* note 98.

[100] Interview with Professor Shraga Shoval, Associate Professor and Head of the Department of Industrial Engineering and Management at Ariel University (June 2016) [hereinafter Shoval Interview]. *See also* Ballard, *supra* note 86, ¶ 61–62.

[101] Shoval Interview, *supra* note 100.

a portable system designed for deployment in the immediate area where signs of activity have been detected by the permanent system.[102]

The United States[103] and Israel[104] have contemplated the use of sensors to limit digging under the U.S.-Mexico border and the Israel-Gaza border, respectively. However, sensors cannot provide a near-perfect solution to tunnel detection for at least two reasons. First, it is not clear how deep sensors can detect digging activity. Tunnels are dug deeper and deeper—as deep as 100 feet. Second, differences in fracturing or saturation of pores in rock or soil, as well as changes in geology caused by rainfall and changing water tables produce some level of inaccuracy.[105] For this reason, according to David Masters who oversees tunnel detecting efforts at the United States Department of Homeland Security, a deep understanding of the geophysics associated with the type of sensor used and the earth investigated is required in order to discriminate between targets and clutter.[106] He adds that "[i]f you have a uniform geology, and a single tunnel, you get a beautiful return."[107] In a more complex terrain, complete with rocks and boulders, the returns are scattered and unpredictable.[108]

In the realm of sensors, remote sensing—that is, the discovery of underground objects and structures from radars and satellites—could well be the way of the future. In 2006, Dan Blumberg of Ben Gurion University, Israel, used microwave subsurface remote sensing to detect the presence of water in desert soil.[109] If the technology can detect water inside the soil, it can detect other subsurface voids. With time, remote sensing will penetrate deeper levels of the earth and become increasingly relevant to the detection of large and small underground structures. The potential of the technology is illustrated, for example, by its successful detection of oil reservoirs[110] and of a 115-foot-long tunnel in Ponar, Lithuania, that was hand-dug and used by Jewish prisoners as an

---

[102] Ballard, *supra* note 86, ¶ 134.

[103] *See also* Meredith Hoffman, *The Future of Border Securing Technology Is Here and It's Terrifying*, VICE (Apr. 10, 2016), https://www.vice.com/en_uk/article/the-new-frontiers-in-border-security-technology.

[104] Jack Moore, *Israel to Install Revolutionary Tunnel Detection System on Gaza Border*, NEWSWEEK (Apr. 17, 2015), http://europe.newsweek.com/israel-install-revolutionary-tunnel-detection-system-gaza-border-323001?rm=eu.

[105] Sandia National Laboratories, *Smuggler's Tunnels: Detecting Tunnels Using Seismic Waves Not as Simple as It Sounds*, SCI. DAILY (Dec. 10, 2012), http://www.sciencedaily.com/releases/2012/12/121210124214.htm.

[106] *Not Easy to Detect a Tunnel*, ISRAEL HOMELAND SECURITY (Mar. 21, 2013), http://i-hls.com/2013/03/not-easy-to-detect-a-tunnel/.

[107] *Id.*

[108] *Id.*

[109] *See* D.G. Blumberg, V. Freilikher, J. Ben-Asher, J. Daniels, Yu. Kaganovskii, A. Kotlyar & L. Vulfson, *Microwave Subsurface Remote Sensing in the Negev Desert: Monitoring of Soil Water-Content*, 16 WAVES IN RANDOM & COMPLEX MEDIA 179 (2006).

[110] Dragana Todorovic-Marinic, *Remote Sensing Underground*, 9 GEO EXPRO 20 (2013), http://www.geoexpro.com/articles/2013/02/remote-sensing-underground.

escape route in 1944.[111] The problem with tunnels, however, is that they are rather small and thus more difficult to detect.

Magnetometers and other metal detectors can detect underground structures that contain metal in the form of wires, pipes, or phone lines.[112] They are helpful in detecting highly sophisticated tunnels that are fortified with metal, but less so in detecting rudimentary tunnels such as those used in Syria.[113] Though they both help detect metal, magnetometers and metal detectors differ in important ways. Whereas magnetometers measure the intensity of the earth's magnetic field on the surface and below, metal detectors respond to the high electrical conductivity of metal targets contained within the normally low conductivity of soil.[114] Each of the two methods presents its own advantages and weaknesses.

Magnetometers can only detect ferrous material (e.g., iron and steel); they cannot detect metals such as tin and aluminum. The effectiveness of a magnetometer can also be significantly compromised by noise, time variable changes in the earth's magnetic field, and spatial variations. Like seismic sensors, they can easily be confused by nearby vibrations and other magnetic objects not related to the tunnel—a problem when the tunnels are located in urban areas. They also need to be placed fairly close to the suspected location in order to yield accurate results.

Metal detectors, on the other hand, can detect any type of metallic material that causes a local conductivity anomaly. Corroded materials are much harder to detect via metal detectors, and high concentration of natural iron bearing minerals, water, acid, and other high conductive fluids will also reduce the effectiveness of a metal detector.[115] Finally, the effectiveness of metal detectors will be influenced by the tunnel's size and depth.

As far back as the Vietnam War, magnetometers were used for tunnel detection—albeit with only limited success. Originally developed in the United States, the results were encouraging: "Theoretically, all you had to do was carry the pack around, set it up, stick the sensor in the ground, wait for a reading—and bingo."[116] But when the "Portable Differential Magnetometer" arrived in Cù Chi weighing 106 pounds, it was too difficult to use: "one operator who tried to carry it in typically heavy vegetation became exhausted and collapsed and was left behind by his own men."[117] Overall, the portal magnetometer

---

[111] *Remote Sensing Technology Reveals WWII Escape Tunnel*, GIM INT'L (Jan. 7, 2016), https://www.gim-international.com/content/news/remote-sensing-technology-reveals-wwii-escape-tunnel.

[112] *Going Deep, supra* note 64, at 21 (the U.S. Navy has used magnetometers on low-flying aircrafts to detect the presence of submarines).

[113] *See* Ballard, *supra* note 86, ¶ 99.

[114] Nalan Tepe, Geophysical Methods: Magnetometry and Metal Detection, Nov. 11, 2003 (unpublished research paper, Villanove University), http://www48.homepage.villanova.edu/andrea.welker/CEE8104/MAGNETOMETRY%20and%20METAL%20DETECTION.pdf.

[115] *Id.* at 5.

[116] MANGOLD & PENYCATE, *supra* note 67, at 208–09 (2005).

[117] *Id.*

was not a great success. Most tunnels were discovered without using it—demonstrating, once again, the incomparable value of human intelligence in tunnel detection.[118]

Electromagnetic induction, another form of metal detection, can be used to detect underground wiring, if it exists—for example, if the tunnels have a system of lights.[119] This technology measures electrical conductivity in the ground, allowing the identification of the materials that lie under a given piece of soil. It is based on the fact that different materials have different electrical conductivity. In the case of tunnels, the air inside a tunnel has a much lower electrical conductivity than the surrounding soil, especially if the soil is moist.[120] The detection will be further facilitated if the tunnel features highly conductive materials such as metal wires. The United States and South Korea have used this method to detect cross-border tunnels.[121]

Electrical resistivity also uses electricity for tunnel detection. Electronic wave machines send pulses into the ground. When the waves hit a tunnel wall, they refract back to the surface.[122] Two geologists, L.S. Palmer and C.M. Bristow, first used this method to find underground caves in the 1980s.[123] The U.S. Army later used it along the Demilitarized Zone in South Korea.[124]

Gravity measurement technology relies on the differences in materials' density to locate tunnels. Different materials yield different gravity field measurements. A deviation of soil and ground consistency can show the presence of a tunnel. Gradiometry has been used for resource exploration since the beginning of the twentieth century, primarily for mapping salt domes for oil exploration. Later, the use of airborne gravity gradiometry grew in the oil and gas industry. The technology has proved useful when seismic data is limited or when the suspected area is large.[125] It is, at the moment, one of the most

---

[118] For more contemporary uses, see R. Alan Clanton, *Major Drug Cartel Tunnel Found near San Diego*, THURSDAY REV. (Oct. 23, 2015), http://www.thursdayreview.com/DrugTunnelTijuana.html; and Peter Andreas & Richard Price, *From War Fighting to Crime Fighting: Transforming the American National Security State*, 3 INT'L STUDIES REV. 31, 39 (2001).

[119] Corey Flintoff, *U.S. to Help Israel Shut Down Smuggling Tunnels*, NPR (Jan. 16, 2009), http://www.npr.org/templates/story/story.php?storyId=99482426.

[120] *Razing Rafah*, *supra* note 49, at 52.

[121] Jose L. Llopis, Joseph B. Dunbar, Lillian D. Wakeley, Maureen K. Corcoran & Dwain K. Butler, *Tunnel Detection Along the Southwest U.S. Border*, SAGEEP 430 (2005); and Larry G. Stolarczyka, Robert Troublefielda & James Battis, *Detection of Underground Tunnels with a Synchronized Electromagnetic Wave Gradiometer*, 5778 PROCEEDINGS OF SPIE 995 (2005), http://www.dtic.mil/dtic/tr/fulltext/u2/a434554.pdf.

[122] Michael Lipin, *Ground Game: Tunnels in Gaza, Korean Peninsula*, VOICE AM. NEWS (Aug. 21, 2014), http://www.voanews.com/content/ground-game-tunnels-in-gaza-korean-peninsula/2423631.html.

[123] T.E. Owen, *Detection and Mapping of Tunnels and Caves*, in DEVELOPMENTS IN GEOPHYSICAL EXPLORATION METHODS 161 (A.A. Fitch ed., 1983).

[124] Lipin, *supra* note 122.

[125] M. Dransfield, *Airborne Gravity Gradiometry in the Search for Mineral Deposits*, in PROCEEDINGS OF EXPLORATION 07: FIFTH DECENNIAL INTERNATIONAL CONFERENCE ON MINERAL EXPLORATION 341, 351 (B. Milkereit, ed., 2007), http://www.dmec.ca/ex07-dvd/E07/pdfs/20.pdf.

promising ways of detecting objects and resources deep underground. In 2014, an underground water reservoir (6 miles underground) was detected on one of Saturn's moons using gravity measurement.[126]

Airborne gravity technology can also help detect deeply buried facilities, as the structures yield a different gravity than their immediate surroundings. Lockheed Martin is one of the most experienced companies in this field.[127] It began in the late 1990s working with the U.S. Air Force on the detection of deeply buried facilities.[128] They conducted experiments to test whether the technology could detect known underground facilities. In one of these experiments conducted in Texas, the tunnel dimensions predicted by the gradiometer came very close to the actual tunnel dimensions. The direction of the tunnel relative to the survey area was also estimated with good accuracy, demonstrating the potential of the technology in the specific area of tunnel detection.[129]

Decades later, in response to a tender issued by DARPA,[130] Lockheed Martin landed a year-long $4.8 million contract to launch the GATE program—Gravity Anomaly for Tunnel Exposure.[131] The technology thus developed can "distinguish man-made voids from naturally occurring features like topography and geology."[132] It can be placed on aerial vehicles, ships, and submarines—with potential applications in the fields of aquifer detection, underwater collision avoidance and exploration, hydrocarbon, mineral, and geothermal exploration. Lockheed has also partnered with the U.S. Department of Homeland Security to develop a radar system for the detection of tunnels at the Mexico border.[133] In 2014 the company opened an office in Israel—but it is not clear whether or how it is involved in Israel's anti-tunnel operations.[134]

Changes in ground elevation can also be detected using **radar**. The Geodar system, a ground penetrating radar, was developed in the mid-1960s under DARPA sponsorship

---

[126] *Deep Ocean Detected Inside Saturn's Moon*, NAT'L AERONAUTICS & SPACE ADMIN. (Apr. 3, 2014), https://science.nasa.gov/science-news/science-at-nasa/2014/03apr_deepocean.

[127] *See Gravity Gradiometry*, LOCKHEED MARTIN (Feb. 20, 2017), http://www.lockheedmartin.com/us/products/gravity-gradiometry.html.

[128] *See Going Deep*, *supra* note 64, at 38.

[129] *Id.* at 43.

[130] GRAVITY ANOMALY FOR TUNNEL EXPOSURE (GATE), STRATEGIC TECHNOLOGY OFFICE, DARPA (Mar. 13 2009), https://www.fbo.gov/download/obb/obbb4887d04b404e5648dfbb4a743f44/GATE.pdf.

[131] Katie Drummond, *Lockheed Using Gravity to Spot Subterranean Threats*, WIRED (July 15, 2010), https://www.wired.com/2010/07/lockheed-using-gravity-to-spot-subterranean-threats.

[132] Eric Beidel, *Secret Tunnels Can't Hide from Gravity*, NAT'L DEF. MAGAZINE (Sept. 2010), http://www.nationaldefensemagazine.org/archive/2010/September/Pages/SecretTunnelsCantHideFromGravity.aspx.

[133] *New Radar to Detect Terror Tunnels*, ISRAEL HOMELAND SEC. (Mar. 26, 2014), http://i-hls.com/2014/03/new-radar-detect-terror-tunnels/; Inbal Orpaz, *Israeli High-Tech Is Great, but Not Yet for Finding Hamas' Tunnels*, HAARETZ (July 24, 2014), http://www.haaretz.com/israel-news/business/.premium-1.606658; and David Hambling, *Pentagon Scientists Target Iran's Nuclear Mole Men*, WIRED (Dec. 1, 2010), https://www.wired.com/2010/01/irans-nuclear-molemen/.

[134] *Lockheed Martin Opens New Office in Israel*, LOCKHEED MARTIN (Apr. 9, 2014), http://www.lockheedmartin.com/us/who-we-are/global/israel/news/Lockheed-Martin-Opens-New-Office-In-Israel.html.

at the request of the U.S. Army, which was having difficulty with tunnels in Vietnam.[135] The success of an experimental system, which radiated electromagnetic energy directly into the ground, led to the development of a prototype for a field test. An improved version, known as the Geodar Mark II, was completed and tested successfully on natural and experimental tunnels in North Carolina and Massachusetts.[136]

Ground penetrating radars helped locate and map British tunnels dating from World War I.[137] They can also be mounted on an aircraft flying above the region where tunnels are suspected, such as the Underground Focusing Spotlight Synthetic Aperture Radar (UF-SL-SAR).[138] The radar then transmits electromagnetic waves at multiple frequencies, which are scattered by the ground and the tunnel.[139] Unlike tunnels, which can be found using this type of radar, natural caves with unclear shapes are harder to detect.[140]

The efficiency of a radar also depends on the consistency of the soil.[141] Whereas it can penetrate only through a few feet of concrete, it can penetrate through tens of feet of loose sand and gravel.[142] Its efficiency may be impaired in urban areas where infrastructure is built on heavy concrete, but the radar may perform very well in open areas. It is especially advantageous when conducting surveillance over foreign territory. Because radars allow for the remote identification of movement patterns they can also play a critical role in detecting tunnel entrances.[143]

Finally, **thermal imagery** can detect changes or differences in heat signatures. It can, for example, detect human presence around the ingress or egress points of tunnels, as well as tunnels equipped with generators.[144] Although this method can be helpful, relying solely on thermal imagery raises a number of issues. It is easy to distort heat signals by creating

---

[135] Thomas G. Bryant, Gerald B. Morse, Leslie M. Novak & John C. Henry, *Tactical Radars for Ground Surveillance*, 12 LINCOLN LABORATORY J. 341, 343 (2000).

[136] *Id.*

[137] Peter Jackson, *WWI Underground: Unearthing the Hidden Tunnel War*, BBC MAG. (June 10, 2011), http://www.bbc.com/news/magazine-13630203.

[138] Fernando Quivira, Kristen Fassbender, Jose A. Martinez-Lorenzo & Carey M. Rappaport, *Feasibility of Tunnel Detection Under Rough Ground Surfaces Using Underground Focusing Spotlight Synthetic Aperture Radar*, 2010 IEEE INTERNATIONAL CONFERENCE ON TECHNOLOGIES FOR HOMELAND SECURITY (HST) 357, 358 (2010), http://ieeexplore.ieee.org/document/5654932/.

[139] Fernando Quivira, Jose A. Martinez-Lorenzo & Carey M. Rappaport, *Impact of the Wave Number Estimation in Underground Focused SAR Imaging*, 32 PROGRESS IN ELECTROMAGNETICS RESEARCH LETTERS 29 (2012).

[140] Jose A. Martinez-Lorenzo, Carey M. Rappaport & Fernando Quivira, *Physical Limitations on Detecting Tunnels Using Underground-Focusing Spotlight Synthetic Aperture Radar*, 49 IEEE TRANSACTIONS ON GEOSCI. & REMOTE SENSING 65 (2011).

[141] Interview with Dan Blumberg, Prof., Head of the Earth and Planetary Image Facility, at Ben Gurion University of the Negev (Aug. 2015) [hereinafter Blumberg Interview].

[142] *How GPR Works*, GLOBAL GPR SERVICES (Feb. 20, 2017), http://www.global-gpr.com/gpr-technology/how-gpr-works.html.

[143] Haydock, *supra* note 85 (referring specifically to the Vehicle and Dismount Exploitation Radar (VADER) developed by Northrop Grumman).

[144] *Going Deep*, *supra* note 64, at 17.

other heat sources to confuse the enemy. In addition, as Dan Blumberg of Ben Gurion University points out, a number of factors such as ground composition and water deposits affect the accuracy of thermal measurements.[145] Thermal imagery would have to be used in conjunction with at least one other method to account for these shortcomings.

As a matter of fact, the same could be said in relation to virtually all of the methods of tunnel mapping and detection. Like thermal imagery, most methods cannot detect all types of tunnels in all terrains. In the realm of underground warfare, one cannot advocate a certain method or technology. The key is to pick the right method for a given situation, and adequately combine the methods for optimal results. The type of soil, the environment (urban or not), the size of the tunnel and its depth will make it more or less difficult to detect the tunnel, and affect the rate of success of any given method. In addition, states should keep in mind applicable legal limitations, as suggested here and analyzed in greater depth in chapters 6 and 7.

The drawbacks inherent to all detection methods—the level of expertise they require, and their cost—have often discouraged states from engaging in detection in the first place. Because mapping is uncertain, time-consuming, and expensive, states have preferred to skip detection and mapping. In the hope of eliminating the threat here and now, they opt instead for methods of random tunnel destruction in suspected areas. I refer to this as the "no mapping" approach: even when a tunnel is detected, there will be no attempt at mapping its route or structure. States that do not invest financial and human resources in mapping tunnels will pay the price later as the information gathered in the mapping process plays a significant role in neutralization, destruction, and monitoring.

Although the no-mapping approach has been portrayed as a valuable strategy against tunnels,[146] I argue that it is not. Quite the contrary: based on my review of state practice, the no-mapping approach reveals much ignorance about tunnels and the absence of a well-thought-out strategy. It holds some advantages in cases of emergency but it cannot and should not replace a long-term strategy that includes mapping—at least for those states likely to face the threat again. At best, the no-mapping approach can be used to minimize an immediate threat, in order to "buy" time. At worst, it can jeopardize the remainder of anti-tunnel operations. At an Israeli cabinet meeting in the summer of 2014, then Economy Minister Naftali Bennett specifically asked about the implications of the no-mapping approach: "Would aerial bombing of some of the openings make it harder

---

[145] Calev Ben David, *Maze of Secret Gaza Tunnels Targeted by Israeli Offensive*, BLOOMBERG (July 21, 2014), https://www.bloomberg.com/news/articles/2014-07-20/israel-gaza-ground-war-puts-maze-of-attack-tunnels-in-its-sights.

[146] Boaz Hayun, Tamar Group, Presentation at IPS (Institute for Policy and Strategy) Conference on *Tunnels and the Underground in Israel's Security Doctrine*, Sept. 28, 2014.

later to identify the course of the tunnels and then destroy them effectively in a ground operation?"[147] As a matter of fact, it did.[148]

With these caveats in mind, it is important to explain what the no-mapping approach consists of. It includes a number of measures—all of which seek to eliminate suspected tunnels whose precise location and route have not been established with certainty.

First, when the presence of tunnels is suspected but their precise location is unknown, states may choose to conduct random drilling (also known as sample drilling), which consists in drilling holes in the ground at fixed intervals. Drilling within a delineated radius according to systematic coordinates can help find the tunnels. This tactic heavily relies on human intelligence, and it is highly resource- and time-consuming. It is not suitable when there is no prior intelligence pointing to the approximate location of the tunnel(s). Moreover, the larger the potential area, the less likely a tunnel will be detected through random drilling. There are additional drawbacks with this technique: it can give away forces' location, endanger them, and give up on the element of surprise. It also creates risks for civilians, as discussed further in Chapter 7.

South Korea used this method to detect tunnels dug by North Korean forces under the Demilitarized Zone. UN peacekeeping forces had been in the area to examine a previously discovered tunnel. When they entered the tunnel, they encountered a strong explosion, killing one peacekeeper and severely injuring another. American and South Korean forces decided to conduct systematic drilling to uncover other suspected tunnels in the vicinity. A contracted oil drilling crew drilled numerous holes, each less than half-a-mile deep, in a set pattern covering most of the area, ultimately discovering two additional tunnels.[149]

Second, instead of random drillings, states have at times chosen to detonate explosives on strips of land along a border when cross-border tunnels are suspected. Although this method can alleviate immediate danger, most tunnels destroyed in this way can be rebuilt in just a few days or weeks.[150]

A third measure that can be undertaken as part of a no-mapping approach is random targeting from the air. The principle is the same, only the strikes are conducted from the air. The strikes can be conducted over a certain area at set intervals with ground penetrating weapons. On at least one occasion, Israel dropped Joint Direct Attack Munitions (JDAM) bombs to locate a tunnel in the Kerem Shalom area.[151] An examination of the

---

[147] Amos Harel, *How Israel Missed and Underestimated Threat of Hamas' Terror Tunnels*, HAARETZ (May 13, 2016), http://www.haaretz.com/israel-news/.premium-1.719463.

[148] *Id.*

[149] Michael E. Wikan, *Guest Column: The Day We Found the Tunnel*, MILITARY.COM (Sept. 8, 2003), http://www.military.com/NewContent/0,13190,Defensewatch_090803_Tunnel,00.html; *Going Deep, supra* note 64, at 21–22.

[150] Blumberg Interview, *supra* note 141.

[151] Gili Cohen, *IDF Soldiers Tasked with Tunnel Destruction Not Trained for Primary Mission*, HAARETZ (Aug. 7, 2014), http://www.haaretz.com/israel-news/.premium-1.609345.

impact on the ground can help determine the route of the tunnel. This method, however, is less than commendable for the uncertain results it achieves and the unnecessary and large bearing it has on the environment. Interestingly, Hamas has tried to counter the method by digging tunnels in a zigzag formation, with many arteries.[152] It requires more tunneling resources, but it makes detonating the entire tunnel from above nearly impossible. Bulldozers offer a better alternative against this type of tunnels.

The no-mapping approach was adopted, intentionally or not, by Egypt—using a variety of methods. Egypt has used bulldozers on strips of land along the Gaza border.[153] Egypt also dug a 1,600-foot-deep buffer zone in order to destroy existing cross-border tunnels and prevent the digging of new ones.[154] The buffer zone encompasses all of Rafah, a town of some 78,000 people that lies directly on the border, as well as large areas of agricultural land around it.[155] The creation of the buffer zone—originally planned to measure 1,600 feet, quickly extended to a half mile in November 2014[156] and to 3 miles a month later[157]—was criticized by human rights organizations, as civilian homes were destroyed with little notice and no appropriate compensation.[158] Egypt's response was that they were simply moving the town a few miles from its current location, providing housing and services to the displaced.[159]

Egypt's experience underscores the limits of the no-mapping approach. While the zero-tolerance policy of Egypt caused a serious blow to Hamas's underground cross-border enterprise, minimizing the security and economic threat to Egypt, it also strongly affected Egypt's own civilian population.[160] More importantly, Egypt's random destruction strategy must be repeated regularly to prevent the rebuilding of tunnels.

The methods employed by Egypt also raise serious legal concerns when carried out in urban areas. This is true even when anti-tunnel measures are carried out by a state on its

---

[152] Ron Ben-Yishai, *An Underground Breakthrough*, YNET (Apr. 18, 2016), http://www.ynetnews.com/articles/0,7340,L-4793159,00.html.
[153] *Tunnel Business in Gaza Declines due to Egypt's Security Measures*, Xinhua News (Sept. 27, 2013), http://news.xinhuanet.com/english/indepth/2013-09/27/c_132757285.htm.
[154] *Egypt Carries Out "Mass Home Demolitions" in Sinai*, AL JAZEERA (Sept. 22, 2015), http://www.aljazeera.com/news/2015/09/egypt-carries-mass-home-demolitions-sinai-150922110538479.html.
[155] *Id.*
[156] Jack Khoury, *Egypt to Expand Buffer Zone to 1 km; 12 New Tunnel Openings Found*, HAARETZ (Nov. 18, 2014), http://www.haaretz.com/middle-east-news/1.627017.
[157] *Gaza Buffer Zone to Increase to 5 km: North Sinai Governor*, DAILY NEWS EGYPT (Dec. 19, 2014), http://www.dailynewsegypt.com/2014/12/29/north-sinai-governor-says-gaza-buffer-zone-increase-5km/.
[158] *Rafah Residents Forced to Leave Their Homes*, AL-MONITOR (Nov. 2, 2014), http://www.al-monitor.com/pulse/originals/2014/11/rafah-egypt-government-evacuation-palestinians.html#; and *Razing Rafah, supra* note 49.
[159] *Egypt to Remove Border City Rafah for Buffer Zone*, MA'AN (Jan. 8, 2015), http://www.maannews.net/eng/ViewDetails.aspx?ID=752455 (Governor Abd al-Fattah Harhour tried to justify his government's actions: "A new Rafah city is being established with residential zones appropriate to the nature and traditions of the residents of Rafah.").
[160] *Another Homeland, supra* note 6, at 18.

own territory. In principle, the state has sovereignty over its own territory and is entitled to carry out whatever operations it deems necessary—provided such operations comply with domestic law. One might assume that international law has little say when states carry out anti-tunnel operations on their territory or on territory over which they have effective control, but Egypt's experience demonstrates precisely the opposite. Even when conducted on Egyptian territory by Egyptian authorities, the methods used to counter the threat of Hamas tunnels raise concern under international law.[161]

To conclude, the no-mapping approach is certainly not as operationally simple and legally straightforward as it seems. Operationally, it merely provides temporary relief from the threat. The measures—drilling or targeting from the air—must be repeated regularly to ensure continued security. The population living in the surrounding areas will likely suffer from these recurring measures. The better strategy consists in detecting tunnels first, and mapping them later. By combining these two important steps into one, the no-mapping approach leaves behind a heavy footprint, with no security guarantees in the short- or long-term. For these reasons, mapping is the more responsible, sensible, humane, and effective approach. This essential and indispensable step must form an integral part of states' strategy.

2. Neutralization and/or Destruction

The destruction of the tunnel usually follows its detection and mapping. Here again, however, states may choose not to destroy or eliminate the tunnel for a variety of reasons. Consider the United States and South Korea, facing the looming threat of cross-border tunnels from Mexico and North Korea, respectively. Both states have decided, for strategic reasons, not to destroy the tunnels that they know exist. Even when states opt *not* to take any kinetic measures, this decision must be informed by an understanding of the risks. It should not come at the expense of an assessment of the dangers posed by the tunnels, intensive intelligence gathering and surveillance, and operational preparedness in case kinetic measures (i.e., the destruction of the tunnels) become necessary. This is because all tunnels pose an inherent threat, which may or may not materialize depending on the circumstances. This threat persists as long as the tunnel itself exists. As a Border Patrol Chief once said about the cross-border tunnels between Mexico and the United States:

> Regardless of whether a tunnel is simply a crude, hand-dug passage or a sophisticated, reinforced passage with lights, all tunnels create viable means for smugglers to enter the U.S. and pose a potential threat to national security.[162]

---

[161] *Id.* The impact of tunnels on civilian populations on both sides will be further discussed in Chapter 7.
[162] *See What Lies Beneath, supra* note 53.

The need to destroy tunnels can arise in three scenarios. First, if the tunnels pose an imminent threat requiring an immediate response following discovery. Second, in the case of a known tunnel, if something changes in the modus operandi of the party that dug the tunnels. For example, if explosives are found in a smuggling tunnel, or if unusual movement of equipment or personnel has been witnessed. Third, if another party makes use or takes control of the tunnel. The latter, on which I elaborate further in Subsection (3) below, is known as the phenomenon of "inheritance," whereby a tunnel is "inherited" by a new party, with potentially different intentions. All of these scenarios could happen with little or no notice, catching a state by surprise.

The risk of inheritance strongly advocates in favor of the complete elimination of tunnels. Other options—leaving the tunnel intact, the temporary neutralizations of tunnels, or the localized destruction of tunnels that leaves parts of the tunnel intact—cannot achieve this objective. Complete destruction is the only way to prevent the use of tunnels in a future conflict, as explained in the U.S. Army Field Manual No. 90-8: "[b]unkers [and tunnels] are destroyed or occupied to prevent the enemy from reoccupying them through another tunnel."[163]

Complete destruction must therefore be distinguished from the mere neutralization of tunnels. Neutralization, often referred to as a functional kill, renders the tunnel impracticable and unusable, but does not destroy it. Destruction, often referred to as a hard kill, implies "the direct destruction of the facility, causing the walls, facility roof and/or tunnels to collapse. This is an effective method, but it is becoming harder and harder to accomplish as facilities [and tunnels] go deeper underground."[164]

Before tunnels are neutralized or eliminated, and particularly when states opt *not* to fully destroy the tunnel, states should keep a record of the location and physical characteristics of the tunnels. This increases their preparedness in case the situation evolves, and can help detect the digging of new tunnel networks in the long run.

Let us begin with neutralization. It can be achieved by flooding the tunnel, injecting gas inside the tunnel to make it uninhabitable, or using cement to block access to the tunnel.

FLOODING. Depending on the features of the tunnel and the quantities of water used, flooding can be used to render a tunnel unwelcoming or to trigger full collapse. The problem, however, is that the effects of flooding are difficult to predict as they depend on factors such as, but not limited to, construction, terrain, water quantity, and water pressure.

Israel has used this technique on a few occasions,[165] but the practice of tunnel flooding is most associated with Egypt. Under the leadership of Mohamed Morsi, Egypt initiated

---

[163] U.S. Army Field Manual, *supra* note 56, at Appendix A, A-12.
[164] *See Going Deep, supra* note 64, at 12.
[165] Cohen, *supra* note 151.

a systematic campaign of flooding beginning in 2013, following an attack on Egyptian soldiers in the Sinai Peninsula.[166] Egypt also used sewage water to flood cross-border tunnels.[167] The use of sewage water raises both humanitarian and environmental concerns, as discussed in Chapter 7.

The legal issues notwithstanding, the efficacy of flooding remains uncertain and reactions to the method have been inconsistent. Although some Hamas smugglers prefer aerial bombing to flooding, as the latter reportedly causes irreparable harm to the tunnels,[168] others have noted that if water is pumped and sand and sawdust are used to reinforce the ceiling, repairs would only take a few weeks.[169] Tunnels can also be reinforced with cement and steel bars to make them waterproof, or dug deeper in the hope that water does not reach that far.[170]

Either way, water may not offer the quick and easy fix one might think. It has the potential of neutralizing the tunnel but results are not guaranteed.

GAS. Gas has been used in the context of underground warfare for reasons as varied as mapping, clearing, and neutralizing tunnels. In the realm of tunnel neutralization, gas can be used to render a tunnel unusable by the enemy (although the tunnel itself remains intact) or drive its users to surrender. Depending on the type and quantity of gas used, the effects vary: they can be short-lived or long-lasting, incapacitating or fatal. They incapacitate the target through irritation and pain to exposed eyes, skin, nasal and oral areas, and airways. Tear gas either drives the insurgents out of the confined space into the open or incapacitates its occupants long enough for military forces to gain control of the tunnel. Either way, the occupants end up at a disadvantage.

U.S. soldiers used tear gas in Vietnam.[171] The objective was to force the Vietcong out of hiding and prevent their return—but U.S. forces were not always successful. Many American soldiers lost their lives as they entered tunnels that they thought had been cleared, only to find enemy fighters ready to attack them. The Vietnamese, for their part, suffered mass casualties from suffocation and were left with soil that was periodically poisoned from above and below.[172] Decades later, Egypt used poisonous gas to

---

[166] See Diaa Hadid & Wissam Nassar, *As Egypt Flood Gaza Tunnels, Smugglers Fear an End to Their Trade*, N.Y. TIMES (Oct. 7, 2015), https://www.nytimes.com/2015/10/08/world/middleeast/as-egypt-floods-gaza-tunnels-smugglers-fear-an-end-to-their-trade.html?_r=0.

[167] *The Enemy Below, supra* note 60, at 117.

[168] Hadid & Nassar, *supra* note 166.

[169] *Id.*

[170] *Id.*

[171] *The Enemy Below, supra* note 60, at 76.

[172] Thomas Dethlefs, *Tear Gas and the Politics of Lethality: Emerging from the Haze*, 2 YALE HISTORY REV. 83, 101–02 (2013); Richard Muller, *The Weapons Paradox*, MIT TECH. REV. (May 21, 2003), https://www.technologyreview.com/s/401923/the-weapons-paradox/.

clear smuggling tunnels emanating from Gaza.[173] There, too, the tactic failed at times to achieve its objective: Hamas pumped air in and continued using the tunnels.[174]

Beyond these operational failures, the use of gas in war raises serious legal concerns. The use of riot control agents as a method of warfare is expressly prohibited under the Chemical Weapons Convention, to which nearly all states are parties.[175] In contrast, tear gas is not a chemical weapon and its use is generally allowed in the context of law enforcement and riot control.[176] Assuming no armed conflict exists between Gaza and Egypt, the use of tear gas to clear tunnels burrowing under the Gaza-Egypt border is in principle lawful. That said, the European Court of Human Rights has indicated that the legality of such a measure might still depend on how the gas is used. It has, for example, distinguished between the use of tear gas and the launch of a tear-gas grenade at a demonstrator.[177] Although it did not object to the former, it held that launching a tear-gas grenade in a manner that causes severe injuries can amount to inhuman or degrading treatment or punishment under the European Convention on Human Rights.[178]

This jurisprudence raises the question of how tear gas would behave in a subterranean environment. Based on experiments conducted in confined spaces, the use of tear gas underground does not seem to raise any specific concern. Thirty-four participants exposed to chlorobenzylidene malonitrile, also known as CS gas or tear gas, in a confined space for 10 minutes did not report any long-term harm.[179] All the symptoms they experienced during their exposure to the gas—burning sensations in the nose and throat, involuntary closure of eyelids, and unceasing tears—disappeared after their release. Nevertheless, some authors have noted that the gas becomes more lethal in confined spaces, as the walls keep it from propagating.[180]

The legal analysis does not yield straightforward findings of (il)legality. Relevant considerations include the context (war versus peace), the type of gas (poisonous or not, as this was a core concern driving the regulation), and its effects in confined spaces. Because

---

[173] Rizek Abdel Jawad, *Hamas: Egypt Kills 4 Tunnel Smugglers with Gas*, NBC News (June 29, 2010), http://www.nbcnews.com/id/36835066/ns/world_news-mideastn_africa/#.WKsECPkrLIU.

[174] Fares Akram & David D. Kirkpatrick, *To Block Gaza Tunnels, Egypt Lets Sewage Flow*, N.Y. Times (Feb. 20, 2013), http://www.nytimes.com/2013/02/21/world/middleeast/egypts-floods-smuggling-tunnels-to-gaza-with-sewage.html?_r=0.

[175] *See, e.g.*, Declaration (IV, 2) Concerning Asphyxiating Gases, Jul. 29, 1899; the Geneva Gas Protocol of 1925 (Protocol for the Prohibition of the Use in War of Asphyxiating, Poisonous or other Gases, and of Bacteriological Methods of Warfare, June 17, 1925, 94 U.N.T.S. 65); and the Convention on the Prohibition of the Development, Production, Stockpiling and Use of Chemical Weapons and on Their Destruction, Jan. 13, 1993, 1974 U.N.T.S. 35.

[176] *Ataman v. Turkey* Eur. Ct. H.R. 74552/01 (2006) ¶ 17, 25.

[177] *Yaşa v. Turkey* Eur. Ct. H.R. 44827/08 (2013) ¶ 42.

[178] *Id.* ¶ 50–51.

[179] Y. G. Karagama, J. R. Newton & C.J.R. Newbegin, *Short-Term and Long-Term Physical Effects of Exposure to CS Spray*, 96 J. Royal Soc'y Med. 172 (2003), https://www.ncbi.nlm.nih.gov/pmc/articles/PMC539444/.

[180] James D. Fry, *Contextualized Legal Reviews for the Methods and Means of Warfare: Cave Combat and International Humanitarian Law*, 44 Colum. J. Transnat'l L. 453, 507 (2006).

its legality depends on a plethora of factors, any use of gas for purposes of tunnel neutralization needs to be carefully weighed both operationally and legally. The risks of violating the law are high, and the operational rewards often limited.

CEMENT. States have also neutralized tunnels by filling them with cement. U.S. Border Police and Homeland Security used this technique to seal off smuggling and trafficking tunnels between Mexico and the United States. It has not proven successful: smugglers found ways to continue using the main body of the tunnel by digging new arteries that connect to the existing underground structure.[181] These operational limitations led the United States to modify its strategy. Instead of sealing off entrances and exits, it began filling the entire body of the tunnel with cement.

The cost of cement remediation, however, is considerable. Between 2007 and 2015, the U.S. Department of Homeland Security spent $8.7 million on the remediation of cross-border tunnels at the Mexican border.[182] In addition, the use of cement will raise legal objections if people are present in the tunnel at the time of the operation, as discussed in Chapters 6 and 7.

It becomes clear that none of the methods envisaged here to neutralize tunnels provides entirely satisfactory results. Beyond the legal issues, which I purposefully did not focus on here, the operational value of these methods appears doubtful. In many cases tunnel-diggers have succeeded in overcoming the damage caused to tunnels. Many of the methods require a high level of control to work properly and achieve the desired results. Even then, some uncertainty remains. Cement, for instance, requires expert handling, and its cost is high. Unlike other methods, however, it has the advantage of achieving a permanent result in little time: remediation only takes half an hour once the cement arrives at the scene.[183] In this respect, it achieves better and more predictable results than flooding and gas.

When destroying tunnels, states have a slightly broader array of options: from bulldozers, explosives and aerial strikes to flamethrowers and thermobaric weapons. As with mapping and neutralization, each of these techniques has advantages and disadvantages depending on the type of soil, and the depth, length, and location of the tunnel(s).

Bulldozers can raze fields and buildings in order to destroy tunnels that lie beneath.[184] The Caterpillar D9, for example, provides a high level of control, and the ability to move

---

[181] *The Enemy Below, supra* note 60.

[182] U.S. Department of Homeland Security, Cross-Border Tunnels and Border Tunnel Prevention 9 (2015), https://assets.documentcloud.org/documents/3038045/DHS-Report-to-Congress-on-Cross-Broder-Tunnels.pdf.

[183] *Agents Find, Seal Border Tunnel Before Drugs Flow Through*, AZ CENTRAL (May 23, 2014), http://www.azcentral.com/story/news/politics/2014/05/24/arizona-border-tunnel-drugs-sealed/9529883/.

[184] *See* Peter Beaumont, *Israeli Military Uncovers First Hamas Tunnel into Israel Since 2014 War*, GUARDIAN (Apr. 18, 2016), https://www.theguardian.com/world/2016/apr/18/israeli-military-uncovers-first-hamas-tunnel-israel-2014-war-gaza; *Egyptian Bulldozers Raze Fields Looking for Tunnels to Gaza*, MIDDLE EAST MONITOR (Feb. 5, 2014), https://www.middleeastmonitor.com/20140205-egyptian-military-bulldozers-

significant quantities of earth.[185] That said, bulldozing will generally require the physical entry of a state's troops into enemy territory, placing them at greater risk than they face when conducting aerial bombings. It is better suited as a means to destroy tunnels on one's own territory, provided the destruction of civilian infrastructure is kept in check.

Alternatively, states may destroy tunnels using thermobaric weapons, flamethrowers, or liquid explosives. Standard bombs can also be used, although some experts claim that their impact is very local and does not cause enough damage to prevent the enemy's use of segments of the tunnel at a later stage.[186] Moreover, if they are not equipped with a guidance system, as the Daisy Cutter bombs used in Vietnam, they may raise legal issues.

Thermobaric weapons release heat and consume the oxygen in their surrounding environment to intensify their detonation impact. Their blast wave is larger than that of conventional weapons especially in confined spaces such as tunnels, caves, or bunkers.[187] In this terrain, the dispersion of the fuel produces high temperatures. The high destructive capability of thermobaric weapons is not only due to the lack of oxygen (the vacuum effect) they cause but also to the injuries resulting from the negative pressure that follows the positive pressure phase of the explosion.[188] The United States used thermobaric weapons in Afghanistan,[189] and reports indicate that Assad's forces used them in Syria—although it is unclear for what purpose.[190]

Bunker busters, developed during the first Gulf War by the U.S. Air Force, are designed to penetrate the ground deeper than any other weapon.[191] This is made possible thanks to their weight (approximately two tons), and their narrow tube-like shape that enables maximum penetration of the ground. One model, known as GBU-28, can penetrate 100 feet of earth or 20 feet of concrete.[192] Bunker busters detonate only once the bomb has penetrated the ground, thereby ensuring the highest level of destruction. This impressive

---

raze-fields-searching-for-tunnels-to-gaza/; and Yaakov Lappin, *Battalion Commander Tells "Post" How Reservists Uncovered Tunnels Under Fire*, JERUSALEM POST (Aug. 8, 2014), http://www.jpost.com/Defense/Battalion-commander-tells-Post-how-reservists-uncovered-tunnels-under-fire-370455.

[185] Baz Ratner, *Israeli Troops, Using Sniffer Dogs and Robots, Hunt for Gaza Tunnels*, NEWSWEEK (July 30, 2014), http://europe.newsweek.com/israeli-troops-using-sniffer-dogs-and-robots-hunt-gaza-tunnels-262164?rm=eu.

[186] Mitch Ginsburg, *The Treacherous Task of Tunnel Demolition*, TIMES OF ISRAEL (July 18, 2014), http://www.timesofisrael.com/the-treacherous-task-of-tunnel-demolition/.

[187] *Going Deep*, supra note 64, at 15.

[188] Lemi Türker, *Thermobaric and Enhanced Blast Explosives (TBX and EBX)*, 12 Defense Technology 423, 423 (2016).

[189] *Pentagon to Use New Bomb on Afghan Caves*, CNN (Dec. 23, 2011), http://edition.cnn.com/2001/US/12/22/ret.new.weapon/.

[190] Torie Rose DeGhett, *A New Kind of Bomb Is Being Used in Syria and It's a Humanitarian Nightmare*, VICE (Aug. 29, 2015), https://news.vice.com/article/a-new-kind-of-bomb-is-being-used-in-syria-and-its-a-humanitarian-nightmare.

[191] Marshall Brain, *How Bunker Busters Work*, HOW STUFF WORKS (Apr. 3, 2003), http://science.howstuffworks.com/bunker-buster.htm.

[192] *Id.*

performance makes bunker busters attractive when fighting concrete-fortified or deeply-buried underground structures.

In 2017, the United States used its most powerful conventional weapon, the Massive Ordnance Air Blast (MOAB), on an Islamic State of Iraq and Syria-Khorasan tunnel complex in Achin district, Nangarhar province, Afghanistan, near the border with Pakistan.[193] MOAB contains more than ten tons of TNT, measures almost thirty feet, and costs $16 million.[194] These characteristics and its acronym have earned the GBU-43/B the nickname "Mother of All Bombs." Dropped from the air and GPS-guided, it explodes before reaching the ground, creating very high pressure over a large, one mile, radius.[195] This radius, and the size of the resulting blast, produce "a large mushroom cloud resembling that of a nuclear detonation."[196] It is seen "as a particularly useful weapon for 'shock and awe' type tactics."[197] This was the first time the U.S. used it[198]—reportedly with no civilian casualties.[199]

Liquid explosives, too, have proven efficient in destroying tunnels and could become increasingly popular in the future. Unlike thermobaric weapons, MOAB, and flamethrowers, they inflict only limited damage on the tunnel's surroundings. The United States used liquid explosives against the Vietcong. Long tubes were thrown down tunnel shafts, filled with liquid explosives, and detonated.[200] Nowadays, liquid explosives can be injected directly into the ground and remotely detonated after the soldiers have left the scene. Israel relies heavily on this technique, which it considers one of the safest and most efficient ways of eliminating tunnels.[201] The IDF has developed a unique solution known as "emulsion," which consists of two liquids that are harmless on their own but turn into

---

[193] *U.S. Bombs, Destroys Khorasan Group Stronghold in Afghanistan*, Department of Defense (April 13, 2017), https://www.defense.gov/News/Article/Article/1151139/us-bombs-destroys-khorasan-group-stronghold-in-afghanistan/.

[194] Michael Schmitt and Lt. Cdr. Peter Barker, *"The Mother of All Bombs": Understanding the Massive Ordnance Air Blast Weapon*, JustSecurity (April 15, 2017), https://www.justsecurity.org/40022/the-mother-bombs-understanding-massive-ordnance-air-blast-weapon/?utm_source=Regular+Newsletter&utm_campaign=0e49c28ab4-EMAIL_CAMPAIGN_2017_04_23&utm_medium=email&utm_term=0_c55805 61c1-0e49c28ab4-36731565.

[195] *36 ISIS Militants Killed in US 'Mother of All Bombs' Attack Afghan Ministry Says*, The Guardian (April 14, 2017).

[196] *See supra* note 194.

[197] *Id.*

[198] *Id.*

[199] *US Military Defends Dropping 'Mother of All Bombs' on ISIS in Afghanistan*, CNN (April 14, 2017), http://edition.cnn.com/2017/04/14/asia/afghanistan-isis-moab-bomb/.

[200] *Historical Vignette 062—How Army Engineers Cleared Viet Cong Tunnels*, U.S. ARMY CORPS OF ENGINEERS (Jan. 2003), http://www.usace.army.mil/About/History/HistoricalVignettes/MilitaryConstructionCombat/062VietCongTunnels.aspx.

[201] Amir Buchbut, *After the Incident: The Special Tool That Destroyed the Tunnel in Gaza*, WALLA (Nov. 2, 2013), http://news.walla.co.il/item/2691024 (in Hebrew); and Cohen, *supra* note 151.

a very powerful explosive when mixed with each other. Major Isam Abu Tarif, responsible for the development of specialized equipment in the IDF, stressed the advantages of injecting liquid explosives into tunnels: "soldiers can reach the tunnel accompanied only by a relatively small team, inject the explosive, and come back with high chances of success and minimum risk."[202] The IDF reportedly intends to use this method in a future confrontation with Hezbollah in Lebanon.[203]

In spite of these promising technological avenues, it is important to keep in mind that no perfect solution exists for tunnel destruction (as with detection and mapping). States would be wise to familiarize themselves with the various options, so that they are able to choose the most appropriate and effective method(s) when a threat emerges.

3. Prevention and Monitoring

The third step in an effective strategy consists in anticipating future threats by preventing the construction of new tunnels, and monitoring areas where tunnels once existed. Much like detecting, mapping, and eliminating tunnels, preventing the construction of tunnels raises a number of challenges.

The experience of Israel and Egypt with Hamas's tunnels demonstrates the difficulty of preventing the construction of tunnels. The Israeli government faced criticism for not having successfully prevented tunnel construction in the years leading up to the conflict in 2014.[204] But the fact of the matter is that neither Israel nor Egypt was able to prevent the construction of tunnels by Hamas. At best, they took measures to prevent the construction of new tunnels once they became aware of the existence of the threat—such as the creation of the buffer zone by Egypt along the Egypt-Gaza border.[205] The buffer zone makes it virtually impossible to conceal the movements and physical changes associated with tunnel-digging and typically only visible via imagery: tunnel construction can no longer be concealed by hangars; tunnel exits can no longer be concealed by civilian dwellings. Those involved in tunnel building are much more likely to get caught and

---

[202] *Supporting Forces*, Israeli Ground Forces (2011), http://mazi.idf.il/6511-9882-he/IGF.aspx (in Hebrew).

[203] Yoav Zeitun, *Preparing for a Third Lebanon War: Blowing Up "Hezbollah Tunnels,"* YNET (Jan. 22, 2017), http://www.ynet.co.il/articles/0,7340,L-4910843,00.html.

[204] Yonah Jeremy Bob, *Comptroller Sounded Alarm on Gazan Terror Tunnels in 2007*, JERUSALEM POST (July 31, 2014), http://www.jpost.com/Operation-Protective-Edge/Comptroller-sounded-alarm-on-Gazan-terror-tunnels-in-2007-369497; STATE COMPTROLLER, OPERATION DEFENSIVE EDGE: CABINET DECISION-MAKING PROCEDURES REGARDING GAZA BEFORE AND AT THE BEGINNING OF OPERATION DEFENSIVE EDGE; COPING WITH THE TUNNEL THREAT (2017), http://www.mevaker.gov.il/he/Reports/Report_568/bd318994-ccaa-4e25-9aff-02561eccadea/zuk-eitan-20.pdf (in Hebrew) (criticizing Israel's response to the tunnel threat, particularly during the 2014 war, in the fields of intelligence, military planning, and research and development).

[205] Reuters, *Egypt May Relocate Thousands of Bedouin to Widen Buffer Zone near Gaza Border*, HAARETZ (Oct. 26, 2014), http://www.haaretz.com/middle-east-news/1.622751.

punished. The buffer zone makes tunnel construction more visible (and thus less likely), however it does not eliminate the possibility of tunnel-digging altogether. Intelligence and monitoring remain indispensable.[206] The same is true with respect to Egypt's other preventive measure—also contemplated by Israel—the creation of an underground fence.[207] Underground fences may make tunneling more difficult, time-consuming, and costly, but they do not make it impossible as even a steel wall can be circumvented with enough time and tools.

The challenge of preventing tunnel construction has led states to come up with other solutions to slow down construction. Israel, for example, has put limitations on the import of cement to Gaza. In additional to being used for tunnels, cement is of course needed to build vital civilian infrastructure such as hospitals, schools, and civilian housing. For this reason, preventing tunnel construction by withholding the materials used for its construction cannot offer a viable solution in the long run.

Ultimately, technology, underground fences, and buffer zones can help prevent and detect existing tunnels and mitigate the threat emanating from them—but they cannot fully prevent tunnel-digging. States still have to engage in monitoring, including the monitoring of existing underground civilian infrastructure (such as subways, maintenance tunnels under universities, and sewage or drainage tunnels).[208]

Monitoring thus fulfills an indispensable preventive function. It helps detect the digging of new tunnels and the inheritance of old tunnels. It limits the looming menace of the sudden discovery of large tunnel networks, and minimizes the risks that tunnels pose in post-conflict situations.

Monitoring constitutes the most effective way for states to remain abreast of the threat before it emerges in full-force, and to destroy an incipient tunnel before it evolves into a full-scale network whose destruction can be challenging. It must complement the creation of buffer zones, underground barriers, and other measures. If resources are scarce, monitoring should be preferred over other alternatives. The investment of time and

---

[206] Note that Israel, too, has demolished houses along the Israel-Gaza border—though it has not created an official buffer zone. According to Human Rights Watch, the demolition of houses that hosted entrances and exits to tunnels was the primary modus operandi of the Israel Defense Forces until 2003: "This tactic," the group said, "caused much destruction and homelessness" but left "tunnels largely intact." See *Razing Rafah, supra* note 49, at 5.

[207] The construction of Egypt's underground fence began in November 2009. Speculations on the depth of the steel fence, which will cover the entire border between Egypt and the Gaza Strip, range from 60 feet and 100 feet in depth. See Wil Longbottom, *Egypt Installs Underground Steel Wall to Block Smugglers' Tunnels Along Gaza Border,* DAILY MAIL (Jan. 5, 2010), http://www.dailymail.co.uk/news/article-1240824/Egypt-installing-underground-steel-wall-block-smugglers-tunnels-Gaza-border.html; see also Sarah A. Topol, *Gaza Border: Why Egypt Is Building a Steel Underground Wall,* CHRISTIAN SCI. MONITOR (Dec. 14, 2009), http://www.csmonitor.com/World/Middle-East/2009/1214/Gaza-border-Why-Egypt-is-building-a-steel-underground-wall.

[208] At the U.S.-Mexico border, the drainage systems (and/or storm drains) are used to smuggle. See *What Lies Beneath, supra* note 53 (also noting that the U.S. team uses a robot to investigate pipes).

resources is particularly important on the part of states that have faced underground threats in the past: an enemy that already has the know-how—regardless of whether previous attempts succeeded—will likely try again.

Monitoring tunnels not only enables states to keep track of new digging, it also alerts them of the inheritance of underground structures by new actors. Even when states do map and eliminate tunnels, a risk remains that part of the structure may not have been discovered. Any such remaining structure, no matter how small or impaired by anti-tunnel measures, presents irresistible appeal. Inheritance saves time and resources—particularly valuable assets to belligerents who are at a military or logistical disadvantage. The human and logistical costs of excavating new tunnels, not to mention the disruption it causes and the attention it attracts, are high. It is irrelevant, for purposes of inheritance, whether the tunnels were initially naturally or artificially formed, or used by the previous party for similar purposes. Expanding any type of existing underground structure is cheaper, easier, and faster than digging tunnels from scratch. A hostile actor can take possession of an underground segment, regardless of its size or level of sophistication, and use it to dig a larger underground structure. The soil will be more amenable to digging in these circumstances. States should carefully monitor underground structures likely to be used or taken over for hostile purposes.

In addition, monitoring mitigates the risks posed by tunnels to civilians in post-conflict situations. Much like landmines, tunnels pose a long-term threat that is difficult to permanently eliminate, even after the conflict ends.[209] Unlike landmines, however, tunnels are not regulated under international law, and never commanded the same level of attention from legal scholars. Yet tunnels do expose civilians to long-term risks from the beginning of the digging until their complete destruction.[210] Only by monitoring tunnel-prone areas, particularly those located near civilians, will states protect those in harm's way.

For all these reasons, states must invest time and resources in monitoring tunnel-prone regions. Although the task can seem daunting and at times unnecessary, it offers the best hope of preventing and countering potential underground threats. Timing is of the essence: the longer it takes for a state to become aware of a tunnel construction, inheritance, or expansion, the more difficult it will be to eliminate the threat. States can do so through satellite imaging,[211] the training of local agents, and of course by using technology such as airborne ground penetrating radars. As none of these methods are infallible, monitoring still embodies the best method to preempt the use and reuse of underground spaces for hostile purposes.

---

[209] Convention on the Prohibition of the Use, Stockpiling, Production and Transfer of Anti-Personnel Mines and on their Destruction, Mar. 1, 1999, 2056 U.N.T.S. 211.

[210] *See infra* Chapter 7.

[211] *North Korea May Have Resumed Tunneling at Nuclear Test Site: U.S. Report*, REUTERS (Apr. 21, 2016), http://www.reuters.com/article/us-northkorea-nuclear-site-idUSKCN0XH2HV.

4. Cooperation: Countering the Diffusion of Tactics

Anti-tunnel strategies should include cooperation with like-minded states. The complexity of the threat and its changing nature make it indispensable for states to share, consult, and exchange experiences. The diffusion of the tactic has shown that what works in one battlefield spreads to the next. Knowing and understanding how tunnels are used elsewhere will therefore enable states to anticipate and prepare for upcoming challenges. In a context where so little information is available, the importance of cooperation only grows.

More often than not, states are reluctant to publish information about the challenges they face, and the type of measures they take, in relation to underground threats. Information is scarce, for example, about the use of the subterranean by al-Qaeda elements in Mali. Similarly, the United States has not volunteered many details about its Underground Facilities Analysis Center. UFAC, as the facility is known, has no website of its own, and the Defense Intelligence Agency's website only explains briefly that "UFAC uses national intelligence and non-intelligence resources to find, characterize, and assess underground facilities used by adversarial state and non-state actors. The UFAC Director reports jointly to the Secretary of Defense and the DNI [Director of National Intelligence] through DIA [Defense Intelligence Agency]."[212] The desire to keep the information confidential can certainly be understood in the charged context of national security. Still, one hopes that, at least at some level, cooperation does exist among like-minded states.

The nascent partnership between Israel and the United States offers an interesting example of what cooperation might mean in the realm of underground warfare. The two countries have sought to create a framework enabling cooperation on the development of anti-tunnel technology. A proposed bill introduced in 2015 authorized the United States to provide up to $200,000,000 assistance to Israel in order to establish an anti-tunneling defense system, among other purposes. According to Rep. Senator Lamborn, one of the bill's sponsors:

> We know that if Hamas has used tunnels in successful terrorist attacks, it is only a matter of time before terrorists elsewhere use tunnels as well. Tunnels are a threat to American bases and embassies around the world, and are already a serious threat on our own southern border. For all these reasons, it only makes sense to partner with Israel, like we have done on missile defense, to learn with them about how to defend against tunnels.[213]

---

[212] Intelligence Community (IC) Members, U.S. DEP'T OF HOMELAND SEC. FUSION CENTER (Dec. 9, 2013), http://fusioncenter.golearnportal.org/3bb/; *see also* Michael Crowley, *Plan B for Iraq*, POLITICO (June 24, 2015), http://www.politico.com/magazine/story/2015/06/plan-b-for-iran-119344.

[213] Rebecca Shimoni Stoil, *Plan for US-Israel Anti-Tunnel R&D Project Clears First House Hurdle*, TIMES OF ISRAEL (Apr. 30, 2015), http://www.timesofisrael.com/bid-for-us-israel-anti-tunnel-partnership-clears-first-house-hurdle/.

Although this bill was not successful, both the House and Senate agreed to the allocation of $40 million for cooperation on a joint anti-tunnel project in the 2016 fiscal year.[214] The bill provides an example of what cooperation could look like, including a sharing of costs and the establishment of a framework to negotiate the rights to any intellectual property developed jointly.

Regardless of the form cooperation takes, states like the United States and Israel have much to gain by working together.[215] The task force established by the Jewish Institute for National Security of America in the wake of the 2014 war between Israel and Gaza, made up of former U.S. high-level military officials, recommended that "the United States work with Israel and other allies to develop technologies and capabilities to address this threat."[216] Members states of the North Atlantic Treaty Organization should enter into similar arrangements to enhance states' individual and collective readiness in the face of fast-spreading underground threats.

To conclude, the components of a comprehensive tunnel strategy can be summarized as follows:

i. Detection and mapping: once the presence of tunnel(s) is suspected, intelligence gathering and technology should be used in tandem to identify and record the route of the tunnel(s). Information obtained on the physical characteristics of an underground structure such as its length and depth, and the location, number, and type of its entrance and exit points will significantly impact subsequent measures. No technology achieves perfect results, and states are advised to combine methods for optimal outcomes.

ii. Neutralization (using water, gas, or cement) and/or destruction (by bulldozers, explosives, or aerial bombardments). There is no one-size-fit-all method; measures must be carefully tailored to the threat.

iii. Prevention and monitoring: the limits of prevention advocate in favor of monitoring tunnel-prone areas so as to detect the construction of new tunnels, keep abreast of the inheritance of remaining structures for hostile

---

[214] President Barack Obama vetoed the bill in October 2015. *See* Library of Congress. (2015). *Actions—H.R. 1735: National Defense Authorization Act for Fiscal Year 2016*, https://www.congress.gov/bill/114th-congress/house-bill/1735/actions; and Rebecca Shimoni Stoil, *Senate Passes Defense Bill That Supports U.S.-Israel Partnerships*, TIMES OF ISRAEL (Oct. 8, 2015), http://www.timesofisrael.com/senate-passes-defense-bill-that-supports-us-israel-partnerships/. *See also Technologies to Enhance Warfighter Capabilities in Subterranean Environments*, Request for Information by the U.S. Army (Dec. 11, 2013), https://www.fbo.gov/?s=opportunity&mode=form&id=0f2c0a2cf8d85db75729b08a1a5a7aaf&tab=core&_cview=1.

[215] In a similar spirit of cooperation, U.S. defense secretary Ashton Carter pledged to enhance strategic cooperation with Israel—including in relation to tunnels (*see* Barbara Opall-Rome, *Carter Pledges to Boost Israel's Military Edge*, DEF. NEWS (Oct. 28, 2015), http://www.defensenews.com/story/defense-news/2015/10/28/carter-pledges-boost-israels-military-edge/74728056/).

[216] *2014 Gaza War Assessment: The New Face of Conflict: A Report by the JINSA-Commissioned Gaza Conflict Task Force* (2015), http://www.jinsa.org/files/2014GazaAssessmentReport.pdf, at 13.

purposes, and minimize the long-term threat posed by tunnels in civilian populated areas.

iv. Cooperation: states seeking to counter the threat should enhance preparedness by sharing information and best practices.

Common to all stages is their complexity and lack of certainty: a strategy that proves effective for one tunnel, or one state, may not adequately answer the needs of another. Considering this, states should familiarize themselves with the available options before they are faced with an underground threat. States sitting on a network of ancient, natural, or other underground structures, and states having encountered underground threats in the past should engage in monitoring on a regular basis. If and when a threat emerges, states should remain apprised of the options for dealing with their particular situation—which may, indeed, differ from what they had anticipated.

Conclusion

This chapter has tackled some of the very first questions that arise when an underground threat emerges—even if the threat seems rather limited in time and scope. When an underground threat emerges, states must identify the applicable legal framework, assess the legality of various counter-measures, and understand the methods available to detect and destroy the tunnel(s). These threshold matters greatly influence state actions in the realm of underground warfare. They embody an important part of the political, legal, and military decision-making processes and must be handled at the outset—before any other seemingly urgent matter overshadows them. The cost, later on, would simply be too great.

The discovery of a tunnel or, more significantly, a tunnel complex, leaves little time for deliberation or research. States must make important decisions under intense time pressure. For this reason, I recommend that states—in particular those facing (or having faced) underground threats in the past—set up a long-term strategy to enhance their readiness.

This long-term strategy should include detecting and mapping the tunnels, destroying the tunnels, monitoring the terrain, and cooperating with other states. Detecting and mapping require a combination of human intelligence and technology. As no foolproof technology exists, optimal results are obtained by using different and complementary methods. Although mapping is both time-consuming and costly, it embodies an essential step in the process. It ensures that anti-tunnel measures are pinpointed and effective, and it enables records to be kept and amended over time. It should not be skipped.

Tunnels must then be neutralized or destroyed to ensure that the threat is eliminated. As partially destroying the tunnels merely slows down the completion of the tunnel, full elimination is preferable. Tunnels can be neutralized and/or destroyed using a variety of methods, some of which raise legal issues—such as gas or flooding with sewage water. The advantages and legality of these methods should be carefully assessed before decisions are made on how to proceed. Once the tunnels have been eliminated, monitoring of the terrain should continue to prevent the digging of new tunnels and the takeover of any remaining structures by new actors. Even when the tunnels are believed to have been fully destroyed, some segments may not have been discovered, and a risk always persists that the tunnels could be used again for hostile purposes. Finally, cooperation presents significant advantages, from raising awareness to choosing the right method and exchanging best practices. Through the sharing of information, states would also better counter the diffusion of tunnel tactics to more theaters of operation.

5

UNDERGROUND WARFARE AND THE *JUS AD BELLUM*

THE U.S. CUSTOMS Service spokeswoman described it as "something out of a James Bond movie."[1] In May 1990, after months of speculation, the first cross-border tunnel between Mexico and the United States was discovered. The tunnel, which had been dug 30 feet underground over the course of six months, was 270 feet long, 5 feet high, and 4 feet wide. The sophisticated underground passageway, equipped with electricity, concrete reinforcement, and storage rooms, was used to store and smuggle large quantities of cocaine from Mexico to the United States. U.S. authorities only discovered it six months after its completion: inside a luxury home in Agua Prieta, Mexico, a hydraulic system raised a pool table, revealing a narrow shaft leading to the tunnel.[2] Since then, U.S. Border Patrols have discovered close to 200 cross-border tunnels.[3]

The United States could have taken a variety of measures in reaction to the cross-border threat. It decided to monitor the use of existing tunnels and the digging of new tunnels, but did not take any further action. This decision was likely influenced by many

---

[1] AP, *Agents Find Drug Tunnel to US*, N.Y. TIMES (May 19, 1990), http://www.nytimes.com/1990/05/19/us/agents-find-drug-tunnel-to-us.html; Douglas Jehl, *$1-Million Drug Tunnel Found at Mexico Border: Narcotics: The Passageway Ends at a Warehouse in Arizona. It Was Used to Bring Cocaine into the U.S.*, L.A. TIMES (May 19, 1990), http://articles.latimes.com/1990-05-19/news/mn-65_1_mexico-border.
[2] *Agents Find Drug Tunnel*, supra note 1.
[3] U.S. DEPARTMENT OF HOMELAND SECURITY, CROSS BORDER TUNNELS AND BORDER TUNNEL PREVENTION: FISCAL YEAR 2015 REPORT TO CONGRESS 6 (2016). This number does not include incomplete tunnels, that is, those discovered prior to crossing the border.

Underground Warfare. Daphné Richemond-Barak.
© Oxford University Press 2018. Published 2018 by Oxford University Press.

factors, including but not limited to the identity of the perpetrators, the purpose of the tunnels, and an assessment of the security risk posed to the United States. These considerations form the heart of the analysis below, which seeks to uncover the decision-making process underlying a state's reaction to an underground cross-border threat.

The discovery of a cross-border tunnel—fully completed or not—must trigger an assessment of the threat, and an examination of the options available to protect the state's sovereignty, security, and territorial integrity. Should the victim state wish to destroy the cross-border tunnel(s), and assuming the border has already been crossed, it can certainly take measures against the portion of the tunnel located on its own territory. The question is whether the victim state might be entitled to destroy the portion of the tunnel located on foreign territory. Legally, anti-tunnel operations undertaken on the territory of a foreign state do not raise issues when the latter consents to the operations—whether the operations are carried out by the victim state or by a skilled third party. If a nonstate actor digs a tunnel without the territorial state's consent, that state could decide to destroy or neutralize the tunnel on its own initiative or at the request of the victim state. This would seem sensible given the potential risks posed by tunnels to the territorial state's own population and infrastructure.

In situations where the victim state cannot rely on the support of the territorial state, the victim state would still, in certain circumstances, be legally justified in destroying the portion of the tunnel located on the opposite side of the border. Whether states choose to make use of this right is not a legal decision—it is a strategic one. The United States has decided, for strategic reasons, not to destroy the cross-border tunnels emanating from Mexico. That the United States has a legal right to do so, however, is an entirely different matter. This right originates in state sovereignty and territorial integrity. Cross-border tunnels violate both. The scope of the victim state's options to uphold its sovereignty and territorial integrity falls within the ambit of a body of law known as the *jus ad bellum*, which regulates the entry into war—that is, states' resort to force.[4]

The *jus ad bellum* suffers from an intrinsic weakness in that it allows states to respond only to acts whose perpetrator is known. This weakness, albeit factually grounded, can complicate the application of the law. Consider, for example, cyberattacks: even when the right to respond exists, identifying the perpetrator of the act (and therefore the target of the response) might prove impossible, leaving the victim state with only very limited options. Beyond its impact on the availability of self-defense, the identification of the perpetrator also matters for the attribution of responsibility.

Luckily, the question of attribution does not arise with as much force in the context of tunnels as in other contexts, such as cyber. The identity of a tunnel-digger or tunnel-user can be deduced from the location of the tunnel, as well as the type of relationship entertained with the neighboring state. States typically know where the tunnel emanates from—if not its precise location, at least the portion of territory on which the tunnel is located. The state governing that territory would of course be the most likely culprit

---

[4] *See supra* Chapter 4 for an overview of the applicable legal regimes.

unless a nonstate armed group, hostile to the victim state, has a presence there. A difficult situation could emerge if several nonstate armed groups—all hostile to the victim state—operate on that territory. The rapport between the various actors, combined with the location of the tunnels, should help narrow down the possibilities.

Responsibility for the digging or use of the tunnel can be imputed to the state, even though it did not directly contribute to it,[5] if the nonstate group is under the direction or control of the state[6] (though the relevant standard—effective or overall control—remains debated)[7] or if the state embraces the actions of the group as its own.[8] Provided all other requirements are met, the target state would then be entitled to take action against the state and the nonstate actor.[9] The state could also be held responsible under an obligation of due diligence, that is, the obligation "not to knowingly allow its territory to be used for acts contrary to the rights of other States."[10] This obligation varies depending on whether the state is *unable* to prevent the digging of the tunnel or *unwilling* to prevent it. However,

---

[5] In the more straightforward situations where the tunnel is built by one of the state's organs or a parastatal entity, it would also be attributable to the state for purposes of imputing responsibility (*see* Articles on Responsibility of States for Internationally Wrongful Acts in the Rep. of the Int'l Law Comm'n, 53rd Sess., Apr. 23–June 1 and July 2–Aug. 10, 2001, U.N. Doc. A/56/10; GAOR, 56th Sess., Supp. No. 10 (2001) [hereinafter: Draft Articles], at arts. 4 and 5, respectively).

[6] *Id.* at art. 8.

[7] Applying an *effective* control test: Application of the Convention on the Prevention and Punishment of the Crime of Genocide (Bosn. & Herz. v. Serb. & Montenegro), 2007, I.C.J. 43, ¶ 400 (Feb. 26) [hereinafter Bosnian Genocide]; Military and Paramilitary Activities in and against Nicaragua (Nicar. v. U.S.), 1986, I.C.J. 14, ¶ 116 (June 27) [hereinafter Nicaragua]; applying an *overall* control test: Prosecutor v. Thomas Lubanga Dyilo, Case No. ICC-01/04-01/06 Judgment Pursuant to Article 74 of the Statute, ¶ 342 (Mar. 14, 2012), https://www.icc-cpi.int/CourtRecords/CR2012_03942.PDF; Prosecutor v. Tadić, Case No. IT-94-1-A, Appeals Chamber Judgment, ¶ 120 (Int'l Crim. Trib. for the Former Yugoslavia July 15, 1999).

[8] Draft Articles, *supra* note 5, at art. 11.

[9] NOAM LUBELL, EXTRATERRITORIAL USE OF FORCE AGAINST NON-STATE ACTORS 48 (2010).

[10] Corfu Channel (U.K. v. Albania), 1949, I.C.J. 4, 22 (Apr. 9) [hereinafter Corfu]. *See also* TALLINN MANUAL ON THE INTERNATIONAL LAW APPLICABLE TO CYBER WARFARE 26 (Michael N. Schmitt ed., 2013). Similar to the general duty of due diligence is the state's specific obligation to prevent terrorism from within its borders. This duty, which can be regarded as customary (*see* MARJA LEHTO, INDIRECT RESPONSIBILITY FOR TERRORIST ACTS: REDEFINITION OF THE CONCEPT OF TERRORISM BEYOND VIOLENT ACTS 382 (2009), is shown inter alia in the 1970 Declaration on Friendly Relations (G.A. Res. 2625 (XXV), U.N. GAOR, 25th Sess., ¶ 1, U.N. Doc. A/RES/25/2625 (Oct. 24, 1970): "Every State has the duty to refrain from organizing, instigating, assisting or participating in acts of civil strife or terrorist acts in another State, or acquiescing in organized activities within its territory directed towards the commission of such acts, when the acts referred to in the present paragraph involve a threat or use of force."); the 1994 Declaration on the Measures to Eliminate Terrorism (*see* G.A. Res. 49/60, U.N. Doc. A/RES/49/60 (Dec. 9, 1994) requires that states must "... refrain from organizing, instigating, facilitating, financing, encouraging or tolerating terrorist activities and to take appropriate practical measures to ensure that their respective territories are not used for terrorist installations or training camps, or for the preparation or organization of terrorist acts intended to be committed against other States or their citizens"); and Security Council Resolution 1373 (S.C. Res. 1373, U.N. Doc. SC/RES/1373 (Sept. 28 2001)). Indeed, complicity in the form of actual involvement of the state, tolerance or failure to suppress activities threatening foreign interests, or negligence with regard to their punishment or prevention, has led to international responsibility (*see* LEHTO, *supra*, at 382).

a consensus has yet to emerge on how these two scenarios affect the responsibility of the territorial state. Some scholars, including Reinold and Bethlehem, concede that harboring or not being able to prevent hostile activities would be sufficient to trigger state responsibility—with some possible adjustments in the interpretation of necessity and proportionality.[11] When the standards for imputing responsibility to the territorial state, albeit unclear, are met, the victim state is entitled to act against the nonstate actor without the consent of the territorial state (for example, Israel against Hezbollah in Lebanon, or the United States against a hostile group having taken over the smuggling tunnels in Mexico).

How can states prevent a finding of responsibility under the obligation of due diligence for the digging of cross-border tunnels? Due diligence has much to do with predictability. If a nonstate group has dug cross-border tunnels in the past, the state would be more likely to be held responsible for the digging of new tunnels on its territory. The obligation includes mitigating damage (destroying the tunnel(s) and prosecuting those involved), and preventing recurrence (at least by warning the target state).[12] It is an obligation of conduct, not of result,[13] which requires the state to employ all means reasonably available[14] based on its knowledge and capacity to avert harm to other states.[15] The standard of conduct is variable,[16] based on the state's actual capabilities. Location plays a role here, too. The fact that a tunnel emerges from a state's territory is an important factor in determining whether or not the state knew—or should have known—about the tunnel's existence,[17] but is not in and of itself determinant.[18] It could be best considered as an *indication*, though not proof, of state involvement.[19] If, for example, the area from which the tunnel emerges is on the state's territory but under the control of an armed group, the state's obligation to know and prevent the digging of a tunnel would be reduced. Due diligence would similarly lose its relevance in the (increasingly frequent) situation where no functioning state governs the territory in question—for example, in Iraq and Syria.

Attribution and due diligence—like sovereignty and nonintervention, analyzed later in this chapter—are overarching principles that permeate the application of international law generally, and of the *jus ad bellum* more specifically. Before turning to the law, however, I analyze the strategic factors that affect a state's reaction to underground threats.

---

[11] Daniel Bethlehem, *Principles Relevant to the Scope of a State's Right of Self-Defense Against an Imminent or Actual Armed Attack by Non-state Actors*, 106 AM. J. INT'L L. 1, 11 (2012); and Theresa Reinold, *State Weakness, Irregular Warfare and the Right to Self-Defense Following 9/11*, 105 AM. J. INT'L L. 244 (2011).

[12] Alabama Claims (U.S. v. U.K.), 29 U.N.R.I.A.A. 125, 129–31 (1872); North Sea Continental Shelf (Ger. V. Den.; Ger. v. Neth.), 1969, I.C.J. 4, at 83 (Feb. 20).

[13] Bosnian Genocide, *supra* note 7, ¶ 430.

[14] *Id.*

[15] United States Diplomatic and Consular Staff in Tehran (U.S. v. Iran), 1980, I.C.J. 3, ¶ 68 (May 24).

[16] Responsibilities and Obligations of States Sponsoring Persons and Entities with Respect to Activities in the Area, Advisory Opinion, Feb. 1, 2011, ITLOS Rep. 10, ¶ 117; Bosnian Genocide, *supra* note 7, ¶ 430.

[17] Boyd (U.S. v. Mex), 4 U.N.R.I.A.A. 380 (1928); Pulp Mills on the River Uruguay (Arg. v. Uru.), 2010, I.C.J. 14, ¶ 197 (Apr. 20).

[18] Corfu, *supra* note 10, at 18; Nicaragua, *supra* note 7, ¶ 155.

[19] TALLINN MANUAL, *supra* note 10, at Rule 7.

I. Strategic Factors Affecting the *Jus ad Bellum* Analysis

As in all matters affecting states' essential security interests, the law is hardly the only factor at play. A whole array of legal and non-legal factors influence a state's reaction in the aftermath of the discovery of cross-border tunnel(s) or an attack carried out via cross-border tunnel(s). These factors include tunnel-specific parameters that states may not be familiar with—especially if they are confronted by underground cross-border threats for the first time. Summarized in Table 5.1 below, these tunnel-specific parameters help determine the gravity and scope of the threat and, as such, can work as a first-aid kit for decision-makers. The idea is not to offer a clear-cut formula on when cross-border tunnels justify war, but rather to develop a qualitative method for assessing the threat.

WHEN. This chapter deals exclusively with the use of cross-border tunnels in peacetime—that is, situations in which cross-border tunnels are dug outside of an armed conflict but could lead to the outbreak of war. If the parties are already at war, the victim state's response to the digging or use of cross-border tunnels is subject to different rules and principles, analyzed in Chapter 6.

WHERE. Location further affects the scenario under consideration. This chapter addresses the discovery, in peacetime, of one or more cross-border tunnel(s) between the territories of two states (or between a state and an internationally recognized entity). Within such a paradigm, the specific location of the tunnel also matters, that is, whether it begins/exits/burrows under uninhabited, mountainous, or urban areas. The answer to this question is important for at least two reasons. First, it helps with the assessment of the security threat, and second, it may provide some insight as to

TABLE 5.1
ASSESSING CROSS-BORDER UNDERGROUND THREATS

When	Peacetime
Where	Cross-border
	Non-urban vs. urban
What	How many?
	Digging stage completed?
	Already been used?
	Internal features?
Why	Assumption of hostile intent
By whom	State vs. nonstate armed group (and, if so, the level of control of the state over nonstate group)
Against whom	Civilians vs. combatants

the intended target of the tunnel attack (the *"against whom"* query, analyzed further below)—assuming the tunnel has not yet been used and this aspect remains cloaked with uncertainty. The two, incidentally, do not always go hand in hand: the tunnel would constitute a significant threat if it burrows under civilian populated areas, even if the intended target is not civilian. Either of these aspects will therefore influence a state's reaction to the tunnel(s).

WHAT. This query touches upon the tunnels' specific features. Some of the basic facts regarding the tunnels—such as how many there are, and whether they cross the border—can provide insight on the important and difficult question of *why* the tunnels were dug (assuming no attack has yet occurred).

Accordingly, authorities should, first and foremost, establish how many tunnels have been dug under or near the border. The more tunnels there are, the greater the threat. That does not mean that a single tunnel poses no threat, however. While numbers matter, it was a single tunnel that led to the kidnapping of Cpl. Shalit—an incident with immense strategic and security implications for Israelis and Palestinians.[20] The "Aleppo Earthquake" operation, also discussed in Chapter 1, similarly demonstrates the destruction that a single mined tunnel can bring about.

In addition, authorities should establish the level of advancement of the tunnels: Has the digging stopped? Have the tunnels already crossed the border? If one or more of the tunnels has already been used, that would certainly be relevant. Finally, efforts should be made to identify some of the tunnels' internal features: Are the tunnels equipped with electricity? Fortified with cement or wood planks? Knowing whether the tunnels are dug on different levels or feature separate rooms or areas can also be helpful. As explained in Chapters 1 and 2, construction features provide information as to the intended use of a tunnel—as an ammunition cache, living quarters, tunnel mining, or smuggling route.

WHY. The "why" behind a tunnel can be very difficult to ascertain with precision. The answer is not always readily available, even with the help of sophisticated intelligence gathering. Yet a state's reaction to cross-border tunnels largely depends on how that state perceives the digger's intentions. States may not react to cross-border smuggling tunnels as they would to tunnels designed to carry out an attack against the civilian population. Tunnels used for human trafficking, illegal infiltrations, or the smuggling of drugs and weapons are unlikely to trigger the use of force. That states may decide *not* to resort to force does not mean they do not possess such a right, however. The right may exist

---

[20] Shalit was released in October 2011, more than five years after he was kidnapped, in exchange for 1,027 Palestinian prisoners being held in Israel. *See supra* Chapter 1 for more details on this incident.

independently of the purpose for which the tunnel was built. In other words, the purpose of the tunnel affects the strategic decision—not the legal entitlement to use force.

BY WHOM. As I explained in Chapter 2, nonstate armed groups have become the main users of the underground. The possibility remains, however, that a state may have dug under the border. The identity of the tunnel-digger bears on (1) the anticipated use of the tunnel, and (2) the legal framework applicable.

States and non-state actors have used the underground for slightly different purposes. States, at least those that possess high-level military capabilities, tend to use the underground for long-term, defensive goals. They dig deep and large structures (known as deeply buried facilities) to shield their most sensitive personnel and equipment and ensure the continuity of the command-and-control chain in time of crisis.

> The dawn of the atomic age forced militaries to dig even deeper underground to protect the chains of command from nuclear attack. So the United States built supposedly nuclear-bomb-proof shelters, including a five-acre network of tunnels buried under 2,000 feet of solid granite built into Cheyenne Mountain, Colorado, to house the North American Aerospace Defense Command; and the Presidential Emergency Operations Center, located 120 feet under the East Wing of the White House. Fortunately, neither one has been put to that ultimate test, although the PEOC was used by Vice President Dick Cheney during the 9/11 crisis.[21]

Nonstate actors, who tend to possess lesser military capabilities, have demonstrated a preference for short-term, offensive uses of the underground (tunnel mining or other). Although these patterns are by no means universal, they reflect broad trends and can assist in conducting preliminary strategic and legal assessments of cross-border underground threats. Knowing *who* is behind the tunnel can help ascertain the *why*, and vice versa.

Knowing *who* is behind the tunnels also bears on the victim state's possible menu of responses. International law in general, and the *jus ad bellum* in particular, make important distinctions based on statehood. International lawyers have discussed for years whether the right to self-defense enshrined in Article 51 of the United Nations Charter affords such a right in response to an armed attack emanating from a nonstate actor—as opposed to a state. The state-centric nature of international law has somewhat eroded with, inter alia, the emergence of powerful nonstate actors and the proliferation of weak and failed states. The state/nonstate divide upon which international law rests can certainly be criticized—and I would support such criticism. *De lege lata*, however, there is no

---

[21] Arthur Herman, *Notes from the Underground: The Long History of Tunnel Warfare*, FOREIGN AFFAIRS (Aug. 26, 2014), https://www.foreignaffairs.com/articles/middle-east/2014-08-26/notes-underground. *See also History of the Diefenbunker*, DIEFENBUNKER (Feb. 20, 2017), http://diefenbunker.ca/history-of-cfs-carp/ (Canada's Diefenbunker is built 75 feet underground, with 100,000 square feet of space over four levels).

escaping the dichotomy for the time being. Whether cross-border tunnels were dug by a state or by a nonstate actor affects the options available to the victim state under the law, as I explain in the remainder of this chapter.

AGAINST WHOM. The intended target of an imminent tunnel-based attack will also affect the decision to go to war. A state will be more inclined to take forceful anti-tunnel measures when the tunnels are aimed at harming civilians than when they aim at armed forces stationed at the border. South Korea, which perceives tunnels as military tools, has opted for a close monitoring of the other side's moves rather than the destruction of the tunnels dug by North Korea under the Demilitarized Zone.

Ultimately, the importance of strategic factors cannot be underestimated. Even in situations where the law affords states the right to use force, they may elect not to exercise that right—for reasons that go beyond the law. The United States and South Korea have chosen not to destroy the tunnels emanating, respectively, from Mexico and North Korea. This is because, under current strategic calculations, the cost of destroying the tunnels outweighs the benefits. The two states could certainly change their minds, and the law would sanction the use of tougher measures against the tunnels.

II. Underground Threats Giving Rise to a Right of Self-Defense

The discovery of a cross-border tunnel may or may not trigger the right to use force in self-defense. Delineating the scope of the right to self-defense in the context of underground warfare is essential. When can states use military force in response to an underground cross-border threat? The answer to this question builds on the existing framework known as the *jus ad bellum*, as explained above. The general principles laid down in the *jus ad bellum* apply in the underground context as they apply in other domains of war, such as, for example, the cyber context.[22]

Situations giving rise to the right to self-defense are purposefully very limited under the post-WWII normative order. The United Nations Charter prohibits unilateral resort to force, unless a state has been the victim of an armed attack. Only some cross-border underground threats qualify as armed attacks, allowing the victim state to use military force in response. Under a broader reading of Article 51 of the United Nations Charter, where the "inherent" right of self-defense of states is enshrined, the use of force might be acceptable *before* an armed attack occurs and/or where the threat emanates from a nonstate actor. This right is known as anticipatory self-defense.

---

[22] TALLINN MANUAL, *supra* note 10, at 13.

A. TUNNEL(S) AS ARMED ATTACK

Only underground threats that rise to the threshold of an armed attack in the meaning of Article 51 of the United Nations Charter will trigger the right to self-defense. The implications are far-reaching, as the victim state becomes entitled by law to use military force.

Article 51 does not define "armed attack," but the International Court of Justice (ICJ) has identified two criteria: it has measured both the "scale and effects"[23] of the attack and its "magnitude and duration,"[24] with "scale and effects" being the more prominent test.[25] Can underground cross-border threats ever meet this high threshold? That depends on whether "armed attack" refers to the use of the tunnel or the digging of the tunnel. The *use* of a single cross-border tunnel can trigger the right to self-defense provided the tunnel-based attack meets the threshold of Article 51. The analysis of this scenario would likely consider the scale and effects of the attack, with the tunnel having little incidence on the outcome. I should add that for a minority of scholars who believe that *any* use of armed force constitutes an armed attack, any cross-border tunnel attack would trigger the right to self-defense—regardless of the attack's scale and effects.[26]

The more relevant and interesting situation arises when the cross-border tunnel *has not yet been used*. Could the *digging* of a single cross-border tunnel trigger the right to self-defense? Yoram Dinstein's analysis of "interceptive" self-defense strikes a chord in this very specific context. It could justify actions in self-defense against unused cross-border tunnels that have already crossed the border.[27] Under this analysis of self-defense, the mere presence of foreign troops on one's territory suffices to trigger the right to self-defense:

> It may start when massive Arcadian armoured or infantry divisions storm, with blazing guns, a Utopian line of fortifications. But an invasion may also be effected when a smaller military Numidian force crosses the Ruritanian frontier and then halts, positioning itself in strategic outposts well within the Ruritanian territory . . . *When a country sends armed formations across an international frontier, without the consent of the local Government, it must be deemed to have triggered and armed attack.*[28]

The cross-border tunnel achieves the same effects as the physical presence of troops on foreign territory. The existence of the tunnel is what matters, not the presence of troops

---

[23] Nicaragua, *supra* note 7, ¶ 195.
[24] Armed Activities on the Territory of the Congo (Dem. Rep. Congo v. Uganda), 2005, I.C.J. 168, ¶ 165 (Dec. 19) [hereinafter Armed Activities].
[25] TALLINN MANUAL, *supra* note 10, at 54.
[26] ELIZABETH WILMSHURST, THE CHATHAM HOUSE PRINCIPLES OF INTERNATIONAL LAW ON THE USE OF FORCE IN SELF DEFENCE BY STATES 6 (2005).
[27] YORAM DINSTEIN, WAR, AGGRESSION AND SELF-DEFENCE 170 (5th ed., 2011).
[28] *Id.* (emphasis added).

inside it. The tunnel is akin to the troops; it amounts to an armed attack in the same way. In fact, the actual presence of troops is much less relevant in the underground context than it is aboveground. Once a tunnel exists, troops can penetrate territory undetected. It may not even be possible to determine, for that matter, whether troops are present in the tunnel or whether they have crossed the border. The only way to verify it is by entering the tunnel, as U.S. border officials regularly do at the Mexican border—but this cannot and should not be envisaged in all situations.[29] Verification of this sort seems overly dangerous and cannot be expected as a standard, let alone required, procedure.

For those willing to accept interceptive self-defense, the action taken in response does not amount to anticipatory self-defense, but to self-defense as such. The armed attack begins with the digging of the cross-border tunnel.[30] Albeit under a different reasoning, the ICJ acknowledged that an attack against a single military vessel could amount to an armed attack.[31]

Finally, the digging of a cross-border tunnel could be regarded as a frontier incident. It is, after all, a frontier incident. According to the ICJ, however, frontier incidents do not trigger the right to self-defense.[32] I disagree. Certain frontier incidents can rise to the armed attack threshold. Judge Fitzmaurice elegantly put it: "[t]here are frontier incidents and frontier incidents."[33] I see no reason why certain frontier incidents—including cross-border tunnels—could not amount to armed attacks.

Regardless of the legal justification, the more cross-border tunnels there are, the stronger the argument. The discovery of several cross-border tunnels would amount to an armed attack—even if each tunnel, individually, does not meet the threshold. A series of low-scale attacks can, taken in the aggregate, be considered an armed attack. This "accumulation of events" theory gives expression to important policy considerations: *not* acknowledging cumulative small-scale attacks as triggering self-defense would encourage more states to make use of under-the-threshold force, in the hope that they would not become subject to reactionary measures.[34] The theory has been invoked by several states,

---

[29] Jason McCammack, *What Lies Beneath*, U.S. CUSTOMS AND BORDER PROTECTION (Feb. 20, 3027), https://www.cbp.gov/frontline/what-lies-beneath.

[30] DINSTEIN, *supra* note 27, at 172 (Sir Humphrey Waldock, cited by Dinstein, embraces this interpretation even when the threat has not yet passed the frontier. The case of the cross-border tunnel—which has indeed passed the frontier—seems all the more convincing). Anticipatory self-defense would become relevant, as I explain below, in the case of uncompleted cross-border tunnels.

[31] Oil Platforms (Iran v. U.S.), 2003 I.C.J. 161, ¶ 72 (Nov. 6) [hereinafter Oil Platforms]. For a different view, see Eri. v. Eth., Partial Award, Jus ad Bellum, Ethiopia's Claims 1–8, XXVI R.I.A.A. 457, ¶ 11 (Eri. Eth. Claims Commission, Dec. 19, 2005) ("[l]ocalized border encounters between small infantry units, even those involving the loss of life, do not constitute an armed attack for purposes of the Charter."). *See also* David Kretzmer, *The Inherent Right to Self-Defense and Proportionality in* Jus ad Bellum, 24 EUR. J. INT'L L. 235, 243 (2013).

[32] Nicaragua, *supra* note 7, at ¶ 195.

[33] G. G. Fitzmaurice, *The Definition of Aggression*, 1 INT'L & COMP. L.Q. 137, 139 (1952).

[34] William H. Taft IV, *Self-Defence and the Oil Platforms Decision*, 29 YALE J. INT'L L. 295, 300–01 (2004). However, for a critical view of the doctrine, see Christian J. Tams, *The Use of Force Against Terrorists*, 20 EJIL 359, 390 (2009); and Kreztmer, *supra* note 31, at 244.

including Russia, Iran, Israel, Liberia, the United States, and Sudan.[35] Its relevance was also inferred by the ICJ in the *Oil Platforms* and *Armed Activities* cases, even though in both situations the Court ultimately concluded that there was no right of self-defense.[36] This broad acceptance, however, should not detract from the difficulty of assessing proportionality in these cases. Take, for example, the discovery of multiple cross-border tunnels.[37] Two options exist: assessing proportionality in relation to each tunnel, or in relation to the tunnels as "accumulated into a whole which would then be considered an armed attack."[38] I would favor the latter interpretation.

If the victim state does not possess the technology or expertise to deal with underground threats, it could request the assistance of a third state under the doctrine of collective self-defense. In *Nicaragua*, for example, the United States claimed to be acting on behalf of El Salvador in exercise of the right of collective self-defense. More recently, various countries invoked this same right in assisting the United States in the wake of the 9/11 attacks.[39] Under this doctrine, the victim state must declare itself the victim of armed attack, and ask for assistance.[40] The legality of the response would also, and importantly, depend on the occurrence of an armed attack.

Even in situations where the right to self-defense does exist—be it individual or collective self-defense—limitations apply. Military steps taken in self-defense must, for their entire duration, comply with the *jus ad bellum*'s necessity and proportionality requirements.[41] These requirements, well-entrenched in the law, do not require an in-depth treatment here; an explanation of how they apply in the context of underground warfare will suffice.

Necessity means that states can resort to military force only as a last resort, when other means would not suffice. Put differently, it means that the attack—whether imminent or underway—can only be repelled via the use of force. Who makes the call? According to the ICJ, the test is an objective one.[42] Yet the Tallinn Manual on the International Law

---

[35] Tom Ruys, "Armed Attack" and Article 51 of the UN Charter: Evolutions in Customary Law and Practice 172, 174 (2010) (noting that the evidence of the acceptance of the "accumulation of events" doctrine is not unequivocal, first and foremost because it has been used by states to justify disproportionate responses to attacks).

[36] *See* Oil Platforms, *supra* note 31, ¶ 64; Armed Activities, *supra* note 24, ¶ 147.

[37] *See* Bethlehem, *supra* note 11, at 6.

[38] Lubell, *supra* note 9, at 53.

[39] Ruys, *supra* note 35, at 87.

[40] Nicaragua, *supra* note 7, ¶¶ 195, 237. In practice, the declaration by the victim state that it has been the victim of an armed attack is not decisive in determining the legality of collective self-defense. *See* Ruys, *supra* note 35, at 88. Indeed, in the discussion of collective self-defense in the *Oil Platforms* case, the criterion was not reiterated. Oil Platforms, *supra* note 31, ¶ 53.

[41] Legality of the Threat or Use of Nuclear Weapons, Advisory Opinion, 1996, I.C.J. 226, ¶¶ 40–41 (July 8) [hereinafter Nuclear Weapons]; Nicaragua, *supra* note 7, ¶¶ 176, 194; Oil Platforms, *supra* note 31, ¶¶ 43, 73–74, 76.

[42] *See* Olivier Corten, *Necessity*, *in* The Oxford Handbook of International Law in Armed Conflict 861, 869 (Andrew Clapham & Paola Gaeta eds., 2014); and Dinstein, *supra* note 27, at 232.

Applicable to Cyber Warfare (hereinafter "the Tallinn Manual") takes the view that the existence of necessity is judged by the victim state.[43] Regardless, in the face of an underground cross-border threat, it seems reasonable to allow the victim state to take forceful action, as there is no *effective* means to respond to the attack other than by using force.[44] Subterranean threats can only be fully eliminated via destruction. I should add that the victim state does not need to prove that all peaceful means have been exhausted before resorting to force. As noted by Daniel Bethlehem, "[a]rmed action in self-defense should be used only as a last resort in circumstances in which no other effective means are *reasonably available* to address an imminent or actual armed attack."[45] The test is whether a reasonable alternative exists, *in abstracto*, to stop or repel the armed attack. Noam Lubell adds another requirement when the attack emanates from a nonstate actor, namely that the victim state should reach out to the territorial state to find a peaceful solution.[46] The victim state could certainly ask the territorial state if it would agree to destroy the tunnels. However, I am doubtful that this amounts to a legal obligation *de lege lata*.

Anti-tunnel measures taken in self-defense would also have to be proportionate—a requirement very different in the context of the *jus ad bellum* than in the *jus in bello* (during war). *Ad bellum* proportionality emphasizes the general objective of the use of force—acting or repelling the attack—rather than the modalities of such use of force: "What matters is the result to be achieved by the defensive action, and not the forms, substance and length of the action itself . . . Its lawfulness cannot be measured except by its capacity for achieving the desired result."[47] Judges Schwebel (in his dissenting opinion in the *Nicaragua* case)[48] and Higgins (in her dissenting opinion to the *Nuclear Weapons* advisory opinion)[49] both adopted this approach. Similarly, in his Separate Opinion in the *Armed Activities* case, Judge Kooijmans measured the proportionality of Uganda's actions against the general aims of repelling attacks and securing borders from attacks by anti-Ugandan rebels.[50]

This is not the only approach to *ad bellum* proportionality, however. *Ad bellum* proportionality has also been measured against the size and scope of the armed attack.[51] In this case, proportionality includes considerations such as "as the geographical and

---

[43] TALLINN MANUAL, *supra* note 10, at 62.
[44] *Id.* at 59; Giovanni Distefano, *Use of Force*, in THE OXFORD HANDBOOK OF INTERNATIONAL LAW IN ARMED CONFLICT, *supra* note 42, at 554; and DINSTEIN, *supra* note 27, at 232.
[45] Bethlehem, *supra* note 11, at 6.
[46] LUBELL, *supra* note 9, at 46.
[47] Robert Ago, *Addendum to the Eighth Report on State Responsibility*, [1980] 2 Y.B. Int'l L. Comm'n 13, at 60, ¶ 121, U.N. Doc. A/CN.4/318/ADD.5–7 (1980).
[48] Nicaragua, *supra* note 7, at 367–69 (Dissenting Opinion of Judge Schwebel).
[49] Nuclear Weapons, *supra* note 41, at 538 (Separate Opinion of Judge Higgins).
[50] Armed Activities, *supra* note 24, at 315 (Separate Opinion of Judge Kooijmans).
[51] Theodora Christodoulidou & Kalliopi Chainoglou, *The Principle of Proportionality from a Jus ad Bellum Perspective*, in THE OXFORD HANDBOOK ON THE USE OF FORCE IN INTERNATIONAL LAW 1187, 1192 (Marc Weller ed., 2015).

destructive scope of the response, the duration of the response, the selection of means and methods of warfare and targets and the effect on third States."[52] This interpretation brings *ad bellum* proportionality (too) close to *in bello* proportionality.[53] As such, it is in my view less relevant than the first test, which focuses on the general objective of the use of force. I should add that some scholars, such as Oscar Schachter, combine the two interpretations of proportionality—insisting that acts taken in self-defense do "not exceed *in manner or aim* the necessity provoking them."[54] Akande and Liefländer are right to assert that "a profound lack of clarity and consensus" permeates this aspect of the *jus ad bellum*.[55]

In an effort to overcome this lack of clear legal guidance, I would argue that the right to self-defense may arise in response to (1) the digging of one or more cross-border tunnels, assuming such tunnels have already burrowed under the border; and (2) an armed attack conducted via one or more cross-border tunnels. The type of response regarded as necessary and proportionate would evolve depending on the circumstances: a response to one or few cross-border tunnels would have to be directed at and limited to the tunnels (destruction and prevention),[56] whereas the discovery of a multitude of tunnels would likely justify actions of a broader reach and higher intensity. Destroying the tunnel, even on foreign territory, is what is needed to eliminate the threat. There is no alternative.

Although the victim state might conceive of the response differently depending on whether a state or nonstate actor dug the tunnel(s), it would not fundamentally affect its right to self-defense under Article 51 of the UN Charter. The measures outlined above will be available regardless of whether the underground threat emanates from a state or a nonstate actor. The view that Article 51 of the UN Charter, where the inherent right of self-defense is enshrined, applies beyond the state-to-state relationship has gained traction in recent years[57]—and rightly so—with only a few

---

[52] Judith Gardam, Necessity, Proportionality and the Use of Force by States 162 (2004).

[53] *See* Dapo Akande & Thomas Liefländer, *Clarifying Necessity, Imminence and Proportionality in the Law of Self-Defense*, 107 Am. J. Int'l L. 563, 566 (2013) (suggesting that this constitutes a third interpretation of *ad bellum* proportionality requiring that the "damage inflicted in self-defense not be disproportionate in comparison to the pursued objective").

[54] Oscar Schachter, *The Right of States to Use Armed Force*, 82 Mich. L. Rev. 1620, 1637 (1984) (emphasis added); *see also* Gardam, *supra* note 52, generally.

[55] Akande & Liefländer, *supra* note 53, at 566.

[56] Gardam, *supra* note 52, at 165 (noting that, according to Christopher Greenwood, the United Kingdom had the right to use force not only to retake the Islands but also to guarantee their future security against further attack (citing to Christopher Greenwood, Command and the Laws of Armed Conflict 7–8 (1993)).

[57] This has been expressed in separate and dissenting opinions in ICJ rulings, (Armed Activities, *supra* note 24, ¶¶ 26–30 (Separate Opinion of Judge Kooijmans) and ¶¶ 7–12 (Separate Opinion of Judge Simma)) and recognized by the Security Council (S.C. Res. 1368, U.N. Doc. S/RES/1368 (Sept. 12, 2001); and S.C. Res. 1371, U.N. Doc. S/RES/1371 (Sept. 26, 2001)). Regarding ISIS, UNSC Res. 2249 (2015) recognized ISIS as a threat to peace and security, opening the door to the application of Chapter VII (S.C. Res. 2249, U.N. Doc. S/RES/2249 (Nov. 20, 2015)). State practice also seems to be moving in this direction (Ruys, *supra*

exceptions.[58] The same standards would apply: an armed attack by a nonstate actor does not have to meet a higher threshold than an armed attack emanating from a state to trigger the right to self-defense.[59]

B. PREEMPTIVE AND ANTICIPATORY SELF-DEFENSE

Under a strict interpretation of Article 51 of the United Nations Charter, the victim state would have to wait for the tunnel to be used—that is, for the armed attack to have occurred—to exercise its right to self-defense. However, scholars and practitioners are increasingly making exceptions for cases in which offensive action has already begun but not yet resulted in attack under a doctrine known as anticipatory self-defense.[60]

One justification behind this more relaxed view of Article 51 has its roots in pre-Charter law, as formulated in the wake of the infamous *Caroline* incident of 1837. In the midst of the Canadian rebellion, British armed forces entered United States territory and attacked and destroyed a vessel owned by U.S. citizens who had been offering support to Canadian rebels. The vessel, *The Caroline*, was later thrown down the Niagara Falls. Following the incident, the Americans and the British discussed the legality of the attack. In the ensuing diplomatic exchange, U.S. secretary of state Daniel Webster insisted that the British actions would be lawful if a "necessity of self-defence, instant, overwhelming, leaving no choice of means and no moment for deliberation" could be shown. Even if so, Webster further noted, "the act, justified by the necessity of self-defence, must be limited by that necessity, and kept clearly within it."[61]

Under the *Caroline* doctrine, states may exercise self-defense in response to an *imminent* attack—not to be confused with a *potential* attack. Whereas the former, known as "anticipatory" self-defense, is widely recognized as legal, the latter, known as "preemptive" self-defense, generally is not. Michael Reisman explains the difference between anticipatory and preemptive self-defense as follows (and his definitions are those adopted herein):

[Preemptive self-defense] is a claim of authority to use, unilaterally and without international authorization, high levels of violence in order to arrest a development

---

note 35, at 487), with strong backing from academia (*inter alia*, Ashley Deeks, *Taming the Doctrine of Pre-Emption*, in THE OXFORD HANDBOOK OF THE USE OF FORCE IN INTERNATIONAL LAW, *supra* note 51, at 493; Kretzmer, *supra* note 31, at 247; DINSTEIN, *supra* note 27, at 228).

[58] Legal Consequences of the Construction of a Wall in the Occupied Palestinian Territory, Advisory Opinion, 2004 I.C.J. 136, ¶ 39 (July 9) [hereinafter Wall Advisory Opinion]; Armed Activities, *supra* note 24, ¶ 147; generally, Reinold, *supra* note 11.

[59] *See* LUBELL, *supra* note 9, at 51 (suggesting a different approach).

[60] Distefano, *supra* note 44, at 560; Deeks, *supra* note 57, at 665.

[61] Correspondence between Great Britain and the United States, respecting the Arrest and Imprisonment of Mr. McLeod, for the Destruction of the Steamboat Caroline 1138 (Mar.–Apr. 1841).

that is not yet operational and hence is not yet *directly* threatening, but which, if permitted to mature, could be neutralized only at a high, possibly unacceptable, cost. A credible claim for [anticipatory self-defense] must point to a palpable and imminent threat; a claim for [preemptive self-defense] need only point to a possibility, a contingency.[62]

Indicators have emerged in recent years supporting the right of anticipatory self-defense, and making imminence the touchstone of this right. A threat is considered imminent when it leaves "no moment for deliberation"[63] and any further delay will result in the inability to act effectively.[64] This happens when a state becomes aware, on the basis of reliable evidence, that an attack is being planned against it.[65] A level of uncertainty persists as to how much planning must have already taken place for the circumstances to give rise to the right of self-defense, what type of evidence is needed, or how much. It depends in large part on the scope and nature of the threat, and on whether there might be further opportunity in the future to stop the attack from happening.[66] Imminence also has much to do with visibility and permanency. It matters, in this regard, that tunnels are as difficult to detect as they are to eliminate: they combine low visibility with high permanency.

In the subterranean context, imminence can refer either to the completion of the tunnel or to the use of the tunnel to conduct an attack. If one accepts that the *digging* of a cross-border tunnel constitutes a threat of the use of force, as I argue below, it makes sense for the *completion* of such a tunnel to trigger a right to anticipatory self-defense. The nature of the underground threat makes it unreasonable to expect the state to remain idle until the tunnel has crossed the border. This is particularly true given the difficulty of ascertaining whether the tunnel has actually crossed the border.[67]

The Tallinn Manual identifies helpful criteria in delineating the right to anticipatory self-defense. Although the criteria were developed in the cyber context, they resonate exceptionally well in the realm of underground warfare. Importantly, the Tallinn Manual does not measure imminence within a temporal scale but, rather, in terms of the ability of the victim state to protect itself from the impending attack:[68]

> [A] State may act in anticipatory self-defence against an armed attack, whether cyber or kinetic, when the attacker is clearly committed to launching an armed

---

[62] W. Michael Reisman, *Self Defense in an Age of Terrorism*, 97 AM. SOC'Y INT'L. L. PROC. 142, 143 (2003) (emphasis in original).
[63] Schachter, *The Right of States, supra* note 54, at 1635.
[64] WILMSHURST, *supra* note 26, at 8.
[65] DINSTEIN, *supra* note 27, at 200.
[66] WILMSHURST, *supra* note 26, at 8.
[67] *See What Lies Beneath, supra* note 29.
[68] TALLINN MANUAL, *supra* note 10, at 64.

attack and the victim State will lose its opportunity to effectively defend itself unless it acts. In other words, it may act anticipatorily only during *the last window of opportunity* to defend itself against an armed attack that is forthcoming. This window may present itself immediately before the attack in question, or, in some cases, long before it occurs.[69]

The discovery of a cross-border tunnel *not having yet crossed the border* would therefore entitle the neighboring state to act in anticipatory self-defense, provided the tunnel is designed for launching an attack and the opportunity to destroy the tunnel and avert the attack will not present itself later. Other types of tunnels may not meet the requirement: the requirement of imminence is met only if the perpetrator has actually decided to conduct an armed attack using the tunnel. It is the combination of capability and intention that justifies the right to anticipatory self-defense. Anticipatory self-defense could also arise in relation to an old tunnel that has been sitting idle—as long as the victim state can reasonably believe that an attack, using that tunnel, is imminent.

In determining the intention of the tunnel-user, the past relationship between the two entities and the proximity of the emerging tunnel to civilian populated areas matter. They can help establish the existence of intent and capability. If a tunnel has already been used for attack and another is being built, the state could respond by attacking the tunnel-in-progress in anticipatory self-defense, as the attack that has already taken place shows both imminence and hostile intent. This is the basis on which the United States and United Kingdom justified their 2001 intervention in Afghanistan:[70] a *completed* attack can give rise to a right to respond anticipatorily to another potential attack.[71] Hostile intent could be presumed even if the aggressor has used tunnels in the more remote past. In the case of completed cross-border tunnels, exits located in proximity to civilian populated areas could also help ascertain the intention of the tunnel-diggers.

In conclusion, provided the imminence requirement is met, anticipatory self-defense is widely—though not universally[72]—considered legal[73] and even, by some scholars,

---

[69] *Id.* at 64–65 (emphasis added).

[70] U.N. Security Council, Letter dated Oct. 7, 2001 from the Permanent Representative of the U.S. to the U.N. addressed to the President of the Security Council, U.N. Doc. S/2001/946 (Oct. 7, 2001); Letter dated Oct. 7, 2001 from the Chargé d'affaires of the Permanent Mission of the United Kingdom of Great Britain and Northern Ireland to the United Nations addressed to the President of the Security Council, U.N. Doc. S/2001/947 (Oct. 7, 2001).

[71] WILMSHURST, *supra* note 26, at 5.

[72] CHRISTINE GRAY, INTERNATIONAL LAW AND THE USE OF FORCE 165 (3d ed., 2008); DINSTEIN, *supra* note 27, at 197–98.

[73] U.N. SECRETARY-GENERAL, REPORT OF THE HIGH-LEVEL PANEL ON THREATS, CHALLENGES AND CHANGE, A MORE SECURE WORLD: OUR SHARED RESPONSIBILITY ¶¶ 188–89 (2004), http://www.un.org/en/peacebuilding/pdf/historical/hlp_more_secure_world.pdf; Nicaragua, *supra* note 7, ¶ 173 (Dissenting Opinion of Judge Schwebel) (indicating that art. 51 is only one form of self-defense); DINSTEIN,

customary.[74] In contrast, preemptive self-defense is mostly regarded as too remote to justify the use of military force.[75] When Israel attacked Iraq's Osirak nuclear facility in 1981, the majority view was that the requirement of imminence had not been met. The attack was condemned by the Security Council,[76] and not recognized as a lawful act of self-defense, although Israel had thus justified its actions.[77] States that recognize the validity of anticipatory self-defense in case of an imminent attack, pursuant to the *Caroline* doctrine, denied that the conditions were met in that case, which was more akin to preemptive self-defense than anticipatory self-defense.[78] Legal scholars continue to resist preemptive self-defense, and rightly so.[79]

III. Underground Threats *Not* Giving Rise to a Right of Self-Defense

As explained in Chapter 3, even cross-border tunnels that do not rise to the threshold of an armed attack violate some fundamental international norms: states' rights to territorial integrity and sovereignty. The victim state should be entitled to uphold these rights. Two questions arise: first, whether, in the specific context of underground warfare, the rights are violated when a tunnel emanating from foreign territory comes close to the border, but without actually crossing it; and second, how states can uphold such rights.

A. VIOLATION OF SOVEREIGNTY AND TERRITORIAL INTEGRITY

Cross-border tunnels embody a violation of the victim state's sovereignty and territorial integrity. As such, tunnels differ from cyberattacks: the latter violate the sovereignty (at a minimum when they cause damage), but not the territorial integrity, of the victim state.[80]

Territorial integrity, an "essential foundation of international relations,"[81] refers to a state's right to the exclusive exercise of sovereign powers within its own

---

supra note 27, at 196; U.N. Secretary-General, *In Larger Freedom: Towards Development, Security and Human Rights for All*, ¶ 124, U.N. Doc. A/59/2005 (Mar. 21, 2005) [hereinafter *In Larger Freedom*].

[74] Distefano, *supra* note 44, at 561.

[75] This is true in spite of the doctrine's endorsement by the United States in the so-called "Bush doctrine" (NSC, THE NATIONAL SECURITY STRATEGY OF THE UNITED STATES OF AMERICA (2006), at 26: "If necessary, however, under long-standing principles of self-defense, we do not rule out the use of force before attacks occur, even if uncertainty remains as to the time and place of the enemy's attack"; Deeks, *supra* note 57, at 667).

[76] S.C. Res. 487, U.N. Doc. S/RES/487 (June 19, 1981).

[77] UNITED NATIONS, REPERTOIRE OF THE PRACTICE OF THE SECURITY COUNCIL 1981–1984, at 203, http://www.un.org/en/sc/repertoire/81-84/Chapter%208/81-84_08-6-Complaint%20by%20Iraq%20.pdf.

[78] Schachter, *The Right of States*, *supra* note 54, at 1635.

[79] Tams, *supra* note 34, at 390; Kretzmer, *supra* note 31, at 248; Terry D. Gill & Paul A.L. Ducheine, *Anticipatory Self-Defense in the Cyber Context*, 89 INT'L L. STUD. 438, 470 (2013).

[80] TALLINN MANUAL, *supra* note 10, at 16.

[81] Corfu, *supra* note 10, at 35.

borders.[82] Although it has existed since the eighteenth century "as a basic rule of co-existence,"[83] it was formally expressed following World War I in Article 10 of the League of Nations Covenant: "The members of the League undertake to respect and preserve as against external aggression the territorial integrity and existing political independence of all Members of the League." It was later incorporated into many international legal instruments and treaties—up until 1945 and the affirmation of states' obligation not to violate other states' territorial integrity in the UN Charter.[84] Though the principle has been reiterated in instruments such as the Charter of the Organization for African Unity[85] and the Helsinki Final Act of 1975,[86] and is regarded as a fundamental pillar of inter-state relations,[87] it has generated surprisingly little legal scholarship.

Violations of territorial integrity have been found in boundary disputes where a state was present on the territory of another,[88] where one state's forces entered the territory of another without permission,[89] or in cases of military invasion and occupation.[90] In all these situations, State A is on State B's territory without State B's consent. The difference between the various scenarios lies in the *intention* of State A, that is, whether the incursion on the territory of State B is intentional or merely accidental.

In the case of cross-border tunnels, intention can be presumed: a state (or other entity) does not dig a tunnel reaching into the territory of another based on the mistaken assumption that the territory is its own. For this reason, it can be presumed that cross-border tunnels are dug with hostile intent. The data retrieved from the *New York Times* archives confirms this: most reported uses of tunnels in armed conflict embody some kind of hostile purpose.

What remedies are available to the victim state in such a situation? The victim state might wish to uphold its right to sovereignty and territorial integrity by turning to

---

[82] MALCOLM SHAW, INTERNATIONAL LAW 377, 838 (7th ed. 2014); Island of Palmas (Neth. v. U.S.), 2 R.I.A.A. 829 (Perm. Ct. Arb. 1928).

[83] Mark W. Zacher, *The Territorial Integrity Norm: International Boundaries and the Use of Force*, 55 INT'L ORG. 215, 217–18 (2001) (citing HEDLEY BULL, THE ANARCHICAL SOCIETY 34–37 (1977)).

[84] Zacher, *supra* note 83, at 219.

[85] Charter of the Organization of African Unity, Preamble, art. II, May 25, 1963, 479 U.N.T.S. 39.

[86] The Final Act of the Conference on Security and Cooperation in Europe, Preamble (Section IV), Aug. 1, 1975, 14 I.L.M. 1292.

[87] Accordance with International Law of the Unilateral Declaration of Independence in Respect of Kosovo, Advisory Opinion, 2010 I.C.J. 403, ¶ 80 (July 22) [hereinafter Kosovo Advisory Opinion].

[88] Land and Maritime Boundary between Cameroon and Nigeria (Cam. v. Nig: Eq. Guinea Intervening), 2002 I.C.J. 303 (Oct. 10) [hereinafter Land and Maritime Boundary]; Certain Activities Carried Out in the Border Area (Costa Rica v. Nic.), 2015 I.C.J. 1 (Dec. 16) [hereinafter Certain Activities]; Temple of Preah Vihear (Cam. v. Thai.), 1962 I.C.J. 6 (June 15) [hereinafter Preah Vihear]; Territorial Dispute (Libya v. Chad), 1994 I.C.J. 6 (Feb. 3) [hereinafter Territorial Dispute].

[89] Corfu, supra note 10, at 35; Nicaragua, *supra* note 7, ¶ 251.

[90] S.C. Res. 822, U.N. Doc. S/RES/822 (Apr. 30, 1993); S.C. Res. 853, U.N. Doc. S/RES/853 (July 29, 1993); S.C. Res. 874, U.N. Doc. S/RES/874 (Oct. 14, 1993); S.C. Res. 884, U.N. Doc. S/RES/884 (Nov. 12, 1993).

the United Nations Security Council or the ICJ. These institutions have taken a variety of measures in reaction to violations of territorial integrity, by issuing declarations of illegality—qualifying as such the incursion of the United Kingdom into Albania's territorial waters[91]—or by calling for the withdrawal of forces (for example, following Eritrea's military action against Djibouti in Ras Doumeira and Doumeira Island).[92] The Security Council has regularly reaffirmed "the inviolability of international borders," including, inter alia, in the wake of Iraq's invasion of Kuwait[93] and in the context of Zaire in 1997.[94] At times, the Security Council has reacted to violations of territorial integrity by calling for negotiations and cooperation between the parties[95] or by creating UN missions charged with maintaining security.[96] When the violation of territorial integrity results from the presence of foreign actors in disputed areas, both the ICJ and the Security Council have called for withdrawal from those areas.[97] In a 2011 Order of Provisional Measures in the *Request for Interpretation of the Judgment of 15 June 1962 in the Case Concerning the Temple of Preah Vihear*, the ICJ ordered Cambodia and Thailand to withdraw *beyond* the disputed area and create a demilitarized zone.[98]

Declarations of illegality, condemnations, calls for cooperation and negotiation, and the creation of demilitarized zones could all be relevant in the context of cross-border tunnels. The creation of a demilitarized zone on both sides of the border seems

---

[91] Corfu, supra note 10, at 35; Land and Maritime Boundary, *supra* note 88, ¶ 319; Certain Activities, *supra* note 88, ¶¶ 97, 99.

[92] S.C. Pres. Statement 2008/20, U.N. Doc. S/PRST/2008/20 (June 12, 2008) (regarding the conflict between Djibouti and Eritrea).

[93] S.C. Res. 687, paras. 2, 4, U.N. Doc. S/RES/687 (Apr. 3, 1991).

[94] S.C. Pres. Statement 1997/5, para. 3, S/PRST/1997/5 (Feb. 7, 1997). For another example (the conflict between Armenia and Azerbaijan and the seizure of territory in the Nagorno-Karabakh region in southwestern Azerbaijan), see S.C. Res. 853, *supra* note 90, ¶ 1.

[95] S.C. Res. 2046, U.N. Doc. S/RES/2046 (May 2, 2012) (regarding the conflict between Sudan and South Sudan); S.C. Res. 1862, U.N. Doc. S/RES/1862 (Jan. 14, 2009) (regarding the conflict between Djibouti and Eritrea).

[96] S.C. Res. 1990, U.N. Doc. S/RES/1990 (June 27, 2011) (establishing the United Nations Interim Security Force for Abyei (UNISFA)).

[97] *See, inter alia*, S.C. Res. 822, *supra* note 90; S.C. Res. 1990, *supra* note 96; S.C. Res. 2032, U.N. Doc. S/RES/2032 (Dec. 22, 2011); S.C. Res. 2046, *supra* note 95; S.C. Res. 1862, *supra* note 95; Frontier Dispute (Burkina Faso v. Mali), Provisional Measures, Order of January 1986, 1986 I.C.J. 3, ¶ 13 (Jan. 10); Land and Maritime Boundary between Cameroon and Nigeria (Cam. v. Nig.), Provisional Measures, Order of Mar. 15, 1996, 1996 I.C.J. 13, ¶ 49(3) (Mar. 15); Certain Activities Carried Out by Nicaragua in the Border Area (Costa Rica v. Nic.), Provisional Measures, Order of Mar. 8, 2011, 2011 I.C.J. (I) 27, ¶ 86(1) (Mar. 8); Preah Vihear, *supra* note 88, at 37; Territorial Dispute, *supra* note 88; Land and Maritime Boundary, *supra* note 88, ¶¶ 315, 319; Certain Activities, *supra* note 88, ¶ 92.

[98] Request for Interpretation of the Judgment of 15 June 1962 in the Case concerning the Temple of Preah Vihear (Camb. v. Thai.), Provisional Measures, Order of 18 July 2011, 2011, I.C.J. 537, ¶¶ 61–63. Several judges criticized this order on the ground that it prohibited both states from entering territory of their own that was not disputed, thereby overstepping the Court's authority (see ¶¶ 9–11 (Dissenting Opinion of Judge Owada); ¶ 27 (Dissenting Opinion of Judge Donoghue); 75 (Dissenting Opinion of Judge Xue); 565 (Dissenting Opinion of Judge Al-Khasawneh)).

particularly promising, as it could prevent the use of existing tunnels, their expansion, and the digging of new tunnels. Although the measure raised objections in the *Preah Vihear* Request for Interpretation—namely, that international institutions cannot demand that states withdraw from their *own* territory—for lack of alternatives such a measure could be warranted in the case of cross-border tunnels.[99]

In sum, the violation of territorial integrity by cross-border tunnel(s) can and should be condemned by the ICJ and/or the United Nations Security Council. It is then up to the relevant institution to take additional steps such as ordering withdrawal, establishing a demilitarized zone, or calling for a peaceful resolution of the dispute. For these measures to offer some solace to the victim state, they ought to be adopted shortly after the discovery of the tunnel(s), and their implementation carefully monitored to ensure that the digging effectively comes to a halt.

B. ILLEGAL INTERVENTION IN THE AFFAIRS OF ANOTHER STATE

In addition to constituting a violation of territorial integrity, tunnels may at times also qualify as illegal intervention in the affairs of the victim state. An illegal intervention is one that uses coercion—not necessarily in the form of force—in a field under the state's exclusive control[100] such as their political, economic, social and cultural system, or the formulation of foreign policy.[101] Intervention can take many forms, "from the notion of any interference at all in the state's affairs at the one end, to the concept of military intervention at the other."[102] As Rosalyn Higgins further explains, "one cannot simply indicate a particular point along the spectrum and assert that everything from there onwards is an

---

[99] Xue, *supra* note 98, ¶¶ 76–77.
[100] Nicaragua, *supra* note 7, ¶ 205; Armed Activities, *supra* note 24, ¶ 164.
[101] Nicaragua, *supra* note 7, ¶ 205. The prohibition on intervention is not expressly formulated in the UN Charter but can be derived from its Articles 2(1) and 2(4). The 1965 Declaration on the Inadmissibility of Intervention in the Domestic Affairs of States and the Protection of Their Independence and Sovereignty further provides as follows:

1. No State has the right to intervene, directly or indirectly, for any reason whatever, in the internal or external affairs of any other State. Consequently, armed intervention and all other forms of interference or attempted threats against the personality of the State or against its political, economic and cultural elements, are condemned.

2. No State may use or encourage the use of economic, political or any other type of measures to coerce another State in order to obtain from it the subordination of the exercise of its sovereign rights or to secure from it advantages of any kind. Also, no State shall organize, assist, foment, finance, incite or tolerate subversive, terrorist or armed activities directed towards the violent overthrow of the regime of another State, or interfere in civil strife in another State.

G.A. Res. 2131 (XX), ¶¶ 1–2, U.N. Doc. A/Res/20/2131 (Dec. 21, 1965).
[102] Rosalyn Higgins, *Intervention and International Law*, in INTERVENTION IN WORLD POLITICS 30 (Hedley Bull ed., 1984).

unlawful intervention and everything prior to that point is a tolerable interference, and one of the things we put up with in an interdependent world."[103]

Illegal interventions include, inter alia, the manipulation of elections,[104] attempts at changing domestic public opinion,[105] and interference in civil wars, whether directly or by proxy.[106] Certain cross-border tunnels fall within this spectrum. Smuggling tunnels, for example, can have a dramatic impact on a state's economy. Cross-border tunnels would also amount to an unlawful intervention if they are designed to assist rebel forces in the victim state, or otherwise attempt to overthrow or undermine that state's government.

Beyond this traditional application of noninterference, the digging of a tunnel could, *in and of itself,* constitute an illegal intervention: states have exclusive competence regarding their own borders, and digging a tunnel underneath those borders undermines the victim state's sovereign authority in that regard. The principles of sovereignty and territorial integrity, as well as the prohibition on the use of force (discussed in the next section), are deeply intertwined and can be difficult to untangle: a use of force constitutes an illegal intervention,[107] which can entail a violation of territorial integrity.[108] Digging a tunnel on another state's territory could, arguably, constitute all three: an illegal intervention because it interferes with a state's control of its borders, a violation of territorial integrity because it infringes upon a sovereign's territory without its consent, and a use of force by virtue of the digging itself, as I further explore below.[109]

C. ILLEGAL THREAT OR USE OF FORCE

Unless the construction of a tunnel is claimed to be an act of self-defense by the digging state (a situation I envisage above), the digging of a tunnel may constitute an illegal threat or use of force. Force, prohibited under Article 2(4) of the UN Charter, is generally interpreted as referring to *armed* force rather than economic or political coercion.[110]

---

[103] *Id.*
[104] TALLINN MANUAL, *supra* note 10, at 47.
[105] Terry Gill, *Non-intervention in the Cyber Context, in* PEACETIME REGIME FOR STATE ACTIVITIES IN CYBERSPACE 217, 234 (Katharina Ziolkowski ed., 2013).
[106] Nicaragua, *supra* note 7, ¶ 242; Armed Activities, *supra* note 24, ¶ 280.
[107] Nicaragua, *supra* note 7, ¶ 204.
[108] Niki Aloupi, *The Right to Non-intervention and Non-interference,* 4 CAMBRIDGE J. INT'L & COMPARATIVE L. 566, 572 (2015).
[109] However, the fact that all three might exist does not mean that all would need to be dealt with separately, or even identified independently: for example, in the 2015 *Certain Activities in the Border Area* case, the ICJ decided that a finding of a violation of territorial integrity by Nicaragua against Costa Rica made it unnecessary to examine whether the incident also constituted a use of force. Certain Activities, *supra* note 88, ¶ 97.
[110] Albrecht Randelzhofer, *Article 2(4), in* 1 THE CHARTER OF THE UNITED NATIONS: A COMMENTARY 112, 117 (Bruno Simma, Daniel-Erasmus Khan, Georg Nolte & Andreas Paulus eds., 3d ed. 2012); DINSTEIN, *supra* note 27, at 86; Matthew C. Waxman, *Cyber-Attacks and the Use of Force: Back to the Future of Article 2(4),* 36 YALE J. INT'L L. 421, 427 (2011).

It can be exercised using any type of weapon, kinetic or not.[111] Computers and chemical and biological agents certainly count as weapons in this context.[112] The ICJ has qualified acts as different as the arming of rebels[113] and frontier incidents[114] as uses of force. Even tunnels that are not currently in use could therefore amount to "force" in the meaning of Article 2(4). In the view of the experts who compiled the Tallinn Manual, the method of warfare employed is not the determinant factor in the qualification of a cyberattack as use of force. Instead, the International Group of Experts placed the emphasis on the effects of the attack:[115]

> It is universally accepted that chemical, biological, and radiological attacks of the requisite scale and effects to constitute armed attacks trigger the right of self-defence. This is so, despite their non-kinetic nature, because the ensuing consequences can include serious suffering or death. Identical reasoning would apply to cyber operations.[116]

Severity is treated by the Tallinn Manual as the determining factor behind the qualification as use of force. It refers to any physical harm resulting from the act—damage, destruction, injury, or death—as opposed to inconvenience or irritation. The Tallinn Manual offers seven additional criteria to assess whether a cyberattack amounts to a use of force. In the terms of the manual itself, these are "merely factors that influence States making use of force assessments" rather than formal, or exhaustive, legal criteria. In addition to severity, the list includes immediacy (whether the harmful effects have immediate consequences or take weeks or months to materialize), directness (the causal link between the act and its effects), invasiveness (to what extent the act intrudes into the target state, contrary to that state's interests), the measurability of effects (visibility, quantifiability, and identifiability of the consequences of the act—as opposed to acts whose consequences are subjective or difficult to measure), military character (nexus with military operations), state involvement (level of connection to the state), and presumptive legality (lawful acts are less likely to be considered as uses of force).[117]

All these criteria are met in the case of cross-border tunnels, with the exception of state involvement if the tunnel was dug or used by a nonstate actor. That the digging of the tunnel—the kinetic aspect of the attack—was already completed days, decades,

---

[111] Nuclear Weapons, *supra* note 41, ¶ 39.
[112] Marco Roscini, *World Wide Warfare—"Jus ad Bellum" and the Use of Cyber Force*, 14 MAX PLANCK Y.B. OF U.N. L. 85, 106 (2010).
[113] Nicaragua, *supra* note 7, ¶ 228.
[114] *Id.* ¶ 175.
[115] TALLINN MANUAL, *supra* note 10, at 49.
[116] *Id.* at 54–55.
[117] *Id.* at 48–52.

or perhaps even millennia ago does not preclude the tunnel from producing immediate harmful effects. Even if some preexisting tunnels (naturally-formed caves or preexisting underground civilian infrastructure such as subways and sewage systems) may not meet the immediacy and directness requirements under the Tallinn test, the *use* of those structures would amount to a use of force. (It could also amount, as I explain below, to an armed attack or give rise to anticipatory self-defense.) More importantly, tunnels that come close to the border, without actually crossing it, qualify as a use of force provided they are designed for the purpose of carrying out an attack. This is because the tunnel then serves as a weapon of sorts. In other situations—that is, when the intention of the tunnel-diggers cannot be established with certainty—such uncompleted tunnels would merely amount to a threat of the use of force.

Threats of the use of force are also prohibited under Article 2(4). Such threats consist of "an express or implied promise by a government of a resort to force conditional on non-acceptance of certain demands of that government."[118] In general, a threat is illegal when the force threatened, if carried out, would be considered illegal.[119] Beyond these general guidelines, a lack of consistency and clear-cut criteria permeates the interpretation and finding of a threat of the use of force.

At times a threat has been recognized even though it did not meet all the above criteria.[120] For example, the Security Council has twice condemned Iran's unconditional threats to "wipe Israel off the face of the earth," even though the threat was not conditional on non-acceptance of certain demands.[121] Similarly, threats have been recognized even when they were merely implicit.[122] Engaging in overt military maneuvers, deploying certain weapons, and moving army units into proximity of the target can constitute implicit threats of the use of force.[123] However, armament does not, in and of itself, constitute a threat.[124]

---

[118] IAN BROWNLIE, INTERNATIONAL LAW AND THE USE OF FORCE BY STATES 364 (1963).

[119] *Id.* at 364; Nuclear Weapons, *supra* note 41, ¶ 47.

[120] Nicholas Tsagourias, *The Prohibition of Threats of Force, in* RESEARCH HANDBOOK ON INTERNATIONAL CONFLICT AND SECURITY LAW 13 (Nigel White & Christian Henderson eds., 2012), http://ssrn.com/abstract=2074015; Marco Roscini, *Threats of Armed Force and Contemporary International Law*, 54 NETH. INT'L L. R. 229, 235 (2007); DINSTEIN, *supra* note 27, at 89.

[121] Press Release, Security Council, Security Council Press Statement on Iran, U.N. Press Release SC/8542 (Oct. 28, 2005); Press Release, Security Council, Security Council Press Statement on Remarks by Iran's President, U.N. Press Release SC/8576 (Dec. 9, 2005).

[122] Documents of the Forty-First Sess., [1989] 2 Y.B. Int'l L. Comm'n, U.N. Doc. A/CN.4/SER.A/1989/Add. 1, at 68 [hereinafter YILC]; Romana Sadurska, *Threats of Force*, 82 AM. J. INT'L. L. 239, 242 (1988); Roscini, *supra* note 120, at 235.

[123] Sadurska, *supra* note 122, at 243.

[124] Nicaragua, *supra* note 7, ¶ 269 ("In international law there are no rules, other than such rules as may be accepted by the State concerned, by treaty or otherwise, whereby the level of armaments of a sovereign State can be limited...").

A lack of consensus also exists as to whether the threat should be analyzed objectively or in its political, geographical, and historical context.[125] In the view of the International Law Commission, the threat must be objective in the sense that any state would believe that aggression was being threatened.[126] In contrast, some scholars emphasize the importance of context and the impact of the threat on the behavior of the intended target.[127] The *Guyana v. Suriname* Arbitral Award of 2007 aptly illustrates this approach. Surinamese naval officers warned a Guyanese vessel, the *C.E. Thornton*, to leave Surinamese waters within 12 hours, "or the consequences would be theirs."[128] One of the witnesses who had been onboard the ship understood the warning "to mean that if the *C.E. Thornton* and its support vessels did not leave the area within twelve hours, the gunboats would be unconstrained to use armed force against the rig and its service vessels."[129] Despite the fact that the Surinamese Navy claimed to have had no such intention,[130] the arbitral tribunal found that the warning amounted to a threat of force based on the subjective perceptions of those onboard:

> . . . in the circumstances of the present case, this Tribunal is of the view that the action mounted by Suriname on 3 June 2000 seemed more akin to a threat of military action rather than a mere law enforcement activity. This Tribunal has based this finding primarily on the testimony of witnesses to the incident.[131]

The pressure resulting from the threat played a significant role in the arbitral tribunal's reaching this conclusion—an element highly relevant in the context of tunnels, which are known to create fear and anxiety.[132]

Considering these diverging views, it is difficult to reach a conclusive determination as to when a tunnel, once dug across the border, may constitute a threat of the use of force. As the ICJ has indicated, penetration into foreign territory is not the sole determinant of whether a threat exists. In the case of cross-border tunnels, the infringement of

---

[125] OLIVIER CORTEN, THE LAW AGAINST WAR: THE PROHIBITION ON THE USE OF FORCE IN CONTEMPORARY INTERNATIONAL LAW 109–10 (2010).

[126] YILC, *supra* note 122.

[127] Tsagourias, *supra* note 120, at 16 and 244 ("Only communications that arouse the anticipation of severe deprivation or destruction of values in the target audience and, hence, trigger a reaction of stress that leads to accommodating or adaptive behavior as the only reasonable alternative can be regarded as a threat.").

[128] The Delimitation of the Maritime Boundary between Guyana and Suriname (Guy. v. Sur.), 30 R.I.A.A. 1, ¶¶ 436–39, 445 (Perm. Ct. Arb. 2007) [hereinafter Guyana v. Suriname].

[129] *Id.* ¶ 433 (emphasis added).

[130] *Id.* ¶ 437.

[131] *Id.* ¶ 445.

[132] STATE OF ISRAEL, THE 2014 GAZA CONFLICT REPORT: FACTUAL AND LEGAL ASPECTS ¶¶ 60–61 (2015); U.N. Human Rights Council, *Rep. of the Detailed Findings of the Independent Commission of Inquiry Established Pursuant to Human Rights Council Resolution S-21/1*, ¶ 74, U.N. Doc. A/HRC/29/CRP.4 (June 24, 2015). *See infra* Chapter 7 for a discussion of the use of tunnels near and against civilians.

sovereignty and territorial integrity and the threat of a tunnel-based attack are accompanied by a strong psychological impact. Although proof of hostile intent is not indispensable to show a violation of Article 2(4), it increases the likelihood of a finding that a threat exists. For example, if weapons or explosives are found inside the tunnel or if the target state has been the victim of tunnel attacks in the past, the tunnel would be more likely to be regarded as a threat of the use of force. In conclusion, the digging of a cross-border tunnel that has not yet crossed the border constitutes a threat of the use of force (though not a use of force) under Article 2(4) of the UN Charter. A completed cross-border tunnel would amount to both a threat of the use of force and a use of force under this provision. In any event, in both cases the range of permitted responses is the same.

This analysis is conditional on the use of force itself being unlawful. What if the tunnel was dug/used as part of a state's claim to self-defense? Whether the digging or use of a tunnel can constitute a measure validly taken in self-defense turns, once again, on the concept of imminence.[133] As explained above, self-defense enables states to address urgent, imminent threats: "Immediacy is hereby understood as referring to the temporal relation between the armed attack and the self-defence response. Requirement of immediacy would mean that the victim of the armed attack needed to respond without delay in order for the self-defence to be legitimate."[134]

This does not mean that the action in self-defense must be taken exactly at the time the right crystallizes, as states need time to identify the attacker and prepare a response. The standard is one of reasonableness.[135] The digging of a tunnel takes months, if not years, of planning and labor. As such, it would be an odd expression of self-defense. The use of preexisting tunnels—as opposed to the digging of fresh ones—could conceivably meet the relevant criteria and be considered a lawful exercise of self-defense.

D. POSSIBLE RESPONSES

1. Countermeasures

Provided a state has dug the tunnel, the victim state can respond via countermeasures in all the scenarios envisaged so far—namely when the tunnel constitutes a violation of sovereignty and territorial integrity, unlawful interference in the affairs of another state, or a threat or use of force.

Countermeasures are widely accepted in principle. The International Law Commission's Draft Articles on State Responsibility for Internationally Wrongful Acts ("Draft Articles"), and their commentary, lay out fundamental and well-established rules. Yet there is little in terms of legal scholarship analyzing or applying these rules. The Tallinn

---

[133] *See supra* Section II(B) for a discussion of imminence.
[134] LUBELL, *supra* note 9, at 44.
[135] TALLINN MANUAL, *supra* note 10, at 62.

Manual discusses at length the meaning and limits of countermeasures in the context of cyber, and as such significantly contributes to this relatively under-theorized area of international law. In the view of the experts in the Tallinn process, countermeasures are available when a violation of sovereignty (such as a cyberattack) does not rise to the level of an armed attack.[136]

Countermeasures are defined as "[s]tate actions, or omissions, directed at another State that would otherwise violate an obligation owed to that State and that are conducted by the former in order to compel or convince the latter to desist in its own internationally wrongful acts or omissions."[137] Countermeasures do not have to be in kind. The victim state of a cross-border tunnel could use cyber means, for example, to exercise pressure on the tunnel-digger. One could even imagine a corollary to Duncan Hollis's "duty to hack"[138] under the *jus ad bellum*: perhaps the victim state should be *obligated* to use cyber if it offers the least damaging way to avert the danger created by the wrongful digging (for example, by convincing the tunnel-digger not to move forward with the attack)? Though intellectually appealing, cyber countermeasures would not destroy the tunnels. The threat would remain.

In principle, countermeasures can only be employed against states, and only insofar as a state is responsible for an internationally wrongful act.[139] Assuming that nonstate armed groups dug a cross-border tunnel, they could not, *de lege lata*, be made the subject of countermeasures. At a time when responsibility for internationally wrongful acts increasingly reaches beyond the state to international organizations[140] and corporations,[141] the Draft Articles' state-centric view of countermeasures seems anachronistic. Armed groups can also be held accountable for violations of IHL under Common Article 3 or Additional Protocol II, and individual members may be criminally liable.[142] These forms of responsibility, however, differ from the liability of states for internationally wrongful

---

[136] *Id.* at Rule 9.

[137] Michael N. Schmitt, *"Below the Threshold" Cyber Operations: The Countermeasures Response Option and International Law*, 54 VIRGINIA J. INT'L L. 697, 700–01 (2013).

[138] Duncan B. Hollis, *Re-thinking the Boundaries of Law in Cyberspace: A Duty to Hack?*, in CYBERWAR: LAW & ETHICS FOR VIRTUAL CONFLICTS 42 (Jens David Ohlin, Kevin Govern & Claire Finkelstein eds., 2014) ("IHL should require States to use cyber-operations in their military operations when they are expected to be the least harmful means available for achieving military objectives.")

[139] Draft Articles, *supra* note 5, at art. 22.

[140] *Draft Articles on the Responsibility of International Organizations, in the* Rep. of the Int'l L. Comm'n, 63d Sess., Apr. 26–June 3, July 4–Aug. 12, 2011, U.N. Doc. A/66/10; GAOR 66th Sess., Supp. No. 10 (2011), ¶ 87 [hereinafter "DARIO"].

[141] U.N. Human Rights Council, Report of the Special Representative of the Secretary General on the issue of human rights and transnational corporations and other business enterprises, John Ruggie: Guiding Principles on Business and Human Rights: Implementing the United Nations "Protect, Respect and Remedy" Framework, U.N. Doc. A/HRC/17/31 (Mar. 21, 2011).

[142] David Weissbrodt, *The Roles and Responsibilities of Non-state Actors*, in THE OXFORD HANDBOOK OF INTERNATIONAL HUMAN RIGHTS LAW 734–35 (Dinah Shelton ed., 2013). These points will be further addressed in Chapter 7.

acts.[143] Whereas the focus of state responsibility is *restorative*—it is designed to allow the victim state and the violator state to return to normal relations[144]—the responsibility of nonstate armed groups is criminal, with a punitive goal.[145] Nevertheless, some scholars have argued that armed groups could, or at least should, be subject to the regime of international responsibility.[146]

Accepting that states can take countermeasures against nonstate armed groups implies that the latter owe states certain obligations. When a nonstate group digs a cross-border tunnel, does it violate the neighboring state's territorial integrity, sovereignty, or norms on the use of force? It is far from clear that nonstate actors are bound by these norms, and can be held accountable for not respecting them under the rules governing countermeasures.[147] Even if one takes the view that countermeasures can be undertaken against nonstate actors, other limitations would of course still apply.

The state invoking the countermeasures must call upon the state in violation to comply with its obligations, notify the violating state of the decision to take countermeasures, and offer to negotiate. The countermeasures must be cancelled or suspended if the wrongful act ceases and the dispute is submitted in good faith to a body with the authority to make a decision binding on the parties.[148] Notwithstanding, the wronged state may take "such urgent countermeasures as are necessary to preserve its rights" prior to notification,[149] specifically where notification would allow the target state to protect itself from the impending countermeasures.[150] Countermeasures must also, as far as possible, be temporary, allow the future resumption of the mutual obligations of the two states,[151] and aim at inducing the attacking state to comply with its obligations under international law.[152] They must facilitate the resumption of lawful interaction and lead to the cessation of

---

[143] Assuming that in almost any case, the group will not fall under the definition of an international organization, defined as "an organization established by a treaty or other instrument governed by international law and possessing its own international legal personality. International organizations may include as members, in addition to States, other entities" (DARIO, *supra* note 140, at art. 2(a)).

[144] JAMES CRAWFORD, THE INTERNATIONAL LAW COMMISSION'S ARTICLES ON STATE RESPONSIBILITY: INTRODUCTION, TEXT AND COMMENTARIES 283 (2002) [hereinafter DRAFT ARTICLES COMMENTARY].

[145] Kimberley Tripp, *Shared Responsibility and Non-state Terrorist Groups*, 62 NETH. INT'L L. REV. 141, 147 (2015).

[146] *See, e.g.,* Nicholas Tsagourias, *Non-state Actors, Ungoverned Spaces and International Responsibility for Cyber Acts*, 21 J. CONFLICT & SEC. L. 455 (2016); Veronika Bílková, *Armed Opposition Groups and Shared Responsibility*, 62 NETH. INT'L L. REV. 69, 75 (2015).

[147] Kosovo Advisory Opinion, *supra* note 87, ¶ 80 (noting that the principle of territorial integrity is relevant in inter-state relations).

[148] Draft Articles, *supra* note 5, at art. 52; DRAFT ARTICLES COMMENTARY, *supra* note 144.

[149] Draft Articles, *supra* note 5, at art. 52(2).

[150] Yuji Iwasawa & Naoki Iwatsuki, *Procedural Conditions*, in THE LAW OF INTERNATIONAL RESPONSIBILITY 1149, 1154 (James Crawford, Alain Pellet & Simon Olleson eds., 2010).

[151] *Id.*

[152] Draft Articles, *supra* note 5, at art. 49.

the wrongful act—without triggering escalation. Though countermeasures should not be punitive in nature, in practice states have often resorted to punitive countermeasures (i.e., bringing the violating state into conformity with international law was not the only goal pursued by the countermeasures).[153] State practice notwithstanding, scholars continue to uphold their illegality.[154] In this regard, countermeasures must be distinguished from acts of retorsion, such as the cutting of diplomatic ties, which are legal but "unfriendly," and *can* be punitive in nature.[155]

Countermeasures must also be proportionate to the injury suffered by the victim state.[156] They may not prejudice the interests of third-party states. Finally, countermeasures may not entail the use of force or violate a norm of *jus cogens*.[157] These latter aspects are arguably the most debated in the context of countermeasures.

In relation to the former—the (il)legality of forceful countermeasures[158]—an interesting compromise was suggested by Judge Simma in the *Oil Platforms* case. In his separate opinion, Judge Simma advocates "proportionate defensive measures," namely forceful countermeasures used in response to an attack *not* rising to the level of an armed attack.[159] In cases where the victim state suffered from a use of force *not* amounting to an armed attack, defensive action below the level of armed attack would be permitted in response. In the realm of underground warfare, it would enable the victim state to use limited, forceful countermeasures aimed exclusively at the destruction of the cross-border tunnel(s) on foreign territory.[160] Arguably, such forceful countermeasures would also be available in situations where cross-border tunnels come close to, but without actually crossing, the border. Though this view has gained some support in the past decade, it does not enjoy universal acceptance.[161]

---

[153] TALLINN MANUAL, *supra* note 10, at 49; Press Release, U.N. General Assembly, "Archaic, Punitive" Embargo Must Be Consigned to History Books, Say Speakers, as General Assembly, for Twenty-First Year, Demands End to Cuban Blockade, U.N. Press Release GA/11311 (Nov. 13, 2012), http://www.un.org/press/en/2012/ga11311.doc.htm.

[154] Roger O'Keefe, *Proportionality, in* THE LAW OF INTERNATIONAL RESPONSIBILITY, *supra* note 150, at 1162; Monica Hakimi, *Unfriendly Unilateralism*, 55 HARV. INT'L L. J. 105, 119 (2014); Tom Ruys, *Sanctions, Retorsions and Countermeasures: Concepts and International Legal Framework, in* RESEARCH HANDBOOK ON UN SANCTIONS AND INTERNATIONAL LAW 1, 2 (Larissa Van den Herik ed., forthcoming 2017).

[155] Thomas Giegerich, *Retorsion, in* 8 MAX PLANCK ENCYCLOPAEDIA OF INTERNATIONAL LAW (2012); DRAFT ARTICLES COMMENTARY, *supra* note 144, at 128.

[156] Draft Articles, *supra* note 5, at art. 51; Schmitt, *supra* note 137, at 723.

[157] Draft Articles, *supra* note 5, at art. 50; Nicaragua, *supra* note 7, ¶ 249.

[158] As noted, *inter alia*, in Nuclear Weapons, *supra* note 41, ¶ 46; CORTEN, *supra* note 125, at 224.

[159] Oil Platforms, *supra* note 31, ¶ 12 (Separate Opinion of Judge Simma).

[160] Importantly, if the victim state destroys the part of the tunnel located *on its own territory*—this would not amount to a countermeasure.

[161] *See* LUBELL, *supra* note 9, at 76 (rejecting this interpretation); Olivier Corten, *Judge Simma's Separate Opinion in the* Oil Platforms *Case: To What Extent Are Armed "Proportionate Defensive Measures" Admissible in Contemporary International Law? In* FROM BILATERALISM TO COMMUNITY INTEREST: ESSAYS IN HONOUR OF BRUNO SIMMA (Ulrich Fastenrath, Rudolph Geiger, Daniel-Erasmus Khan, Andreas Paulus, Sabine Schorlemer & Christoph Vedder eds., 2011).

The second heavily debated aspect relates to the conformity of the countermeasure to norms of *jus cogens*. Just as states remain bound by *jus cogens* norms in their treaty relations, they remain bound by them when undertaking countermeasures.[162] Accordingly, if the prohibition on the use of force amounts to *jus cogens*, forceful countermeasures would be prohibited. Even though most states generally regard the use of force as a peremptory norm, this is not without caveats—particularly considering many proposed new exceptions in the context of the "war on terror."[163] The ICJ has called the prohibition on the use of force a "fundamental or cardinal principle,"[164] and the unlawful use of force an egregious violation of international law,[165] but has not explicitly called it *jus cogens*. In the Commentaries of the Vienna Convention on the Law of Treaties, the ILC offered the prohibition on the use of force as a "conspicuous example of a rule in international law having the character of *jus cogens*."[166] However, in its Draft Articles, the ILC does not mention the prohibition on the use of force in the list of *jus cogens* prohibitions, which includes aggression, genocide, slavery, racial discrimination, crimes against humanity, torture, and the right to self-determination.[167] This does not exclude the use of force per se, of course. Yet there is a difference, in gravity and scope, between the violation of the enumerated norms and a limited tunnel-destruction operation. A limited incursion on foreign territory aimed *exclusively* at destroying a tunnel cannot be compared to aggression, genocide, slavery, or crimes against humanity—all of which suggest violations on a large scale.[168]

2. The Plea of Necessity

The plea of necessity offers the victim state another avenue for relief: it allows localized and pinpointed actions designed to put an end to the security threat posed by the cross-border tunnel(s).

This limited response would allow the victim state to respond to the infringement of sovereignty and territorial integrity, while limiting the outbreak of further violence. As

---

[162] Vienna Convention on the Law of Treaties, art. 53, May 23, 1969, 1155 U.N.T.S. 331; DRAFT ARTICLES COMMENTARY, *supra* note 144, at 132.
[163] Nico Schrijver, *The Ban on the Use of Force in the UN Charter*, *in* THE OXFORD HANDBOOK OF THE USE OF FORCE IN INTERNATIONAL LAW 465, 485–86 (Marc Weller ed., 2015); James A. Green, *Questioning the Peremptory Status of the Prohibition on the Use of Force*, 32 MICH. J. INT'L L. 215, 217 (2011).
[164] Nicaragua, *supra* note 7, at ¶ 190.
[165] Kosovo Advisory Opinion, *supra* note 87, at ¶ 81.
[166] Reports of the International Law Commission on the Second Part of its 17th Sess. and on its 18th Sess., [1966] 2 Y.B. Int'l L. Comm'n 169, U.N. Doc. A/CN.4/SER. A/1966/Add. 1, at 247.
[167] DRAFT ARTICLES COMMENTARY, *supra* note 144, at 85.
[168] For extensive discussion of state, doctrinal, and case-law support for this point, see CORTEN, *supra* note 126, at 201–13. For further discussion on the definition of aggression, *see infra* note 221.

such, the invocation of a state of necessity by the victim state would be an appropriate response to the discovery of a tunnel, or several tunnels, in situations not giving rise to a right to self-defense.

The plea of necessity, however, must remain an exceptional remedy.[169] According to the Draft Articles, *a state* can invoke necessity as a circumstance precluding wrongfulness of an act not in conformity with its international obligations provided (1) that this is the "only way for the State to safeguard an essential interest against a grave and imminent peril";[170] and (2) that this "does not seriously impair an essential interest of the State or States towards which the obligation exists, or the international community as a whole."[171] Necessity cannot be invoked when the victim state has contributed to the situation giving rise to necessity, or when the obligation in question excludes the possibility of invoking necessity.[172] The latter refers to situations in which "the non-availability of the plea of necessity emerges clearly from the object and purpose of the rule [that would be violated]."[173] These provisions are recognized as customary.[174]

The first requirement—that the measures undertaken under the plea of necessity be "the only way for the State to safeguard an essential interest against a grave and imminent peril"—consists of two elements: one related to the threat ("a grave and imminent peril"), and the other related to the response (that it be "the only way" to safeguard the endangered interest). The ICJ held in *Gabčíkovo-Nagymaros* that "a peril appearing in the long term might be held to be 'imminent' as soon as it is established, at the relevant point in time, that the realization of that peril, however far off it might be, is not thereby any less certain and inevitable."[175] The word "peril" invokes the idea of risk, meaning that damage need not have *actually* been caused.[176] Although "a measure of uncertainty" does not preclude a state from invoking necessity,[177] the peril must be "clearly established based on the evidence available at the time."[178] A peril that is "merely apprehended or contingent" cannot justify the invocation of necessity.[179]

---

[169] Gabčíkovo-Nagymaros Project (Hung. v. Slov.), 1997 I.C.J. 7, ¶ 51 (Sept. 25) [hereinafter Gabčíkovo]; Draft Articles Commentary, *supra* note 144, at 83.
[170] Draft Articles, *supra* note 5, at art. 25(1)(a).
[171] *Id.* at art. 25(1)(b).
[172] *Id.* at art. 25(2).
[173] Draft Articles Commentary, *supra* note 144, at 84.
[174] Gabčíkovo, *supra* note 169, ¶¶ 51–52; Wall Advisory Opinion, *supra* note 58, ¶ 140; CMS Gas Transmission v. Arg., I.CSI.D Case No. ARB/01/8, ¶ 315 (2005).
[175] Gabčíkovo, *supra* note 169, ¶ 54.
[176] Sarah Heathcote, *Circumstances Precluding Wrongfulness in the ILC Articles on State Responsibility: Necessity*, in The Law of International Responsibility, *supra* note 150, at 497.
[177] Draft Articles Commentary, *supra* note 144, at 83.
[178] *Id.*
[179] Draft Articles Commentary, *supra* note 144, at 83; Heathcote, *supra* note 176, at 497.

Under the plea of necessity, accordingly, a state could justify the destruction of a tunnel before it has been used for a deadly attack, or even before it has crossed the victim state's borders. It can do so because tunnels can be harnessed discretely and quickly, such that their very existence constitutes a grave and imminent peril for the victim state. Underground threats, by nature, leave little room for action once they materialize.

For a plea of necessity to conform to the law, the response of the victim state—in this case the destruction of the tunnel(s)—must constitute the only way to safeguard its endangered interests. If other means exist, even if they are more costly or less convenient, they ought to be preferred.[180] The factors analyzed in Section I become relevant here. In a scenario where one cross-border tunnel has been discovered in an uninhabited area, with no past history suggesting hostile intent, and there is a functional government on the digging side, the tunnel poses only a relatively low risk. A plea of necessity would not be justified. However, if the tunnel intrudes into a civilian area, or was dug by a party who has dug in the past for hostile purposes, destroying the tunnel(s) completely would be the only way to truly neutralize the risk posed to the victim state. In this situation, a plea of necessity would meet applicable legal standards.

The second requirement posits that measures taken under a plea of necessity cannot "seriously impair an essential interest of the State or State towards which the obligation exists, or the international community as a whole."[181] This is a balancing requirement,[182] which leaves the victim state a lot of leeway in choosing which method to employ. Importantly, the interest being protected must outweigh all other considerations, not only from the point of view of the competing state but also from the perspective of the international community as a whole.[183] Thus, the interest being safeguarded must be of greater importance than that which is temporarily disregarded:[184] for example, the safety of the victim state's civilians must outweigh the territorial integrity of the state from which the tunnel emanates.

Weighing the interests of the victim state against the interests of "the international community as a whole" seems trickier, however. It would matter that the measures taken under a plea of necessity violate erga omnes obligations, that is, obligations that are "the concern of all states" and in whose protection all states share a legal interest.[185] The ICJ has enumerated a number of such obligations, among which aggression, genocide, slavery, and racial discrimination.[186]

---

[180] *Id.*
[181] Draft Articles, *supra* note 5, at art. 25(1)(b).
[182] Roman Boed, *State of Necessity as a Justification for Internationally Wrongful Conduct*, 3 YALE HUM. RIGHTS & DEVELOPMENT J. 1, 18–19 (2000); TALLINN MANUAL, *supra* note 10, at 43.
[183] DRAFT ARTICLES Commentary, *supra* note 144, at 83–84.
[184] Heathcote, *supra* note 176, at 498.
[185] Case Concerning the Barcelona Traction, Light and Power Company, Ltd. (Belg. v. Sp.), 1970 I.C.J. 3, ¶¶ 33–34 (Feb. 5).
[186] *Id.*; Boed, *supra* note 182.

Without undermining the prohibition on the use of force, this is not a situation where the interests of the international community as a whole would have to be part of the equation. The balancing act would be limited to the consideration of the interests of both entities. I would therefore argue, as in the example above, that the interest of the victim state to safeguard its civilians would have to be weighed against the right to territorial integrity of the state from which the tunnel emanates.

Once the respective individual interests have been placed on the balance, the determination whether an "essential interest" has been affected is made on a case-by-case basis, and cannot be prejudged.[187] The plea of necessity is an ex-post, ad hoc defense, and not an ex-ante set of guidelines.[188] In most cases, a limited, pinpointed strike intended to *prevent* escalation and additional uses of force would meet the legal standards set forth under necessity.

More specifically, two additional questions arise when the plea of necessity is invoked to justify measures involving the use of force—namely the physical destruction of the cross-border tunnel(s). First, whether allowing the plea of necessity in the context of the use of force would contradict a *jus cogens* norm, as prohibited under Article 26 of the Draft Articles. Second, whether arguing necessity in such a context would contradict the Draft Articles' directive that Article 25 not be invoked in relation to a primary norm that already contemplates such considerations.

According to the Draft Articles, which provide the most comprehensive elucidation of the plea of necessity to date, necessity (like countermeasures) cannot preclude wrongfulness if the measure undertaken violates a *jus cogens* prohibition.[189] Given the discussion above on the *jus cogens* status of the prohibition on the use of force, how does this affect the invocation of necessity in the situation at hand? The heated debate over the availability of necessity to excuse humanitarian intervention offers some valuable insight. In both cases—in underground warfare as in humanitarian intervention—necessity would be used to excuse a limited use of force on the territory of a foreign state.

The debate is not only heated, but also dated. The relationship between necessity and humanitarian intervention had been raised by the International Law Commission's Special Rapporteur on State Responsibility Roberto Ago in 1980. In a lengthy analysis, Ago contemplated the use of necessity to justify humanitarian intervention—a question he thought should be addressed by the International Law Commission.[190] Ago's successor James Crawford, however, decided not to clearly take a position on the matter. In the end, according to the Draft Articles, "the question whether measures of forcible

---

[187] DRAFT ARTICLES COMMENTARY, *supra* note 144, at 83.
[188] Ian Johnstone, *The Plea of "Necessity" in International Legal Discourse: Humanitarian Intervention and Counter-terrorism*, 43 COLUM. J. TRANSNAT'L L. 337, 365 (2004).
[189] Draft Articles, *supra* note 5, at art. 26.
[190] *See Addendum to the Eighth Rep. on State Responsibility*, *supra* note 47, ¶¶ 1–82; and Andreas Laursen, *The Use of Force and (the State of) Necessity*, 37 VAND. J. TRANSNAT'L L. 485, 513–14 (2004).

humanitarian intervention, not sanctioned pursuant to Chapters VII or VIII of the Charter of the United Nations, may be lawful under modern international law is not covered by article 25."[191]

The debate continues. Some authors advocate in favor of necessity as a lesser evil. They view a narrowly construed necessity as preferable to adding exceptions to the prohibition on the use of force[192] or formulating a new rule allowing humanitarian intervention.[193] Others have put forward the view that "necessity should not, in advance and as a matter of some principle, be rejected as an international law justification for humanitarian intervention or other uses of force."[194] Even Olivier Corten, for whom necessity cannot justify the use of force, concedes that there might be room for distinction between large-scale, grave uses of force and limited ones (such as Israel's capture of Eichmann on Argentinian territory, for example).[195] In situations where the threshold of the use of force under the Charter is not met, a state could invoke necessity.[196]

Beyond the issue of *jus cogens*, some commentators have argued that the *jus ad bellum* takes into account considerations of necessity ab initio in that it allows for exceptions (self-defense and the involvement of the Security Council as part of the collective security system). Put differently, this argument holds that necessity would not be relevant to the prohibition on the use of the force as the norm itself—the primary norm delineating states' obligation—already incorporates similar concerns.

The Draft Articles generally take the view that circumstances precluding wrongfulness should be dealt with via the primary norm. The primary norm is the norm that would be violated were it not for the plea of necessity precluding wrongfulness.[197] If the norm *already* acknowledges situations of necessity, either by accepting them or rejecting them as invalid, the plea of necessity (the secondary norm) is not available: "As embodied in article 25, the plea of necessity is not intended to cover conduct which is in principle regulated by the primary obligations."[198]

To illustrate this, the Draft Articles mention the *jus in bello* concept of military necessity and note that "considerations akin to those underlying article 25 . . . are taken into account in the context of the formulation and interpretation of the primary obligations."[199] In other words, the plea of necessity is of only limited availability in situations where considerations of necessity are already built into the primary norm itself.

---

[191] DRAFT ARTICLES COMMENTARY, *supra* note 144, at 83.
[192] Johnstone, *supra* note 188, at 354.
[193] OSCAR SCHACHTER, INTERNATIONAL LAW IN THEORY AND PRACTICE 126 (1991).
[194] Ole Spiermann, *Humanitarian Intervention as a Necessity and the Threat or Use of* Jus Cogens, 71 NORDIC J. INT'L L. 523, 543 (2002).
[195] *See* Corten, *Necessity*, *supra* note 42, at 867.
[196] *Id.*
[197] DRAFT ARTICLES COMMENTARY, *supra* note 144, at 14–16, 85.
[198] *Id.* at 84.
[199] *Id.* at 85.

This seemingly doctrinal point takes on more concrete meaning when one considers the invocation of necessity in relation to the use of force. Although the plea of necessity is, in principle, unavailable if the applicable primary rule already takes into account considerations akin to those of Article 25, practice tells a different story.[200] Robert Sloane deplores the fact that even though formulations and interpretations of *jus ad bellum* rules do incorporate (or displace) similar concerns, Article 25 has been used as an "additional layer," allowing states to get "two bites at the apple" of necessity.[201]

The ICJ has allowed this application of necessity in at least two instances. In its *Nuclear Weapons* Advisory Opinion, the Court concluded that "the threat or use of nuclear weapons would generally be contrary to the rules of international law applicable in armed conflict"—admitting, however, that it "cannot conclude definitely whether the threat or use of nuclear weapons would be lawful or unlawful in an extreme circumstance of self-defense, in which the very survival of a State would be at stake."[202] The ICJ's tacit reliance on necessity does not sit well with the Draft Articles' command that necessity not apply where the primary norm—here the prohibition on the threat or use of force—*already* acknowledges similar situations. The Court engaged in a similar analysis in its *Wall* opinion: after a discussion on whether Israel's actions violated the *jus ad bellum*, the Court inquired as to the availability of necessity.[203] Although it eventually rejected the argument on the ground that the measures were not the only way to safeguard Israel's interests against the "peril which it has invoked as justification,"[204] it is noteworthy that the ICJ even considered the availability of necessity in that context. In both the *Wall* and the *Nuclear Weapons* Advisory Opinions, the Court distanced itself from the approach advocated by the International Law Commission in the Draft Articles.

---

[200] Robert D. Sloane, *On the Use and Abuse of Necessity in the Law of State Responsibility*, 106 AM. J. INT'L L. 447, 494 (2012).

[201] *Id.* at 494, 497. The *Caroline* incident, most commonly referred to as an incident of self-defense, was, according to the International Law Commission, an instance of necessity—but at a time (1837) when the law regarding use of force was different from the current regime (*see* DRAFT ARTICLES COMMENTARY, *supra* note 144, at 179). In more contemporary times, Belgium has argued necessity twice (once with the backing of the UK (*see* Johnstone, *supra* note 188, at 363))—first to justify its military intervention in the Congo in 1960 (*see* DRAFT ARTICLES COMMENTARY, *supra* note 144, at 84 (quoting to Official Records of the U.N. Security Council, Fifteenth Year, 873rd meeting, July 13–14, 1960, ¶¶ 144, 182 and 192; 877th meeting, July 20–21, 1960, paras. 31 *et seq.* and para. 142; 878th meeting, July 21, 1960, ¶¶ 23 and 65; and 879th meeting, July 21–22, 1960, ¶ 80 *et seq.* and ¶¶ 118 and 151)), and a second time before the ICJ in relation to the NATO bombings in Kosovo (*see* Laursen, *supra* note 190, at 514). Other instances of state practice that have been interpreted as relying on necessity and are, in my view, much less convincing, include Turkey's justifications for various types of incursions and air strikes conducted in Northern Iraq against Kurds (*see* Laursen, *supra* note 190, at 515; and THE INDEPENDENT INTERNATIONAL COMMISSION ON KOSOVO, THE KOSOVO REPORT 4 (2000) [hereinafter KOSOVO REPORT]).

[202] *See* Nuclear Weapons, *supra* note 41, ¶ 105; and Sloane, *supra* note 200, at 496.

[203] Wall Advisory Opinion, *supra* note 58, ¶ 140.

[204] *Id.* ¶¶ 140–142.

In my view, limited incursions designed to destroy cross-border tunnels correspond to what Roberto Ago had in mind when he advocated that "certain actions by States in the territory of other States which, although they may sometimes be coercive in nature, serve only limited intentions and purposes bearing no relation to the purposes characteristic of a true act of aggression," be covered by Article 25. In fact, I would argue that pinpointed operations against cross-border tunnels would at times even meet Ago's stringent test of necessity: "it must be impossible for the peril to be averted by any other means, even one which is much more onerous but which can be adopted without a breach of international obligations."[205]

The reliance of states, scholars, and the ICJ on necessity in the *ad bellum* context—despite the Draft Articles' commands to the contrary—suggests, at a minimum, that the matter remains unresolved. If necessity has not been ruled out in the context of humanitarian intervention, it should not pose any significant obstacle to limited anti-tunnel operations on foreign territory either. Even if necessity is available, the victim state would still have to establish that the cross-border tunnel(s) meet(s) the imminent peril test of Article 25, use restricted measures, and demonstrate awareness of their exceptional nature.

Based on the analysis of the plea of necessity in the context of cyber, the victim state could invoke necessity to destroy a tunnel even if the perpetrators have not been identified. As per the Tallinn Manual, "in cases where the exact nature and, in particular, origin of a cyberattack are unclear, certain protective (cyber) measures may be justified on the basis of necessity. For example, if a cyber-incident endangers a State's essential interests, it may in some cases temporarily shut off certain cyber infrastructure even if doing so affects cyber-systems in other states. Similarly, if faced with significant cyber operations against a State's critical infrastructure, the plea of necessity could justify a State's resort to counter-hacking."[206] This is because, unlike countermeasures, the invocation of necessity does not find its legal justification in the wrongful act of another state, but rather as an extreme measure to safeguard a right from an urgent peril. The issue of attribution is therefore of lesser importance in the context of necessity. There, the priority lies in the right being protected, assuming the conditions analyzed above are complied with.

To conclude, the plea of necessity allows states—and only states—to safeguard their security interests and their right to sovereignty and territorial integrity, while limiting situations of all-out war. Accepting this in no way undermines the exceptional character of necessity as a circumstance precluding wrongfulness. Rather, it prevents the escalation of underground cross-border threats into full-on wars. Oscar Schachter describes necessity as a "safety valve"—making an act "excusable though not legal."[207] Necessity, in his view,

---

[205] *Addendum to the Eighth Rep. on State Responsibility, supra* note 47, ¶ 56, quoted in Sloane, *supra* note 200, at 502. According to Sloane, "[n]either states nor tribunals (or other decision makers) will be likely to construe Article 25 so stringently" (at 502).
[206] TALLINN MANUAL, *supra* note 10, at 43.
[207] Oscar Schachter, *The Lawful Use of Force by a State Against Terrorists in Another Country*, 19 ISR. Y.B. HUMAN RIGHTS 209, 229–30 (1989).

"recognizes that threatened States may be compelled to act against hit-and-run criminals who operate across national borders but not as belligerents in an inter-State armed conflict."[208] Mindful of the need to carefully circumscribe necessity, I believe that it would justify the destruction of a segment of a cross-border tunnel located on another state's territory. Absent the option of destroying it in an isolated, time-limited operation, states are more likely to regard the cross-border tunnel as an armed attack or an act justifying anticipatory self-defense. The exercise of the right to self-defense in response to the digging of cross-border tunnels, albeit justified in some circumstances, is likely to have a more devastating impact—and yet, in practice, to achieve no more than a pinpointed operation under the plea of necessity.

3. Involvement of the UN Security Council

While international law holds states to stringent rules regarding the use of force, the Security Council can take measures involving force in situations presenting a "threat to the peace," a "breach of the peace," or "aggression."[209] The question is whether the discovery of cross-border tunnel(s) could qualify as any of these three options and justify action by the Security Council under Chapter VII of the United Nations Charter. In the case of threats to and breaches of the peace, no actual or potential violation of international law is required—thus giving the Security Council a much broader mandate to act.[210] As explained by then-UN secretary-general Kofi Annan, "where threats are not imminent but latent, the Charter gives full authority to the Security Council to use military force, including preventively, to preserve international peace and security."[211]

When might a cross-border tunnel threat qualify as a threat to the peace under Article 39 of the UN Charter? Of the three situations contemplated in that Article, "threat to the peace" is the broadest and most important—and almost the only one used by the Security Council in practice.[212] A threat to the peace differs from the threat of force, but a threat of force could be sufficient to constitute a threat to peace. The existence of a "threat to the peace" is not contingent on any actual (or even potential) use of force.[213] The UN Security Council has interpreted the meaning of a "threat to the peace" quite loosely. A typical threat to the peace is an impending or already initiated armed conflict between states, but the Security

---

[208] *Id.*
[209] Charter of the United Nations arts. 39, 41 and 42, June 26, 1945, 1 U.N.T.S. XVI (1945).
[210] Nico Krisch, *Article 39, in* 2 THE CHARTER OF THE UNITED NATIONS: A COMMENTARY 1278 (Bruno Simma, Daniel-Erasmus Khan, Georg Nolte & Andreas Paulus eds., 3d ed. 2012) [hereinafter Article 39 Commentary].
[211] *In Larger Freedom, supra* note 73, ¶ 125.
[212] Article 39 Commentary, *supra* note 210, at 1278.
[213] DINSTEIN, *supra* note 27, at 309–10.

Council has also recognized several other types of "threats to the peace". These include proliferation and arms control, terrorism, internal armed conflict, piracy, and, in recent years, threats to human security and human rights violations. The idea of "threat to the peace" has also expanded to include the prevention of conflict and instability in a more general way, such as combatting HIV/AIDS and climate change.[214] Where states have been limited in their ability to respond to threats under the law, the Security Council has enjoyed much more flexibility to act.

A cross-border tunnel would qualify as a threat to the peace. When cross-border tunnels are dug or used by nonstate armed groups, the state on whose territory the group is acting could find itself the target of Chapter VII measures, due to its support for or failure to prevent the attack.[215] Even before the September 11th attacks, the Security Council took measures under Chapter VII of the UN Charter against Libya for the Lockerbie bombing[216] and against Afghanistan for its support of al-Qaeda in the late 1990s.[217]

The second category triggering Security Council action—breaches of the peace—generally supposes the breakout of hostilities between two states. In such cases, a *threat* to the peace has already materialized. The Security Council qualified as "breach of the peace" the situation in the Falkland Islands following Argentina's invasion, and in Kuwait following Iraq's invasion.[218]

Aggression, the third category, presumes the direct or indirect use of force, and always constitutes a breach of the peace as well. It includes, inter alia, armed attacks under Article 51 of the Charter.[219] The United Nations General Assembly has formulated a definition for aggression,[220] later recognized by the ICJ as customary,[221] and referred to in the International Criminal Court's provisions on the crime of aggression.[222]

---

[214] *See* Article 39 Commentary, *supra* note 210, at 1280–91.

[215] *Id.* at 1281.

[216] S.C. Res. 731, U.N. Doc. S/RES/731 (Jan. 21, 1992); S.C. Res. 748, U.N. Doc. S/RES/748 (Mar. 31 1992); S.C. Res. 883, U.N. Doc. S/RES/883 (Nov. 11 1993).

[217] S.C. Res. 1267, U.N. Doc. S/RES/1267 (Oct. 15, 1999); S.C. Res. 1333, U.N. Doc. S/RES/1333 (Dec. 19, 2000).

[218] S.C. Res. 502, U.N. Doc. S/RES/502 (Apr. 3 1982); S.C. Res. 660, U.N. Doc. S/RES/660 (Aug. 2, 1990); Article 39 Commentary, *supra* note 210, at 1293.

[219] Article 39 Commentary, *supra* note 210, at 1293.

[220] Definition of Aggression, G.A. Res. 3314 (XXIX), U.N. Doc. A/RES/3314 (Dec. 14, 1974), art. I ("Aggression is the use of armed force by a State against the sovereignty, territorial integrity or political independence of another State, or in any other manner inconsistent with the Charter of the United Nations, as set out in this Definition." *See* Ruys, *supra* note 35, at 137.

[221] Nicaragua, *supra* note 7, ¶ 195.

[222] Article 39 Commentary, *supra* note 210, at 1293; Amendments to the Rome Statute of the International Criminal Court on the Crime of Aggression, June 11, 2010, U.N. Doc. C.N.651.2010.TREATIES-8, at art. 8 *bis* (2): "For the purpose of paragraph 1, 'act of aggression' means the use of armed force by a State against the sovereignty, territorial integrity or political independence of another State, or in any other manner inconsistent with the Charter of the United Nations. Any of the following acts, regardless of a declaration of war, shall,

Could a cross-border tunnel amount to an act of aggression? At times, limited attacks have been considered aggression—such as an Israeli air raid on Palestinian Liberation Organization's targets in Tunisia in 1985 in response to a PLO attack on Israeli civilians.[223] The Security Council also demanded that South Africa cease "all acts of aggression" against Angola.[224] Ultimately, however, "[t]he determination of an act of aggression by the Security Council is a political, not a judicial finding. It primarily opens the way for enforcement action and helps unite the international community against the aggressor. Thus its effects remain, in general, limited to peace enforcement action."[225] Perhaps in light of its political character, aggression is rarely invoked. In most situations corresponding to aggression, the collective security system will be triggered by other means.

To conclude, states are by no means helpless when cross-border underground threats do not reach the threshold of armed attack—whether the perpetrator is a state or a non-state actor. States should uphold their sovereignty and territorial integrity by turning to either the Security Council or the ICJ. Hopefully these institutions can condemn the act and, without delay, take measures to minimize the threat to the victim state. Should they not take appropriate or sufficient measures, the victim state would be entitled to take limited anti-tunnel actions on the territory from which the threat emanates—incursions that would be excused under the plea of necessity provided they meet all applicable legal requirements. This solution is preferable to a broadening of the right to self-defense: it keeps violence to a minimum while recognizing the grave and imminent peril that cross-border underground threats embody.

---

in accordance with United Nations General Assembly resolution 3314 (XXIX) of 14 December 1974, qualify as an act of aggression:

a) The invasion or attack by the armed forces of a State of the territory of another State, or any military occupation, however temporary, resulting from such invasion or attack, or any annexation by the use of force of the territory of another State or part thereof;
b) Bombardment by the armed forces of a State against the territory of another State or the use of any weapons by a State against the territory of another State;
c) The blockade of the ports or coasts of a State by the armed forces of another State;
d) An attack by the armed forces of a State on the land, sea or air forces, or marine and air fleets of another State;
e) The use of armed forces of one State which are within the territory of another State with the agreement of the receiving State, in contravention of the conditions provided for in the agreement or any extension of their presence in such territory beyond the termination of the agreement;
f) The action of a State in allowing its territory, which it has placed at the disposal of another State, to be used by that other State for perpetrating an act of aggression against a third State;
g) The sending by or on behalf of a State of armed bands, groups, irregulars or mercenaries, which carry out acts of armed force against another State of such gravity as to amount to the acts listed above, or its substantial involvement therein.

[223] S.C. Res. 573, U.N. Doc. S/RES/573 (Oct. 4, 1985).
[224] S.C. Res. 577, U.N. Doc. SC/RES/577 (Dec. 6, 1985).
[225] Article 39 Commentary, *supra* note 210, at 1294.

Conclusion

The discovery of each new tunnel burrowing under the North Korean border comes as an unwanted surprise to South Korea. The United States has invested immense resources in the detection of tunnels emanating from Mexico, and Egypt has taken drastic measures to counter the threat of Hamas's tunnels. Although these situations have not led to full-fledged wars between their respective protagonists, they harbor the potential for conflict. The discovery of more tunnels or the ever-slightest change in circumstances could trigger a military escalation.

Situations in which cross-border tunnels *can* lead to war must be distinguished from those in which they *do* lead to war. In this sense, cross-border threats do not significantly differ from other threats. As with other cross-border tensions, legal rights and security interests do not necessarily align: states may possess the right to react using military force but not make use of such right. This is because, unsurprisingly, war goes beyond law. A whole array of strategic concerns weigh on the decision-making process leading to the exercise of military force.

In this chapter, I have laid out the factors that might influence a state to use force following the discovery of one or more cross-border tunnels—assuming the state in question possesses that right under the law. All the scenarios examined in this chapter relate to the discovery of cross-border tunnel(s) in peacetime. In such situations, states' reactions to the discovery will be influenced by parameters including the location of the tunnel(s) (in or near civilian populated areas); the number of tunnels, their stage of completion, and internal features; the predicted purpose of the tunnel(s); the identity of diggers and users (state versus nonstate group, and the type of relationship entertained by the victim state and such entities); and the anticipated target of the cross-border attack (civilians versus combatants). These parameters may tilt the balance one way or another—leading a state not to take any action, or to adopt measures rather suddenly because strategic needs have evolved.

The law, for its part, does not always afford the victim state the right to launch a full-fledged war. Circumstances in which cross-border threats amount to armed attacks in the meaning of Article 51 of the UN Charter are few and far between. "Armed attack" corresponds to the "most grave forms"[226] of use of force. This, as well as other applicable legal limitations, affects the type of measures states can lawfully adopt in reaction to completed and uncompleted cross-border tunnel(s). It is best to think of it as a spectrum of options.

---

[226] Nicaragua, *supra* note 7, ¶ 110.

Self-defense is available when tunnel(s) have already been used to conduct a cross-border attack, provided the scale and effects of the attack rise to the required threshold. If *several tunnels have crossed the border but no attack has occurred yet*, the victim state might be entitled to self-defense by virtue of the existence of the completed cross-border tunnels under Dinstein's interceptive self-defense analysis. For those who do not embrace Dinstein's approach, anticipatory self-defense would remain available. In either case, the victim state may choose not to make use of the right to use military force for strategic or other reasons.

Moving towards the middle of the spectrum, the discovery of *several tunnels that have not yet crossed the border* could also give rise to the right of anticipatory self-defense, depending on a variety of factors—such as the past relationship with the actor and the proximity to civilians, for example.

At the far end of the spectrum, the discovery of *a single tunnel that has not yet crossed the border* (or several such tunnels in situations where anticipatory self-defense is not available) will amount to a threat of the use of force or a use of force. International institutions such as the UN Security Council or the ICJ may intervene to acknowledge the violation and/or take measures to put an end to it. Yet the victim state will not be entitled to take countermeasures or invoke necessity—let alone self-defense under any of its forms.

In all situations, the victim state can make use of retorsions—the most muted form of retaliation under international law, consisting of measures that, "while harming the interests of the subject that infringed the state's right," do not "conflict with an international obligation towards that other subject."[227] Retorsion is unfriendly, but it does not need to be excused as it is not per se unlawful.[228] As a result, states enjoy relative freedom when using measures of retorsion: they can embody a punitive element, and do not need to be temporary or proportionate. Their appeal, however, should not detract from the fact that they would remain of little avail against cross-border underground threats. Exercising pressure by way of retorsion might limit the digging of new tunnels, but would not eliminate the threat posed by existing ones. Only destruction would.

For these reasons, I have argued in favor of the plea of necessity—which can be invoked in almost all the above scenarios (except the digging of *a single tunnel that has not yet crossed the border*). Necessity offers the best hope as an exceptional measure likely to preserve the interests of the victim state, without leading to escalation. Though its availability in cases involving the use of force has been debated for decades, states, scholars, and

---

[227] *Addendum to the Eighth Rep. on State Responsibility, supra* note 47, ¶ 94.
[228] Lassa Oppenheim, International Law: A Treatise 134 (Hersch Lauterpacht ed., 7th ed. 1952).

the ICJ continue to invoke and rely on the doctrine. Arguments that international norms regulating the use of force already incorporate considerations akin to necessity, and those relating to a possible violation of *jus cogens*, have not had any real effect in practice. To all intents and purposes, the plea of necessity therefore remains an option as a response to cross-border underground threats—subject to the usual legal requirements (that the peril be grave and imminent, inter alia). When several options are available under the law, say necessity and anticipatory self-defense, the victim state can choose that which best fits its strategic and other interests.

6

UNDERGROUND WARFARE AND THE *JUS IN BELLO*

General Considerations

SUN TZU WROTE that "as water has no constant form, there are in war no constant conditions."[1] French and Chadian forces fighting al-Qaeda in Mali in 2013 quickly took measure of what the lack of constant conditions means in a mountainous terrain. Al-Qaeda in the Islamic Maghreb had entrenched in caves and underground structures, confronting the forces with surprise after surprise:

> It took time for the French forces to realize the major role played by the Ametetai Valley for AQIM. It was impossible to guess its importance via aerial surveillance. It was only during the first assault, around February 18 [2013], that French troops understood what they were really dealing with. The first elements were approaching the Valley when they hit a major obstacle: "We were 47 and suddenly we saw 50 guys get up in front of us—it led to a tough engagement," says one of the participants. The next day, a French soldier died. Then, unexpectedly, AQIM leaders turned on their phones to communicate, perhaps because they were surprised by the arrival of the French forces, even though virtually nothing had been heard on their waves for weeks.[2]

---

[1] SUN TZU, THE ART OF WAR 101 (Samuel B. Griffith trans., Oxford University Press, 1971).
[2] Jean-Philippe Rémy, *Mali: "On a Cassé le Donjon d'AQMI"*, LE MONDE (Mar. 7, 2013), http://mobile.lemonde.fr/afrique/reactions/2013/03/07/mali-a-tessalit-on-a-casse-le-donjon-d-aqmi_1844273_3212.html (translation by author).

Underground Warfare. Daphné Richemond-Barak.
© Oxford University Press 2018. Published 2018 by Oxford University Press.

From the uselessness of aerial surveillance, to surprise attacks and the enemy's changing patterns of communication, contending with subterranean warfare requires adaptability at the operational and tactical levels. Adaptability may also be needed on the part of the law: it is important to understand how the underground affects the application of the law, and how the law affects underground operations.

Rather surprisingly, little guidance is available. The laws of war do not directly mention the underground—neither in their ancient nor in their more contemporary formulations. The threat emanating from the underground has not only been overlooked by the community of states, security experts, and public opinion, but also remains underexplored under the law. It is difficult to reconcile the law's silence with the widespread nature of the tactic and the difficulties it creates on the ground.

Skeptics might attribute this silence to the fact that underground warfare does not raise distinct legal issues. They might also argue that, by remaining mum, the law conveys a permissive message as to the use of tunnels in war. This chapter puts these arguments to rest.

Underground warfare amplifies many of the well-known dilemmas arising in contemporary conflicts, such as target identification or the pervasive noncompliance problem characteristic of conflicts involving nonstate actors.[3] Underground combat also calls into question the legality of certain weapons and the ability of military commanders to take precautionary measures in order to protect civilians in time of war.[4] Weapons must be chosen in accordance with the threat, and so as to minimize the harm caused to civilians.[5] In the context of underground warfare, however, the unknown factor makes it difficult to assess the level of the threat. How can force levels be fine-tuned given the difficulty of obtaining intelligence on what is going on inside tunnels? In the face of such uncertainty, states may be tempted to use powerful weapons capable of taking out a more serious threat. Military commanders will also find it challenging to provide advance warning to civilians ahead of a strike. Methods that have become increasingly common (leaflets, text messages, and social media) will be of limited use below ground. The underground could well present forces with a situation in which, as the law contemplates, "the circumstances do not permit" any such warning to be given. Regardless of whether one accepts this difficult conclusion, the dilemma illustrates how profoundly underground warfare challenges the accepted moral and legal standards of behavior in war.

Underground warfare also takes us outside the familiar frames of reference for proportionality. Destroying a tunnel may involve bombing from above, or finding its access points and destroying it from within. A strike conducted against one segment of a tunnel—even if that segment is in an unpopulated area—may inflict unforeseen damage

---

[3] Eyal Benvenisti, *The Legal Battle to Define the Law on Transnational Asymmetric Warfare*, 20 DUKE J. COMP. & INT'L L. 339, 340 (2010); M. Cherif Bassiouni, *The New Wars and the Crisis of Compliance with the Law of Armed Conflict by Non-state Actors*, 98 J. CRIM. L. & CRIMINOLOGY 711, 715 (2008).

[4] Protocol Additional to the Geneva Conventions of 12 August 1949, and relating to the protection of victims of international armed conflicts, art. 57(2)(c), June 8, 1977, 1125 U.N.T.S. 3 [hereinafter AP I].

[5] Michael Schmitt, *The Interpretive Guidance: A Critical Analysis*, 1 HARV. NAT'L SEC. J. 5, 33 (2010).

on different and potentially unknown segments. The interconnected infrastructure impedes the determination of whether collateral damage resulting from the destruction of a tunnel might be excessive in relation to the military advantage anticipated from that destruction. Even careful mapping of a tunnel ahead of a strike may not suffice to ascertain collateral damage, as tunnels can be expanded rapidly, often escaping detection. A military commander will therefore find it difficult to foresee with precision the collateral damage likely to result from a strike against a tunnel, regardless of the method used (aerial strikes with bunker-busting munitions, or ground strikes and the manual detonation of tunnel entrances).

Underground warfare also raises unique legal questions, particularly pertaining to the nature and status of tunnels. As international humanitarian law does not address tunnels as such, one could argue, as mentioned above, that the law condones their use. Under a rather outdated view of international law, whatever is not expressly outlawed is permitted.[6] This view, albeit attractive, can hardly provide answers to all of the pertinent questions: Does the underground embody a new domain of war? Are tunnels weapons? Do they constitute military objectives? Does it make a difference, for the status of tunnels, that a tunnel may not have been excavated for belligerent use in the first place? The nature of tunnels—including the distinction, if any, between digging tunnels and using tunnels—remains unclear.

The breadth and depth of these issues significantly undermine the skeptics' arguments that underground warfare raises no specific issues in war or that the law takes a permissive stance vis-à-vis tunnels. That is not to say that underground warfare requires the adoption of new laws or principles. Some of these questions certainly *can* be answered under existing law. Because the relevant questions have not been addressed in legal scholarship, however, it is necessary to consider how the existing legal framework applies to this re-emerging, violent phenomenon. The focus is on applying the law (the *how*), not on reinventing it. Even in situations where law is lacking, a central pillar of the laws of war, known as the Martens clause, posits that "[i]n cases not covered by this Protocol or by other international agreements, civilians and combatants remain under the protection and authority of the principles of international law derived from established custom, from the principles of humanity and from the dictates of public conscience."[7] The following analysis therefore proceeds under the assumption that there can be no vacuum under international humanitarian law (IHL)—only matters of interpretation.

---

[6] *See* S.S. Lotus (Fr. v. Turk.), 1927 P.C.I.J. (ser. A) No. 10 (Sept. 7). For a recent application of this principle, see Accordance with International Law of the Unilateral Declaration of Independence in Respect of Kosovo, Advisory Opinion, 2010 I.C.J. 403, ¶ 84 (Jul. 22).

[7] AP I, *supra* note 4, at art. 1(2). The clause differs slightly from the original formulation in the Preamble of The Hague Convention II of 1899; it also appears in the four Geneva Conventions of 1949. The International Court of Justice has recognized the Martens clause as customary law. *See* Legality of the Threat or Use of Nuclear Weapons, Advisory Opinion, 1996 I.C.J. 226, ¶ 87 (July 8) [hereinafter Nuclear Weapons Advisory Opinion].

In this chapter and the following one, I examine legal questions that arise when armed forces engage in or against tunnels. Whereas the present chapter focuses on general questions pertaining to the legality and status of tunnels under the law of armed conflict, the following chapter zooms in on the impact of underground warfare on civilians.

I. Legality and Status of Tunnels under IHL

Here, in contrast to Chapter 5, I examine the use of tunnels and other underground structures as part of an *existing* armed conflict. As explained above, it is the existence of an armed conflict that triggers the application of IHL. IHL refers to the body of law governing war—a subset of international law also known as "the laws of war" or "the law of armed conflict." Before delving into the application of IHL to underground warfare, let me briefly recall the main tenets of this legal framework.

A. THE APPLICABLE LEGAL FRAMEWORK: KEY PRINCIPLES

Under IHL, an armed conflict may be of two types: international or non-international. The distinction between international and non-international armed conflict constitutes a *summa divisio* under IHL, with different rules applying to each type of conflict. In practice, the distinction has created recurring challenges for the classification of contemporary conflicts involving nonstate actors. Conflicts featuring elements of underground warfare are no stranger to this issue, particularly as they increasingly involve nonstate actors.[8]

If tunnels are dug by a state or state-sponsored entity onto the territory of a foreign state, the conflict qualifies as an international armed conflict (IAC) in the meaning of Common Article 2 of the Four Geneva Conventions of 1949. The sole determining factor with respect to the existence of an international armed conflict is whether the conflict pits two states against each other. The law does not specify any threshold of duration or intensity.[9] The Geneva Conventions, applicable in such a conflict and widely ratified, establish standards of humanitarian treatment for those affected by the hostilities: the wounded, sick, and shipwrecked, prisoners of war, and civilians.

---

[8] The data retrieved from *NYT* reports suggests that the use of tunnels in armed conflict at the hands of nonstate actors as a share of total use rose from 56 percent between 1969 and 2000 to 83 percent thereafter (2000–2015).
[9] INTERNATIONAL COMMITTEE OF THE RED CROSS, COMMENTARY ON THE FIRST GENEVA CONVENTION: CONVENTION (I) FOR THE AMELIORATION OF THE CONDITION OF THE WOUNDED AND SICK IN ARMED FORCES IN THE FIELD ¶ 236 (2d ed. 2016), https://ihl-databases.icrc.org/ihl/full/GCI-commentary [hereinafter 2016 GC I COMMENTARY]; JEAN S. PICTET, I–IV COMMENTARY ON THE GENEVA CONVENTIONS OF 12 AUGUST 1949, at 32 (1952).

The First Additional Protocol to the Conventions of 1977 (AP I),[10] also applicable in IAC but less widely ratified,[11] would also apply in most international armed conflicts.

Non-international armed conflicts (NIAC) are less heavily regulated. Only one provision of the four Geneva Conventions (known as Common Article 3) addresses "armed conflict not of an international character occurring on the territory of one of the High Contracting Parties."[12] A NIAC may exist between a state and a nonstate armed group, or between two such armed groups,[13] but in order to be a party to a NIAC, the armed group(s) must reach a certain threshold of organization.[14] A degree of intensity is also required for the armed conflict to exist. IHL applies only to those internal conflicts that meet both the intensity and organization thresholds. "Internal disturbances and tensions, such as riots, isolated and sporadic acts of violence and other acts of a similar nature" do not qualify as armed conflict for they do not meet these thresholds.[15]

Additional Protocol II was adopted in 1977 to enhance the regulation applicable to non-international armed conflicts. Nonetheless, its scope is much narrower than that of Common Article 3: it applies only to conflicts between the armed forces of a contracting state and an organized armed group that operates under responsible command, exercises territorial control, and has the capacity to implement the Protocol.[16] This test is stricter than that put forward in customary law.[17] In the latter, there is no requirement for territorial control: it is sufficient that the abovementioned intensity and organization thresholds be met.

These legal technicalities notwithstanding, the legal regimes governing international and non-international armed conflicts have converged in recent years[18]—particularly thanks to the broad application of customary norms.[19] Several specific weapons

---

[10] AP I, *supra* note 4.

[11] Many of its provisions, such as Article 48, are regarded as customary law. *See* JEAN-MARIE HENCKAERTS & LOUISE DOSWALD-BECK, CUSTOMARY INTERNATIONAL HUMANITARIAN LAW, VOL. 1: RULES Rule 1 (2005) [hereinafter ICRC Customary Law Study].

[12] Convention (I) for the Amelioration of the Condition of the Wounded and Sick in Armed Forces in the Field, art. 3, Aug. 12, 1949, 75 UNTS 31 [hereinafter GC I]; Convention (II) for the Amelioration of the Condition of Wounded, Sick and Shipwrecked Members of Armed Forces at Sea, art. 3, Aug. 12, 1949, 75 U.N.T.S. 85 [hereinafter GC II]; Convention (III) Relative to the Treatment of Prisoners of War, art. 3, Aug. 12, 1949, 75 U.N.T.S. 135 [hereinafter GC III]; Convention (IV) Relative to the Protection of Civilian Persons in Time of War, art. 3, Aug. 12, 1949, 75 U.N.T.S. 287 [hereinafter GC IV].

[13] Dapo Akande, *International Law and the Classification of Conflicts*, *in* INTERNATIONAL LAW AND THE CLASSIFICATION OF CONFLICTS 51 (Elizabeth Wilmshurst ed., 2012).

[14] *Id.* at 51; Prosecutor v. Tadić, Case No. IT-94-1-A, Decision on Defense Motion for Interlocutory Appeal on Jurisdiction ¶ 70 (Int'l Crim. Trib. for the Former Yugoslavia, Oct. 2,1995) [hereinafter Tadić].

[15] 2016 GC I COMMENTARY, *supra* note 9, ¶¶ 386–87; Protocol Additional to the Geneva Conventions of 12 August 1949 and relating to the protection of victims of non-international armed conflicts, art. 1(2), June 8, 1977, 1125 U.N.T.S. 609 [hereinafter AP II]; Tadić, *supra* note 14, ¶ 70.

[16] AP II, *supra* note 15, at art. 1(1).

[17] Akande, *supra* note 13, at 54.

[18] *Id.* at 35.

[19] Tadić, *supra* note 15, ¶ 127; ICRC Customary Law Study, *supra* note 11, at xxix; Akande, *supra* note 13, at 35–36.

conventions, such as the Biological Weapons Convention of 1972,[20] the Chemical Weapons Convention of 1993,[21] and the Convention on Conventional Weapons,[22] apply to both types of conflict. Additionally, the Rome Statute of the International Criminal Court defines war crimes in both international[23] and non-international[24] armed conflict, though the former remains far more robust. Among the important distinctions that endure, one must note prisoner of war status—which exists only in international armed conflicts.[25]

The qualification of conflicts as international or non-international becomes increasingly complicated in the context of asymmetrical, transborder conflicts—for example, if State A takes action against a tunnel dug by a nonstate actor on the territory of State B. This would be the case, hypothetically, if the United States were to use force against Hezbollah or al-Qaeda in Mexico following a takeover by such groups of the vast network of cross-border smuggling tunnels.[26] There are several views as to how such a conflict would be classified.[27] Regardless of classification, the core tenets of international humanitarian law will apply.

---

[20] Convention on the Prohibition of the Development, Production and Stockpiling of Bacteriological (Biological) and Toxin Weapons and on Their Destruction, Apr. 10, 1972, 1015 U.N.T.S. 163.

[21] Convention on the Prohibition of the Development, Production, Stockpiling and Use of Chemical Weapons and on Their Destruction, art. (1), Jan. 13, 1993, 1974 U.N.T.S. 45 [hereinafter Chemical Weapons Convention].

[22] Convention on Prohibitions or Restrictions on the Use of Certain Conventional Weapons which may be deemed to be Excessively Injurious or to have Indiscriminate Effects (with Protocols I, II and III), art. 1, Oct. 10, 1980, 1342 U.N.T.S. 137 (as amended in 2001) [hereinafter CCW].

[23] Rome Statute of the International Criminal Court, arts. 8(2)(a) and 8(2)(b), July 17, 1998, 2187 U.N.T.S 3 [hereinafter Rome Statute].

[24] *Id.* at arts. 8(2)(c) and 8(2)(e).

[25] 2016 GC I COMMENTARY, *supra* note 9, ¶ 391.

[26] *See* Dawn L. Bartell & David H. Gray, *Hezbollah and Al Shabaab in Mexico and the Terrorist Threat to the United States*, 3 GLOBAL SEC. STUD. 100 (2012); Warren Richey, *Are Terrorists Crossing the US-Mexico Border? Excerpts from the Case File*, CHRISTIAN SCI. MONITOR (Jan. 15, 2017), http://www.csmonitor.com/USA/Justice/2017/0115/Are-terrorists-crossing-the-US-Mexico-border-Excerpts-from-the-case-file.

[27] One approach would regard any armed conflict crossing the borders of a state as international (HCJ 769/02, Public Committee Against Torture in Israel v. Gov't of Israel 62(1) PD 507 ¶¶ 18, 21 [2006] (Isr.). Alternatively, actions taken by State A on the territory of State B against an armed group, without State B's permission, could be seen as giving rise to *jus ad bellum* violations and as creating an international armed conflict between States A and B (in our case between the United States and Mexico). This international armed conflict would exist alongside the NIAC between State A and the nonstate armed group(s), that is, between the United States and Hezbollah/al-Qaeda (Akande, *supra* note 13, at 73). The issues with this approach are beyond the scope of the discussion (Noam Lubell, *The War (?) against Al-Qaeda*, *in* INTERNATIONAL LAW AND THE CLASSIFICATION OF CONFLICTS 421, 432 (Elizabeth Wilmshurst ed., 2012)). Further, as discussed regarding the *jus ad bellum*, insofar as the actions of the nonstate armed group can be attributed to a state—if the nonstate armed group is essentially an organ of a state or if it is acting under the control or direction of a state—the conflict will, in fact, be an international armed conflict (Responsibility of States for Internationally Wrongful Acts, G.A. Res. 56/83, Annex U.N. Doc. A/RES/56/83, arts. 4 and 8 (Jan. 28, 2002)). Absent these unique circumstances, situations in which a state acts against a nonstate actor on the territory of a foreign state will generally be classified as a non-international armed conflict (Yahli Shereshevsky, *Politics by Other Means: The Battle over the Classification of Asymmetrical Conflicts*, 49 VAND. J. TRANSNAT'L L. 455, 495 (2016)). The idea that transborder conflicts between a state and a nonstate armed group should be classified as NIAC—even

IHL rests on four pillars, all of which are relevant to the use of tunnels in war, in all types of armed conflict. Because I repeatedly refer to them throughout this chapter and the following one, I introduce them shortly here.

First, the principle of distinction demands that the parties to the conflict distinguish between civilians and combatants, and between civilian objects and military objectives. Strikes cannot be intentionally directed at civilian targets.[28] This principle was consecrated as a "cardinal principle" of international law by the International Court of Justice and is regarded as customary.[29] Importantly, in cases of doubt, objects and persons are presumed to be civilian.[30]

Second, the principle of proportionality posits that an attack must not cause harm to civilians that would be excessive in relation to the concrete and direct military advantage anticipated from it.[31] Disproportionate attacks must be aborted,[32] and if a choice is available between several possible military objectives that would bring about the same advantage, the one that would cause the least harm to civilians should be preferred.[33]

Third, parties to the conflict must take constant care to spare the civilian population and civilian objects during military operations. Belligerents must do everything feasible to verify the nature of their objectives, choose means or methods of attack that avoid or minimize harm to civilians, and give advance warning to civilians ahead of strikes.[34]

---

though they take place on the territory of two states—stems from a residual view of NIAC as *any conflict not pitting two states against each other*. The NIAC regime is arguably more equipped to address nonstate actors (Benvenisti, *supra* note 3, at 343; Bassiouni, *supra* note 3, at 787), and states would likely be reluctant to grant combatant and prisoner of war status to members of a nonstate armed group (Lubell, *supra*, at 434; David Kretzmer, *Rethinking the Application of IHL in Non-international Armed Conflicts*, 42 Isr. L. Rev. 33 (2009)). These arguments lose much of their relevance, however, vis-à-vis well-organized and well-armed nonstate groups that are also more capable of complying with IHL norms (Shereshevsky, *supra* note 27, at 478–79). For these reasons, a number of scholars have advocated the application of customary law (David Kretzmer, *Targeted Killings of Suspected Terrorists: Extra-Judicial Executions or Legitimate Means of Defense?*, 16 Eur. J. Int'l L. 171, 195 (2005); Roy S. Schöndorf, *Extra-State Armed Conflicts: Is There a Need for a New Legal Regime?*, 37 N.Y.U. J. Int'l L. & Pol. 1, 54 (2005); or the recognition of a hybrid category of armed conflict (Geoffrey Corn, *Hamdan, Lebanon, and the Regulation of Hostilities: The Need to Recognize a Hybrid Category of Armed Conflict*, 40 Vand. J. Transnat'l L. 295, 330 (2007)).

[28] AP I, *supra* note 4, at art. 48; AP II, *supra* note 15, at art. 13(1); ICRC Customary Law Study, *supra* note 11, at Rules 1 and 7.

[29] Nuclear Weapons Advisory Opinion, *supra* note 7, ¶ 78.

[30] AP I, *supra* note 4, at arts. 50(1) and 52(3). Interestingly, the ICRC Customary Law Study notes that this principle was considered unrealistic by some states. It therefore suggested a more permissive interpretation, which emphasizes the importance of information: "when there is a doubt [as to the character of a person] a careful assessment has to be made under the conditions and restraints governing a particular situation as to *whether there are sufficient indications to warrant an attack*. One cannot automatically attack anyone who might appear dubious" (ICRC Customary Law Study, *supra* note 11, at Rule 6; emphasis added).

[31] AP I, *supra* note 4, at art. 57(2)(b); ICRC Customary Law Study, *supra* note 11, at Rule 14.

[32] AP I, *supra* note 4, at art. 57(2)(b).

[33] *Id.* at art. 57(3).

[34] *Id.* at arts. 57(1), 57(2)(a)(i), 57(2)(a)(ii), 57(2)(c); ICRC Customary Law Study, *supra* note 11, at Rule 15.

Fourth, means or methods of warfare that cause superfluous injury or unnecessary suffering may not be used, including against combatants.[35] This principle is embodied, inter alia, in bans on the use of specific weapons, such as biological and chemical weapons.

I should also note, in the specific context of underground warfare, the duty of parties to the conflict to preserve the environment.[36] Although the law only specifically prohibits causing intentional or expected damage to the environment that is widespread, long-term, and severe,[37] environmental concerns come into play in the proportionality calculus.[38]

B. DEFINING A TUNNEL UNDER IHL

Since 9/11, the application of IHL has been challenged from a temporal and geographical perspective.[39] Underground warfare adds a physical dimension to this debate—one that should have been discussed long ago but has strangely been left out of the conversation. It is not clear how IHL characterizes a tunnel. Is a tunnel a weapon or a tactic of war, and what difference does it make? Arguably, the underground could also be treated as a type of warfare, such as submarine, aerial, or cyberwarfare, to which special rules apply alongside core IHL principles. With time, IHL has embraced a slightly differential approach to its applicability from which underground warfare could benefit.

The expression "means of warfare" typically refers to the use of weapons in armed conflict, including weapon systems and other platforms employed for purposes of attack.[40] "Weapons" has a broader meaning than means of warfare, in the sense that a weapon can be used outside of armed conflict. In contrast, the term "methods of warfare" refers "to how attacks and other hostile actions are conducted."[41] The Manual on International Law Applicable to Air and Missile Warfare, prepared under the auspices of the Program on Humanitarian Policy and Conflict Research at Harvard University (hereinafter the "HPCR Manual"), similarly

---

[35] AP I, *supra* note 4, at art. 35(2); ICRC Customary Law Study, *supra* note 11, at Rule 70.
[36] Jean-Marie Henckaerts & Dana Constantin, *Protection of the Natural Environment*, in THE OXFORD HANDBOOK OF INTERNATIONAL LAW IN ARMED CONFLICT 480 (Andrew Clapham & Paola Gaeta eds., 2014).
[37] AP I, *supra* note 4, at art. 55(1); Rome Statute, *supra* note 23, at art. 8(2)(b)(iv).
[38] Nuclear Weapons Advisory Opinion, *supra* note 7, ¶ 30.
[39] Emily Crawford, *The Temporal and Geographic Reach of International Humanitarian Law*, in OXFORD GUIDE TO INTERNATIONAL HUMANITARIAN LAW (Ben Saul & Dapo Akande eds., forthcoming 2018).
[40] CLAUDE PILLOUD, JEAN PICTET, YVES SANDOZ, CHRISTOPHE SWINARSKI & BRUNO ZIMMERMAN, COMMENTARY ON THE ADDITIONAL PROTOCOLS OF 8 JUNE 1977 TO THE GENEVA CONVENTIONS OF 12 AUGUST 1949 ¶ 1402 (1987) [hereinafter COMMENTARY TO AP I] ("The words 'methods and means' include weapons in the widest sense, as well as the way in which they are used"); PROGRAM ON HUMANITARIAN POLICY AND CONFLICT RESEARCH AT HARVARD UNIVERSITY, HPCR MANUAL ON INTERNATIONAL LAW APPLICABLE TO AIR AND MISSILE WARFARE, Section E, Rule 1(t) and accompanying Commentary (2010), [hereinafter HPCR MANUAL].
[41] *Id.* at Rule 1(v).

defines methods of warfare as "attacks and other activities designed to adversely affect the enemy's military operations or military capacity," such as bombing.[42]

The qualification of tunnels depends on how a tunnel is used. In tunnel mining, the tunnel *is* the object used to conduct the attack and therefore serves as a weapon. However, when tunnels serve to smuggle weapons, hide, or host command-and-control centers, they should be treated as methods of warfare. Determining whether a tunnel qualifies as a means or method of warfare matters because IHL regulates the use of weapons by prohibiting or limiting their use, and imposing procedures designed to verify the legality of new weapons. Regardless of how one defines a "new" weapon,[43] tunnels do not fall under the purview of Article 36 of Additional Protocol I, which sets forth the obligation for states to carry out weapon review for new weapons:

> In the study, development, acquisition or adoption of a new weapon, means or method of warfare, a High Contracting Party is under an obligation to determine whether its employment would, in some or all circumstances, be prohibited by this Protocol or by any other rule of international law applicable to the High Contracting Party.

Tunnel mining has been used, as explained in Chapter 1, from the American Civil War through World War I, and in virtually every conflict since 9/11. It would not, under any interpretation, be subject to weapons review.[44]

In sum, tunnels could qualify as either means or methods of warfare. Tunnels constitute a weapon or a means of warfare when they are used for tunnel mining. This still would not make tunnels amenable to weapons review—a process set up for new weapons, something tunnels undeniably are not. In other situations, they are more akin to methods of warfare.

An interesting question remains as to whether underground warfare might constitute an entirely different type of warfare, like aerial warfare, naval warfare, or cyberwarfare. IHL acknowledges that different rules may apply to different types of warfare—without referring to them explicitly as domains:

> [T]he provisions of this Section apply to . . . all attacks from the sea or from the air against objectives on land but do not otherwise affect the rules of international law applicable in armed conflict at sea or in the air.[45]

---

[42] *Id.*
[43] On whether Article 36 is limited to new weapons, see James D. Fry, *Contextualized Legal Reviews for the Methods and Means of Warfare: Cave Combat and International Humanitarian Law*, 44 COLUM. J. TRANSNAT'L L. 453, 481 (2006) ("By modifying the weapon or using it in a new way, the state is introduced to a 'new' weapon in terms of its new capabilities.").
[44] For a discussion of weapons review, *see infra* Section III(A).
[45] AP I, *supra* note 4, at art. 49(2).

For IHL to treat underground warfare as a special type of warfare, as it treats naval, aerial, or cyberwarfare, means embracing it as an acceptable dimension of war. This does not seem to be IHL's preference, because it has at times recognized other types of warfare—and yet has never even mentioned underground warfare.

Other types of warfare have been expressly or implicitly recognized over the years via treaty law, state practice, or more informal processes. IHL has also accepted that some adjustments can and must be made in situations other than land warfare. Consider, for example, the Tallinn Manual on the International Law Applicable to Cyber Warfare, the HPCR Manual on International Law Applicable to Air and Missile Warfare, and the San Remo Manual on International Law Applicable to Armed Conflict at Sea.[46]

The Tallinn Manual acknowledges unique features of the cyberspace—such as the interconnectivity of cyberspace and the high probability that cyber operations will affect civilian systems—and envisages their implications for the conduct of military operations. For example, it suggests, in a rather unusual move, that "mission planners should, where feasible, have technical experts available to assist them in determining whether appropriate precautionary measures have been taken."[47]

The application of IHL to armed conflicts occurring partly or fully at sea has similarly been seen as calling for certain adjustments. Sovereignty at sea is not a uniform concept: the rights of states vary greatly from one area to the next (say from territorial waters to exclusive economic zones). To account for these variations, which do not exist on land, the San Remo Manual recognizes the right to conduct hostilities on the territorial sea and internal waters, the land territories, the exclusive economic zone and continental shelf of belligerent states; the high seas; and, to some extent and quite remarkably, the exclusive economic zone and the continental shelf of neutral states.[48] That said, when taking hostile action on the high seas or the exclusive economic zone of a nonbelligerent, states must act with due regard for the right of neutral states to exploration and avoid causing damage to cables and pipelines laid on the seabed that do not exclusively serve the belligerents.[49] These precisions are designed to account for the specificity of naval

---

[46] *See also* Treaty on Principles Governing the Activities in the Exploration and Use of Outer Space, including the Moon and Other Celestial Bodies, art. I, Oct. 10, 1967, 610 U.N.T.S. 205; INTERNATIONAL INSTITUTE OF HUMANITARIAN LAW, SAN REMO MANUAL ON INTERNATIONAL LAW APPLICABLE TO ARMED CONFLICTS AT SEA, Rule 10 (1994) [hereinafter SAN REMO MANUAL]; HPCR MANUAL, *supra* note 40, at 1, art. 1(a); MANUAL ON INTERNATIONAL LAW APPLICABLE TO MILITARY USES OF OUTER SPACE (Feb. 20, 2017), https://www.mcgill.ca/milamos/home.

[47] TALLINN MANUAL ON THE INTERNATIONAL LAW APPLICABLE TO CYBER WARFARE, Rule 52 and accompanying Commentary (Michael N. Schmitt ed., 2013) [hereinafter TALLINN MANUAL].

[48] SAN REMO MANUAL, *supra* note 46, at arts. 10, 34, 35.

[49] *Id.* arts. 36 and 37. "Exclusive economic zone" and "high seas" are respectively defined as "an area beyond and adjacent to the territorial sea," which extends for up to 200 nautical miles, and "all parts of the sea that are not included in the exclusive economic zone, in the territorial sea or in the internal waters of a State, or in the archipelagic waters of an archipelagic State." United Nations Convention on the Law of the Sea, arts. 55, 57, 86, Dec. 10, 1982, 1833 U.N.T.S. 397.

warfare, without modifying the applicability of core IHL principles. The HPCR Manual does the same when it delineates the scope of the aerial "battlefield," particularly with respect to "no-fly" and "exclusion" zones.[50]

The legal considerations notwithstanding, the recognition of underground warfare as a distinct type of warfare would also be felt at the operational level. The recognition of new domains of war affects the decision-making process, organizational structure, and preparedness of organizations and institutions.[51] NATO's recent acknowledgment of cyber as a new domain of operations is a case in point.[52]

Given this background—and without going as far as advocating the recognition of the underground as a new domain of warfare—one has to wonder whether subterranean warfare may nevertheless justify some adjustments on the part of IHL akin to those realized in the realms of cyber, air, or naval warfare. Best characterized as a subset of land warfare,[53] subterranean warfare warrants some internal adjustments within a state's armed forces in terms of recruitment, training, communication tools, and decision-making processes. One could envisage, much like in cyber, the involvement of a designated "underground warfare expert" who would attend meetings and advise commanders when an operation displays elements of underground warfare.

Additional adjustments may be needed to account for the difficulty of gathering intelligence in a subterranean environment. The law imposes a range of information-seeking duties on commanders—from determining whether a target constitutes a military objective to verifying the presence of civilians in its vicinity. The commander then makes decisions based on the information collected. The lack of available information on what is going on below ground, which is precisely the feature that makes this terrain so attractive, complicates the application of the law.

Despite the difficulties, issues regarding the nature of the underground, the status of tunnels, and the unavailability of information are not insurmountable. They can be overcome, provided those applying the law (commanders, legal advisers, and decision-makers)

---

[50] For a discussion on the differences between exclusion zones and other methods of warfare, see HPCR Manual, *supra* note 40, Section P and accompanying Commentary, ¶¶ 9–11.

[51] *See*, for example, William J. Lynn III, *Deputy Secretary of Defense, Defending a New Domain: The Pentagon's Cyberstrategy*, 89 FOREIGN AFFAIRS 97, 101 (2010). *See also* Herb Lin, *NATO's Designation of Cyber as an Operational Domain of Conflict*, LAWFARE (June 15, 2016) (discussing how the recognition of cyber as a domain would affect the exercise of collective self-defense by NATO), https://www.lawfareblog.com/natos-designation-cyber-operational-domain-conflict. It has also been reported that the U.S Department of Defense might define the electromagnetic spectrum as a new domain of war (*see* Sidney Freedberg, *DoD CIO Says Spectrum May Become Warfighting Domain*, BREAKING DEFENCE (Dec. 9, 2015), http://breakingdefense.com/2015/12/dod-cio-says-spectrum-may-become-warfighting-domain/).

[52] *NATO Recognizes Cyberspace as a "Domain of Operations" at Warsaw Summit*, NATO COOPERATIVE CYBER DEFENCE CENTER OF EXCELLENCE (July 21, 2016), https://ccdcoe.org/nato-recognises-cyberspace-domain-operations-warsaw-summit.html.

[53] Telephone Interview with Lieutenant General (ret.) Richard F. Natonski, Former Commander of U.S. Marine Corps Forces Command, Jan. 8, 2017.

and opining on its application (members of a commission of inquiry or judges) are familiar with and mindful of how underground warfare affects the conduct of hostilities. The underground cannot be treated as a side note in a conflict, given how deeply it affects military operations and the application of the law. Provided this is kept in mind, only minimal adjustments, if at all, will be needed.

C. THE LEGALITY OF DIGGING AND USING TUNNELS IN WAR

The analysis above suggests that the excavation and use of tunnels in armed conflict is considered lawful. I find it difficult to accept, however, that IHL takes a one-size-fit-all approach to tunnels, condoning their use in all circumstances. Arguably the question was not of great importance when underground warfare was used by combatants against other combatants. Today, however, tunnels are dug in or near populated areas, and tunnel attacks are at times directed at civilians. Tunnel warfare has grown into something more complicated and threatening than the tactic of war it once was, requiring more detailed answers.

A significant advantage of tunnels lies in their invisibility. Nearly impossible to detect, underground structures enhance a belligerent's mobility and flexibility. They create confusion as to the scope of their users' destructive capabilities when they are used for weapons storage. They introduce an element of uncertainty, hold a major surprise effect potential, turn the battlefield into a sphere in geospatial terms, and can deceive the enemy in endless ways.

In war, deceiving the enemy is part of the game. IHL recognizes this by allowing acts "which are intended to mislead an adversary or to induce him to act recklessly but which infringe no rule of international law applicable in armed conflict and which are not perfidious."[54] Ruses of war, as such acts are known, are lawful. They include camouflage, mock operations, feigned attacks or retreat, and communicating with nonexistent units.[55] Even ruses of war, however, must be carried out in accordance with IHL principles.[56]

Deception is permissible, but the law's tolerance ends with perfidy. Perfidy refers to an "act inviting the confidence of an adversary to lead him to believe that he is entitled to, or obliged to accord, protection under the rules of international law applicable in armed conflict, with intent to betray that confidence."[57] Such acts also constitute war crimes in both international and non-international armed conflicts.[58] Booby-trapping wounded or dead bodies and children's toys, and feigning a ceasefire amount to perfidy.[59]

---

[54] AP I, *supra* note 4, at art. 37(2).
[55] GARY D. SOLIS, THE LAW OF ARMED CONFLICT: INTERNATIONAL HUMANITARIAN LAW IN WAR 464 (2d ed. 2016) [hereinafter SOLIS].
[56] AP I, *supra* note 4, at art. 37(2).
[57] AP I, *supra* note 4, at art. 37(1).
[58] Rome Statute, *supra* note 23, at arts. 8(2)(b)(vii), 8(2)(b)(xii), and 8(2)e(ix).
[59] SOLIS, *supra* note 55, at 460.

Jus in Bello | 173

The distinction between ruses and perfidy, albeit intellectually satisfying, is far from intuitive. State practice reveals that the line between perfidious acts and ruses is thin at best, confusing at worst. During the Te-Leeng-See battle, fought during the Russo-Japanese war in 1904, Russian troops allegedly advanced under Japanese flags, a maneuver that led the Japanese artillery to cease fire. The Japanese government lodged a protest against the Russians for violating an international custom and Article 23 of The Hague Regulations, which forbids using national flags, military insignia, or uniforms of the enemy. However, ultimately, the incident was qualified as a ruse and not as perfidy.[60] Even today, despite Additional Protocol I's explicit prohibition against the use of the adversary's military uniform, flags, or other insignia to shield, favor, protect, or impede military operations, it is still not clear whether the use of the enemy's military uniform is prohibited as perfidy.[61]

Similarly, and somewhat surprisingly, flying a false flag at sea is not regarded as perfidy so long as true colors are revealed before engagement. During World War I, a German cruiser entered the port of Penang in Japan flying the false flag of Japan. Just before attacking a Russian cruiser and sinking it, it revealed its German flag. Although the German cruiser was heavily armed, disguised as a merchant ship, and flying false colors, the act was not considered perfidy.[62]

Several military manuals acknowledge the difficulty of distinguishing between ruses and perfidy. While the Netherlands' Military Manual refers to the "narrow borderline"[63] between perfidy and ruses of war, the UK's concedes that "it is difficult to lay down hard and fast rules in the matter."[64] The U.S. Manual for Military Commissions, while recognizing that "[t]he line of demarcation between legitimate ruses and forbidden acts of perfidy is sometimes indistinct," makes a point of clarifying the matter by establishing some guidelines:

> It would be an improper practice to secure an advantage of the enemy by deliberate lying or misleading conduct which involves a breach of faith, or when there is

---

[60] Dieter Fleck, *Ruses of War and Prohibition of Perfidy*, 13 MIL. L. & L. WAR REV. 269, 280 (1974).

[61] See AP I, *supra* note 4, at art. 39(2) In favor of regarding the use of an enemy uniform as perfidious, see ICRC Customary Law Study, *supra* note 11, at Rule 62; and Valentine Jobst III, *Is Wearing the Enemy's Uniform a Violation of the Laws of War?*, 35 AJIL 435, 440 (1941) ("it is not without significance that in . . . the Hague Regulations, enemy uniforms are included in the same paragraph as flags of truce and the distinctive insignia of the Geneva Convention; . . . When . . . the soldiers of one army wear, not their own uniforms but those of the enemy for purposes of deceiving the latter . . . there would seem to be a breach of faith amounting to forbidden perfidy."). For a different view, see Peter Rowe, *The Use of Special Forces and the Laws of War*, 33 MIL. L. & L. WAR REV. 207, 214 (1994).

[62] SOLIS, *supra* note 55, at 468.

[63] ICRC Customary Law Study, *supra* note 11, Practice related to Rule 65 (citing to Netherlands, *Humanitair Oorlogsrecht: Handleiding*, Voorschift No. 27-412, Koninklijke Landmacht, Militair Juridische Dienst, 2005, ¶ 0413).

[64] ICRC Customary Law Study, *supra* note 11, Practice related to Rule 65 (citing to United Kingdom, *The Law of War on Land Being Part III of the Manual of Military Law*, The War Office, HMSO, 1958, ¶¶ 308, 310).

a moral obligation to speak the truth. For example, it is improper to feign surrender so as to secure an advantage over the opposing belligerent thereby. So similarly, to broadcast to the enemy that an armistice had been agreed upon when such is not the case would be treacherous. On the other hand, it is a perfectly proper ruse to summon a force to surrender on the ground that it is surrounded and thereby induce such surrender with a small force.[65]

To sum up, in order to amount to perfidy, tunnels must first be intended to kill or injure (and, according to some, capture).[66] Even when they are so intended—and it is not the case with all tunnels—they must also mislead the adversary into believing that they enjoy protection under IHL. Tunnels generally do not, to paraphrase the Commentary, "claim any legal protection."[67] One exception could be envisaged, namely if underground facilities officially designated as civilian shelters are in reality used for belligerent purposes.[68] Such a use would, in any event, violate the prohibition on human shields and/or the requirement to take precautionary measures against the effects of attack under Article 58 of AP I.[69] Given that state practice only rarely and seemingly reluctantly qualifies an act as perfidy, tunnels are unlikely to amount to perfidy.[70]

The law's take on submarine warfare further confirms this conclusion. The question of perfidy arose in the early twentieth century in relation to submarines, which, by definition, seek to conceal, surprise, and mislead. Viewing submarine warfare as perfidious in nature, the British engaged in efforts to legally ban the practice.[71] Germany, in contrast, believed in unrestricted submarine warfare: vessels encountered within the limits of a declared so-called "war zone" were sunk without warning.[72] Other states, such as France, suggested instead that submarines be allowed, with some limitations. The French rejected

---

[65] UNITED STATES MANUAL FOR MILITARY COMMISSIONS, Part IV, 15 (2010).

[66] COMMENTARY TO AP I, *supra* note 40, ¶ 1496.

[67] *Id.* ¶ 1500.

[68] According to the Israeli Ministry of Foreign Affairs Report on the 2014 Gaza conflict, "[s]hafts were often placed near vantage points that provided a military advantage for attacks on approaching IDF troops, and were often concealed within or placed near sensitive civilian sites (such as residential houses, mosques, and medical clinics) that IDF forces might avoid entering or attacking" (STATE OF ISRAEL, THE 2014 GAZA CONFLICT: FACTUAL AND LEGAL ASPECTS 43 (2015) [hereinafter 2014 GAZA REPORT]).

[69] MARCO SASSÒLI & ANTOINE BOUVIER, 1 HOW DOES LAW PROTECT IN WAR? ch. 9, 17 (3d ed. 2011); Eric Talbot Jensen, *Cyber Attacks: Proportionality and Precautions in Attack*, 89 INT'L L. STUD. 198, 216 (2013).

[70] It could well be that tunnels amount to neither perfidy nor ruses—like feigning being wounded with the intent of surrendering when the enemy's successful attack subsides. Such an act, Gary Solis notes, is "not perfidy because it involves no intent to kill, wound, or capture, and it is not a ruse because . . . it is not done in the interest of military operations for the purpose of misleading the enemy" (see SOLIS, *supra* note 55, at 462).

[71] INGRID DETTER, THE LAW OF WAR 310 (2d ed. 2000) [hereinafter DETTER].

[72] Wolf Heintschel Von Heinegg, *The Law of Armed Conflict at the Sea*, *in* HANDBOOK OF INTERNATIONAL HUMANITARIAN LAW 518 (Dieter Fleck ed., 3d ed. 2013). *See also* Howard Levie, *Submarine Warfare: With Emphasis on the 1936 London Protocol*, *reprinted in* 70 INT'L L. STUD., LEVIE ON THE LAW OF WAR 293, 298 (Michael Schmitt & Leslie C. Green eds., 1997).

Germany's position, which they viewed as incompatible with the law of war, and that of Britain, which they said confused ruses and perfidy.[73]

The matter was settled in 1930 with the signing of the London Agreement on Naval Armament, which subjected submarines to the general rules governing naval warfare "in their action with regard to merchant ships"—essentially equating submarines, for purposes of the law, to surface vessels.[74] A submarine could not attack a merchant vessel, even when it flew under an enemy flag, unless the vessel refused to stop or be searched, and without "having first placed passengers, crew and ship's papers in a place of safety."[75] The same rule was later reaffirmed in the London Protocol of 1936.[76]

Subjecting submarines to the visit-and-search provision comes with its share of contradictions, as a submarine's effectiveness relies on its sailing submerged. The compromise reflected in the legal instruments adopted in 1930 and reaffirmed in 1936 may not, from this perspective, be entirely practical. Nevertheless, it demonstrated the acceptance of submarine warfare as a lawful practice in war, and embodied a clear rejection of the claim that submarines ought to be banned as perfidious. Still, one is tempted to ask whether equally impractical solutions should be transposed to tunnels as conditions of their lawfulness. Should tunnel users reveal tunnel exits and routes? Should belligerents making use of the underground be expected to place flags near tunnel shafts to prevent civilians from approaching them? As in submarine warfare, such solutions would be impractical. States are unlikely to embrace in practice a ban of underground warfare, or a requirement to notify the enemy of tunnel routes. The law will continue to accept a level of invisibility, which comes close to deception but is key to military success, as part of the reality of war. Ultimately, the debate over whether to ban or regulate submarine warfare on grounds of perfidy and the soundness of the visit-and-search provision underscores the difficulty of distinguishing between ruses and perfidy. It also highlights the challenge of applying IHL wholesale to different types of warfare.

One last question must now be addressed, namely whether the law should approach the *use* and the *digging* of tunnels in the same way. Although I reach the conclusion that there is no reason to distinguish between the two under IHL, the question deserves to be raised. With respect to the legality of tunnels, it is difficult to envisage a situation where the use of a tunnel is lawful but the digging of a tunnel is not. An a contrario reasoning advocates in favor of the legality of both activities under the law of armed conflict. In the context of targeting, I would similarly see no objection to treating a tunnel-in-the-making as a military objective. An uncompleted tunnel could certainly qualify as a legitimate target on account of purpose, use, location, or nature—as long as it makes

---

[73] DETTER, *supra* note 71, at 310.
[74] Limitation and Reduction of Naval Armament (London Naval Treaty), art. 22, Apr. 22, 1930.
[75] *Id.* art. 22(2).
[76] London Submarine Protocol, Rule 2, Nov. 6, 1936.

an effective contribution to military action. The qualification as military objective on account of purpose resonates particularly well in the context of tunnel-digging. A tunnel may, in its initial phases of excavation, be regarded as a lawful target in light of its *future use*. I return to this in Section D. Finally, the question of digging matters for the application of Article 49 of Additional Protocol I. Article 49 provides that attacks are "acts of violence against the adversary, whether in offence or in defence."[77] Only acts that qualify as "attacks" must comply with core IHL principles. If a tunnel qualifies as an attack, it must be directed only at military targets. What about tunnel-digging? These questions find no straightforward answers in the law—and are reminiscent, in many ways, of those arising in cyberspace. Experts were initially quite divided as to the meaning of "attack" in the context of cyberwarfare.[78] Ultimately, they agreed upon an outcome-based test: cyberattacks constitute "attacks" provided they produce death or injury.[79] The test could easily apply to tunnel warfare: a tunnel would have to comply with IHL insofar as it is likely to cause death or injury. According to the Tallinn Manual, nonviolent operations would generally not qualify as attacks.[80] This approach would therefore exclude underground smuggling, transportation, and command-and-control structures from the scope of "attacks." However, it would include tunnel mining and cross-border tunnels designed to launch an attack on a foreign state. More controversially—and of high relevance for underground warfare—the Tallinn Manual notes that cyberattacks can amount to attacks to which IHL fully applies, even when they form part of a broader operation.[81] This means that even when elements of underground warfare are integrated into broader operations, forming only a small component thereof, IHL would apply.

To conclude, in the absence of guidance from the law, there are many ways to conceptualize underground warfare under IHL. The regulatory history of submarine warfare offers a glimpse of the various approaches states can take on the issue. One approach would validate the use of tunnels in war under all circumstances. Another would view tunnel warfare as perfidious, and therefore unlawful per se. The better approach, advocated in this book, takes a permissive view of underground warfare subject to limitations imposed by IHL. Although IHL tolerates the digging and use of tunnels in armed conflict *in principle*, it should unequivocally condemn the use of tunnels to harm civilians, immunize military targets from attack, and spread fear among the civilian population. IHL should also prohibit the use of underground structures for civilian and military purposes simultaneously—which can only lead to disastrous outcomes, such as bombing of the Al Firdos bunker (sometimes also referred to as Al Firdus) during Operation Desert Storm.

---

[77] AP I, *supra* note 4, at art. 49.
[78] *See* Heather A. Harrison Dinniss, *Regulation of Cyber Warfare under the* Jus in Bello, *in* Cyber Warfare: A Multi-disciplinary Analysis 129 (James A. Green ed., 2015).
[79] Tallinn Manual, *supra* note 47, at Rule 30 and accompanying Commentary.
[80] *Id.* ¶ 2 to Commentary.
[81] *Id.* ¶ 16 to Commentary.

To all intents and purposes, the bunker looked like and operated as a major Iraqi military command and control center. Unbeknownst to the United States, however, civilians regularly sought shelter in the bunker's basement. Hundreds of them died in the attack. This devastating incident advocates in favor of a broad reading of "attack"—broader than that of the Tallinn Manual—in the context of underground warfare.[82] The digging and use of tunnels in conflict, to the extent it is likely to cause harm to civilians, which would include virtually the digging or use of any tunnel near civilian populated areas, should abide by the principles of distinction, proportionality, and precautions.

D. THE LEGAL STATUS OF TUNNELS UNDER IHL

I have now established that IHL does not extend a blanket prohibition on the digging and/or use of the underground in armed conflict. Neither does IHL condone the use of tunnels in all situations. Certain limitations do apply, as explained above. From the point of view of belligerents in an armed conflict, an additional question arises whenever underground structures are concerned: Does every underground structure used in war constitute a legitimate target?

1. Tunnels as Military Objectives

A tunnel can be built or used for a variety of purposes ranging from illegal smuggling of food or weapons, to the transportation of people, tunnel mining, the storage of ammunition, and command-and-control centers. The purpose of a tunnel might also shift with time or, more complicated yet, alternate between civilian and military purposes. Does the purpose of a tunnel matter for the application of IHL? Does IHL view smuggling tunnels differently than it views tunnel mining? The answers to these questions have tangible implications for targeting.

Like all other objects, tunnels can be targeted provided they qualify as military objectives. Although international humanitarian law does not directly address the status of tunnels, it provides a general definition of what constitutes a military object. Article 52(2) of AP I defines a military objective as

> those objects which by their nature, location, purpose or use make an effective contribution to military action and whose total or partial destruction, capture or neutralization, in the circumstances ruling at the time, offers a definite military advantage.[83]

---

[82] This incident is discussed further in *supra*, Chapter 7.
[83] AP I, *supra* note 4, at art. 52(2).

This provision sets forth two cumulative conditions:[84] First, that the object makes an effective contribution to military action by its nature, location, purpose, or use; and, second, that the object's partial destruction, capture, or neutralization offers a definite military advantage.

The first condition tends to create some confusion because of the "intertwining of nature, location, purpose, and use."[85] Oftentimes, "a military object will be included in more than one of those descriptive categories."[86] This holds true in the case of tunnels. In some circumstances, a tunnel or other underground structure may qualify as a military objective by it. This is the case when a tunnel is used by armed forces (or groups akin thereto) on a regular basis—just as they would use weapons, equipment, transports, fortifications, depots, or buildings. According to the ICRC Commentary, "all objects directly used by the armed forces" should be regarded as military objectives by nature.[87] These objects possess an inherent attribute that contributes to the military effort.[88] Command and control centers and major highways and railroads that serve the military would also qualify as such.[89]

This view, however, has been challenged on the ground that it confuses nature and use.[90] "Military objectives by nature," Jachec-Neale argues, refers instead to objects whose "normal condition is to be used intrinsically for military purposes *only*."[91] Under this narrow interpretation of "nature," military objectives by nature are only those objects that are *exclusively* military in nature.[92] An object cannot qualify as a military objective by nature if it has many applications. Nature, unlike use, is not context-dependent. The nature of an object cannot change, and "objects performing both military and civilian functions could not be considered legitimate targets due to their nature."[93]

It is less than certain that this view reflects the general understanding of what "military objective by nature" means. A view of tunnels as lines of communication, and, accordingly, as military objectives by nature, seems more in line with practice. Lines of communication are defined as "routes (land, water, and air) that connect a military force with a base of operations, along which supplies and troops move."[94] When tunnels serve as lines of communication, military headquarters, means of offensive warfare, or weapons

---

[84] COMMENTARY TO AP I, *supra* note 40, ¶ 2018.
[85] SOLIS, *supra* note 55, at 510.
[86] *Id.* at 510.
[87] COMMENTARY TO AP I, *supra* note 40, ¶ 2020.
[88] YORAM DINSTEIN, THE CONDUCT OF HOSTILITIES UNDER THE LAW OF ARMED CONFLICT 110 (3d ed. 2016).
[89] SOLIS, *supra* note 55, at 510–11. *See also* DINSTEIN, *supra* note 88, at 110–11.
[90] AGNIESZKA JACHEC-NEALE, THE CONCEPT OF MILITARY OBJECTIVES IN INTERNATIONAL LAW AND TARGETING PRACTICE 47 (2014).
[91] *Id.* (emphasis added).
[92] *Id.* at 46–47.
[93] *Id.* at 48.
[94] *Id.* at 52.

caches, they resemble military bases, ammunition depots, and other objects that have traditionally been regarded as military by nature. I see no reason to oppose a qualification as military objective by nature in such circumstances. As for tunnels dug or used for tunnel mining—that is, for the specific purpose of placing and detonating explosives under a target—they qualify as military objectives by nature under both interpretations.

One way to get around the uncertainty surrounding the meaning of "nature" is to regard tunnels as military objectives by virtue of their *location*. Location matters in conflicts where geographical features matter. In such conflicts, belligerents exploit the natural landscape to gain a military advantage—for example, natural crevices or ridgelines in deep valleys surrounded by mountain ranges, or extensive vegetation or foliage in the jungle.[95] According to the Commentary to Article 52 of AP I, a military objective by location refers to "a site which is of special importance for military operations in view of its location, *either because it is a site that must be seized or because it is important to prevent the enemy from seizing it*."[96] Even an unused underground structure could meet that definition simply on account of being located underground. Natural or preexisting tunnels that are taken over by a party to a conflict, or at risk of being so used, can qualify as military objectives based on their location. A party fighting in an arena full of natural caves and tunnels, for example in the mountainous regions of Afghanistan or Mali, would want and need to prevent the other party from gaining control of these structures. Location would also justify the targeting of a tunnel located in proximity to a military base, compound, or a place of other tactical importance[97]—as it justifies the targeting of land at the entrance of a harbor.[98] The importance of preventing the enemy from seizing the object (cave, bridge,[99] or otherwise) is what drives the qualification as a military objective in these cases.

Purpose refers to an object's intended future use (as opposed to its present function, which corresponds to its *use*). As noted above, this category is particularly relevant in the context of tunnel-digging. Uncompleted tunnels or tunnels in early stages of excavation can constitute military objectives on account of their future use. The difficulty is that the enemy's intent as to the future use of an object is not always clear. As Michael Schmitt

---

[95] *Id.* at 64.
[96] COMMENTARY TO AP I, *supra* note 40, ¶ 2021 (emphasis added).
[97] JACHEC-NEALE, *supra* note 90, at 62 ("Location can turn a purely civilian object into a military objective if such an object is regarded as obstructing a clear line of fire, or preventing the execution of certain military operations ... Tactically important mountain passes, routes through natural or man-made obstacles, a bridgehead, footbridges, crossroads, hills and tunnels can all be perceived as military objectives by virtue of their location.").
[98] COMMENTARY TO AP I, *supra* note 40, ¶¶ 2020–23; DINSTEIN, *supra* note 88, at 115.
[99] DINSTEIN, *supra* note 88, at 115–16; COMMENTARY to AP I, *supra* note 40, ¶ 2021 ("there are objects which by their nature have no military function but which, by virtue of their location, make an effective contribution to military action. This may be, for example, a bridge or other construction."). However, others view bridges as military objectives based on their use or purpose (*see, e.g.*, Terry D. Gill, *Some Considerations Concerning the Role of the* Ius ad Bellum *in Targeting*, *in* TARGETING: THE CHALLENGES OF MODERN WARFARE 106 (Paul A.L. Ducheine, Michael N. Schmitt & Frans P.B. Osinga eds., 2016)).

rightly puts it, "how certain must be an attacker of the intended future military use of an object that was not designed for military purposes?"[100] With the help of the typology laid out earlier in this book,[101] the designation of a tunnel could be determined based on past history and the structure and type of tunnel, without conceding too much to speculation. As an example of where clarity as to intent does exist, the HPCR Manual tells the story of an apartment building being renovated in order to serve as military barracks.[102] The ongoing excavation of a tunnel closely resembles these circumstances, making it possible for a tunnel (albeit uncompleted) to constitute a legitimate target.

The *use* of an object, in contrast, refers to the way an object is *presently* employed. Use is, by definition, context-dependent: "[A] school or a hotel is a civilian object, but if they are used to accommodate troops or headquarters staff, they become military objectives."[103] A civilian object can thus become a military objective if used by the armed forces. There is a presumption, however, that civilian objects are used for civilian purposes. For a civilian object to become a military objective, the presumption would have to be rebutted.[104] Consider, for example, the case of an underground shelter. Like civilian infrastructure, the civilian shelter is protected from attack. It could, however, lose its protection if it is used for military purposes, or if it is connected to other underground structures serving the military or organized armed groups. Civilian objects used simultaneously for civilian and military functions—so-called "dual use" objects—therefore constitute military objectives, with the civilian nature taken into consideration under duties of precautions and proportionality.[105]

The analysis above purposefully avoids placing too much weight on a tunnel's designation. The appeal of tunnels lies, as repeatedly explained in this book, in their versatility. A smuggling tunnel can turn into a means of infiltrating territory to carry out a murderous attack, a sewage system can be used to flee after a terrorist attack, and the basement of a house can be used to connect tunnels serving as lines of communication. The list goes on. For this reason, conceptualizing tunnels solely based on their designation would fly in the face of the reality on the ground, and introduce unwarranted uncertainty and unpredictability into the targeting process.

Even when an object qualifies as a military objective under the first requirement of Article 52, it must fulfill the second requirement—that its destruction or neutralization offers the targeting party a definite military advantage—to be regarded as a legitimate target. The assessment of the military advantage to be gained from the neutralization

---

[100] Michael N. Schmitt & Eric Widmar, *The Law of Targeting*, in TARGETING: THE CHALLENGES OF MODERN WARFARE, *supra* note 99, at 147.
[101] *See supra* Chapter 2.
[102] HPCR MANUAL, *supra* note 40, at 117.
[103] COMMENTARY TO AP I, *supra* note 40, ¶ 2022.
[104] AP I, *supra* note 4, at art. 52(3); DINSTEIN, *supra* note 88, at 112.
[105] Michael Schmitt, *The Law of Cyber Targeting*, TALLINN PAPER NO. 71, 11 (2015).

or destruction of a target is never an easy exercise. This is not the place to revisit these debates. I would only mention two issues that are relevant to the calculation of the military advantage in subterranean warfare.

Any given strike cannot eliminate an entire tunnel at once. It will typically be directed at a segment of a tunnel—in the hope of hindering the use of the tunnel as a whole. Imagine, then, a strike hitting point P somewhere along the route of a kilometers-long tunnel. The question is whether the military advantage gained from the strike should be measured based on the destruction of the segment where point P is located, or on the lack of functionality of the tunnel as a whole. Analyzing this from the perspective of the segment where point P is located means that the destruction of *the targeted segment* must offer a "definite military advantage."[106] Assuming that the same approach applies to the proportionality calculus later on in the targeting process, the military commander would have to make difficult determinations (such as who uses the tunnel and whether any civilians are present inside it) in relation to a rather small section of the tunnel. It is difficult enough to gain information on the use of a tunnel as a whole, but going down to this level of detail—at any stage of the targeting process—complicates the task that much more. Moreover, the use of the tunnel may change along its route: while one part of a tunnel may be used by civilians as a makeshift home of sorts (as in Sarjah, Syria),[107] others may be used by militants as sleeping quarters and ammunition caches. It should also be noted that tunnels can branch out or spread over different levels, connecting several rooms, mountains, or houses. Determining where "a tunnel" begins and ends is therefore not as easy as it seems.

In any event, the determination of what constitutes a tunnel for the purpose of assessing the target's contribution to military action is likely to raise some issues. Experts warn against too narrow a view in this context. If a strike is carried out along the route of a tunnel, the calculation of the military advantage obtained from each strike should be performed in relation to the entire tunnel and not to each targeted section individually.[108] In my view the standard should be one of reasonableness: commanders should not assess the military advantage with respect to too small or too large a portion of the tunnel.

A second-order question arises when a tunnel entrance is located inside a civilian home—say under the kitchen sink or in the basement.[109] Does the entire house become a military objective or only the entrance to the tunnel itself? Assuming that the tunnel entrance can be isolated and targeted with precision without damaging the house, states should do so. However, from a strictly legal standpoint, I believe hosting a tunnel

---

[106] I am indebted to Professor Michael Schmitt for this point.
[107] C.J. Chivers, *Jammed in Roman Caves, Ducking Syria's War*, N.Y. TIMES (Mar. 23, 2013), www.nytimes.com/2013/03/24/world/middleeast/syrians-fleeing-home-crowd-in-roman-caves.html.
[108] Interview with Maj. Gen. (Ret.) Yaakov Amidror, Former National Security Advisor of Israel, June 8, 2016.
[109] I am indebted to Adv. Ido Rosenzweig for this point.

entrance is sufficient for a house to lose its protection under IHL. The legality of a strike against that house would then become a matter of proportionality and precautions.

Ultimately, most underground structures used in war—other than those used exclusively by civilians—constitute military objectives. Treating (most) tunnels as military objectives best ensures the protection of civilians. Civilians should know that tunnels are highly vulnerable to explosions, collapses, and accidents, and serve as a confined death trap when used by military forces. The better course of action is for civilians to stay away from tunnels—assuming that they have a safer alternative, which admittedly is not always the case. The law, as a matter of policy, must ensure that tunnels remain separated, as much as possible, from civilians. The raison d'être of the principle of distinction is to impose, preserve, and facilitate the distinction between military and civilian objects. The principle of proportionality later applies to account for the presence of civilians inside the tunnels, and possibly render the strike unlawful.

2. Tunnels as War-Sustaining Objects

Tunnels that do not meet the treaty definition of military objective as per the analysis above could still be regarded as legitimate targets—albeit under a more controversial interpretation of the law. Certain tunnels, such as smuggling tunnels, could amount to war-sustaining objects if the revenues they generate serve to fuel the war effort, however indirectly. Consider, for example, the cross-border tunnels dug by Hamas and Islamic Jihad between Gaza and Egypt. Assuming that an armed conflict exists between Gaza and Egypt, the smuggling tunnels could constitute war-sustaining objects, as the smuggling activity significantly benefits the economy of the Gaza Strip and Hamas's military activities.[110]

The term "war-sustaining objects" refers to objects that make an indirect contribution to military action, in contrast to the treaty definition which requires that military objects make an "effective" contribution to military action. The concept, which arguably finds support in the Lieber Code,[111] has been championed in contemporary times by the United States:

> It is not necessary that the object provide immediate tactical or operational gains or that the object make an effective contribution to a specific military operation. Rather,

---

[110] Hazem Balousha, *Hamas Faces Financial Crisis After Egypt Tunnel Closure*, AL MONITOR (July 15, 2013), http://www.al-monitor.com/pulse/iw/originals/2013/07/hamas-financial-crisis-gaza-egypt-morsi.html; Ben Piven, *Gaza's Underground: A Vast Tunnel Network That Empowers Hamas*, AL JAZEERA (July 23, 2014), http://america.aljazeera.com/articles/2014/7/23/gaza-undergroundhamastunnels.html.

[111] Instructions for the Government of Armies of the United States in the Field (Lieber Code), art. 15, Apr. 24, 1863 ("Military necessity . . . allows of all destruction of property, and obstruction of the ways and channels of traffic, travel, or communication, and of all withholding of sustenance or means of life from the enemy.").

the object's effective contribution to the war-fighting or war-sustaining capability of an opposing force is sufficient.[112]

The United States has been consistent in promoting this broad conception of military objective—mindful, of course, that it does not align with the treaty-law definition.[113] The upshot is that, in the United States' view, "economic objects associated with military operations or with war-supporting or war-sustaining industries" constitute legitimate targets.[114] Examples of war-sustaining objects include those providing logistical and administrative support surrounding military operations, lines of communication, industries (such as oil, drugs,[115] crops), electric power stations, and most recently—money itself.[116] The justification lies in the capacity of such activities to sustain the conflict.[117] Underground structures of many sorts could fall under this interpretation, certainly as economic objects or lines of communication.

The competing, narrower, more mainstream view, which is also closer to the wording of the definition of military objective under Additional Protocol I, would not view smuggling tunnels as military objectives unless they are used by an adversary to support its military effort directly. According to Yoram Dinstein, the U.S. interpretation goes too far, as war-sustaining activities are too remote and lack the required nexus to "warfighting."[118] As a counter to the potential broadening of the concept to money and financial institutions, Dinstein notes that "the stock exchange, banking system and money markets of the enemy State—albeit, perhaps, vital to its economic staying power in the armed conflict—do not, as such, constitute lawful military objectives."[119] Dinstein is not alone in resisting the U.S. approach. The HPCR Manual also identified this matter as one on which experts are divided.[120]

Even though the notion remains unacceptable to most legal academics, a growing body of state practice suggests that a change may nevertheless be underway.[121]

---

[112] U.S. Dep't of Defense, Law of War Manual, 210, ¶ 5.7.6.2 (2015) [hereinafter U.S Law of War Manual].
[113] *Id.* at 210.
[114] *Id.* at 213.
[115] Michael N. Schmitt, *Targeting Narcoinsurgents in Afghanistan: The Limits of International Humanitarian Law*, 12 YB Int'l Humanitarian L. 301, 320 (2009).
[116] Daphné Richemond-Barak, *Is Money a Legitimate Target?*, Just Security (Feb. 10, 2016), https://www.justsecurity.org/29255/money-legitimate-target/.
[117] W. Hays Parks, *Asymmetries and the Identification of Legitimate Military Objectives*, in International Humanitarian Law Facing New Challenges 100 (Wolff Heintschel von Heinegg & Volter Epping eds., 2007).
[118] Dinstein, *supra* note 88, at 109.
[119] *Id.*
[120] HPCR Manual, *supra* note 40, at Rule 23 ¶ 2.
[121] *See* Ryan Goodman, *The Obama Administration and Targeting "War-Sustaining" Objects in Non international Armed Conflict*, 110 Am. J. Int'l L. 663 (2016), https://papers.ssrn.com/sol3/papers.cfm?abstract_id=2783736.

As Kenneth Watkin rightly points out, actions taken against ISIS's cash depots and oil facilities support a more flexible and controversial understanding of the notion of military objective—particularly if these attacks "are intended to stop the sale of smuggled oil, the proceeds of which provide 'fuel' for Islamic State activities, only part of which includes military action."[122]

To conclude, the law's rather permissive take on digging and using tunnels in times of war comes with an unapologetic view of their status: with the obvious exception of civilian shelters, underground structures generally constitute legitimate targets in war. They qualify as such under either a narrow or broad understanding of the concept of military objective. Tunnels used for tunnel mining and command-and-control structures amount to military objectives by nature. Many underground structures—such as caves and cavities—qualify as military objectives by virtue of their location. Uncompleted tunnels, even in early stages of excavation, can be regarded as legitimate targets on account of their intended future use. Smuggling tunnels may fall under the definition of war-sustaining activities in situations where they do not meet the stricter and more widely accepted treaty-based test. Be this as it may, the nature of tunnels and the multifaceted functions they fulfil on the battlefield make it difficult to specify under which rationale they amount to military objectives. Tunnels may constitute military objectives under one or more of the grounds listed in Article 52. For this and other reasons, states are unlikely to indicate the precise legal justification for targeting. Suffice it to say that, in most situations, the non-civilian use of underground structures in armed conflict provides belligerents the legal justification to use lethal force against these structures (provided other requirements, such as proportionality and precautions, are met).

II. The Unknown Factor and Its Implications for IHL

Clausewitz coined the phrase "war is the province of uncertainty."[123] One might have expected modern warfare to change this. When it comes to tunnel warfare, however, Clausewitz's words remain as relevant as ever. In fact, underground warfare goes beyond the realm of uncertainty: it conceals people, objects, and intentions, in an almost infallible way. I refer to this unique feature of underground warfare as the "unknown factor." Interestingly, it has not always been the main motivation for the use of tunnels and underground structures. Once upon a time, their appeal lay in affording a way to overcome fortifications and walls. In contemporary warfare, however, the underground most attractively bridges the gap between the low-tech and

---

[122] Kenneth Watkin, *Targeting "Islamic State" Oil Facilities*, 90 INT'L L. STUD. 499, 505, 512 (2014).
[123] CARL VON CLAUSEWITZ, ON WAR (1832), Book I, at 25.

high-tech capabilities of belligerents. This aspect is best illustrated by the U.S. tunnel rats in Vietnam:

> After Operation Crimp, as tunnel rat volunteers began to step forward, experience soon showed that the knife, the pistol, and the flashlight were to be the basic tools for combat and survival inside the tunnels of Cù Chi. Indeed, the very reverse of high-tech weapons development took place within the tiny ranks of the tunnel rats. They had to relearn the whole business of carefully planned face-to-face combat, one on one, as they called it, without [the] support, and without weapons superiority. The rats were to become obsessive about the most minute details of their equipment, lauding one pistol over another, one knife edge over another. They rediscovered the satisfaction of old fashioned unarmed combat, where individual strength, guts, and cunning counted for much more than massive air and artillery support.[124]

As militaries become more technology-savvy, the appeal of the underground only grows. The improvements in intelligence, surveillance, and reconnaissance capabilities, combined with the desire to keep soldiers out of harm's way and avoid "boots on the ground," strengthen the resolve of technology-inferior belligerents to hide. The race toward better technology, in other words, exacerbates the urge to conceal intentions, people, and objects. The underground remarkably enables belligerents to restore some level of symmetry on the modern battlefield.

As the tunnel rats understood in Vietnam, the use of the subterranean inevitably calls for a rethinking of basic assumptions—from the operational to the tactical. Aboveground, tunnels transform the battlefield into a sphere, making it necessary for soldiers to remain alert not only to what is above and ahead of them, but also to what is behind and below them. The realm of what they cannot see—the uncertainty and the unknown—expands dramatically. It is no longer sufficient for soldiers to secure the rear, as tunnels can emerge from anywhere. Even for well-trained soldiers, the multidimensional aspect of the subterranean threat is not easy to handle.[125]

The unknown factor permeates virtually every aspect of anti-tunnel operations—from knowing where the enemy hides to assessing the extent of its destructive capabilities and localizing the threat. Gaining access to this information requires an investment of time

---

[124] Tom Mangold & John Penycate, The Tunnels of Cù Chi: A Harrowing Account of America's "Tunnel Rats" in the Underground Battlefields of Vietnam 107 (2005).

[125] Testimonies of U.S. soldiers who fought in Vietnam point to the grave moral and psychological effects of fighting in tunnels. *See* Peter Gorner, *Life of a Tunnel Rat: Fighting Fear in "Nam,"* Chi. Trib. (June 28, 1985), http://articles.chicagotribune.com/1985-06-28/features/8502110841_1_cu-chi-american-tunnel-rats-john-penycate; Gerard DeGroot, *The Enemy Below: Why Hamas Tunnels Scare Israel So Much*, Wash. Post (July 25, 2014), https://www.washingtonpost.com/opinions/the-enemy-below-why-hamas-tunnels-scare-israel-so-much/2014/07/25/c7ef0902-1281-11e4-9285-4243a40ddc97_story.html?utm_term=.cf6310eea7c0.

and resources in any war. Below ground, however, information is so well guarded that it is beyond the reach of traditional intelligence-gathering methods. Gaining access to *that* information requires commanders to go out of their way, with few chances of success. Even the aftermath of attacks is imbued with greater uncertainty and unpredictability in the realm of underground warfare than in "aboveground" warfare. The consequences of simple operations—such as blowing up an entrance or destroying a segment of a tunnel—cannot be fully predicted, for reasons having to do with the tunnel's structure and the soil's geological makeup. In the case of cross-border tunnels, when tunnels are dug underneath a state's *own* populated areas, the unknown factor also affects the ability to predict the outcome of anti-tunnel operations on one's own territory.

Skeptics might take issue with the claim that the fog of war affects underground warfare more than it affects other types of warfare. Urban warfare makes it exceedingly difficult to gain information about the location and identity of fighters—who not only look like civilians but also purposefully operate from civilian populated areas. Acknowledging the unique challenge of underground warfare should not, in any way, be interpreted as minimizing the challenge of urban warfare (or other types of warfare, for that matter). The fog of war characterizes warfare of all types. My research shows, however, that the unknown factor affects underground warfare at levels exponentially higher than urban warfare. Examples abound, from the underground battles of WWI where belligerents struggled to locate each other's tunnels, to Vietnam where the United States tried, in vain, to detect the Vietcong's complex underground structures by bringing new technology to the battlefield, and the surprises encountered by French forces in the mountains of Mali in 2013. The difficulty in detecting tunnels and accessing enemy communication hinders the identification of targets and sometimes even the most basic understanding of the enemy's modus operandi (including, for example, potential cooperation with other groups, organizational structure, and available arsenal).

In this section, I examine how the unknown factor bears on IHL's application, particularly on the fulfillment of IHL's many knowledge- and information-based obligations. IHL expects military commanders to know, foresee, and act based on information. It assumes, and builds on, a military commander's knowledge of certain facts. For example, Article 52(2) of AP I asks that a commander gain some knowledge regarding the nature, location, purpose, or use of a given object before launching a strike. The assumption is that the commander *may* gain such knowledge in war. In a conventional war waged far from civilian centers, the assumption might hold. In urban warfare, it begins to break down: Is the rebel leader using this house to sleep, or also to plan attacks and coordinate operations? The question is difficult to answer—more difficult than determining whether bunkers and trenches located on an actual and well-delineated battlefield constitute military objectives. When urban warfare meets underground warfare, as explained in Chapter 7, commanders face the task of untangling the complexity of the former in the unknown environment inherent to the latter.

IHL requires both information *and* knowledge. Whereas information refers to "facts about a situation, person, event, etc.,"[126] knowledge is commonly defined as the "understanding of or information about a subject that you get by experience or study, either known by one person or by people generally."[127] Whereas information is raw, knowledge involves a human element: the interpretation of information. Norms governing the conduct of hostilities require the commander to possess both knowledge and information. The unknown factor makes the performance of these duties overly burdensome as, by definition, the underground conceals information in a virtually foolproof manner.

IHL imposes three types of knowledge-based duties. The first type consists of those duties inherent to distinction, proportionality, and precautions. Upholding the basic tenets of IHL makes it necessary to gather and analyze information about the identity of targets, their location, activities, and potential membership in a hostile group. This exercise in intelligence gathering, sometimes referred to as establishing a "pattern of life," is aimed at collecting as much information as possible about the target.[128] It also helps to minimize the impact of the strike on civilians. Verifying the nature of the target involves "focusing intelligence, surveillance, reconnaissance (ISR) and target acquisition resources to satisfy the commander's intelligence and information requirements."[129] Similarly, in the realm of proportionality, the law asks a commander to foresee the collateral damage that will ensue from the strike. The problem is that these resources and capabilities are precisely (and intentionally) those hindered by the underground. Either way, the commander must make his or her assessment based on the information available at the time.[130] It is unclear, however, how much information the commander needs to fulfill this obligation—particularly in extreme situations where information is scarce and hardly available. I return to this later.

The second type of IHL knowledge-based duties consists of those that commanders and states owe for actions (or omissions) carried out by their subordinates, or entities under their control. Article 86(2) of AP I provides that superiors are responsible for a subordinate's violations "if they knew, or had information which should have enabled them to conclude in the circumstances at the time, that he was committing or was going to commit such a breach and if they did not take all feasible measures within their power to prevent or repress the breach." Under customary law, this type of command responsibility "is not limited to situations where the commander/superior has actual knowledge

---

[126] *Information Definition*, CAMBRIDGE DICTIONARY, http://dictionary.cambridge.org/dictionary/english/information.

[127] *Knowledge Definition*, CAMBRIDGE DICTIONARY, http://dictionary.cambridge.org/dictionary/english/knowledge.

[128] HUMAN RIGHTS WATCH, "TROOPS IN CONTACT": AIRSTRIKES AND CIVILIAN DEATHS IN AFGHANISTAN 29–30 (2008), https://www.hrw.org/sites/default/files/reports/afghanistan0908web_0.pdf.

[129] Geoffrey Corn & James A. Schoettler, Jr., *Targeting and Civilian Risk Mitigation: The Essential Role of Precautionary Measures*, 223 MIL. L. REV. 785, 801 (2015).

[130] *Id.* at 802.

of the crimes committed or about to be committed by his or her subordinates."[131] Constructive knowledge is sufficient. Information and knowledge play a more passive role in the fulfillment of these duties: the commander or the state should have knowledge of their subordinates' actions, and could be held responsible for having constructive knowledge of any violation. Although these duties are certainly knowledge-dependent, they are very different from the active information-seeking obligations analyzed above.

A third type of information duties includes the obligation to ensure respect for IHL and disseminate its knowledge to the civilian population and the armed forces.[132] Ensuring respect for IHL, as set forth in Common Article 1 of the Geneva Conventions, requires sharing and inculcating its values. The duty of dissemination is embodied in all four Geneva Conventions,[133] AP I,[134] and numerous military manuals.[135] It is premised on the idea that knowledge is a precondition for compliance. IHL must be not only taught during military training, but integrated into all activity, training, and instruction.[136] In addition, states must ensure that "all officials are aware of the essential rules of law relevant to their actual functions."[137] Both the obligation to ensure respect and the duty to disseminate are regarded as customary.[138]

The major role played by information and knowledge under IHL and the difficulty of obtaining information in the underground realm create undeniable challenges for the warring parties—particularly in the fulfillment of the first category of duties. What is the burden of proof weighing on military commanders ahead of a strike? This question would seem to an IHL-outsider—and certainly to a practitioner—a fundamental one. Yet IHL, here as in so many other areas, has avoided setting forth a ready-made formula. It has left it to practitioners to balance considerations of humanity with military necessity and delineate the scope of information-seeking duties.[139]

IHL's relatively weak attempt at delineating the scope of the information-based obligations weighing on a military commander begins with Article 57(2) of Additional

---

[131] ICRC Customary Law Study, *supra* note 11, at Rule 153. *See also* Rules 149–155.

[132] *Id.* at Rules 139–143.

[133] GC I, *supra* note 12, at art. 47; GC II, *supra* note 12, at art. 48; GC III, *supra* note 12, at art. 127; GC IV, *supra* note 12, at art. 144. All require as follows: "The High Contracting Parties undertake, in time of peace as in time of war, to disseminate the text of the present Convention as widely as possible in their respective countries and, in particular, to include the study thereof [if possible] in their programmes of . . . civilian instruction, so that the principles thereof may become known to the entire population."

[134] AP I, *supra* note 4, at art. 83: "The High Contracting Parties undertake, in time of peace as in time of armed conflict, to disseminate the Conventions and this Protocol as widely as possible in their respective countries and, in particular, to include the study thereof in their programmes of military instruction and to encourage the study thereof by the civilian population, so that those instruments may become known to the armed forces and to the civilian population."

[135] *See* ICRC Customary Law Study, *supra* note 11, at Rules 143 and 144.

[136] 2016 COMMENTARY TO GC I, *supra* note 9, ¶¶ 2776.

[137] *Id.*

[138] *Id.* at Rule 142.

[139] I am indebted to Professor Geoffrey Corn on this point.

Protocol I and the requirement that "[e]ach party to the conflict must do *everything feasible* to verify that the objectives to be attacked are ... military objectives."[140] The obligation derives from the principle of distinction, which calls on military commanders to direct their operations exclusively at military objectives.[141] Upholding the principle of distinction, Article 57 explains, means doing "everything feasible" to verify that a target is in fact a military objective and therefore legally targetable. Although the law arguably tries to clarify the standard, the words "everything feasible" remain vague. At the time the article was adopted, some delegations interpreted "feasible" as meaning "practicable or practically possible."[142] According to the Commentary, which does not embrace this view, information must be actively sought and supplemented by the competent services of the army. The Commentary explains that commanders should not rely exclusively on information readily available:

> [I]n case of doubt, even if there is only slight doubt, they must call for additional information and if need be give orders for further reconnaissance to those of their subordinates and those responsible for supportive weapons (particularly artillery and airforce) whose business this is, and who are answerable to them.[143]

The goal is to keep collecting intelligence from all possible sources in order "to obtain the best possible intelligence."[144] In practice, however, "the commander and the aircrew actually engaged in operations must have some range of discretion to determine which available resources shall be used and how they shall be used."[145] Moreover, limited information does not imply that the commander should abort the attack. The U.S. Law of War Manual, for example, makes it clear that

> Even when information is imperfect or lacking (as will frequently be the case during armed conflict), commanders and other decision-makers may direct and conduct military operations, so long as they make a good faith assessment of the information that is available to them at that time ... The special circumstances of armed conflict often make an accurate determination of facts very difficult ... the importance of prevailing during armed conflict often justifies taking actions based upon limited information that would be considered unreasonable outside armed conflict.[146]

---

[140] AP I, *supra* note 4, at art. 57 (emphasis added).
[141] AP I, *supra* note 4, at art. 48.
[142] *Id.* ¶ 2198.
[143] COMMENTARY TO AP I, *supra* note 40, ¶ 2195.
[144] ICRC Customary Law Study, *supra* note 11, at Rule 15.
[145] NATO BOMBING REPORT, *infra* note 148, ¶ 29.
[146] U.S LAW OF WAR MANUAL, *supra* note 112, at 192.

It would be unrealistic to require commanders to act on "completely accurate information."[147] For this reason, emphasis has been placed on the importance of an effective intelligence-gathering system capable of bringing the required information to the attention of the military commander:

> The obligation to do everything feasible [to verify the nature of a target] is high but not absolute. A military commander must set up an effective intelligence gathering system . . . [and] direct his forces to use available technical means to properly identify targets during operations.[148]

As in the context of cyberwarfare, the question arises of whether doing everything feasible when contending with tunnel warfare includes consulting with an expert.[149] The commander may not possess the background necessary to assess the impact of underground structures on a given operation. Without making it a legal requirement, the presence of an underground warfare expert would certainly benefit the decision-making process whenever operations feature an underground element.

Information-seeking obligations go beyond distinction. As one author notes, "the information that must be gathered before an attack must relate to more than just the nature of the objective. Many other details must be collected, in particular on the immediate surroundings of the target, in order to gain a clear picture of the conditions that will trigger the obligation to apply the principle of proportionality."[150] Proportionality, like distinction, builds on the ability to obtain and assess information.

An attack is considered disproportionate when it "may be expected to cause incidental loss of civilian life, injury to civilians, damage to civilian objects, or a combination thereof, which would be excessive in relation to the concrete and direct military advantage anticipated."[151] Much has been written about proportionality and its indeterminacy.[152] Here, too, the law has avoided clear-cut formulas—leaving states to balance military necessity with humanitarian considerations. One thing is clear: commanders ought to base their

---

[147] Corn and Schoettler, *supra* note 129, at 802.
[148] INTERNATIONAL CRIMINAL TRIBUNAL FOR THE FORMER YUGOSLAVIA: FINAL REPORT TO THE PROSECUTOR BY THE COMMITTEE ESTABLISHED TO REVIEW THE NATO BOMBING CAMPAIGN AGAINST THE FEDERAL REPUBLIC OF YUGOSLAVIA ¶ 29 (June 13, 2000) [hereinafter NATO BOMBING REPORT].
[149] TALLINN MANUAL, *supra* note 47, at Rule 52 and accompanying Commentary, ¶ 6.
[150] Jean-François Quéguiner, *Precautions under the Law Governing the Conduct of Hostilities*, 88 INT'L REV. RED CROSS 793, 798 (2006).
[151] AP I, *supra* note 4, at art. 51(5).
[152] *See, inter alia,* JANINA DILL, LEGITIMATE TARGETS? SOCIAL CONSTRUCTION, INTERNATIONAL LAW AND US BOMBING 95 (2014); Robert D. Sloane, *Puzzles of Proportion and the "Reasonable Military Commander": Reflections on the Law, Ethics and Geopolitics of Proportionality*, 6 HARV. NAT'L SEC. J. 299 (2015); J.D. Ohlin, *Is Jus in Bello in Crisis?* 11 J. INT'L CRIM. JUS. 27 (2013), at 43.

assessment on the information available at the time of an attack.[153] States have embraced this requirement. The U.S DoD Law of War Manual, for example, notes that

> Persons who plan, authorize, or make other decisions in conducting attacks must make the judgments required by the law of war in good faith and on the basis of information available to them at the time . . . Similarly, the expected incidental damage to civilians or civilian objects must be assessed in good faith, given the information available to the commander at the time.[154]

The U.S. Law of War Manual uses the words "in good faith," suggesting that the assessment of the information is an objective one. Similarly, the ICTY, in the Galić judgment, ruled that a disproportionate attack is one in regard to which "a reasonably well-informed person in the circumstances of the actual perpetrator, making reasonable use of the information available to him or her, could have expected excessive civilian casualties to result from the attack."[155] This suggests that information has to be processed objectively by the commander.

Yoram Dinstein takes a different approach on how proportionality needs to be assessed. He argues that, by nature, the proportionality calculus involves a subjective assessment:

> The whole assessment of what injury or damage is "excessive" in the circumstances entails a mental process of weighing in the balance dissimilar considerations—to wit, the expected civilian losses/damage and the anticipated military advantage—and is not an exact science.[156]

That the assessment is subjective does not detract from the obligation to make it in good faith.[157] The two, Dinstein argues quite persuasively, are not incompatible.[158] When making the decision to attack, the commander is, of course, conditioned by a whole array of subjective considerations. I agree that this cannot be avoided. Still, the weighing of the various factors ought to be made in good faith. The same considerations should be kept in mind by those who, in hindsight, will assess this decision—be they investigators, prosecutors, or judges. Their own knowledge and subjective understanding of the situation should not influence the ex-post assessment of a commander's decision.

---

[153] *See, e.g.*, ICRC Customary Law Study, *supra* note 11, at Rule 14.
[154] U.S. LAW OF WAR MANUAL, *supra* note 112, at 96 (noting that the principle is accepted by most states).
[155] Prosecutor v. Galić, Case No. IT-98-29-T, Judgment, ¶ 58 (Int'l Crim. Trib. for the Former Yugoslavia, Dec. 5, 2003).
[156] DINSTEIN, *supra* note 88, at 158.
[157] LESLIE C. GREEN, THE CONTEMPORARY LAW OF ARMED CONFLICT 391 (3d ed. 2008).
[158] DINSTEIN, *supra* note 88, at 159 n.906.

In sum, obtaining information and processing it into reliable, sufficient, and objective knowledge forms the core of a commander's obligations under IHL. Commanders must use much, if not all, of available capabilities to gather information about the target. As noted above, they might even decide to turn to tunnel experts within the army. However, the law cannot expect commanders to know that which is unknowable. The expectations, too, should remain reasonable. The guiding principle that "in case of doubt, additional information must be obtained" offers little relief in the realm of underground warfare.[159] What if more information *cannot* be obtained? Although the situation is by no means unusual in war, the informational dead end occurs earlier in underground warfare. At some point, however, a decision must be made and intelligence collection must cease. This should be kept in mind by all relevant actors, even as militaries continue to develop tools that enhance the collection of information in a subterranean environment.

Until technology overcomes the unknown factor, the underground will continue to complicate military operations and the application of the law alike. In addition to impeding the ability to implement the principles of distinction and proportionality, the underground makes it difficult to take the precautions required under Article 57 of Additional Protocol I. Article 57 provides as follows:

1. In the conduct of military operations, constant care shall be taken to spare the civilian population, civilians and civilian objects.
2. With respect to attacks, the following precautions shall be taken:
   (a) those who plan or decide upon an attack shall:
      (i) do everything feasible to verify that the objectives to be attacked are neither civilians nor civilian objects and are not subject to special protection but are military objectives within the meaning of paragraph 2 of Article 52 and that it is not prohibited by the provisions of this Protocol to attack them;
      (ii) take all feasible precautions in the choice of means and methods of attack with a view to avoiding, and in any event to minimizing, incidental loss of civilian life, injury to civilians and damage to civilian objects;
      (iii) refrain from deciding to launch any attack which may be expected to cause incidental loss of civilian life, injury to civilians, damage to civilian objects, or a combination thereof, which would be excessive in relation to the concrete and direct military advantage anticipated;
   (b) an attack shall be cancelled or suspended if it becomes apparent that the objective is not a military one or is subject to special protection or that the

---

[159] Quéguiner, *supra* note 150, at 798.

attack may be expected to cause incidental loss of civilian life, injury to civilians, damage to civilian objects, or a combination thereof, which would be excessive in relation to the concrete and direct military advantage anticipated;

(c) effective advance warning shall be given of attacks which may affect the civilian population, unless circumstances do not permit.

3. When a choice is possible between several military objectives for obtaining a similar military advantage, the objective to be selected shall be that the attack on which may be expected to cause the least danger to civilian lives and to civilian objects.

4. In the conduct of military operations at sea or in the air, each Party to the conflict shall, in conformity with its rights and duties under the rules of international law applicable in armed conflict, take all reasonable precautions to avoid losses of civilian lives and damage to civilian objects.

5. No provision of this Article may be construed as authorizing any attacks against the civilian population, civilians or civilian objects.[160]

The breadth of these precautionary duties designed to protect the civilian population, as well as the difficulty of upholding them in underground warfare, could mean one of two things. First, the unique operational complexity could be viewed as allowing the commander more flexibility where information cannot be obtained. Alternatively, one could argue that where uncertainty is too high restrictions need to be tightened instead.

The first and more flexible approach acknowledges the unique features of subterranean warfare. As explained above, the idea is not unprecedented. Tailor-made applications of IHL have been embraced in naval warfare, aerial warfare, submarine warfare, and of course cyberwarfare. In yet another example, Article 2(4) of Protocol III to the Convention on Certain Conventional Weapons forbids attacks against forests or other kind of plant cover, except when such natural elements are used to "cover, conceal, or camouflage combatants or other military objectives."[161] This exception, known as the *jungle exception*, recognizes the need for some flexibility in an unusual environment. States could adopt similar exceptions in the context of underground warfare.[162]

An opposite view would restrict the right to use lethal force when the unknown factor hinders the ability to take precautions. Among those, Article 57(2)(b) demands that commanders retain the ability to monitor an attack and cancel it if necessary: "an attack shall be cancelled or suspended" if it becomes apparent that it would be indiscriminate or

---

[160] AP I, *supra* note 4, at art. 57.
[161] Protocol (III) to CCW on Prohibitions or Restrictions on the Use of Incendiary Weapons, art. 2(4), Oct. 10, 1980, *supra* note 22.
[162] DETTER, *supra* note 71, at 226 (noting that "the clause was devised to cater for such situations as that encountered by the United States in Vietnam when fighting the Viet Cong," and encouraging a revision of the protocol).

disproportionate. The ICRC Study on Customary International Humanitarian Law uses a different formula, noting instead that the attacker "must do *everything feasible* to cancel or suspend" an attack in such cases.[163] It is arguable whether a change of circumstances creates an obligation to cancel or suspend an attack. Assuming that it does, can an attack that cannot be monitored ever be lawful? Or, to put it differently, how much control *over an ongoing attack* is required on the part of the attacker for such attack to be lawful?

Unlike on land, in the air, or at sea, common means of communication are either ineffective or not suitable underground. The lack of communication makes it difficult to monitor underground activity. Notifying troops about nearby civilians, ceasefires, or withdrawals may not be feasible while the attack is ongoing and soldiers are inside a tunnel. Based on some accounts, this might have happened when, on August 1, 2014, Hamas broke the ceasefire that had just been agreed upon with Israel. Amos Yadlin, former chief of the IDF's military intelligence directorate, has raised the possibility that Hamas militants had no knowledge of the ceasefire because it had been agreed upon while they were underground.[164] Regardless of the circumstances in that case, the ability to know and maintain control over what goes on underground is inferior to aboveground.

The ability to monitor on ongoing attack—or the lack thereof—has arisen in the context of lethal autonomous weapons. Benvenisti and Lieblich have argued that when operating an intelligent or automated weapon, a commander will "be more inclined to absolve him/herself from exercising discretion by relying on the weapon's discretion instead."[165] Cyberwarfare exhibits similar problems.[166] The lack of control over the effects of an attack and the circumstances in which it evolves has caused concern. Once a code is designed and used for an attack in cyberspace, the attack proceeds as planned: its effects cannot be modified once it has begun. Even when suspending or canceling an attack is possible in cyberspace, the perpetrator would probably refrain from doing so to protect anonymity. Far from questioning the legality of such attacks, however, the Tallinn Manual subjected the perpetrator to heightened scrutiny in the planning stages of an attack:[167]

> Some attacks may be difficult to continuously monitor, thus making it practically difficult to know whether to cancel or suspend them. This would heighten the degree of scrutiny that is merited during the planning and decision phases of the attack.[168]

---

[163] ICRC Customary Law Study, *supra* note 11, at Rule 19 (emphasis added).

[164] Robert Naiman, *Gaza Ceasefire Collapses; What Should We Do Now?*, Huffington Post (Aug. 1, 2014), http://www.huffingtonpost.com/robert-naiman/gaza-ceasefire-collapses-_b_5641634.html.

[165] Eliav Lieblich & Eyal Benvenisti, *The Obligation to Exercise Discretion in Warfare: Why Autonomous Weapons Systems Are Unlawful*, *in* Autonomous Weapons Systems: Law, Ethics, Policy 277 (Nehal Bhuta et al. eds., 2016).

[166] *See* Cordula Droege, *Get Off My Cloud: Cyber Warfare, International Humanitarian Law, and the Protection of Civilians*, 94 Int'l Rev. Red Cross 886 (2012).

[167] Tallinn Manual, *supra* note 47, at Rule 57.

[168] *Id.* at Rule 57 and accompanying Commentary, ¶ 7.

To conclude, the reduced ability to take precautions could, at best, advocate in favor of imposing greater obligations on the commander. It cannot invalidate underground operations altogether. Imposing greater obligations on the commander seems hardly reasonable in the context of underground warfare. As explained above, information-seeking duties already weigh more on commanders in the context of underground operations than in "ordinary" warfare. Imposing a heightened degree of scrutiny in an environment so heavily permeated by the unknown factor would make it virtually impossible to carry out anti-tunnel operations in accordance with the law.

III. Weapons Underground

Underground warfare calls for many adjustments on the part of states—from the institutionalization of a strategy to the development of new technology, communication tools, and rescue procedures. The choice of weapons to contend with underground threats also deserves some attention. Tunnels and other underground structures are characterized by some unique physical features, including limited air flow, and the ability of walls to retain gas and amplify the impact of blasts. Weapons can react differently in this airless environment than they do aboveground. Lethal weapons could become more powerful; non-lethal weapons could become lethal. The question I wish to examine is whether the subterranean can affect the legality of weapons otherwise considered lawful.[169]

According to the International Court of Justice, the legality of weapons is governed by two "cardinal principles":[170] the obligation to discriminate between civilians and combatants, and the prohibition on causing unnecessary suffering to combatants.[171] In the case of the underground, both are of concern. The lack of visibility, intelligence, and real-time control can affect the ability to distinguish between civilians and combatants underground.[172] In addition, a weapon can become more lethal, cruel, or powerful when used in a confined environment—thereby causing unnecessary suffering or superfluous injury to combatants. In addition to these two principles—to which all weapons are subject—the legality of a weapon depends on any specific rule (conventional or customary) applicable to the weapon in question.[173]

There is little doubt that the effect of a weapon may be modified for the worse when used inside a tunnel. When comparing open-air explosions with explosions in buses, scientists have found that the latter cause more severe injuries and a higher mortality rate

---

[169] I focus here on the effects of these weapons on combatants, as effects on civilians are analyzed in depth in Chapter 7.
[170] Nuclear Weapons Advisory Opinion, *supra* note 7, at 78.
[171] *See* CCW, *supra* note 22.
[172] Fry, *supra* note 43, at 490–91, 499.
[173] WILLIAM BOOTHBY, WEAPONS AND THE LAW OF ARMED CONFLICT 233 (2d ed., 2016).

than explosions in the open air.[174] Scientists attempting to measure the impact of walls on the severity of injuries, particularly brain injuries and hearing loss have found that "[t]he walls in the confined space enhance the risk of primary blast injuries considerably because of indirect blast waves transferring a larger amount of damaging energy to the head."[175] In confined spaces, blast waves are concentrated—intensifying the effects of blasts and making them last longer.[176] The brain, for example, "experiences subsequent overpressure loads."[177] Other primary blast injuries, such as "tympanic perforation and blast lung and increasing displacement of the body wall, which may cause a shearing effect on larger organs, especially abdominal viscera," also increase as a result.[178]

These studies underscore the importance of looking into how weapons "behave" underground, and how this unique environment affects their legality.

A. UNNECESSARY SUFFERING AND MILITARY NECESSITY

The prohibition on means and methods that are of a nature to cause superfluous injury or unnecessary suffering is well established under the law of armed conflict. The two expressions "superfluous injury" and "unnecessary suffering" are often used in tandem to reflect both the English wording ("unnecessary suffering") and the French wording ("*maux superflus*," translated into "superfluous injury").[179] Despite the slightly broader meaning of the French wording, both expressions are generally used interchangeably.

The principle was first formulated in the 1868 Saint Petersburg Declaration,[180] and later reiterated in the 1899 Hague Regulations,[181] the 1907 Hague Regulations,[182]

---

[174] D. Leibovici et al., *Blast Injuries: Bus Versus Open-Air Bombings – A Comparative Study of Injuries in Survivors of Open-Air Versus Confined-Space Explosions*, 41 J. TRAUMA & ACUTE CARE SURGERY 1030 (1996).

[175] Andrew J Newman, Sarah H. Hayes, Abhiram S. Raoa, Brian L. Allman, Senthilvelan Manohar, Dalian Ding, Daniel Stolzberg, Edward Lobarinas, Joseph C. Mollendorf & Richard Salvi, *Low-Cost Blast Wave Generator for Studies of Hearing Loss and Brain Injury: Blast Wave Effects in Closed Spaces*, 242 J. NEUROSCIENCE METHODS 82 (2015). *See also* Asghar Rezaei, Mehdi Salimi Jazi & Ghodrat Karam, *Computational Modeling of Human Head Under Blast in Confined and Open Spaces: Primary Blast Injury*, 30 INT'L J. NUMERICAL METHODS IN BIOMEDICAL ENGINEERING 69, 69 and 79 (2014) (investigating "the effect of walls in the confined and semiconfined spaces under different explosion intensities compared with that of the open space" and "the reasons for the harshness of the situations in confined spaces.")

[176] *Id.* at 80.

[177] *Id.*

[178] Eddie Chaloner, *Blast Injury in Enclosed Spaces*, 331 BRIT. MED. J. 119, 119 (2005).

[179] Hague Convention (IV) Respecting the Laws and Customs of War on Land and Its Annex: Regulations Concerning the Laws and Customs of War on Land (Oct. 18, 1907) [hereinafter 1907 Hague Regulations].

[180] Declaration Renouncing the Use, in Time of War, of Explosive Projectiles Under 400 Grammes Weight (Nov. 29/Dec. 11, 1868) ("The only legitimate object which States should endeavor to accomplish during war is to weaken the military forces of the enemy; That for this purpose it is sufficient to disable the greatest possible number of men; That this object would be exceeded by the employment of arms which uselessly aggravate the sufferings of disabled men, or render their death inevitable.")

[181] Convention (II) with Respect to the Laws and Customs of War on Land and its Annex: Regulations Concerning the Laws and Customs of War on Land, art. 23(e) (July 29, 1899).

[182] 1907 Hague Regulations, *supra* note 179, at art. 23(e).

Additional Protocol I,[183] and the Rome Statute of the International Criminal Court.[184] The prohibition is considered customary, and applies in international and non-international armed conflicts.[185]

The principle has been regarded as a tenet of the law of armed conflict for centuries, but its scope has not remained constant. Whereas the 1899 Hague Regulations prohibit the use of "arms, projectiles, or material of *a nature to cause* superfluous injury," the 1907 Hague Regulations prohibit the use of those "*calculated to cause* unnecessary suffering."[186] The Brussels Declaration of 1874,[187] the 1868 Saint Petersburg Declaration, and the Oxford Manual,[188] though arguably of lesser normative force, all adopted the more restrictive wording ("calculated to cause").[189] AP I—the most recent formulation of the principle—prohibits the use of "weapons, projectiles and material and methods of warfare *of a nature to cause* superfluous injury or unnecessary suffering."[190]

What is a weapon *of a nature to cause superfluous injury*? Is it a weapon that was meant to cause such harm (a design-based approach) or, rather, one that could have such effects if used in a particular way (an effect-based approach)? The CCW (Convention on Certain Conventional Weapons) suggests that the former is right. The design-based approach finds support in Protocol I to the CCW on non-detectable fragments, which prohibits the use of "any weapon *the primary effect* of which is to injure by fragments which in the human body escape detection by X-rays,"[191] and in Protocol IV to the CCW, which prohibits "laser weapons *specifically designed*, as their sole combat function or as one of their combat functions, to cause permanent blindness to unenhanced vision."[192] These two prohibitions emphasize a weapon's design, prohibiting only those weapons specifically designed to produce certain effects. The second interpretation—which looks to prohibit a weapon based on its effects regardless of whether the weapon was originally designed to cause them[193]—is much broader and makes less sense in practice. Consider, for example, anti-tank missiles. Despite the horrific effect and the great suffering they may cause to soldiers, no state would regard them as prohibited for causing unnecessary suffering. That anti-tank missiles were not designed for the purpose of burning soldiers in tanks excludes them from the scope of the prohibition.

---

[183] AP I, *supra* note 4, at art. 35(2).
[184] Rome Statute, *supra* note 23, at art. 8(b)(2)(20).
[185] Tadić, *supra* note 14, ¶ 127.
[186] 1907 Hague Regulations, *supra* note 179, at art. 23(e) (emphasis added).
[187] Project of an International Declaration concerning the Laws and Customs of War, art. 13(e) (Aug. 27, 1874).
[188] The Laws of War on Land, art. 9 (Sept. 9, 1880).
[189] For an explanation about the different versions and their legal implications, see DETTER, *supra* note 71, at 165.
[190] AP I, *supra* note 4, at art. 35(2).
[191] Protocol (I) to CCW on Non-Detectable Fragments, Oct. 10, 1980, *supra* note 22 (emphasis added).
[192] Protocol (IV) to CCW on Blinding Laser Weapons, art. 1, Oct. 13, 1995, *supra* note 22 (emphasis added).
[193] WILLIAM BOOTHBY, WEAPONS AND THE LAW OF ARMED CONFLICT 53-54 (2d ed. 2016).

Under all of its iterations and interpretations, the principle is understood as protecting combatants rather than civilians.[194] It prohibits belligerents from inflicting more suffering on enemy soldiers than necessary to bring about their submission or, to borrow the ICJ's words, from inflicting "a harm greater than that avoidable to achieve legitimate military objectives."[195] Weapons that would increase suffering without increasing the military advantage are therefore considered unlawful.[196] As William Boothby puts it,

> [I]t is the aggravation of that suffering without associated usefulness, or, in more modern parlance, without military utility, that would exceed the legitimate object to be accomplished by States in war. If it exceeds that which is legitimate, it is illegitimate and thus unlawful.[197]

The legal test does not require an examination by medical means or *in abstracto*, but, rather subjectively, a balancing act between the anticipated suffering and military necessity. Put differently, IHL permits the infliction of a greater amount of suffering in circumstances when military necessity justifies it. The wording *unnecessary* suffering implies that the infliction of a wide range of "necessary suffering" is legitimate.[198] It is therefore not enough to point to the great amount of suffering a combatant might experience from the use of a weapon in a given terrain; the necessity of the use must be weighed against it in the balance.[199] As the U.S. Law of War Manual explains,

> an artillery shell designed to destroy field fortifications or heavy material causes injuries to enemy personnel that are much greater than those necessary to make enemy combatants *hors de combat*. However, the artillery shell is not prohibited because these military advantages are not clearly disproportionate to the injuries it inflicts.[200]

---

[194] Nuclear Weapons Advisory Opinion, *supra* note 7, at 76.
[195] *Id.* ¶ 78.
[196] Solis, *supra* note 55, at 290.
[197] BOOTHBY, *supra* note 173, at 47.
[198] Geoffrey S. Corn et al., *Belligerent Targeting and the Invalidity of a Least Harmful Means Rule*, 89 INT'L. L. STUD. 536, 554 (2013) [hereinafter Corn et al.].
[199] COMMENTARY TO AP I, *supra* note 40, ¶ 1428 ("[i]n principle it is necessary to weigh up the nature of the injury or the intensity of suffering on the one hand, against the 'military necessity', on the other hand, before deciding whether there is a case of superfluous injury or unnecessary suffering as this term is understood in war.") *See also* Dissenting Opinion of Judge Higgins in the Nuclear Weapons Advisory Opinion, *supra* note 7, ¶¶ 16–17 ("It is this understanding of the principle that explains why States have been able to move to a specific prohibition of dum-dum bullets, whereas certain weapons that cause vastly greater suffering have neither been the subject of specific prohibitions . . . The principle does not stipulate that a legitimate target is not to be attacked if it would cause great suffering.")
[200] U.S. LAW OF WAR MANUAL, *supra* note 112, at 337.

The difficulty of reaching the underground, the depth of the tunnels, and the availability of any other weapons must therefore be taken into account when assessing whether a weapon is likely to cause unnecessary suffering. It is interesting to note in this regard that, according to Michael Schmitt, the GBU 43/B, also known as the "Mother of All Bombs" is not "a weapon that causes superfluous injury or unnecessary suffering, for its effects on combatants are basically the same as those of other blast weapons that rely upon the creation of a pressure wave to injure or kill."[201]

The prohibition on unnecessary suffering applies to all weapons—including lawful weapons.[202] Flamethrowers, white phosphorus, and napalm are lawful, yet they may not be used in a way that causes suffering "substantially disproportional to the military advantage gained."[203] Weapons that have successfully passed weapon's review might still be regarded as illegal when used in an underground environment.

In other words, passing a weapon review with flying colors does not guarantee legality in all circumstances.

Before elaborating further, a few words are in order on weapon reviews. Weapon review, a process required under Article 36 of Additional Protocol I, is routinely carried out by states to assess the legality of new weapons. Most states favor a multidisciplinary assessment involving experts with legal, military, political, technological, or medical backgrounds.[204] Others rely on expertise by way of consultation where it is necessary. The outcome of a weapon's review does not necessarily affect acquisition decisions. It may result, at times, in the modification of system requirements, the formulation of operational directives that prescribe or restrict how a weapon system should be used, or the introduction of training and education processes. The review process examines whether a weapon is inherently indiscriminate, prohibited as part of existing IHL regulations, and/or likely to cause superfluous injury or unnecessary suffering.[205]

---

[201] Michael Schmitt and Lt. Cdr. Peter Barker, *"The Mother of All Bombs": Understanding the Massive Ordnance Air Blast Weapon*, JustSecurity (April 15, 2017), https://www.justsecurity.org/40022/the-mother-bombs-understanding-massive-ordnance-air-blast-weapon/?utm_source=Regular+Newsletter&utm_campaign=0e49c28ab4-EMAIL_CAMPAIGN_2017_04_23&utm_medium=email&utm_term=0_c558056c1-0e49c28ab4-36731565.

[202] Solis, *supra* note 55, at 291; and ICRC Customary Law Study, *supra* note 11, at Rule 70 (noting that divergences of opinion remain "as to whether the rule itself renders a weapon illegal or whether a weapon is illegal only if a specific treaty or customary rule prohibits its use").

[203] Solis, *supra* note 55, at 292.

[204] For example, in the UK, weapons reviews are undertaken by the Development Concepts and Doctrine Centre (DCDC). The DCDC is part of Joint Forces Command, is completely independent from the regular chain of command, and brings together lawyers from the Navy, Army, and Air Force. *See* UNITED KINGDOM MINISTRY OF DEFENCE, U.K. WEAPON REVIEWS (2016), https://www.gov.uk/government/uploads/system/uploads/attachment_data/file/507319/20160308-UK_weapon_reviews.pdf.

[205] *See*, The Third CCW Meeting of Experts on Lethal Autonomous Weapons Systems (LAWS), Apr. 11–15, 2016, *Report of the 2016 Informal Meeting of Experts on LAWS* ¶¶ 48–49.

Beyond these basic guidelines, however, the standards for appropriate review are not clearly spelled out in the Protocol. States can shape their review process pretty much as they see fit. The upshot, as acknowledged by the ICRC Commentary, is that states may reach different conclusions as to the legality of a weapon. In a noteworthy attempt at providing some guidance, the ICRC Guide to the Legal Review of New Weapons, Means and Methods of Warfare notes that the authority responsible for reviewing new weapons must "[bear] in mind that the weapon's effects will result from a combination of its design *and* the manner in which it is to be used."[206] Although it is the duty of the authority conducting the review to consider the various ways in which the weapon can be used, context continues to matter in how the weapon is used going forward. If, as is often the case, the underground context has not been envisaged as part of a weapon's review,[207] it should be taken into consideration prior to the weapon's use. Use therefore matters as part, and independently, of weapon review. The ICTY confirmed this when it held that the M-87 Orkan rocket launcher, though not prohibited per se, was indiscriminate when used from a distance that reduces its accuracy and in a civilian populated area.[208] If a permissible weapon is used in a way that is indiscriminate or causes unnecessary suffering, it will be regarded as unlawful *in these specific circumstances*. Such a finding will not affect the legality of the weapon outside the said circumstances.

To conclude, a weapon's use can be declared illegal at any point in time, even after or independently of a review. Accordingly, military commanders should always consider the anticipated effects of a weapon in unique terrains, including underground—and carefully weigh these effects against military necessity.

Weapons that may be affected by this complex calculation include booby traps, incendiary weapons, white phosphorus, and thermobaric bombs. This list is certainly not exhaustive; its purpose is merely to illustrate the importance of assessing the effects of powerful weapons in an underground context. Importantly, IHL does not treat these weapons as unlawful. They could, however, become unlawful when used underground—even when deployed against combatants.

Protocol II to the CCW defines booby traps as "any device or material which is designed, constructed or adapted to kill or injure and which functions unexpectedly when a person disturbs or approaches an apparently harmless object or performs an apparently safe act."[209] The use of booby traps "designed to cause superfluous injury or

---

[206] INTERNATIONAL COMMITTEE OF THE RED CROSS, A GUIDE TO THE LEGAL REVIEW OF NEW WEAPONS, MEANS AND METHODS OF WARFARE: MEASURES TO IMPLEMENT ARTICLE 36 OF ADDITIONAL PROTOCOL I OF 1977 17 (2006).

[207] Fry, *supra* note 43, at 480.

[208] Prosecutor v. Martić, Case No. IT-95-11, Appeals Chamber Judgment ¶¶ 247–252 (Int'l Crim. Trib. for the Former Yugoslavia, Oct. 8, 2008).

[209] Protocol (II) to CCW on Prohibitions or Restrictions on the Use of Mines, Booby-Traps and Other Devices, art. 2, Oct. 10, 1980, *supra* note 22.

unnecessary suffering,"[210] is prohibited, as well as the use of such weapons in a way "which cannot be directed at a specific military objective"[211] or directly against civilians or civilian objects.[212] Certain booby traps are prohibited "in all circumstances"—that is against both civilians and combatants—when they are hidden in seemingly harmless objects such as food, children's toys, or medical equipment.[213] The latter aspect of the regulation is heavily influenced by rules governing perfidy. The ICRC Customary Law Study confirms that IHL does not impose a blanket prohibition on booby traps but, rather, limits their use in certain situations.[214] The use of booby traps inside tunnels, a practice favored by the Vietcong, would have to be assessed in light of these limitations. The indiscriminate impact (i.e., whether they are likely to harm civilians or combatants) seems the most concerning in this regard, as the effects of booby traps in terms of suffering are probably equivalent above and below ground.

Protocol III of the CCW similarly regulates incendiary weapons by allowing their use against combatants but prohibiting them against or near civilians. This outcome reflects a compromise between states that advocated a complete ban on incendiary weapons, and those (such as the United States and the UK) that objected to a ban even as against combatants alone.[215] The protocol defines incendiary weapons as those *"primarily designed* to set fire to objects or to cause burn injury to persons through the action of flame, heat, or a combination thereof, produced by a chemical reaction of a substance delivered on the target."[216] Weapons that set fire to objects or cause burn injuries, however frequently, are thus not prohibited unless they were primarily designed to produce these effects.[217] Incendiary weapons that do not meet this definition—such as flamethrowers and grenades—are lawful provided they are used only against combatants and not in such a way as to cause unnecessary suffering.[218] The UK Manual aptly captures this compromise. It notes that when used against combatants, weapons such as napalm and flamethrowers "are governed by the unnecessary suffering principle so that they should not be used directly against personnel but against armoured vehicles, bunkers and built up emplacements, even though personnel inside may be burnt."[219]

---

[210] *Id.* art. 6(2).
[211] *Id.* art. 3.
[212] *Id.*
[213] *Id.* art. 7.
[214] This is important as only 95 states are party to Protocol II. ICRC Customary Law Study, *supra* note 11, at Rule 80.
[215] ICRC Customary Law Study, *supra* note 11, at Rule 85. *See also* BOOTHBY, *supra* note 173, at 200 (noting that the words "less harmful" are unclear as they could mean "less painful" or "less long-lasting").
[216] Protocol (III) to CCW, *supra* note 161, at art. 1 (emphasis added).
[217] BOOTHBY, *supra* note 173, at 194.
[218] *Id.*; SOLIS, *supra* note 55, at 291–92, 742.
[219] UNITED KINGDOM MINISTRY OF DEFENCE, JOINT SERVICE MANUAL OF THE LAW OF ARMED CONFLICT, ¶ 6.12.6 (2004) [hereinafter UK LOAC MANUAL].

In light of the above, the position taken by the ICRC in its study of customary IHL is not readily understandable. In Rule 85, the ICRC states rather categorically that "[t]he anti-personnel use of incendiary weapons is prohibited, unless it is not feasible to use a less harmful weapon to render a person hors de combat." The position taken by the ICRC is much more restrictive than that of the protocol. Here is why, according to the study:

> There are very few reports of use of napalm and similar incendiary weapons against combatants since the adoption of the Convention on Certain Conventional Weapons. What reports there are have been in the form of accusations condemning their use and are unconfirmed. It can be concluded from this practice that incendiary weapons may not be used against combatants if such use would cause unnecessary suffering, i.e., if it is feasible to use a less harmful weapon to render a combatant hors de combat.[220]

This seems a weak legal justification for making incendiary weapons unlawful—an outcome certain states have actively resisted. I would therefore conclude that incendiary weapons can continue to be used against caves, bunkers, and tunnels. This conclusion finds support, inter alia, in the terms of Protocol III to the CCW, which, as noted above, prohibits "mak[ing] forests or other kinds of plant cover the object of attack by incendiary weapons except when such natural elements are used to cover, conceal or camouflage combatants or other military objectives, or are themselves military objectives."[221] The purpose of the underground is precisely to provide such cover and concealment to combatants, and the use of incendiary weapons to expose the military objectives therefore cannot be regarded as unlawful per se.

Grenades—another type of incendiary weapon—raise similar issues. Although the use of grenades is not prohibited under IHL, throwing a grenade in a tunnel may accentuate the effect of the shrapnel and shock waves. Beyond its effect on the enemy, using grenades in an underground context can be dangerous for the forces. The blast can lead to the tunnel's collapse—or injure the soldier who threw the grenade.

White phosphorus, which presents some incendiary-like characteristics, is another weapon worth considering in the context of underground warfare. White phosphorus is not prohibited as a chemical weapon.[222] Instead, the law takes a very context-dependent view of its legality—much like it treats incendiary weapons. White phosphorus is not prohibited when it is used to produce a smokescreen to provide cover.[223]

---

[220] ICRC Customary Law Study, *supra* note 11, at Rule 85.
[221] Protocol (III) to CCW, *supra* note 161, at art. 2(4).
[222] BOOTHBY, *supra* note 173, at 232.
[223] *Id.* Notably, however, the UN Fact Finding Mission on the Gaza Conflict took a more restrictive view, contesting the legality of white phosphorus as an illuminant on the ground, asserting that there are "other screening and illuminating means which are free from the toxicities, volatilities and hazards that are inherent in

It is unlawful, however, to use white phosphorus against civilians. Some states also prohibit the use of white phosphorus against military personnel (but not against military objects).[224] The use of white phosphorus in Falluja by the United States and by Israel in Gaza prompted heated debates over the circumstances in which the weapon might be lawful.[225] In 2011, however, states remained divided on the legal status of the weapon.[226]

It was suggested in Chapter 4 that smoke ammunition could lawfully be used to map tunnels, particularly as few methods are available for mapping tunnels. The concern with regard to using white phosphorus over wide areas, which is often brought up, would not arise in the context of mapping tunnels. Although it would get released into the air (possibly near civilians) at egress and ingress points, the rate of dispersion in the air would not reach that of aboveground conditions. In addition, the limited amount of oxygen inside the tunnel would limit the temporal effects of the weapon. The use of white phosphorus for mapping tunnels can even be contemplated when combatants are present inside a tunnel—provided the weapon is not directed at them and the use is justified by military necessity. In fine,

> even if [white phosphorus] were classified as an incendiary weapon, there would be nothing unlawful, stemming from Protocol III, about the "shake and bake" tactics adopted to clear fortified areas or entrenchments of enemy military personnel if that were the only way such military objectives could be neutralised. It is to be hoped, however, that attention will be paid to the principle of humanity and the dictates of public conscience when contemplating antipersonnel uses of [white phosphorus], so that such decisions would be exceptional, when no alternative form of action is

---

the chemical white phosphorous," and concluding that "[t]he use of white phosphorous in any from [sic] in and around areas dedicated to the health and safety of civilians has been shown to carry very substantial risks. The Mission therefore believes that serious consideration should be given to banning the use of white phosphorous as an obscurant." Human Rights Council, *Human Rights in Palestine and Other Occupied Arab Territories: Report of the United Nations Fact-Finding Mission on the Gaza Conflict*, ¶ 901, U.N. Doc. A/HRC/12/48 (Sept. 25, 2009).

[224] *See* UK LOAC MANUAL, *supra* note 219, ¶ 6.12.6; US LAW OF WAR MANUAL, *supra* note 112, ¶ 6.14.2.1 (citing to the use of white phosphorus in Fallujah, Iraq "as a potent psychological weapon against the insurgents in trench lines and spider holes").

[225] *See, e.g.*, David P. Fidler, *The Use of White Phosphorus Munitions by U.S. Military Forces in Iraq*, ASIL INSIGHTS (Dec. 6, 2005), https://www.asil.org/insights/volume/9/issue/37/use-white-phosphorus-munitions-us-military-forces-iraq; HUMAN RIGHTS WATCH, RAIN OF FIRE: ISRAEL'S UNLAWFUL USE OF WHITE PHOSPHORUS IN GAZA (2009).

[226] Fourth Review Conference of the High Contracting Parties to the Convention on Prohibitions or Restrictions on the Use of Certain Conventional Weapons Which May Be Deemed to Be Excessively Injurious or to Have Indiscriminate Effects, Nov. 14–15, 2011, *Final Document of the Fourth Review Conference*, 9, U.N. Doc. CCW/CONF.IV/4/Add.1, Addendum, Part II: Final Declaration (Dec. 15, 2011).

feasible, perhaps authorised only at a suitably high level in the command chain. It should never become a matter of routine.[227]

Thermobaric bombs (also known as bunker busters) are very popular and effective against tunnels and cave complexes. They have been used by the United States in Afghanistan[228] and, according to some reports, by Russia in Syria.[229] Thanks to the combined effect of heat and pressure, they can penetrate considerable thicknesses of concrete. At the same time, however, they suck out the oxygen from inside a tunnel and produce effects for a longer time than conventional weapons. The effects of the use of this weapon in confined spaces are particularly severe:

> Those near the ignition point are obliterated as others at the fringe are likely to suffer many internal, and thus invisible injuries, including burst eardrums and crushed inner ear organs, severe concussions, ruptured lungs and internal organs, and possibly blindness.[230]

The use of thermobaric weapons by Syrian and Hezbollah forces was condemned by the Independent International Commission of Inquiry on the Syrian Republic, established by the UN Human Rights Council, as highly destructive, imprecise, and indiscriminate.[231] Notwithstanding the repeated condemnations and the humanitarian impact, these weapons continue to be used. The UK and Iraq have contemplated acquiring thermobaric weapons precisely for the purpose of driving the enemy out of tunnels and destroying underground structures.[232] Their use, however, can easily cross the bounds of

---

[227] I.J. MacLeod & A.P.V. Rogers, *The Use of White Phosphorus and the Law of War*, 10 Y.B. INT'L HUMANITARIAN L. 75, 96 (2007).

[228] *See* Andrew C. Revkin, A NATION CHALLENGED: ADVANCED ARMAMENTS; *U.S. Making Weapons to Blast Underground Hide-Outs*, N.Y. TIMES (Dec. 3, 2001), http://www.nytimes.com/2001/12/03/world/nation-challenged-advanced-armaments-us-making-weapons-blast-underground-hide.html; Richard Norton-Taylor, *MoD Admits Use of Controversial "Enhanced Blast" Weapons in Afghanistan*, GUARDIAN (May 28, 2009), https://www.theguardian.com/uk/2009/may/28/british-pilots-afghanistan-thermobaric-weapons.

[229] Kareem Shaheen, *"Hell Itself": Aleppo Reels from Alleged Use of Bunker-Buster Bombs*, GUARDIAN (Sept. 26, 2016), https://www.theguardian.com/world/2016/sep/26/hell-itself-aleppo-reels-from-alleged-use-of-bunker-buster-bombs; Torie Rose DeGhett, *A New Kind of Bomb Is Being Used in Syria and It's a Humanitarian Nightmare*, VICE (Aug. 29, 2015), https://news.vice.com/article/a-new-kind-of-bomb-is-being-used-in-syria-and-its-a-humanitarian-nightmare.

[230] HUMAN RIGHTS WATCH, BACKGROUNDER ON RUSSIAN FUEL AIR EXPLOSIVES (Feb. 1, 2000), https://www.hrw.org/report/2000/02/01/backgrounder-russian-fuel-air-explosives-vacuum-bombs (citing CENTRAL INTELLIGENCE AGENCY, CONVENTIONAL WEAPONS PRODUCING CHEMICAL-WARFARE-AGENT-LIKE INJURIES, Feb. 1990 (unclassified document).) *See also* Fry, *supra* note 43, at 28.

[231] Human Rights Council, *Report of the Independent International Commission of Inquiry on the Syrian Arab Republic*, ¶ 201(a), U.N. Doc. A/HRC/24/46 (Aug. 16, 2013).

[232] David Hambling, *Britain's Thermobaric Secret*, WIRED (Aug. 22, 2007), https://www.wired.com/2007/08/britains-thermo/; Patrick Wintour, *Battle for Mosul: Iraq Asks for UK Help to Get Thermobaric*

legality. Such legality should therefore be determined on a case-by-case basis based on the context in which the weapon is intended to be used and military necessity.

In conclusion, a weapon can be unlawful when used underground even if no weapon review took place or if the impact of a given weapon in a subterranean context was never discussed as part of its review. Belligerents must therefore exercise caution before employing weapons in or against tunnels—even when those weapons have been previously and lawfully employed in other contexts or environments. The weapons *may* become unlawful if they can no longer discriminate between civilians and combatants, or if they end up causing unnecessary suffering to combatants. The legality of a weapon underground thus depends on its anticipated effects in the said circumstances as compared to military necessity.

B. NON-LETHAL WEAPONS

The underground may modify the effects of weapons—rendering them unlawful when they cause unnecessary suffering or fail to properly discriminate. Similar concerns arise when states employ non-lethal weapons (NLWs), that is, "weapons, devices, and munitions that are explicitly designed and primarily employed to incapacitate targeted personnel or materiel immediately, while minimizing fatalities, permanent injury to personnel, and undesired damage to property in the target area or environment."[233] Militaries use NLWs to deter and coerce, and develop them in the hope of making warfare less deadly.[234] The option of using non-deadly force affords military commanders more flexibility,[235] and can help reduce disproportionate harm.[236] The intended physical effects of NLWs are also generally temporary and of much smaller degree.[237]

NLWs therefore do not aim to kill but rather to incapacitate the enemy—often to achieve a comparable military advantage. IHL tolerates their use, subject to the same basic principles of discrimination and unnecessary suffering that apply to lethal weapons. Like weapons, NLWs can lead to the commission of war crimes.[238]

Weapons, GUARDIAN (Nov. 17, 2016), https://www.theguardian.com/world/2016/nov/17/battle-for-mosul-iraq-asks-for-uk-help-to-get-thermobaric-weapons.

[233] U.S. DEPARTMENT OF DEFENSE, DoD EXECUTIVE AGENT FOR NON-LETHAL WEAPONS (NLW), AND NLW POLICY, DoD Directive No. 3000.03E (Apr. 15, 2013).

[234] Jared Silberman, *Non-lethal Weaponry and Non-proliferation*, 19 NOTRE DAME J.L. ETHICS & PUB. POL'Y 347, 347 (2005).

[235] David P. Fidler, *The International Legal Implications of "Non-lethal" Weapons*, 21 MICH. J. INT'L L. 51, 88 (1999). *See also* Robin Coupland & David R. Meddings, *Mortality Associated with Use of Weapons in Armed Conflicts, Wartime Atrocities, and Civilian Mass Shootings: Literature Review*, 319 BRITISH MED. J. 407, 409 (1999) (arguing that NLWs not only fail in reducing mortality rate but may also increase it in some circumstances).

[236] M.L. Gross, *The Second Lebanon War: The Question of Proportionality and the Prospect of Non-lethal Warfare*, 7 J. MIL. ETHICS (2008).

[237] Fidler, *supra* note 235.

[238] *Id.* at 91.

The concern is that the underground may affect the way NLWs behave and potentially turn them into deadly weapons, thereby raising questions as to their legality.[239] Even when NLWs are employed in regular circumstances, their effects tend to be poorly understood. One thing, however, is certain: even with NLWs, the risk of causing fatal injury remains.[240] Does that risk increase when NLWs are used underground?

NLWs include a wide variety of tools—from plastic bullets to nets (catching potentially harmless individuals or vehicles), sticky substances (also known as superlubricants, used to prevent the enemy from moving), smelly substances (also known as malodorants), direct-energy weapons that create heat sensations, and low-level acoustics. Some of them could have more severe effects below ground than they have aboveground, such as acoustics for example. The intensity of certain NLWs can be adjusted by the operator to increase or decrease the physiological effect of the weapon on enemy forces,[241] but this is not the case with all of them. In any event, adjusting the intensity of an NLW when used underground may not be practical or feasible.

When a panoply of options is available, commanders should choose non-lethal tools whose effects are least likely to be heavily modified in the confines of tunnels and other underground structures. I would also add that when NLWs undergo review, the authority conducting the review should envisage their effects in unique environments, such as the subterranean. Ultimately, here as in other aspects of IHL's application to underground warfare, states should be mindful of the unique circumstances at play. The environment does not necessarily affect the legality of lethal or NLWs—but it could. Unnecessary suffering and military necessity continue to provide the benchmark for assessing such legality. Considerations of humanity play a significant role in this balancing act, yet states must retain some tools, lethal and non-lethal, to combat underground threats effectively. Too many legal constraints could achieve counterproductive results. For example, banning the use of NLWs underground could impede the promise of these less-than-lethal methods in a particularly challenging environment.

Conclusion

The application of the law of armed conflict to tunnel warfare raises more issues than one would think. The reason IHL does not address tunnels per se remains somewhat of a mystery. One possible explanation is that the tactic, when employed by combatants against other combatants, has never been regarded as problematic. The use of tunnels

---

[239] Non-lethal weapons raise a number of concerns under IHL (see *id.* at 82). I focus here on a relatively narrow aspect, namely the potential illegality of such weapons when used underground.
[240] BOOTHBY, *supra* note 173, at 234.
[241] Fidler, *supra* note 235.

did not formerly draw the stigma it has today—in an era when underground warfare has flourished at the hands of violent nonstate actors. This, however, cannot fully explain the absence of legal attention to tunnels. Even when used against combatants, tunnel warfare raises a plethora of questions, from the effect of weapons underground to the calculation of the military advantage and the nature of a tunnel (as a weapon, means of warfare, or military objective).

In this chapter, I have argued that the law does not prohibit the use of tunnels and other underground structures in times of war. Underground warfare—in any of its many forms—does not amount to perfidy. Tunnels are not weapons, but the digging and use of tunnels must comply with Article 49 of Additional Protocol I. Tunnels and other underground structures must be kept separate from civilians and civilian infrastructure. They should not serve to immunize military objectives or spread terror among the civilian population.

Many of the questions pertaining to tunnels under IHL find no easy answer, and I would not be surprised if scholars and practitioners were to take issue with some of my conclusions. One thing is certain—some adjustments need to be made in light of the unique features of underground warfare and the far-reaching impact of the unknown factor. The nature and extent of these adjustments, however, remain open to debate. My objective has been to expose the difficulties, put an end to the flawed assumption that underground warfare raises no issues of its own under IHL, dismiss any blanket permissive interpretation, and offer a conceptual framework for analyzing tunnels under the law of armed conflict.

7

UNDERGROUND WARFARE IN URBAN AREAS

HAMAS DID NOT have to dig to reap the benefits of operating underneath the Al-Shifa Hospital in Gaza City. The basement of the hospital, allegedly connected to the larger network of Hamas tunnels, has long served as a command-and-control center for the group.[1] Hamas leaders walk freely in the hospital's corridors,[2] conduct interrogations, and hold meetings with the media.[3] According to a doctor interviewed by PBS, Hamas is aware that their activities are putting civilians in harm's way.[4]

As part of the hospital, this basement enjoys arguably the highest level of protection available under the laws of war.[5] It affords Hamas operatives a shield against Israeli strikes, as well as a unique opportunity to operate far from surveillance drones, GPS, and

---

[1] Amos Harel, *Sources: Hamas Leaders Hiding in Basement of Israel-Built Hospital in Gaza*, HAARETZ (Jan. 12, 2009), http://www.haaretz.com/sources-hamas-leaders-hiding-in-basement-of-israel-built-hospital-in-gaza-1.267940.
[2] William Booth, *While Israel Held Its Fire, Militant Group Hamas Did Not*, WASH. POST (July 15, 2014), https://www.washingtonpost.com/world/middle_east/while-israel-held-its-fire-the-militant-group-hamas-did-not/2014/07/15/116fd3d7-3c0f-4413-94a9-2ab16af1445d_story.html?utm_term=.e4f99a7efaa0.
[3] Terrence McCoy, *Why Hamas Stores Its Weapons Inside Hospitals, Mosques and Schools*, WASH. POST (July 31, 2014), https://www.washingtonpost.com/news/morning-mix/wp/2014/07/31/why-hamas-stores-its-weapons-inside-hospitals-mosques-and-schools/?utm_term=.8a50b6b22da8.
[4] *Hamas Hiding in Shifa Hospital?*, PBS WIDE ANGLE (Jan. 13, 2009), http://www.pbs.org/wnet/wideangle/blog/gaza-er-hamas-hiding-in-shifa-hospital/4086/.
[5] *See* Geneva Convention Relative to the Protection of Civilian Persons in Time of War, art. 19, Aug. 12, 1949, 6 U.S.T. 3516, 75 U.N.T.S. 287 [hereinafter "the Fourth Geneva Convention" or "GCIV"].

Underground Warfare. Daphné Richemond-Barak.
© Oxford University Press 2018. Published 2018 by Oxford University Press.

other intelligence-gathering technology. Within the framework of this book, the hospital qualifies as an existing underground civilian infrastructure: although dug for civilian purposes, the underground structure is being used for military purposes. It also embodies a relatively recent trend: the growing proximity of underground warfare to the civilian world. This trend is at the heart of this chapter, which focuses on the impact of underground warfare on civilians in three main situations: when tunnels are used near, by, or against civilians.

The first scenario—tunnels dug in or *near* civilian populated areas—creates a direct and often intentional danger to the civilian population. This danger begins with the digging of the tunnel and only ends when the tunnel is fully eliminated. Equally challenging are the conditions in which these tunnels may be destroyed. Regardless of the method used, anti-tunnel operations bear significant risks not only for those who carry out the operation and those who use the tunnels, but also for those who live in the vicinity of the tunnels. When tunnels are located under civilian structures, their destruction can easily cause disproportionate harm to the population. Like placing civilians on rooftops, digging tunnels in urban areas has the effect of rendering the tunnels virtually legally immune to counterattacks. This operational complexity only makes civilians more vulnerable. Urban tunnels expose civilians to a threat that is very different, by virtue of its geographical and temporal characteristics, from other forms of warfare that come close to the civilian population.

The use of tunnels *by* civilians embodies another manifestation of the growing proximity of underground warfare to civilians. When civilians seek shelter in the same tunnels from which militants or soldiers operate, the outcome can be devastating. Innocent civilians might die as the tunnels are targeted by the other side, or suffer from the tunnel-diggers' lack of experience in operating underground, particularly when manipulating explosives. From the point of view of the other party to the conflict—the one seeking to prevail over the underground threat—civilian presence inside the tunnels (or, for that matter, the very likelihood of such presence) affects the type of measures that can be employed to map, detect, or eliminate the tunnels.

The use of tunnels *against* civilians takes the dilemma to the extreme. Unlike the use of tunnels near and by civilians, a use of the underground *intentionally directed* at civilians departs from historical practice. Tunnels have rarely, if ever, been used against civilians.

I. Underground Warfare Meets Urban Warfare: Tunnels *near* Civilians

Underground warfare has re-emerged in the twenty-first century as a multifaceted, fast-spreading threat. As compared to the use of the subterranean in previous wars and conflicts—setting aside the Vietnam War—contemporary uses of this terrain present innovative and challenging features. One noticeable and concerning trend has brought civilians and tunnels closer together, raising both operational and legal challenges. When underground warfare meets urban warfare, traditional dilemmas intensify and new dilemmas surface.

A. THE SPREAD OF UNDERGROUND WARFARE TO CIVILIAN POPULATED AREAS

Historically, and as shown in Chapter 1, tunnels have been used mostly by and against combatants. The Vietnam War stands out in this respect, as the Vietcong's tunnels served simultaneously as death traps for American soldiers, an operational base for Vietcong fighters, and at times even a safe haven for Vietnamese women to give birth.[6] The tunnels hosted civilian facilities such as hospitals, storage spaces, cinemas, and living compounds, alongside bunkers, ammunition caches, imaginative traps, tunnel mines, and military headquarters. Civilians present in the tunnels were put at risk both by the Vietcong's actions and by the U.S. forces' counterattacks. After the Củ Chi district was designated a free strike zone (i.e., an area "where everybody was deemed hostile and a legitimate target by US forces"),[7] the local civilian population took shelter in the Củ Chi tunnels, alongside the Vietcong.[8] No other pre-9/11 war brought civilians in such proximity to the underground.

In recent years, however, the shift from mountains to cities has become apparent—from Yemen to Egypt, Israel, Iraq, and Syria. Tunnels have been dug in the middle of Sana'a, Yemen, in close proximity to the civilian population.[9] In Syria, tunnels have been found to connect Basateen, a village controlled by anti-Assad militants, with the Boukein area, southeast of Zabadani city on the border with Lebanon. These tunnels, located in the midst of civilian areas, were blown up by Assad's forces.[10] Other tunnels found in the area were reportedly dug by ISIS to smuggle weapons and supplies. Assad himself built

---

[6] Joe Havely, *Củ Chi: The Underground War*, BBC NEWS ONLINE (Apr. 25, 2000), http://news.bbc.co.uk/2/hi/asia-pacific/720577.stm; TOM MANGOLD & JOHN PENYCATE, A HARROWING ACCOUNT OF AMERICA'S "TUNNEL RATS" IN THE UNDERGROUND BATTLEFIELDS OF VIETNAM 93–96 (2005).

[7] MANGOLD & PENYCATE, *supra* note 6, at 291. *See also* Arthur Herman, *Notes from the Underground: The Long History of Tunnel Warfare*, FOREIGN AFFAIRS (Aug. 2014), https://www.foreignaffairs.com/articles/middle-east/2014-08-26/notes-underground.

[8] MANGOLD & PENYCATE, *supra* note 6, at 177–78.

[9] Ali Ibrahim Al-Moshki & Yasser Rayes, *Preparing to Invade Sana'a, Hadi's Forces Amass Hundreds of Armored Vehicles*, MEDIALINE (Sept. 12, 2015), http://www.themedialine.org/news/preparing-to-invade-sanaa-hadis-forces-amass-hundreds-of-armored-vehicles/ (noting that "[t]housands of fighters have been spread throughout the mountains surrounding Sana'a and tunnels and trenches have been dug near the entrances to the city" and near the city's international airport).

[10] *Regime Forces Tighten Noose on Opposition in Zabadini*, AL MONITOR (July 21, 2015), http://www.al-monitor.com/pulse/en/originals/2015/07/syria-zabadani-regime-advance-opposition-besieged.html. *See also Syria Conflict: "Unprecedented" Assault on Zabadani*, BBC (July 22, 2015), http://www.bbc.com/news/world-middle-east-33624215; SHAUL SHAY, THE ISLAMIC STATE (ISIS) AND THE SUBTERRANEAN WARFARE 3 (2015), http://www.herzliyaconference.org/_Uploads/dbsAttachedFiles/ISISshay2015A.pdf [hereinafter SHAY, ISLAMIC STATE].

an underground city consisting of seven floors, complete with paved roads and multiple exits, intended to act as headquarters for security apparatus and military intelligence agencies—all under the city of Harasta, a northern suburb of Damascus.[11]

Underground warfare has also reached the Syrian-Turkish border, where residents have complained of hearing nighttime digging,[12] and tunnels have been discovered by Kurdish forces. The tunnels reportedly originated in proximity to the city of Tel Abyad (known as Girê Spî in Kurdish) and exited in the Turkish border town of Akçakale. The tunnels' length is estimated from 300 to 2,000 feet, allowing ISIS fighters to travel freely from Turkey to Syria, transport equipment, and hide from aerial bombardments. Kurdish fighters have claimed that they have information regarding several additional tunnels in other regions close to the border, including the northern Syrian border-town of Jarabulus connecting to the southeastern Turkish town of Karkamış.[13]

In Iraq, ISIS has reportedly used a network of tunnels originally built by Saddam Hussein's regime connecting Baghdad and its southern suburbs to move around safely and hide from aerial bombardments.[14] However, Saddam's tunnel complex is not the only underground route used by insurgents in Iraq. In December 2013, Iraqi authorities uncovered three cross-border smuggling tunnels between the Iraqi al-Anbar region and the Syrian al-Kamal region.[15] Following ISIS's establishment of the caliphate in the summer of 2014, Coalition forces destroyed tunnels in close proximity to the cities of Huwayjah and Ramadi.[16] An underground network of nearly 40 ISIS tunnels running for several hundred yards each was also discovered in the northern Iraqi town of Sinjar.[17] The network connected different houses and allowed undetected movement.

---

[11] Sirwan Kajjo, *Syrian Rebels Unmask Regime's "Underground City,"* VOICE OF AMERICA (Feb. 16, 2016), http://www.voanews.com/a/syrian-rebels-unmask-regime-underground-city/3193647.html; Ari Solomon, *Report: Assad Built Seven-Story Underground War Bunker,* TIMES OF ISRAEL (Feb. 16, 2016), http://www.timesofisrael.com/report-assad-able-to-wage-war-from-underground-bunker/.

[12] See Erin Cunningham, *The Flow of Jihadists into Syria Dries Up as Turkey Cracks Down on the Border,* WASH. POST (Aug. 1, 2015), https://www.washingtonpost.com/world/middle_east/the-flow-of-jihadists-into-syria-dries-up-as-turkey-cracks-down-on-the-border/2015/07/31/d95f4234-34ad-11e5-b835-61ddaa99c73e_story.html?utm_term=.97c33276b2a4.

[13] *Kurds Find ISIS Tunnel near Turkish Border,* FOX NEWS (June 22, 2015), http://www.foxnews.com/world/2015/06/22/kurds-find-isis-tunnel-near-turkish-border.html. *See also New ISIS Terror Tunnels Discovered by Kurdish Forces in Tel Abyad,* KURDISH DAILY NEWS (Aug. 10, 2015), http://kurdishdailynews.org/2015/08/10/new-isis-terror-tunnels-discovered-by-kurdish-forces-in-tel-abyad/; SHAY, ISLAMIC STATE, *supra* note 10, at 2.

[14] Michael Georgy & Ahmed Rasheed, *Tunneling Through "Triangle of Death", Islamic State Aims at Baghdad from South,* REUTERS (Aug. 4, 2014), http://www.reuters.com/article/us-iraq-security-south-insight-idUSKBN0G41CO20140804.

[15] *Iraq Discovers Smuggling Tunnels at Syria Border,* ALALAM (Dec. 7, 2013), http://en.alalam.ir/news/1542238.

[16] *See Air Strikes Continue Against ISIL Targets in Iraq, Syria,* Combined Joint Task Force Operation Inherent Resolve News Release (Sept. 29, 2015), http://www.defense.gov/DesktopModules/ArticleCS/Print.aspx?PortalId=1&ModuleId=753&Article=620857; SHAY, ISLAMIC STATE, *supra* note 10, at 3.

[17] Salar Salim & Susannah George, *Footage Reveals ISIS Tunnel Network Under Iraqi Town of Sinjar,* HAARETZ (Nov. 25, 2015), http://www.haaretz.com/middle-east-news/1.688221; CBS/AP, *ISIS Used Tunnels to Hide*

Braced with metal arches and fortified with sandbags, the tunnels were connected to local electricity wires, ventilation fans, and lighting. ISIS fighters used the tunnels as living quarters, shelters from air strikes, and storage for vast ammunition caches, medicine, food, and religious artifacts. Video footage showed two tunnels, originating from and exiting in residential houses, through holes knocked in walls or floors.[18] Likewise, in Mosul and the surrounding area, the Islamic State has made use of an extensive network of tunnels, many of them booby-trapped, exiting in restaurants and connecting the basements of various homes.[19] Much as in Syria, the use of underground structures by ISIS pushed Iraqi forces below ground, and reports indicate that tunnels helped Iraqi forces repel ISIS's advances in Anbar province.[20]

With ISIS's influence growing in Libya, similar uses of the underground have been witnessed in Benghazi's Al Sabri district,[21] a district heavily affected by the war.[22] Most civilians left the town after ISIS took over,[23] but several dozen families still lived in the area at the time the tunnels were discovered.[24] Matters could further escalate were ISIS to take hold of Gaddafi's tunnel network. Originally constructed as an irrigation system connecting Tripoli and Benghazi, U.S. intelligence reports believe it was used by Gaddafi and his forces to hide and store ammunition. The tunnel system connects various strategic compounds and cities in Libya.[25]

Under Besieged Iraqi City, CBS NEWS (Nov. 25, 2015), http://www.cbsnews.com/news/isis-tunnel-network-discovered-sinjar-iraq-kurdish-forces/.

[18] *See* SHAY, ISLAMIC STATE, *supra* note 10, at 4; *ISIS Used Tunnels*, *supra* note 17.

[19] Jared Malsin, *Qurans and Solar Cells: Inside the ISIS Tunnels Around Mosul*, TIME (Oct. 21, 2016), http://time.com/4541647/isis-defensive-tunnels-mosul-iraq/; William Booth & Aaso Ameen Shwan, *Islamic State Tunnels Below Mosul Are a Hidden and Deadly Danger*, WASH. POST (Nov. 5, 2016), https://www.washingtonpost.com/world/middle_east/islamic-state-tunnels-below-mosul-are-a-hidden-and-deadly-danger/2016/11/05/5199afcc-a2c7-11e6-8864-6f892cad0865_story.html?utm_term=.b920fc750201.

[20] Erin Bianco, *Sunni Tribes and Iraqi Military Score Victories Against ISIS with "Tunnel Warfare,"* INT'L BUS. TIMES (Mar. 10, 2015), http://www.ibtimes.com/sunni-tribes-iraqi-military-score-victories-against-isis-anbar-tunnel-warfare-1842838.

[21] AlWasat Libya (@alwasatengnews), Twitter (May 6, 2015, 11:27), https://twitter.com/alwasatengnews/status/596018558133469184: "More pictures of the tunnels #ISIS have dug in the Al-Sabri area of #Benghazi. #Libya #Daesh"; Vijay Prashad (@vijayprashad), Twitter (May 5, 2015, 16:28), https://twitter.com/vijayprashad/status/595731762724118530: "ISIS has tunnels in Benghazi (Libya), a five-star hotel in Mosul (Iraq) & lone gunmen in the West."

[22] *Benghazi: A City Going Up in Smoke*, FRANCE 24 (Dec. 11, 2014), http://observers.france24.com/en/20141112-benghazi-destruction-architecture-islamist-militias.

[23] *For Benghazi's Displaced, No Help and No Dignity*, AL JAZEERA (Aug. 28, 2015), http://www.aljazeera.com/news/2015/08/benghazi-displaced-dignity-150824093614799.html (reporting that more than 100,000 people, about one-quarter of Benghazi's population, have been forced to flee their homes, mostly in the el-Blad, Sidi Khribish, and el-Sabri districts).

[24] *Libya: Civilians Trapped in Benghazi: Allow Safe Passage, Aid Access*, HUMAN RIGHTS WATCH (May 25, 2015), https://www.hrw.org/news/2015/05/25/libya-civilians-trapped-benghazi.

[25] Mike Elkin, *Inside Gadhafi's Secret Underground Arsenal*, WIRED (Mar. 3, 2011), https://www.wired.com/2011/03/inside-gadhafis-secret-underground-arsenal/.

The 2014 conflict between Hamas and Israel arguably provides the most poignant manifestation of the growing proximity of tunnels to civilians on the contemporary battlefield. In Gaza, tunnels are dug in civilian homes, pass under entire neighborhoods, and lead into populated areas inside Israel. This enables Hamas to conceal entry and exit points, and facilitates undetected movement and activity. The cross-border nature of these tunnels places the civilian population on both sides of the conflict in harm's way: both Palestinian and Israel civilians have become exposed to a new, direct, and intentional threat.

Cross-border tunnels that either emanate from civilian populated areas, reach into civilian populated areas, or both, raise the same concerns as those dug near or under civilian populated areas on the territory of a single state. All urban tunnels, cross-border or not, directly and intentionally endanger civilians from the very moment the digging commences. One reason is that tunnels dug under civilian populated areas weaken the structures under which they are dug, routinely causing collapses.[26] Although reports do not generally specify whether the victims are civilians or combatants, each and every one of these incidents can cost the life of innocent civilians located anywhere along the tunnel's route. The underground movement of explosives and weapons inside tunnels also causes accidents—as often reported in tunnels between Gaza and Egypt.[27] Civilians continue to be exposed to the risks of collapse and accidents throughout the tunnels' lifespan.

A unique feature of cross-border tunnels is that they spread these risks to civilians living on the other side of the border. As a result, cross-border tunnels end up posing a threat to civilians on both sides of the conflict:

> The attack tunnels Hamas has constructed running from Gaza into Israel have long sown deep fears in the communities on the Israeli side of the border fence, where residents talk of nightmares about militants popping up into their dining rooms or kindergartens. Now, the tunnels are keeping others up at night: the Palestinians who live on the Gaza side of the fence. People living on the edges of Gaza border towns, like the Israelis a few miles away, complain of hearing surreptitious digging in the wee hours, and voice a parallel anxiety about the tunnels being rapidly rebuilt near their homes becoming targets for Israeli strikes.[28]

---

[26] *See, e.g.*, AFP and Times of Israel Staff, *Hamas Operative Killed in Gaza Tunnel Collapse*, Times of Israel (Jan. 20, 2017), http://www.timesofisrael.com/hamas-operative-killed-in-gaza-tunnel-collapse/.

[27] *Hamas Fighter, Civilians Killed in Gaza Tunnels Near Rafah*, Maan News (Feb. 19, 2015), http://www.maannews.com/Content.aspx?id=759515; Saed Bannoura, *Palestinian Killed in Tunnel Accident in Gaza*, IMEMC (Apr. 2, 2015), http://imemc.org/article/63724/.

[28] Diaa Hadid & Majd al Waheidi, *As Hamas Tunnels Back into Israel, Palestinians Are Afraid, Too*, N.Y. Times (May 20, 2016), https://www.nytimes.com/2016/05/21/world/middleeast/hamas-tunnels-gaza-strip-israel.html. *See also Two Years After War, Rebuilding in Gaza is Far From Done, and International Donors are Bailing*, Los Angeles Times (August 16, 2016) ("In private conversations in cafes and on social media, Gazans say they're anxious that Hamas' effort to rebuild its cross-border attack tunnels will one day bring new Israeli destruction to border areas like Shajaiya.")

The parallel between the Israeli and the Palestinian experience is striking. The Palestinians' perception of the underground threat shows that civilians living on the territory from which the tunnels emanate are aware that the digging of tunnels places them in harm's way. In fact, Palestinians have raised harsh criticism against Hamas "for putting people at risk."[29] In addition to the risk of collapses and explosions, Palestinians (like all civilians in a cross-border, urban tunnel situation) also become vulnerable to enemy retaliation.

One could argue that bomb assembly, suicide-vest assembly, or arms factories pose equivalent threats to civilians living nearby. Tanks posted at the border or drones flying above it could perhaps be compared to tunnels burrowing under it. Still, the excavation of tunnels and underground complexes—often by children, and without the engineering know-how necessary to prevent disasters—stretching for miles below civilian homes and religious and cultural sites, raises far greater concerns for the civilians who live in their vicinity. This threat also happens to last unusually long. As explained in Chapter 1, even abandoned tunnels can later be inherited by other factions. The threat therefore only disappears if and when the tunnel itself disappears—keeping in mind that destruction poses its own set of difficulties and risks. As for tanks and drones, unlike cross-border tunnels, they do not directly or tangibly threaten one's own civilians. They mainly endanger the enemy's civilian population.

In conclusion, an analysis of underground warfare in recent conflicts shows that it has come ever closer to civilians. Belligerents who choose to dig tunnels in civilian populated areas directly and long-lastingly endanger their own civilians. In the case of cross-border tunnels, the risks extend to civilians on the other side of the conflict. Exposure to underground threats lasts from the very beginning of the digging until the tunnel is fully eliminated. It includes the risk of collapses and explosions and that of anti-tunnel operations launched by the enemy in retaliation for tunnel-digging. The concern is that, like the Vietcong and Hamas, more actors will voluntarily endanger civilians in their use of the underground during armed conflict. They could place civilians in the tunnels or use existing underground civilian infrastructure such as subways and sewage systems. These potential developments would put more civilians in direct danger and, in turn, considerably complicate the neutralization of underground threats. Whether the tunnels are used *by* civilians, dug *near* civilians, or used *against* civilians, the weaving in of civilian elements raises multiple challenges at the operational and legal levels.

B. STATE PRACTICE AND CIVILIAN PROTECTION

Taking a long-term view of underground warfare, another reason for concern is the scarcity and nature of state practice. Generally speaking, state behavior offers little insight as to how tunnels should be contended with—either because states do not share much about

---

[29] *Id.*

the methods employed, or because no consistent pattern can be identified. However, one thing is certain: states take underground threats very seriously, and have demonstrated a willingness to react aggressively to overcome them.

States faced with underground warfare have resorted to extreme and controversial methods, often causing significant casualties and long-term damage. Take, for example, the United States' experience with the deadly Vietcong tunnels. The operational complexity of fighting inside and outside the tunnels took its toll on U.S. forces, leading them to deploy B-52 bombers with bombs penetrating up to 40 feet into the earth, set to detonate moments after penetration. The collapse of numerous tunnel segments came at a cost: the suffocation of many of their inhabitants by the combination of poisonous agents and destroyed ventilation shafts.[30] U.S. troops also injected acetylene gas and pumped water into the tunnels to force the combatants out of hiding and prevent their return.[31] These measures had devastating effects on combatants and civilians alike, many of whom lost their lives through suffocation or poisoning. Widespread damage was also caused to the environment.

The Soviets faced similar challenges—though importantly not in proximity to large civilian population centers—during the Afghan-Soviet War. They developed special weapons for tunnel warfare, including improved range RPO-A flamethrowers. These weapons, essentially single-use grenade launchers with a range of 2,000 feet, employed three different types of projectiles: thermobaric (combining an explosive charge and highly combustible fuel, which disperses when the target is reached and is then ignited by the charge), incendiary, and smoke. The flamethrowers were lowered into shafts with cords and then activated with the aim of burning down the tunnel.[32] Testimonies also report the use of chemical agents by the Soviets inside a Karez underground canal in the Ghazni province of Afghanistan, killing over 30 villagers who had sought refuge from the hostilities.[33]

In more contemporary times, the reaction of the Egyptian government to the cross-border tunnels dug by Hamas along the Gaza border further demonstrates the lengths to which states are willing to go to eliminate underground threats. Egypt deployed a panoply of measures:[34] from a buffer zone that required the evacuation and destruction

---

[30] MANGOLD & PENYCATE, *supra* note 6, at 269.

[31] Thomas Dethlefs, *Tear Gas and the Politics of Lethality: Emerging from the Haze*, 2 YALE HISTORY REV. 83, 101 (2013); Richard Muller, *The Weapons Paradox*, MIT TECH. REV. (May 21, 2003), https://www.technologyreview.com/s/401923/the-weapons-paradox/; MANGOLD & PENYCATE, *supra* note 6, at 101 and 177.

[32] *Id. See also* Lester Grau & Ali Ahmad Jalali, *Underground Combat: Stereophonic Blasting, Tunnel Rats and the Soviet-Afghan War*, 28 ENGINEER 20 (1998); Kyle Mizokami, *Terrifying Russian "Bumblebee" Flamethrower Shows Up in Syria*, POPULAR MECHANICS (Nov. 4, 2015), http://www.popularmechanics.com/military/weapons/a18067/this-bumblebee-flamethrower-packs-a-mean-stinger/.

[33] M. HASSAN KAKAR, AFGHANISTAN: THE SOVIET INVASION AND THE AFGHAN RESPONSE, 1979–1982, at 220 (1995).

[34] *See* discussion *infra* in Chapter 1.

of civilian homes,[35] to an underground steel barrier,[36] flooding with sewage water,[37] an anti-tunneling legislation imposing a life sentence on tunnel diggers.[38] The United States, for its part, has filled tunnels at the Mexico border with cement[39] and deployed its most powerful conventional weapon to destroy ISIS tunnels in Afghanistan.[40]

States have taken far-reaching measures to eliminate underground threats because they understand that tunnels need to be completely destroyed. Merely ousting their occupants and removing ammunition does not solve the problem; it only neutralizes the threat momentarily. As explained earlier in this book, tunnels can be inherited years later by the same or another enemy, as in Afghanistan (by al-Qaeda and the Taliban) or in Iraq (by ISIS). Tunnels must therefore be destroyed, preferably in their entirety, regardless of their location and purpose at the time of the dismantlement. It is also recommended that states monitor previously used tunnels continuously to prevent their inheritance or rebuilding.[41]

This sets underground warfare apart from urban warfare. If a sniper operates from within a building, the entire building generally need not be destroyed for the threat to be eliminated: the sniper's weapon can be confiscated, disabled, or otherwise impaired. In the worst case scenario, forces will have to destroy part of the building (one of its floors, for example), or target the sniper him/herself. By contrast, the only way to eliminate the threat posed by a tunnel, as noted above, is to destroy the tunnel.[42] This goes beyond the importance of undermining the enemy's motivation to dig tunnels (if a tunnel can be destroyed in a minute, why spend so much time and resources on digging it?). It is about eliminating the threat by making sure that the tunnel cannot be inherited or repaired.

Another factor is at play, too, which becomes apparent when one compares states' reaction to underground warfare to the casualties it causes. The data assembled from the *New York Times* archives is relatively inconclusive as to the quantity and identity of the victims of underground warfare. If anything, it suggests that underground warfare has claimed relatively few victims. This data, albeit consistent with my qualitative

---

[35] HUMAN RIGHTS WATCH, LOOK FOR ANOTHER HOMELAND: FORCED EVICTIONS IN EGYPT'S RAFAH (2009), https://www.hrw.org/report/2015/09/22/look-another-homeland/forced-evictions-egypts-rafah [hereinafter ANOTHER HOMELAND].

[36] *See* Christian Fraser, *Egypt Starts Building Steel Wall on Gaza Strip Border*, BBC (Dec. 9, 2009), http://news.bbc.co.uk/2/hi/8405020.stm.

[37] *See* Fares Akram & David Kirkpatrick, *To Block Gaza Tunnels, Egypt Lets Sewage Flow*, N. Y. TIMES (Feb. 20, 2013), http://www.nytimes.com/2013/02/21/world/middleeast/egypts-floods-smuggling-tunnels-to-gaza-with-sewage.html.

[38] Aswat Masriya, *Cabinet Approves Legislation Maximizing Penalty for Digging Border Tunnels*, EGYPT INDEPENDENT (Apr. 1, 2015), http://www.egyptindependent.com/news/cabinet-approves-legislation-maximizing-penalty-digging-border-tunnels.

[39] *See* Richard Marosi, *Workers Begin to Fill Tunnels at Mexican Border*, L.A. TIMES (May 16, 2007), http://articles.latimes.com/2007/may/16/local/me-tunnel16.

[40] *See supra*, Chapter 4.

[41] *See supra* Chapter 4.

[42] *See supra* Chapter 4.

it difficult to justify the robust measures employed against underground
 do states use such violent and often indiscriminate methods to combat a
ffensive threat? If not the prospect of high casualties, what triggers states' aggressive response to underground threats? The reaction to underground threats is, in large part, the product of the strong psychological impact such threats have on decision-makers and the public alike.[43] Although tunnels do not lead to high casualties, they elicit deep-seated fears and a sense of helplessness. They create the possibility of a first strike (in the *ad bellum* context) and expose the limits of all-powerful technology—leaving the state with a perceived loss of control over the situation. The main feature of tunnels, their invisibility, contributes to these effects.

Regardless of what motivates these desperate attempts to prevail against underground threats—the operational complexity, the fear of inheritance, and/or the existential fear they trigger among states—state practice raises serious concerns for the protection of civilians. When urban warfare meets underground warfare, civilians will pay the ultimate price, particularly if they live inside or near tunnels.

C. THE LEGALITY OF URBAN TUNNELS UNDER IHL

In spite of its potentially devastating impact on the civilian population, the digging of a tunnel does not automatically amount to a war crime under existing law. When a tunnel burrows under borders, it violates sovereignty and territorial integrity regardless of its impact on civilians. When dug on the territory of a single state, the digging of a tunnel might not violate international law at all. At best, the use of a tunnel can *lead to* violations of international law—such as the taking of hostages, the launch of indiscriminate attacks, or the hiring of forced child labor to dig tunnels.[44] Although the digging and/or use of tunnels in urban areas intentionally threatens the civilians and civilian infrastructure and can have a long-lasting psychological and physical impact on these civilians, it is not prohibited as such.

This is not to say that international humanitarian law (IHL) condones such tunnels. Tunnels dug in proximity to or with the help of civilians violate Article 58 of Additional Protocol I, which requires that belligerents endeavor to (1) remove civilians and civilian objects under their control from the vicinity of military objectives, (2) avoid locating military objectives within or near densely populated areas, and (3) protect civilians and civilian objects against the dangers resulting from military operations. The law does not elaborate much beyond these requirements. The assumption is that governments are "sufficiently concerned with sparing their population" and will thus act in their best

---

[43] I am indebted to my colleague, Dr. Sivan Hirsch-Hoefler, for this point.
[44] Nicolas Pelham, *Gaza's Tunnel Phenomenon: The Unintended Dynamics of Israel's Siege*, 41 J. PALESTINIAN STUD. 6, 23 (2012).

interests.⁴⁵ Where tunnels are concerned, however, the groups digging and using tunnels often make deliberate, cynical use of civilian presence in blatant violation of the law.⁴⁶ As explained in the previous chapter, civilians remain protected even when belligerents violate the prohibition on the use of human shields or fail to take precautionary measures against the effects of attacks.

Further strengthening the importance of the command to separate civilian sites from military installations,⁴⁷ the law explicitly condemns the use of the civilian population to render military objectives immune from attack. Article 51(7) of Additional Protocol I would certainly apply to tunnels dug under civilian homes and other civilian objects:

> The presence or movements of the civilian population or individual civilians shall not be used to render certain points or areas immune from military operations, in particular attempts to shield military objectives from attacks or to shield, favor or impede military operations. The Parties to the conflict shall not direct the movement of the civilian population or individual civilians in order to attempt to shield military objectives from attacks or to shield military operations.⁴⁸

This prohibition is customary in both international armed conflicts (IAC) and non-international armed conflicts (NIAC),⁴⁹ and the Rome Statute of the International Criminal Court qualifies the act of using the civilian population to render military objectives immune from attack as a war crime in international armed conflict.⁵⁰ This happens when the perpetrator moves or otherwise takes advantage of the location of civilians or other protected persons, intending to shield a military objective from attack or shield, favor, or impede military operations.⁵¹ The prohibition will be further discussed below, in the context of human shields.

In addition to exposing civilians to physical harm, tunnels also and importantly affect their sense of security. Like the physical risks, the sense of insecurity begins as soon as the digging of tunnels is suspected and ends only when the tunnels are fully eliminated. The

---

[45] CLAUDE PILLOUD, JEAN PICTET, YVES SANDOZ, CHRISTOPHE SWINARSKI & BRUNO ZIMMERMAN, COMMENTARY ON THE ADDITIONAL PROTOCOLS OF 8 JUNE 1977 TO THE GENEVA CONVENTIONS OF 12 AUGUST 1949, ¶ 2253 (1987) [hereinafter COMMENTARY TO AP I].

[46] JEAN-MARIE HENCKAERTS & LOUISE DOSWALD-BECK, CUSTOMARY INTERNATIONAL HUMANITARIAN LAW, VOL. I: RULES, Rule 22 (2005) [hereinafter ICRC Customary Law Study].

[47] See, e.g., id. at Rule 23 (noting that "in 1979, in the context of the conflict in Rhodesia/Zimbabwe, the ICRC appealed to the Patriotic Front to 'clearly separate civilian establishments, particularly refugee camps, from military installations.'").

[48] Protocol Additional to the Geneva Conventions of 12 August 1949, and relating to the Protection of Victims of International Armed Conflicts (Protocol I), art. 51(7), June 8, 1977, 1125 U.N.T.S. 3 [hereinafter AP I].

[49] ICRC Customary Law Study, supra note 46, at Rule 97.

[50] Rome Statute of the International Criminal Court art. 8(b)(xxiii), July 17, 1998, 2187 U.N.T.S 3 [hereinafter: Rome Statute].

[51] INTERNATIONAL CRIMINAL COURT, ELEMENTS OF CRIMES, art. 8(b)(xxiii) (2011).

prospect of having the enemy emerge in one's backyard, without any warning and with no chance of escape, is terrifying. Tunnels are not only invisible and unpredictable; they also create the possibility of a face-to-face encounter with the enemy in the privacy of one's home or neighborhood.

The UN Human Rights Council Report on Operation Protective Edge stressed the "trauma and persistent fear" sustained by Israelis as a result of the cross-border tunnels dug by Hamas:[52]

> The discovery of these tunnels and their use by Palestinian armed groups during the hostilities caused great anxiety among Israelis that the tunnels might be used to attack civilians. One witness told the commission, "When it's quiet we get even more afraid because we don't know what things can come from the ground. Since April, everyone was afraid and uncomfortable about the tunnels." Another witness said, "There was a tunnel just behind the greenhouses. In a way, they are more scary than rockets because with the tunnels there's no chance of being warned. Some people won't let their children go outside.[53]

Yet the psychological harm caused by the tunnels did not affect the Human Rights Council-appointed commission's legal analysis.[54] The commission of inquiry notes that it "cannot conclusively determine the intent of Palestinian armed groups with regard to the construction and use of these tunnels"[55]—as if this finding rendered the incidental psychological harm caused by the tunnels (or the potential risk to civilians) irrelevant. Eliav Lieblich has made a similar observation in the context of a report prepared by Stanford and New York University entitled *Living under Drones*.[56] Lieblich decries the contrast between the report's focus on the psychological trauma drones cause to civilians, on one hand, and the report's legal analysis in which "the issue of mental harm seems to have faded, as if not playing any part beyond a factual situation," on the other.[57] International practice, he writes, has "gloss[ed] over the meaning of civilian harm in the context of proportionality."[58] Lieblich believes that psychological harm should be taken into account under the laws of war, even if it is caused incidentally.

---

[52] U.N. Human Rights Council, *Rep. of the Detailed Findings of the Independent Commission of Inquiry Established Pursuant to Human Rights Council Resolution S-21/1*, ¶ 74, U.N. Doc. A/HRC/29/CRP.4 (June 24, 2015).
[53] *Id.* ¶ 106.
[54] Daphné Richemond-Barak, *Tunnel Vision at the UN*, IDC HERZLIYA INTERNATIONAL INSTITUTE FOR COUNTERTERRORISM (July 29, 2015), https://www.ict.org.il/Article/1447/Tunnel-Vision-at-the-UN.
[55] U.N. Doc. A/HRC/29/CRP.4, *supra* note 52, ¶ 108.
[56] Eliav Lieblich, *Beyond Life and Limb: Exploring Incidental Mental Harm Under International Humanitarian Law*, in APPLYING INTERNATIONAL HUMANITARIAN LAW IN JUDICIAL AND QUASI-JUDICIAL BODIES: INTERNATIONAL AND DOMESTIC ASPECTS 186 (Derek Jinks et al. eds., 2014).
[57] *Id.*
[58] *Id.* at 197.

These reflections acutely resonate in the realm of underground warfare. Tunnels can cause two types of mental harm—intentional or incidental. When tunnels cause intentional harm—that is, when they are meant to spread terror—they explicitly violate the law of armed conflict.[59] Article 51(2) of Additional Protocol I prohibits "[a]cts or threats of violence the primary purpose of which is to spread terror among the civilian population."[60] The rule has been recognized as customary in all types of conflict.[61] Acknowledging that "acts of violence related to a state of war almost always give rise to some degree of terror among the population and sometimes also among the armed forces," the law nevertheless goes the extra step of condemning outright "acts of violence the primary purpose of which is to spread terror among the civilian population without offering substantial military advantage," as well as the threat of such acts.[62]

But what about those acts whose primary purpose may not be to cause terror, but that cause terror anyway? The incidental psychological harm caused by drones, like the incidental harm caused by tunnels, ought to be condemned. When it comes to "incidental" harm, international courts have placed the threshold quite high: serious mental harm was defined by the ICTY as "grave and long-term disadvantage to a person's ability to lead a normal and constructive life."[63] The ICTR noted that a "state of anxiety" would be insufficient.[64] The standard is akin to the diagnostic criteria for post-traumatic stress disorder.[65]

The law also condemns the digging and use of cross-border urban tunnels in peacetime. A landmark decision of the Special Tribunal for Lebanon, which defines the crime of terrorism in times of peace, would apply to the digging and use of cross-border tunnels. It defines terrorism as including the following three elements: (1) the perpetration of a criminal act (such as murder, kidnapping, hostage-taking, arson, and so on), or threatening such an act; (2) the intent to spread fear among the population (which would generally entail the creation of a public danger) or to directly or indirectly coerce a national or international authority to take some action, or to refrain from taking it; and (3) a transnational element.[66] Cross-border tunnels fall within this definition because they extend beyond the territory of a single state, create a public danger, and constitute a criminal act (or the threat thereof).

---

[59] COMMENTARY TO AP I, *supra* note 45, ¶ 1940.
[60] AP I, *supra* note 48, at art. 51(2).
[61] ICRC Customary Law Study, *supra* note 46, at Rule 2.
[62] COMMENTARY TO AP I, *supra* note 45, ¶ 1940.
[63] *Prosecutor v. Tolimir*, Case No. IT-05-88/2-T, Judgment, ¶ 738 (Int'l Crim. Trib. for the Former Yugoslavia, Dec. 12, 2012).
[64] Prosecutor v. Seromba, Case No. ICTR-2001-66-A, Appeals Chamber Judgment, ¶¶ 47–48 (Mar. 12, 2008).
[65] For a discussion of the threshold of harm, see Lieblich, *supra* note 56, at 208.
[66] Interlocutory Decision on the Applicable Law: Terrorism, Conspiracy, Homicide, Perpetration, Cumulative Charging, Case No. STL-11-01/I, ¶ 85 (Special Trib. for Lebanon Feb. 16, 2011).

Under this definition, cross-border tunnel-digging in or near civilian populated areas would amount to terrorism. There is little doubt that tunnel-digging achieves the same ends as the confirmed presence of tunnels. Israelis living near the Lebanese border have heard drilling under their homes at night for years, awakened to "the trembling and noise from a jackhammer," and witnessed vibrations so intense "that picture frames and TV sets have crashed to the floor."[67] Their children, they claim, are afraid to come visit.[68] Palestinians have experienced similar trauma from the digging of tunnels under their homes,[69] as have civilians living at the Syrian-Turkish border.[70] The psychological impact of tunnels can be compared to that of other terrorist threats, which have been shown to lead, inter alia, to symptoms of depression, anxiety, a diminished sense of safety, and post-traumatic stress disorder.[71] That said, much like Article 51(2) of Additional Protocol I applicable in time of war, the Special Tribunal for Lebanon's definition fails to explicitly address the non-intentional infliction of psychological harm.

To conclude, cross-border tunnels (and the threat of such tunnels) violate the law when they intentionally spread terror among the civilian population in times of peace and in times of war (and, under a broader interpretation of the law, also when such terror is inflicted incidentally). In addition and more generally, urban tunnels violate the law of armed conflict when their location effectively renders them immune from attack. In international armed conflicts, this would also amount to a war crime.

II. The Use of Tunnels *by* Civilians

When war rages aboveground, civilians often take refuge below it. In some cases, combatants make use of most of a tunnel, with civilians using only a relatively small part of it. In other cases, tunnels are used simultaneously as lines of communication by fighters, means of "safe" transportation by the civilian population, and/or smuggling routes by criminals.

Civilian use of the underground can happen quite naturally, as in Syria where entire families moved into vacant ancient caves to seek shelter from bombings.[72] For some

---

[67] *See* Adam Ciralsky, *Did Israel Avert a Hamas Massacre?*, VANITY FAIR (Oct. 21, 2014), http://www.vanityfair.com/news/politics/2014/10/gaza-tunnel-plot-israeli-intelligence.
[68] *Id.*
[69] Hadid & al Waheidi, *supra* note 28.
[70] *See* Cunningham, *supra* note 12.
[71] *See* Stevan E. Hobfoll, Daphna Canetti-Nisim & Robert J. Johnson, *Exposure to Terrorism, Stress-Related Mental Health Symptoms, and Defensive Coping Among Jews and Arabs in Israel*, 74 J. CONSULTING & CLINICAL PSYCHOLOGY 207 (2006); Yael Danieli, Brian Engdahl, & William E. Schlenger, *The Psychological Aftermath of Terrorism, in* UNDERSTANDING TERRORISM: PSYCHOSOCIAL ROOTS, CONSEQUENCES, AND INTERVENTIONS 228 (F.M. Moghaddam & A.J. Marsella eds., 2004); Avraham Bleich, Mark Gelkopf & Zehava Solomon, *Exposure to Terrorism, Stress-Related Mental Health Symptoms, and Coping Behaviors Among a Nationally Representative Sample in Israel*, 290 JAMA 612 (2003).
[72] C.J. Chivers, *Jammed in Roman Caves, Ducking Syria's War*, N.Y. TIMES (Mar. 23, 2013), http://www.nytimes.com/2013/03/24/world/middleeast/syrians-fleeing-home-crowd-in-roman-caves.html.

families the caves served as temporary bomb shelters and for others as their dwelling until the end of the war. Existing caves were arranged, organized, and equipped with wood-burning stoves, ventilation shafts, and blankets. Although civilians living in caves often suffer from health issues, they regard these hardships as preferable to the hostilities waging aboveground. The caves of Sarjah, Syria, are reminiscent of elaborate complexes used in historical times to shield local populations.

Tunnels, however, rarely serve *only* civilian purposes in contemporary armed conflicts. Even tunnels used for civilian purposes (such as those in which civilians took refuge in the Vietnam or Afghan-Soviet Wars) were used simultaneously by opposition forces.[73] In fact, as the war continues to progress in Syria, caves and tunnels have come to play a major role for civilians, rebels, and soldiers. Both sides of the conflict have engaged in underground combat—a feature of war not seen for centuries.[74]

The proximity of combatants to civilians as in the Vietcong tunnels has yet to be witnessed in contemporary conflicts. Yet the possibility certainly looms ahead on battlefields where the line between the civilian and military worlds has increasingly faded—and the presence of civilians is ever more exploited.

A. THE UNKNOWN FACTOR AND URBAN TUNNELS

Unlike most means of warfare, tunnels cannot be seen by the naked eye. As discussed, underground warfare offers none of the visibility inherent to aboveground operations. Contending with such a threat thus presents an extraordinary challenge, particularly considering that states have yet to develop intelligence capabilities or technology able to accurately detect and map tunnels without penetrating them. This explains why tunnels between Syria and Turkey, or between Lebanon and Israel, largely remain a matter of speculation.[75] The existence of a tunnel can generally be confirmed with certainty only after the tunnel has been used. By that time, it is often too late.[76] I have referred to this

---

[73] As noted above, during the Vietnam War, civilians used the tunnels alongside combatants—often to receive medical care from the underground hospitals that had been set up to treat the wounded Vietnamese fighters. The civilian population also used the tunnels as shelters from air attacks and living quarters. *See* MANGOLD & PENYCATE, *supra* note 6, at 177 ("Every house in Ben Suc, for example, had an underground shelter connected by tunnel to other shelters.") Nearby, the Vietcong used the tunnels to hide, meet, and launch surprise attacks above and below ground. (*Id.* at 5–6 and 215: one of the biggest finds during operation "Cedar Falls" was a tunnel complex believed to be the underground headquarters of the Vietcong).

[74] *See, e.g.,* Oliver Holmes & Andrew Heavens, *Syrian Soldiers Enter Rebel Tunnels, Find Chemical Agents: State TV*, REUTERS (Aug. 24, 2013), http://www.reuters.com/article/us-syria-crisis-jobar-idUSBRE97N04T20130824; AFP, *Syrians Wage "War of Tunnels" for Damascus*, NEWS 24 (June 6, 2014), http://www.news24.com/World/News/Syrians-wage-war-of-tunnels-for-Damascus-20140606.

[75] *See* Ciralsky, *supra* note 67 (discussing the existence of cross-border tunnels between Lebanon and Israel).

[76] For example, the tunnel used to abduct Israeli soldier Gilad Shalit in 2006 was discovered only after it was used by his kidnappers to bring him into Gaza. *See* Amos Harel, *How Were Palestinian Militants Able to Abduct Gilad Shalit?*, HAARETZ (Oct. 18, 2015), http://www.haaretz.com/how-were-palestinian-militants-able-to-abduct-gilad-shalit-1.390573.

challenge as the "unknown factor." Here I envisage this unique feature of underground warfare through the lens of civilians.

Taking advantage of the element of surprise in warfare is neither unusual nor forbidden, so long as these ruses do not violate the laws of war.[77] In subterranean warfare, the difference is one of degree: the element of surprise permeates virtually every aspect of anti-tunnel operations. For example, in Chapter 6, I addressed the difficulty of applying a body of law that requires states to plan ahead, foresee, and gather evidence in time of war—when information and knowledge are hard to come by.

The difficulties are further exacerbated when civilian lives are at stake. The law's commands, for the most part, aim at minimizing the harm caused to civilians. Yet the underground significantly impedes the ability of military commanders to make the required judgments. It becomes extremely difficult to verify and localize civilian presence within tunnels, so that civilians may be protected or factored into military planning and proportionality assessments. Coalition Forces bombed the Al Firdos bunker in Iraq in 1991, not knowing that the command-and-control center was used simultaneously by some 300 civilians as a shelter.[78]

The mere likelihood of civilian presence could affect anti-tunnel operations in significant ways. Military legal advisers and commanders will probably make similar determinations in cases where the presence of civilians is merely suspected as they do in cases where it is actually confirmed. Clearing procedures will have to be followed; strikes will have to be called off. As a result of the foreseeable presence of civilians—either because civilians have been present in the tunnels in the past, or because intelligence suspects they could be present—any strike against a tunnel runs the risk of being deemed disproportionate. Imaging technology struggles with tunnel detection to begin with; distinguishing between civilians and combatants *inside a tunnel* is likely only achievable through human intelligence, too often beyond reach as it requires maintaining a physical presence in or near the tunnels.

Even a strike on an exclusively military segment of a tunnel could affect civilians inside and outside that tunnel. There is no foolproof method to assess how the destruction of a tunnel will impact homes, hospitals, schools, religious sites, or other civilian facilities located above or in the vicinity of the tunnel's route. Sections of the tunnel could collapse and block the civilians' exit, the fumes and dust resulting from the strike could suffocate them and/or render humanitarian aid unusable, and civilian infrastructure could collapse

---

[77] AP I, *supra* note 48, at art. 37(2); ICRC Customary Law Study, *supra* note 46, at Rule 57. *See* discussion *infra* in Chapter 6.

[78] Nora Boustany, *Bombs Killed Victims as They Slept*, WASH. POST (Feb. 14, 1991), http://www.washingtonpost.com/wp-srv/inatl/longterm/fogofwar/archive/post021391_2.htm; CENTRAL INTELLIGENCE AGENCY, PUTTING NONCOMBATANTS AT RISK: SADDAM'S USE OF "HUMAN SHIELDS" 8 (2003), https://www.cia.gov/library/reports/general-reports-1/iraq_human_shields#09.

and cause civilian casualties. Any or all of these are bound to happen—but knowing what and where with precision is hardly predictable.

The burden placed by tunnel warfare on intelligence services thus goes beyond that experienced in "ordinary" urban warfare. In the latter, military commanders must take all feasible means to verify the presence of civilians before striking a building. Making the determination certainly presents a challenge, and commanders do abort strikes when civilians are spotted through a window or on the roof. However, little can be seen, heard or spotted, when it comes to the underground. The near impossibility of collecting information—and the ease with which such information can be hidden and manipulated underground—embody the main difference between urban and underground warfare.

The lack of visibility inherent to underground warfare, albeit challenging, is not entirely unique. Submarine warfare and cyberwarfare, on which this book builds heavily, also display some of these features. The effectiveness of submarines lies in operating undetected, and cyber can take states by surprise at any time. Submarines, however, belong to the military world: they neither interact with nor threaten civilians, at least not since the Second World War. The same cannot be said about cyber and underground threats—both of which can cause intentional or unintentional harm to civilians and civilian infrastructure. Moreover, cyber, like tunnels, brings with it a wide range of uncertainties as to the origin of the threat, its intended target, and the process in-between. In both cyber and underground warfare, the investment in technology needed to defend against attacks very much outweighs that of launching the attack.

Beyond their many similarities, cyber and underground warfare differ in historical terms. Underground warfare has been present on the battlefield from time immemorial, as explained in Chapter 1. Cyber, in contrast, is relatively new, with fewer cyberattacks recorded, and less state practice to learn from. Based on the state practice available, states' reaction to cyberattacks has been muted in comparison to their reaction to underground threats. Attribution might have something to do with it: identifying the territory from which a tunnel emanates or the identity of those who dug it is much easier than identifying the perpetrator of a cyberattack. In fact, a level of uncertainty remains as to the identity of the perpetrators of the most serious cyberattacks—such as the 2007 Distributed Denial of Service (DDoS) in Estonia, which almost entirely cut off what was then Europe's most-connected country,[79] and the 2010 Stuxnet attack in Iran that destroyed some 10,000 Iranian uranium enrichment centrifuges.[80] Even in cases where attribution has been possible, the response has been relatively mild. The United States qualified the 2014 hacks against Sony, which the FBI attributed to North Korea, as a "very costly" act

---

[79] ENEKEN TIKK, KADRI KASKA & LIIS VIHUL, INTERNATIONAL CYBER INCIDENTS: LEGAL CONSIDERATIONS 14–22 (2010), https://ccdcoe.org/publications/books/legalconsiderations.pdf.
[80] LTC MARCO DE FALCO, STUXNET FACTS REPORT (A TECHNICAL AND STRATEGICAL ANALYSIS) 4 (2012).

of "cybervandalism."[81] In response, the United States imposed sanctions against three North Korean organizations and 10 individuals.[82] The much more problematic hack of the 2016 U.S. elections by Russia led to the expulsion of 35 Russian intelligence operatives from the United States.[83]

Ultimately, the destructive potential of cyber has been neither fully exploited nor exposed. Cyber does not (yet) trigger the same psychological fear and feeling of helplessness as tunnels. The cyber threat remains a somewhat abstract and remote one. In contrast, the impact of tunnel warfare is felt on and off the battlefield in a tangible and very kinetic manner, away from the air-conditioned rooms and somewhat sterilized atmosphere of cyber monitoring teams. Underground warfare contributes to and intensifies the fog of war, taking it to its extreme and expanding its reach to the civilian world.

B. HOW CIVILIAN PRESENCE AFFECTS ANTI-TUNNEL OPERATIONS

Tunnel warfare calls for a systematic and methodical approach. As explained in Chapter 4, states contending with an underground threat must devise a detailed, long-term strategy consisting of four main steps: detecting and mapping tunnels, destroying or neutralizing them, monitoring suspected areas, and information-sharing with other states. In this section, I analyze the first two steps (the third and fourth steps, monitoring and coordination, pose no physical threat to civilians) with a focus on how methods used to map or destroy tunnels impact civilians and civilian infrastructure.[84]

Different methods affect civilians in different ways, but some legal issues arise across the board and must be addressed at the outset. The first issue relates to the status of the tunnel, or a segment thereof. As in Chapter 6, the analysis below assumes that the tunnel in question constitutes a military objective. The second issue, a more factual one, relates to the presence of individuals inside tunnels. When individuals are present in a tunnel, a third question arises—on which I focus here—regarding their legal status. Combatants constitute legitimate targets. But what if the tunnel is being used by civilians? Are they protected?

---

[81] Allen McDuffee, *Obama: North Korea Hack "Cybervandalism", Not Act of War*, ATLANTIC (Dec. 21, 2014), https://www.theatlantic.com/international/archive/2014/12/obama-north-korea-hack-cybervandalism-not-an-act-of-war/383970/.
[82] *Sony Cyber-Attack: North Korea Faces New US Sanctions*, BBC (Jan. 3, 2015), http://www.bbc.com/news/world-us-canada-30661973.
[83] Laurent Gambino, Sabrina Siddiqui & Shaun Walker, *Obama Expels 35 Russian Diplomats in Retaliation for US Election Hacking*, GUARDIAN (Dec. 30, 2016), https://www.theguardian.com/us-news/2016/dec/29/barack-obama-sanctions-russia-election-hack.
[84] Questions related to the impact of these measures on combatants, particularly in relation to the prohibition on inflicting unnecessary suffering, are examined in Chapter 6. Strikes carried out against tunnels are lawful only when the methods used meet both requirements, that is, when they are discriminate (able to distinguish between civilian and combatants) and do not cause unnecessary suffering.

1. Targetable v. Non-targetable Civilians

Civilians can find themselves inside a tunnel for a variety of reasons—ranging from digging the tunnel to seeking shelter from the atrocities, receiving medical treatment, and hoping to shield the tunnel from destruction. The law does not look upon all of these situations in the same way.

In principle, civilians cannot be intentionally targeted in war. They enjoy a high level of protection under the law. The law defines "civilian" negatively as any individual who does not enjoy prisoner of war status or fall under the definition of "combatant," so as to extend protection to as many individuals as possible. Civilians using a tunnel or other underground structure as a shelter are protected, provided they do not get involved in military activities going on inside the tunnel simultaneously.[85] If they do, they will in certain situations lose their protection from attack and become targetable.

These situations correspond to what the law calls "direct participation in hostilities." Civilians may constitute legitimate targets only if they "take a direct part in hostilities" in the meaning of Article 51(3) of Additional Protocol I. Unfortunately the law does not provide a list of the types of conduct that amount to direct participation. The analysis is therefore very much context-dependent and open to interpretation.

The notion of direct participation has generated widespread discussion and debate, with two main views emerging. According to the International Committee of the Red Cross (ICRC), members of organized armed groups belonging to a party to the conflict lose their civilian protection insofar as they maintain a continuous combat function.[86] Being a member of the group, in and of itself, is not enough: an individual's role in the group must involve continuous direct participation in hostilities.[87] In contrast, individuals who are not members of an organized group and engage in hostilities only on a sporadic basis can only be targeted *while* doing so.

An alternative approach, based on membership alone, denies protection to all members of organized armed groups, regardless of their specific function (with the exception of those who become hors de combat and medical and religious personnel).[88] This approach maintains symmetry between the organized armed group and the opposing armed forces, all members of which are targetable regardless of their role.[89]

---

[85] AP I, *supra* note 48, at art. 50(1).
[86] NILS MELZER, INTERPRETATIVE GUIDANCE ON THE NOTION OF DIRECT PARTICIPATION IN HOSTILITIES UNDER INTERNATIONAL HUMANITARIAN LAW 34 (2009) [hereinafter DPH Guide]; Nils Melzer, *The Principle of Distinction Between Civilians and Combatants, in* THE OXFORD HANDBOOK OF INTERNATIONAL LAW IN ARMED CONFLICT 315–17 (Andrew Clapham & Paola Gaeta eds., 2014).
[87] DPH Guide, *supra* note 86, at 37.
[88] Michael Schmitt, *The Interpretive Guidance: A Critical Analysis,* 1 HARV. NAT'L SEC. J. 5, 22–24 (2010) [hereinafter Schmitt, *Critical Analysis*]; STATE OF ISRAEL, THE 2014 GAZA CONFLICT: FACTUAL AND LEGAL ASPECTS ¶ 265 (2015) [hereinafter 2014 GAZA REPORT].
[89] Bill Boothby, *"'And For Such Time As': The Time Dimension to Direct Participation in Hostilities,"* 42 INT'L L. & POL. 741, 743 (2010).

Although the ICRC's approach has been heavily criticized for its impracticality,[90] it represents the prevalent view. The ICRC has identified three cumulative criteria to determine whether a given act constitutes direct participation in hostilities. *First*, the act must be likely to adversely affect the military operations or military capacity of a party to an armed conflict, or cause harm to objects or persons protected from attack (threshold of harm). *Second*, there must be a direct causal link between the act and the harm likely to result from it (direct causation). *Third*, the act must be designed to benefit one party to the conflict to the detriment of another (belligerent nexus).[91] Most tunnel-related activities fit within these parameters: the digging of a tunnel for military purposes, the preparation and perpetration of tunnel-based attacks, and the use of tunnels as a command-and-control center or means of transportation to/from an attack.

Broader interpretations distinguish between acts creating the capacity to undertake military operations in general, and acts preparatory to combat.[92] The latter would also constitute direct participation when combat is "in the contemplation of the actor at the time of the preparatory act."[93] This means that the digging of a tunnel with the explicit purpose of carrying out tunnel mining, kidnapping, or other tunnel-based attack would amount to direct participation.[94]

Considering the risk that tunnels pose, and the complexity of detecting and destroying them, the conclusion that tunnel-related activities amount to direct participation seems both sound and practical. At the policy level, it might deter civilians from engaging in such activities in armed conflict—a relevant consideration for IHL. Importantly, as noted above, this conclusion holds for civilians who participate in the digging or provisioning of tunnels, as well as for those who mastermind tunnel-based attacks—regardless of whether they possess full knowledge of the intended use of the tunnel. It is sufficient for such purpose that the civilians work in the vicinity of or in concert with an armed group and/or under their orders. Even blindfolded individuals who do not know where they are or what is going on around them would fall under this category. The criterion of belligerent nexus is *objective*, and does not look at the mental ability or willingness of participants to take responsibility for their actions.[95] Even children below the legal age of recruitment,[96] although they receive special protection under IHL, can lose their

---

[90] Schmitt, *Critical Analysis, supra* note 88, at 23.
[91] DPH Guide, *supra* note 86, at 16.
[92] Boothby, *supra* note 89, at 750.
[93] *Id.*
[94] *Id.* at 751 (noting that it "seems proper to regard deployment with the explicit purpose of doing something preparatory to an act that itself amounts to direct participation" as amounting to direct participation).
[95] DPH Guide, *supra* note 86, at 59–60.
[96] AP I, *supra* note 48, at art. 77(2); Protocol Additional (II) to the Geneva Conventions of 12 August 1949, and relating to the Protection of Victims of Non-International Armed Conflicts (Protocol II), art. 4(3)(c) June 8, 1977, 1125 U.N.T.S 609; Convention on the Rights of the Child, art. 38(2), Nov. 20, 1989, 1577 U.N.T.S. 3; ICRC Customary Law Study, *supra* note 46, at Rule 137.

protection from attack when they directly participate in hostilities.[97] That said, the amount of force that can lawfully be used against them might differ from that directed at adults.[98]

In terms of timing, the question arises as to when protection begins and ends. As a reminder, for those who belong to organized armed groups and perform a continuous combat function within such a group, the question does not arise. It is relevant only vis-à-vis civilians whose involvement in hostilities is sporadic and limited in time. The ICRC recognizes "deployment and return" from an attack as a part of the temporal scope of participation in hostilities,[99] though here, too, the exact scope is disputed.[100] The question has little incidence in the realm of underground warfare, as the digging of a tunnel in itself constitutes direct participation—rendering a discussion of the meaning of "preparatory act" irrelevant.

An upshot of the temporal scope of IHL protection finds expression in a dilemma known as the revolving door. According to the ICRC, individuals regain their immunity in-between instances of "direct participation." Someone who is a farmer by day, but digs or uses tunnels by night, would remain protected during the day in spite of his recurring night-time activities. Critics of this approach argue that such a person is targetable until he or she unambiguously withdraws from any participation.[101] To illustrate this point, Michael Schmitt gives the example of assemblers of improvised explosive devices (IEDs) and landmines—comparable to the diggers of tunnels as "sometimes the attack does not occur until long after the insurgents have departed the area."[102] It would not make sense, Schmitt argues, for these assemblers to be "safe" until they depart again for an attack.

When civilians who have *not* lost their protection remain in a tunnel at the time of the strike, a final question arises with regard to proportionality. A strike against the tunnel will be lawful only if the harm caused to these civilians is not excessive in comparison to the military advantage anticipated from the destruction or neutralization of the tunnels. The question will not arise if the tunnel has been fully evacuated, or if those present inside it all constitute legitimate targets.

One scenario deserves to be analyzed, however. What if civilians present inside the tunnels have gone underground for purposes of immunizing the tunnel from attack? How should they be counted in the proportionality calculus? In such situations, commonly

---

[97] DPH Guide, *supra* note 86, at 60; Pelham, *supra* note 44.
[98] René Provost, *Targeting Child Soldiers*, EJILTALK! (Jan. 12, 2016), http://www.ejiltalk.org/targeting-child-soldiers/.
[99] DPH Guide, *supra* note 86, at 65.
[100] Boothby, *supra* note 89, at 751.
[101] Michael Schmitt, *Targeting in Operational Law*, in THE HANDBOOK OF THE INTERNATIONAL LAW OF MILITARY OPERATIONS 251 (Terry D. Gill & Dieter Fleck eds., 2010).
[102] Schmitt, *Critical Analysis*, *supra* note 88, at 38.

known as "human shielding," one of the belligerents is plainly taking advantage of the other party's respect for the law, knowing that the enemy will likely refrain from targeting the tunnel if civilians are present inside it. The dilemmas associated with human shielding are a well-known feature of contemporary warfare.

Although the use of human shields to render an otherwise legitimate military target immune from attack violates the law, this violation has no incidence on targeting:

> State practice indicates that an attacker is not prevented from attacking military objectives if the defender fails to take appropriate precautions or deliberately uses civilians to shield military operations. The attacker remains bound in all circumstances, however, to take appropriate precautions in attack and must respect the principle of proportionality even though the defender violates international humanitarian law.[103]

The law's position on this matter gives rise to serious dilemmas on the contemporary battlefield—including regarding the status of civilians who voluntarily take part in human shielding. Interestingly, the ICRC has addressed the latter by drawing a distinction between voluntary human shields who pose a *physical* obstacle to military operations and those who pose merely a *legal obstacle* in the sense that their presence "may eventually lead to the cancellation or suspension of an operation by the attacker."[104] According to the ICRC, only civilians who pose a physical obstacle—that is, those who try "to give physical cover to fighting personnel supported by them or to inhibit the movement of opposing infantry troops" and as such have an "adverse impact on the capacity of the attacker to identify and destroy the shielded military objective"—might, in some circumstances, count as legitimate targets.[105] In cases of doubt, protection continues to apply.[106]

The ICRC's subcategorization of voluntary human shields—differentiating between those who pose a physical obstacle and those who merely pose a legal obstacle—is both surprising and impractical. It encourages cynical uses of the law and upsets IHL's delicate balance between military necessity and humanitarian concerns.[107] In addition, it seems impractical to treat physical obstacles more stringently than so-called legal obstacles. Physical obstacles, unlike legal obstacles, may be removed. Legal obstacles, as defined by the ICRC, cannot.[108] Finally, as the ICRC itself acknowledges, the subjective intent of belligerents cannot always be uncovered during military operations.[109] The nature of

---

[103] ICRC Customary Law Study, *supra* note 46, at Rule 22 (references omitted).
[104] *Id.* (references omitted); DPH Guide, *supra* note 86, at 57.
[105] DPH Guide, *supra* note 86, at 56–57.
[106] *Id.* at 76.
[107] Schmitt, *Critical Analysis, supra* note 88, at 32–33; HCJ 769/02, Public Committee Against Torture in Israel v. Gov't of Israel 62(1) PD 507 ¶ 36 [2006] (Isr.).
[108] Schmitt, *Critical Analysis, supra* note 88, at 32.
[109] DPH Guide, *supra* note 86, at 59 n.150.

tunnel warfare, where gaining information about *who* is in a tunnel, let alone why, is nearly impossible, further underscores the limitations of the ICRC's distinction.

In sum, the law protects most civilians using tunnels. The default rule whereby anyone not considered a combatant is a civilian ensures that this remains the case in all types of warfare. In principle, civilians cannot be intentionally targeted. They may, however, lose their immunity from attack if and when they "take a direct part in hostilities." Civilians who dig tunnels, plan tunnel-based attacks, or use tunnels to carry out an attack would certainly fit within this category. The status of civilians who go underground for the purpose of shielding a tunnel from destruction is less clear legally. These situations would arguably fall within the narrow exception carved out by the ICRC, pursuant to which civilians who have an "adverse impact on the capacity of the attacker to identify and destroy the shielded military objective" could be regarded as legitimate targets. In all cases, the unknown factor and the invisibility of the tunnel must be taken into account when making the relevant legal assessments—as well as proportionality, where relevant.

2. Detection and Mapping

As explained in Chapter 4, states do not look at mapping as an indispensable step of anti-tunnel strategies. Where mapping technology is unavailable, expensive, or too time-consuming, and human intelligence is lacking, states often skip the mapping stage altogether. Instead, they undertake operations designed to destroy any *potential* tunnels. States have used random drilling, controlled explosives, and random targeting from the air as substitutes for systematic mapping. I examine here the impact of these measures on civilians and civilian infrastructure.

RANDOM DRILLING. This method consists in drilling holes in the ground at fixed intervals in places where tunnels are suspected. The United States used random digging and drilling in the Demilitarized Zone on the South Korean side, leading to the detection of four tunnels.[110] Random drilling not only requires time and resources, but is also unsuitable for large suspected areas. The larger the suspected radius, the less adequate random drilling is. Generally, it yields only limited results, as the drilling crew might miss existing tunnels—or, worse, face a last-resort surprise attack when a tunnel is close to being compromised. Beyond the risk to the armed forces or law enforcement authorities, random drilling inevitably disrupts civilian life when carried out in civilian populated areas. As part of the operation, civilians may be evacuated from their homes and/or see their homes destroyed. Egyptian anti-tunnel measures aptly illustrate this risk.

Indeed, in Egypt, widespread home demolitions began taking place in 2013 near the Gazan border as part of an effort to create a "buffer zone" that would allow the tunnel

---

[110] *See supra,* Chapter 4.

threat to be defeated. According to Human Rights Watch, an estimated 3,200 families lost their homes leading to human rights law and humanitarian law violations.[111] Egyptian authorities have coercively evicted people without proper notification or sufficient compensation.[112] Children's education was interrupted because of the unexpected move; lands and jobs were lost. The organization has voiced similar criticism of Israel for evacuating houses located within 1,000 feet of the Israel/Gaza border on both sides.[113]

CONTROLLED EXPLOSIVES. In addition to or instead of random drilling, states may use explosives on strips of land alongside a border to destroy any existing tunnel and prevent entry onto their territory. The same method can also help clear out tunnels before entering them, with smoke and secondary explosions potentially leading to additional levels and exits. This method, however commonly used, can inflict severe damages on civilians taking shelter in the tunnels. The use of explosives in confined spaces can lead to injury upon impact, and partial or complete infrastructure collapse. Detonations can cause suffocation due to the pressure resulting from stereophonic blasts. As such, this tactic can cause damage to civilians and civilian infrastructure located inside a tunnel and along its route.

RANDOM TARGETING FROM THE AIR. Similar issues arise when, again seeking to avoid mapping, states conduct random targeting from the air. Following the same rationale as in random drilling, states often carry out aerial strikes in the hope of destroying suspected tunnels. Based on available intelligence, the strikes are launched in a predelineated area and at set intervals.

Such strikes raise distinct legal challenges in civilian populated areas. Assuming civilians have not been evacuated, the strikes may qualify as indiscriminate, for they would not adequately distinguish between civilians and combatants, and between civilian objects and military objectives. The strikes would also qualify as disproportionate if the damage they cause is excessive in relation to the military advantage anticipated, as set forth in Article 51(5)(b) of Additional Protocol I. The destruction of religious and cultural sites, civilian homes, and other civilian infrastructure (roads, agricultural lands, and electricity, water, and sewage supporting facilities), and any damage caused to the environment, would have to be factored into this calculus. That said, random targeting from the air could offer a valuable alternative when the targeted area qualifies as a military objective. The main challenge, in this case, will be to minimize damage to protected persons and objects.

---

[111] *See* LOOK FOR ANOTHER HOMELAND, *supra* note 35.

[112] *Frontline Sinai: Egypt's Government Turning to Mass Relocation in Desperate Tunnel War*, International Business Times (November 7, 2014), http://www.ibtimes.co.uk/frontline-sinai-egypts-government-turning-mass-relocation-desperate-tunnel-war-1473712.

[113] *See* HUMAN RIGHTS WATCH, RAZING RAFAH: MASS DEMOLITIONS IN THE GAZA STRIP (2004), https://www.hrw.org/report/2004/10/17/razing-rafah/mass-home-demolitions-gaza-strip.

As mapping technologies remain costly, time-consuming, and underdeveloped, many states will continue to find the no-mapping approach attractive. It is important to keep in mind, in addition to other issues raised above, that the no-mapping approach puts forces at risks by relying in large part on human intelligence and requiring the direct, personal involvement of forces (except in the case of random targeting from the air). In the case of cross-border tunnels, it also puts one's own civilians at risk—as well as those living across the border. The no-mapping approach certainly has its limits, both legally and operationally.

When states do choose to detect and map tunnels, they have a variety of methods at their disposal—many of which have no incidence on civilians, such as the use of human intelligence, animals, sensors, magnetometers, gravity measurements, thermal imagery, electromagnetic induction, or electrical resistivity.[114] I therefore do not consider them here. Robots and smoke, however, deserve special mention.

Robots probably offer the most promising method for detecting and mapping tunnels. Equipped with cameras, lasers, and other tools, they already are a fixture in the civilian world,[115] and are increasingly adopted by militaries as well. The i-Robot, unveiled by the IDF in 2014, can map tunnels in a variety of terrains. It can operate in dark environments, stream encrypted images to operatives, and even open fire.[116] Another tunnel-mapping robot, currently under development by the United States, is the Counter Tunnel Exploitation Robot (CTER).[117] The CTER has the ability to carry both a camera and an explosive payload, as well as a fiber-optic communication cable. It has numerous modes of operation, allowing it to function and carry out different tasks in varying environments.[118]

Robots provide the least risky method of mapping, both to one's forces and to civilians. Legally, thoses that are not equipped with firepower capabilities—a function not necessary for mapping—do not raise any legal issues.[119] Those that do possess firepower capabilities must be examined in light of the emerging regulation governing lethal autonomous weapons. Expert meetings have been taking place regularly since 2014 within the

---

[114] *See supra* Chapter 4.
[115] *See* R. Montero, J.G. Victores, S. Martínez, A. Jardón & C. Balaguer, *Past, Present and Future of Robotic Tunnel Inspection*, 59 AUTOMATION IN CONSTRUCTION 99 (2015), http://www.robo-spect.eu/Publications/montero2015past-preprint.pdf.
[116] Israel Defense Forces, *Meet i-Robot: The First Soldier to Enter Terror Tunnels*, IDF BLOG (May 1, 2014), https://www.idfblog.com/blog/2014/05/01/meet-robot-first-soldier-enter-terror-tunnels/.
[117] Jacoby Larson, Brian Okorn, Tracy Pastore, David Hooper & Jim Edwards, *Counter Tunnel Exploration, Mapping, and Localization with an Unmanned Ground Vehicle*, 9084 PROCEEDINGS OF SPIE 3–5 (June 3, 2014), http://www.dtic.mil/get-tr-doc/pdf?AD=ADA607907.
[118] *Id.* at 3.
[119] For different views on the issue of the legality of autonomous weapons systems, see, for example, Michael N. Schmitt, *Autonomous Weapon Systems and International Humanitarian Law: A Reply to the Critics*, HARVARD NATIONAL SECURITY JOURNAL FEATURES (2013); HUMAN RIGHTS WATCH, LOSING HUMANITY: THE

framework of the Convention on Certain Conventional Weapons with the aim of adopting a definition of lethal autonomous weapons systems and clarifying the circumstances in which their use might be lawful.[120] At the opening of a 2016 meeting of experts, a consensus began to emerge that autonomous weapons systems must comply with international humanitarian law and that humans should always remain part of the decision to use lethal force.[121] These principles, should they crystallize in the coming years, will apply to anti-tunnel robots that meet the agreed upon definition of "lethal autonomous weapons."

Smoke raises more concerns from the perspective of civilians. It is one of the most effective methods of mapping tunnels (and can also be used to clear tunnels of their inhabitants, as further explained below). Robots aside, smoke presents none of the disadvantages of other mapping methods—cost, time, or lack of efficacy. It can be used immediately, for instant and accurate results. It will not trigger the collapse of part of the tunnel, and as such does not pose a risk to civilian infrastructure located in its vicinity. The evacuation of civilians need only last a short time; buildings need not be destroyed. However, in an environment where air circulation and ventilation systems are limited, smoke poses risks to civilians located *inside* tunnels. Nevertheless, smoke might still offer a valuable and lawful alternative provided that any civilians present inside a tunnel can be warned of the operation, the smoke is non-lethal, and it is used in small quantities (the minimum needed to map and/or clear the tunnel). Operationally, the only requirement is that the smoke be visible to the naked eye so as to enable the mapping of the underground structure in real time.

3. Neutralization and/or Destruction

After having detected and possibly mapped tunnels, states can employ a multitude of methods to neutralize or eliminate them. Documented methods of neutralization include the use of water to flood tunnels, pumping in toxic gases to make them uninhabitable, or cement to block them. Methods of tunnel elimination include bulldozers, explosives, flamethrowers, thermobaric weapons, and aerial strikes. The need to neutralize and/or eliminate tunnels is undeniable, as explained in Chapter 4. Yet it is important

---

CASE AGAINST KILLER ROBOTS (Nov. 4, 2012), https://www.hrw.org/sites/default/files/reports/arms-1112ForUpload_0_0.pdf.

[120] *See Background: Lethal and Autonomous Weapons*, THE UNITED NATIONS OFFICE AT GENEVA (Feb. 20, 2017), http://www.unog.ch/80256EE600585943/(httpPages)/8FA3C2562A60FF81C1257CE600393DF6?OpenDocument.

[121] Ambassador Michael Biontino, Permanent Representative of Germany to the Conference on Disarmament Geneva, Introductory Statement (Apr. 11, 2016), http://www.unog.ch/80256EDD006B8954/(httpAssets)/6796F4DBA5B2F0D6C1257F9A00441922/$file/2016_LAWS+MX_GeneralExchange_Statements_Germany.pdf.

to acknowledge that these methods all raise legal concerns when used against urban tunnels—albeit to varying extents.

FLOODING. When a tunnel is detected, flooding it with water can deter combatants and civilians from using it, due to fear of collapse and drowning. Israel has used water to intentionally trigger the collapse of cross-border tunnels on a few occasions,[122] but the practice of tunnel flooding is most associated with Egypt.[123]

Water can—intentionally or not—cause a tunnel to collapse, thus creating a risk for those both inside and above the tunnel. Water can also render ventilation shafts useless by blocking or eroding them, increasing the risk of suffocation. Whether a tunnel will collapse as a result of flooding cannot be accurately predicted and depends on a variety of factors, including construction, terrain, water amount, and water pressure. In any case, the commander of the operation must consider a possible collapse when assessing the harm that might result from the operation.

More controversially, Egypt has used sewage water to flood the cross-border tunnels.[124] The use of sewage water raises serious humanitarian and environmental concerns, as sewage is a prime carrier of diseases. Not only does the direct contact with foul sewage water carry a great risk for people inside the tunnels, but the water may also enter into contact with groundwater tables or harm nearby crops.

It is unclear what advantages sewage water holds over clean water, but the impact of sewage water on civilians and the environment is significantly worse. Considering the numerous mechanisms available to destroy and disable tunnels, it is hard to envision a situation in which military necessity would require that sewage water be used.

Methods or means of warfare that are intended, or may be expected, to cause widespread, long-term, and severe damage to the natural environment are prohibited.[125] The natural environment cannot be used as a weapon,[126] or destroyed, unless it is a military objective.[127] Even if the damage does not meet the widespread, long-term, and severe criteria, parties to the conflict have a general duty of due regard for the natural environment,[128] and environmental damage would need to be taken into account as part of a proportionality analysis.[129]

---

[122] Gili Cohen, *IDF Soldiers Tasked with Tunnel Destruction Not Trained for Primary Mission*, HAARETZ (Aug. 7, 2014), http://www.haaretz.com/israel-news/.premium-1.609345.

[123] *See* Hadid & Nassar, *supra* note 28.

[124] Joshua Bowes, Mark Newdigate, Pedro Rosario & Davis Tindoll, *The Enemy Below: Preparing Ground Forces for Subterranean Warfare* (2003) (Thesis, Naval Postgraduate School), at 117.

[125] AP I, *supra* note 48, at art. 35(3); and ICRC Customary Law Study, *supra* note 46, at Rule 45.

[126] *Id.*

[127] *Id.* at Rule 43.

[128] *Id.* at Rule 44; Jean-Marie Henckaerts & Dana Constantin, *Protection of the Natural Environment*, in THE OXFORD HANDBOOK OF INTERNATIONAL LAW IN ARMED CONFLICT 480 (Andrew Clapham & Paola Gaeta eds., 2014).

[129] Legality of the Threat or Use of Nuclear Weapons, Advisory Opinion, 1996 I.C.J. 226, ¶ 30 (July 8).

In addition, flooding, like the use of cement, may at times raise issues of "no quarter". The entrapment of people in a tunnel, whether civilians or combatants, can amount to a declaration that there shall be no survivors—an act prohibited under Article 40 of Additional Protocol I,[130] and customary law.[131] Declaring no quarter also constitutes a war crime in international armed conflicts.[132] This prohibition does not obligate a belligerent to stop using a particular weapon or method—in this case, blocking or flooding a tunnel—but it does prohibit its use in cases that would amount to a refusal to give quarter, and this is true even if there are no civilians involved.[133]

GAS. This method is perhaps the most legally questionable, as it includes the deployment of potentially deadly substances in confined spaces, significantly increasing the chances of suffocation and death. States have used toxic gases to force combatants out of tunnels and/or prevent the tunnels' reoccupation. As mentioned earlier, American forces pumped tear gas into the Vietcong tunnel complexes, which caused suffocation, even with ventilation systems in place.[134] It also poisoned the soil and inflicted long-lasting damage upon the surviving population. Similarly, the Soviets pumped unidentified gases into sections of the Karez irrigation system during the Soviet-Afghan war.[135]

The use of gas during wartime has been prohibited for over a century, whether it is employed against civilians or combatants, as explained in Chapter 4.[136] Tear gas, however, is considered lawful when used in law enforcement contexts, for example to disperse riots. This means that Egypt's reported use of tear gas,[137] although denied by the Egyptian government,[138] could arguably be considered lawful—subject to applicable limitations—so long as Egypt is not engaged in an armed conflict with Gaza. I propose to distinguish between the use of nontoxic, visible gas for mapping purposes, and that of toxic gas for the purpose of eliminating human presence inside a tunnel. Few methods are available to

---

[130] "It is prohibited to order that there shall be no survivors, to threaten an adversary therewith or to conduct hostilities on this basis." AP I, *supra* note 48, at art. 40.
[131] ICRC Customary Law Study, *supra* note 46, at Rule 46.
[132] Rome Statute, *supra* note 50, at art. 8(2)(b)(xii).
[133] COMMENTARY TO AP I, *supra* note 45, ¶ 1598.
[134] MANGOLD & PENYCATE, *supra* note 6, at 89.
[135] *See* Kakar, *supra* note 33.
[136] *See* 1899 Hague Declaration (IV,2) concerning Asphyxiating Gases, the Geneva Gas Protocol of 1925 (Protocol for the Prohibition of the Use in War of Asphyxiating, Poisonous or other Gases, and of Bacteriological Methods of Warfare); Chemical Weapons Convention, Jan. 13, 1993, 1974 U.N.T.S. 45; ICRC Customary Law Study, *supra* note 46, at Rule 75 (customary law prohibits the use of chemical weapons, including riot dispersing agents, in all armed conflicts).
[137] *See Hamas Accuses Egypt of Poisoning Palestinians in Smuggling Tunnel*, TELEGRAPH (Apr. 29, 2010), http://www.telegraph.co.uk/news/worldnews/middleeast/7651685/Hamas-accuses-Egypt-of-poisoning-Palestinians-in-smuggling-tunnel.html.
[138] AP, *Egypt Denies Gassing Gaza Tunnels*, JERUSALEM POST (Apr. 29, 2010), http://www.jpost.com/Middle-East/Egypt-denies-gassing-Gaza-tunnels.

map tunnels, and most of them are highly damaging to civilians and civilian objects. For this reason, the use of nontoxic gas should be allowed for the limited purpose of mapping a tunnel. The use of gas to clear tunnels, however, should remain prohibited not only against civilians but also against combatants.

CEMENT. Blocking a tunnel with cement can neutralize an underground threat rapidly. Contrary to conventional wisdom, however, it does not necessarily eliminate the threat altogether. It is also a costly method that requires expertise, as cement hardens quickly and must be manipulated carefully. No significant legal issues arise when cement is only used to seal off one side or one artery of a tunnel. The use of cement would also be lawful if the area qualifies as a military objective and no one is present in the tunnel at the time it is sealed—because the tunnel has been either evacuated or abandoned. Unlike many other methods, cement does not directly or indirectly affect those living in the vicinity of the tunnel.

Issues do arise, however, if all entrances and exits are sealed off while people are present inside the tunnel. As explained above, if the civilians located inside the tunnel have lost their protection by virtue of their direct participation in hostilities, they will constitute legitimate targets in their own right.[139] If they have not lost such protection, the law continues to protect them from intentional attack; however, their death may also, at times, be justified under the principle of proportionality, depending on the military value of the tunnel in question. Civilian death in the case of a cement remediation would be particularly cruel: it would amount to entrapment and suffocation. If authorities have obtained intelligence as to the presence of innocent civilians inside a tunnel, the method should not be used: methods that render death inevitable are prohibited under IHL, even against combatants. Authorities would be able to use cement remediation only if civilians and combatants evacuate the tunnel.

Ultimately, the legality of anti-tunnel measures must be assessed on a case-by-case basis. It all very much depends on the value of the tunnel and the military advantage anticipated from its elimination or neutralization, as required under the principle of proportionality. When weighing the relevant elements, decision-makers will likely struggle with the unknown factor. Mapping out and neutralizing a tunnel is hard enough, let alone determining whether any parts of it (and which) are used for civilian purposes or occupied by civilians at any given time. These challenges should be kept in mind when choosing anti-tunnel measures and assessing their respective impact on the local population.

Destroying tunnels goes beyond neutralization or remediation, providing a more suitable answer to underground threats in the long run. Various methods exist: bulldozers, explosives, and targeted aerial bombardments are all capable of inflicting sufficient

---

[139] Issues of unnecessary suffering might arise. See supra Chapter 6.

damage to destroy tunnels. States typically resort to these methods in the aftermath of mapping, but they can also do so immediately upon discovering the tunnel(s).

BULLDOZERS. Unlike explosives, bulldozers provide troops with optimal control over the destruction. However, manually destroying a tunnel is a daunting task that places one's own forces at prolonged risk, as they must enter enemy territory and operate in the open, often while engaging in active combat.[140] This method also usually requires pre-mapping and a better understanding of the type and route of the tunnel. Both Israel and Egypt have used bulldozers to destroy tunnels near their Gaza borders.[141]

Bulldozers do not pose a threat to civilian life as much as to civilian infrastructure and the environment. Bulldozer operators will typically watch for the presence of civilians. The real-time control over the destruction and the direct visual contact with civilian presence make this method relatively safe from the perspective of civilian lives. In addition, if the operation is properly planned and monitored it should not cause any significant damage to civilian infrastructure or the environment.

EXPLOSIVES. Explosives can be dropped, fired, or deployed manually against tunnels or segments thereof. Manually placed explosives should be favored against heavily fortified tunnels that might be difficult to destroy otherwise, but do not necessitate an aerial operation. This is a quick, efficient, and highly controllable method.[142] Ground engagement generally minimizes civilian casualties. That said, the unknown factor is still present and the manual placement of explosives places forces in harm's way.[143] In addition, the explosion can destroy existing infrastructure and harm civilians close to weapons caches and hidden exits. The precise extent of the destruction, and the ensuing damage to civilian and civilian infrastructure, depends on the type of explosives used.

Thermobaric weapons—whose destructive capability exceeds that of conventional high-explosives munitions of comparable size—also raise concern when employed in civilian populated areas. Although, as explained in Chapter 6, these weapons "are

---

[140] Amos Harel, *Analysis: As Bulldozers Destroy Hamas' Underground Network, IDF Sees Light at End of Tunnel*, HAARETZ (Aug. 1, 2014), http://www.haaretz.com/israel-news/.premium-1.608293. I discuss the issue of force protection below in Section IV.

[141] *Egyptian Bulldozers Raze Fields Looking for Tunnels to Gaza*, MIDDLE EAST MONITOR (Feb. 5, 2014), https://www.middleeastmonitor.com/20140205-egyptian-military-bulldozers-raze-fields-searching-for-tunnels-to-gaza/; *Israel Military Increases Activity to Find Tunnels in Gaza Territory: Report*, TIMES OF ISRAEL (June 2, 2016), https://www.i24news.tv/en/news/international/115359-160602-israeli-military-increases-activity-to-find-tunnels-in-gaza-territory-report.

[142] Yoav Zitun, *IDF Unveils New Method for Destroying Terror Tunnels*, YNET (Mar. 4, 2015), http://www.ynetnews.com/articles/0,7340,L-4633580,00.html.

[143] *See Supporting Forces*, Israeli Ground Forces (2011), http://mazi.idf.il/6511-9882-he/IGF.aspx (in Hebrew) (noting the injuries sustained by an IDF soldier seeking to inject liquid explosives into a tunnel in 2013). For more details see discussion in *infra* Chapter 4.

not currently banned under international humanitarian law," Human Rights Watch has cautioned against their use in or near population centers.[144] Echoing this view, the U.S. Law of War Manual notes that "[i]nflicting blast injury is not prohibited by the law of war," and makes a specific reference to the use of these weapons in underground warfare:[145]

> Pioneers, sappers and combat engineers engaged in tunneling operations under enemy lines in the American Civil War, World War I, and Korea employed substantial amounts of high explosives. Enemy personnel above the detonation became blast casualties. Artillery barrages generally will produce a number of enemy casualties, including fatalities, from blast alone, as will heavy aerial bombardment.[146]

Similar weapons were used—for similar reasons—by American forces in Afghanistan against underground shafts, with an equally strong impact, though not in proximity to civilians.[147] Human Rights Watch cautioned Russia over the potential use of vacuum bombs "in towns and cities where Chechen fighters are dug in."[148] Although the efficiency of these weapons against tunnels, caves, and bunkers leaves no doubt,[149] the concern is that the effects of vacuum bombs cannot be limited to combatants when used in urban settings, and that they will burn civilians, collapse buildings, and destroy vegetation and agricultural crops.[150]

AERIAL STRIKES. Where states identify or suspect the existence of tunnels, they often resort to aerial strikes in order to find the tunnels and destroy them. This method limits the troops' exposure to some of the dangers mentioned above. When backed up by reliable and precise intelligence, pinpointed aerial bombardments can help eliminate tunnels, or at least segments of them. As is often the case with aerial warfare, however, aerial methods of tunnel destruction could pose graver risks to civilians and existing

---

[144] HUMAN RIGHTS WATCH, BACKGROUNDER ON RUSSIAN FUEL AIR EXPLOSIVES ("VACUUM BOMBS") (Feb. 1, 2000), https://www.hrw.org/report/2000/02/01/backgrounder-russian-fuel-air-explosives-vacuum-bombs [hereinafter FUEL AIR EXPLOSIVES].
[145] U.S. DEPARTMENT OF DEFENSE, LAW OF WAR MANUAL ¶ 6.5.5 (2015) [hereinafter LAW OF WAR MANUAL].
[146] Id. at 327 n.90 (citing W. Hays Park, Special Assistant to the Judge Advocate General, U.S. Army, Memorandum re: 40mm Thermobaric Munition: Legal Review (Apr. 2, 2003)).
[147] Pentagon to Use New Bomb on Afghan Caves, CNN (Dec. 23, 2001), http://edition.cnn.com/2001/US/12/22/ret.new.weapon/.
[148] FUEL AIR EXPLOSIVES, supra note 144.
[149] Torie Rose DeGhett, A New Kind of Bomb Is Being Used in Syria and It's a Humanitarian Nightmare, VICE (Aug. 28, 2015), https://news.vice.com/article/a-new-kind-of-bomb-is-being-used-in-syria-and-its-a-humanitarian-nightmare.
[150] FUEL AIR EXPLOSIVES, supra note 144. See also Max Boot, INVISIBLE ARMIES, at 361.

infrastructure than ground methods of destruction. Moreover, the more powerful the blast, and the closer the proximity to civilians and civilian infrastructure, the more dubious is the legality of the strike. In each given case, whether conducted prior to the strike or ex post facto, the analysis should be made on a case-by-case basis, based on the intelligence available to the commander at the time of the strike.

To conclude, civilian presence affects the choice of anti-tunnel operations in significant ways. Although the use of flamethrowers and other highly devastating weapons can be contemplated in uninhabited mountainous areas, their deployment in urban areas would likely qualify as indiscriminate and/or disproportionate. With a focus on the impact of mapping, neutralizing, and elimination methods on civilians and civilian infrastructure, this section has called for a strict application of the core IHL principles of distinction and proportionality. Regardless of the method used, the area/tunnel must constitute a legitimate target, the damage to civilians and civilian infrastructure should not be "excessive" in relation to the military advantage anticipated from the attack on the tunnel, and all feasible precautions should be taken to evacuate civilians ahead of the operation. In the unique context of underground warfare, where the unknown factor rules, the mere likelihood of civilian presence will likely trigger the same processes and decisions as the confirmed presence of civilians. This outcome could impede anti-tunnel operations and render tunnels virtually untouchable—a result states will not easily accept.

III. The Use of Tunnels *against* Civilians

Historically tunnels have been used mainly against fighters and their positions. Even though the years since 9/11 have seen a re-emergence and evolution of underground warfare—with caves and tunnels featuring in theaters of operations from Afghanistan to Mali[151] and Libya[152]—this has remained largely unchanged. Operation Aleppo Earthquake, for example, targeted a command-and-control center of Assad's forces inside the Carlton Hotel of Aleppo, Syria.

This is likely to change in the coming years, however. As aptly noted by the former IDF Chief of General Staff, Rav Aluf Benny Gantz, the fear is that "an explosives-laden tunnel

---

[151] Adam Nossiter & Eric Schmitt, *Facing the French, Mali Rebels Dig in and Blend in,* N.Y. TIMES (Jan. 15, 2013), http://www.nytimes.com/2013/01/16/world/africa/mali-islamists-dig-in-for-a-long-military-struggle.html; MICHAEL SHURKIN, FRANCE'S WAR IN MALI: LESSONS FROM AN EXPEDITIONARY ARMY (2014), https://www.rand.org/content/dam/rand/pubs/research_reports/RR700/RR770/RAND_RR770.pdf.

[152] Raymond Bonner, *Libya's Vast Desert Pipeline Could Be Conduit for Troops,* N.Y. TIMES (Dec. 2, 1997), http://www.nytimes.com/1997/12/02/world/libya-s-vast-desert-pipeline-could-be-conduit-for-troops.html; Oana Lungesu, NATO Spokesperson & Mike Bracken, Operation "Unified Protector" Military Spokesperson, Press Briefing on Libya (July 7, 2011), http://www.nato.int/cps/en/natolive/opinions_76163.htm. *See also* Oana Lungesu, NATO Spokesperson & Roland Lavoie, Operation "Unified Protector" Military Spokesperson, Press Briefing on Libya (Sept. 13, 2011), http://www.nato.int/cps/en/natolive/opinions_77984.htm.

would be detonated under a kindergarten near the border."[153] Tunnel attacks directed at civilians will increase, even if they do not fully replace the more traditional use of tunnels against combatants. Behind this change lies a combination of factors, including a general trend bringing warfare in closer contact with civilians, and the transformation and diffusion of underground warfare in recent years.[154]

The versatility of tunnels makes it easy to predict a wide variety of attacks against civilians—from tunnel mining to kidnapping—mirroring the multifaceted use of the underground against combatants. Tunnels may allow chemical agents to come in contact with the civilian population, crops, or irrigation systems. In contemporary times, the tunnels dug by Hamas under the Gaza/Israel border provide the most vivid example of the digging of man-made underground structures to reach, inter alia, civilians. Other, arguably less striking examples include ISIS's imprisonment of approximately 1,500 individuals—most of them civilians—in an underground facility.[155]

Tunnels dug solely for launching attacks against enemy combatants and other related uses do not violate international law. In contrast, as explained above, tunnels dug in civilian populated areas do violate international law. I focus here on tunnels dug for the purpose of harming civilians. Such tunnels violate the principle of distinction and spread fear among the civilian population. The challenge, however, is to show the diggers' intention. Relevant indicators include the route of the tunnel, the diggers' modus operandi, the type of warfare they are generally engaged in (guerilla, insurgency, or terrorism), their IHL compliance record, declarations they might have made as to their intentions, and any past relationship between the parties. Intent is a subjective criteria, and disagreement could arise as to the true purpose of a tunnel.[156] The purpose of a tunnel can change with time: an irrigation or sewer system, a smuggling tunnel, or a tunnel built to shelter civilians can be overtaken by combatants. It can then be used to attack civilians, combatants, or both. All of this makes it difficult to ascertain with precision the purpose of a tunnel and whether it aims specifically and intentionally at harming civilians. Nevertheless, when the specific purpose of attacking civilians *can* be shown, the digging and/or use of the underground constitutes a violation of international law.

---

[153] *Israeli Military Video Shows Soldiers Detonating Tunnel*, ITV NEWS (July 31, 2014), http://www.itv.com/news/2013-10-17/the-terror-tunnels-that-threaten-the-fragile-israeli-palestinian-peace-process/.

[154] Eyal Benvenisti, *The Legal Battle to Define the Law on Transnational Asymmetric Warfare*, 20 DUKE J. COMP. & INT'L L. 339, 343 (2010). For a discussion of these factors, *see supra* Chapter 2.

[155] *See Report: Underground ISIS Jail Holding 1,500 Prisoners Liberated by Iraqi Forces*, HAARETZ (Apr. 2, 2016), http://www.haaretz.com/middle-east-news/1.712321.

[156] U.N. Doc. A/HRC/29/CRP.4, *supra* note 52, ¶ 108 (noting that "[t]he commission cannot conclusively determine the intent of Palestinian armed groups with regard to the construction and use of these tunnels. However, the commission observes that during the period under examination, the tunnels were only used to conduct attacks directed at IDF positions in Israel in the vicinity of the Green Line, which are legitimate military targets."). *See also* Exodus 22:1 and Babylonian Talmud, Sanhedrin Tractate 72 (a burglar who entered a house via a tunnel is presumed to have bad intentions).

Consider, for example, Hamas's use of the basement of Al-Shifa hospital as a command-and-control center. It embodies a unique manifestation of the intersection of the civilian world with the underground: the use of an existing underground civilian infrastructure for offensive purposes, which combines the use of the underground by *and* against civilians. The use of existing underground civilian infrastructures is unique in many other ways. Remarkably, the mapping stage becomes redundant when it comes to this type of underground structures. Delineating the structure's path does not pose any challenge: authorities can easily obtain the map of the subway or sewage system in question. In addition, and in contrast to other scenarios where the presence of civilians has to be established, here such presence should be taken as axiomatic. The unknown factor, in other words, has a lesser effect on operations undertaken against existing civilian underground infrastructure than on other types of anti-tunnel operations. The use of the facility *by* civilians should not only be presumed but also carefully weighed in when planning the operation. Finally, the goal of the operation differs: it will focus on stopping an attack or putting an end to the military use of the infrastructure rather than on eliminating the structure altogether. Interestingly, the use of existing civilian underground infrastructure can take place in times of war like in Gaza, or in times of peace. The 1995 release of sarin gas in the Tokyo subway by members of the Aum Shinrikyo cult—which killed 13 and left thousands sick or injured—illustrates the latter.

Let us examine the situation in which an existing civilian underground structure is taken over, in whole or in part, for military purposes during an armed conflict. The underground structure—be it a hospital, subway, or sewage system—is a civilian object and thus protected from attack under the law. Such protection is reinforced under the terms of Article 52(2) of Additional Protocol I. Yet the article also contemplates the loss of the protection in situations where the underground structure is being used to make an effective contribution to military action: "In case of doubt whether an object which is normally dedicated to civilian purposes, such as a place of worship, a house or other dwelling or a school, *is being used to make an effective contribution to military action*, it shall be presumed not to be so used."[157]

Civilian objects are protected unless they become military targets, along with the presumption of civilian character in cases of doubt. This rule is customary.[158] Both the grant of protection and the possibility of having it removed feature as a silver lining within IHL, with respect to medical units and personnel,[159] and cultural property.[160]

---

[157] AP I, *supra* note 48, at art. 52(3) (emphasis added).
[158] ICRC Customary Law Study, *supra* note 46, at Rule 10.
[159] AP I, *supra* note 48, at arts. 12 and 13; ICRC Customary Law Study, *supra* note 46, at Rule 28; Geneva Convention for the Amelioration of the Condition of the Wounded and Sick in Armed Forces in the Field (First Geneva Convention), art. 19, 12 August 1949, 75 U.N.T.S. 31; Geneva Convention Relative to the Protection of Civilian Persons in Time of War, art. 18, Aug. 12, 1949, 6 U.S.T. 3516, 75 U.N.T.S. 287.
[160] Convention for the Protection of Cultural Property in the Event of Armed Conflict, art. 4(2), May 14, 1956, 249 U.N.T.S. 240; ICRC Customary Law Study, *supra* note 46, at Rule 38.

The protection of objects, like the protection of persons, is thus strong yet not absolute. Assuming a commander can show that the underground civilian infrastructure "is being used to make an effective contribution to military action," protection will be lost. Before the strike can be considered lawful, however, the commander must overcome another hurdle: the principle of proportionality. He or she will also have to take all feasible precautions to minimize civilian casualties resulting from the attack.

Alternatively, the attack may be directed at specific individuals located inside the underground civilian infrastructure, rather than at the facility itself. The targeted individuals must constitute legitimate targets, and the damage caused to the structure (and any civilians in or above it) must remain proportionate. In other words, the damage to the structure and civilians cannot be excessive in relation to the military advantage gained from neutralizing or killing the hostile individuals.

Outside of armed conflict, in a law enforcement context, the civilian-military distinction ceases to apply: attacks are viewed through the prism of the right to life, which prohibits arbitrary depravations of life[161] but allows the use of lethal force in the protection of life and limb.[162] This is the framework that applies in cases of domestic terrorism, in which the underground has been and will continue to be harnessed. Examples include the above-mentioned sarin gas attack inside the Tokyo subway system,[163] and the escape of the Al-Shabbab perpetrators of the deadly 2013 Westgate Shopping Mall attack through the mall's sewage system.[164] Outside an armed conflict, lethal force must be a last resort[165] and remains subject to proportionality and absolute necessity.[166]

---

[161] International Covenant on Civil and Political Rights, art. 6, Dec. 12, 1966, 999 U.N.T.S. 171.

[162] U.N. Human Rights Comm., Draft General Comment 36, Article 6: Right to life, ¶ 16, U.N. Doc. CCPR/C/GC/R.36/Rev.2 (Sept. 2, 2015) 18 [hereinafter Draft General Comment 36]; Christof Heyns, *Report of the Special Rapporteur on extrajudicial, summary or arbitrary executions*, ¶ 58, U.N. Doc. A/HRC/26/36 (2014).

[163] Tomohiro Osaki, *Deadly Sarin Attack on Tokyo Subway Recalled 20 Years On*, JAPAN TIMES (Mar. 20, 2015), http://www.japantimes.co.jp/news/2015/03/20/national/tokyo-marks-20th-anniversary-of-aums-deadly-sarin-attack-on-subway-system/#.

[164] Russell Myers, *The Escape Route Tunnel Used by Terrorists After Shopping Centre Massacre*, DAILY MIRROR (Sept. 29, 2013), http://www.mirror.co.uk/news/world-news/nairobi-attack-escape-route-tunnel-2314873.

[165] Draft General Comment 36, *supra* note 162, ¶ 18.

[166] Code of Conduct for Law Enforcement Officials, art. 3, Adopted by General Assembly Resolution 34/169 (Dec. 17, 1979); Basic Principles on the Use of Force and Firearms by Law Enforcement Officials, art. 5, Adopted by the Eighth United Nations Congress on the Prevention of Crime and the Treatment of Offenders, Havana, Cuba, 27 August to 7 September 1990.

IV. Urban Tunnels and Reflexive Obligations under IHL

Urban tunnels raise additional issues under international humanitarian law. Like the tunnels themselves, anti-tunnel operations launched by a belligerent against urban tunnels located (even partially) on its territory will impact its own civilians. In the case of cross-border tunnels, commanders must consider not only how the operations will affect enemy civilians, but also how they will affect their own civilians and civilian infrastructure. The problem is that IHL provides little guidance on how states should factor in potential damage to their own civilians in war.

IHL's difficulty has its roots in the law's primarily causative nature. The regulation of war focuses on the treatment of a state's opponent(s)—that is, enemy civilians and, to a lesser extent, enemy combatants: "As IHL developed as the law of international armed conflicts covering, in conformity with the traditional function of international law, inter-State relations, it aimed essentially to protect 'enemies' in the sense of enemy nationals."[167]

The focus on the protection of enemy nationals has left the protection of one's own nationals in time of war largely unregulated.[168] There is nothing inherently wrong with IHL's harm-focused approach; the law *should* be concerned with the harm caused to enemy civilians and combatants by a state party.[169] However, contemporary warfare increasingly requires the law to stretch beyond its causative nature, thereby exposing the limits of the causative approach.

In the context of underground warfare, this gap becomes apparent when, for example, a belligerent digs tunnels in urban areas—thereby intentionally creating a threat to its own population—or undertakes anti-tunnel operations against cross-border tunnels exiting on its own territory.

These issues touch upon the relationship between a belligerent and its own nationals in time of war—a relationship that has not traditionally been the focus of the law of armed conflict. Such law primarily regulates how belligerents ought to behave vis-à-vis each other in times of war: the types of weapons they may use, the level of harm they may inflict, the tactics they may employ, whom they should spare, and so on. To put it differently, IHL regulates the type and level of harm that can be caused to the enemy or its civilians.

The focus on causative factors is a function of IHL's history and evolution. Traditionally understood as the body of law governing state conduct in time of war, IHL has two main objectives: to protect enemy civilians from hostilities, and to authorize the targeting of combatants in armed conflicts. An essential purpose of IHL is to ensure that war is not unlimited, that is, that international norms restrict the level of harm that can be inflicted

---

[167] *See* MARCO SASSÒLI & ANTOINE BOUVIER, 1 HOW DOES LAW PROTECT IN WAR? 32 (2011).

[168] For another manifestation of this gap, see Daphné Richemond-Barak & Ayal Feinberg, *The Irony of the Iron Dome: Intelligent Defense Systems, Law and Security*, 7 HARV. J. NAT'L SEC. 479 (2016).

[169] For further discussion, see Janina Dill, *The 21st Century Belligerent's Trilemma*, 26 EUR. J. INT'L L. 83 (2015).

on the other side to achieve victory. A plethora of contemporary norms give expression to this concern for the other side—from prisoner of war status to advance warning, proportionality, distinction, and unnecessary suffering. Few humanitarian norms, however, dictate how belligerents ought to treat their *own* people in times of war, be they civilians or combatants. Such *reflexive* considerations were at best of secondary importance at the time of the law's inception, and have remained much less developed to this day.[170]

Examples of reflexive norms include those governing non-international armed conflicts, and the rules governing the identification of hospitals and civil defense teams, as they impose norms on states for the protection of their *own* population.[171] Similarly, Article 58 of Additional Protocol I imposes a triple duty on states to protect *their* civilian population from the effects of attacks.[172] This article "is not concerned with laying down rules for the conduct to be observed in attacks on territory under the control of the adversary, but with measures which every Power must take in its own territory in favour of its nationals, or in territory under its control."[173] The sacrosanct principle of distinction, for its part, embodies both causative and reflexive concerns. It gives expression to *causative* concerns in that it requires military commanders to direct strikes at military targets only (in order to minimize the harm caused to enemy civilians), but it is also a *reflexive* norm in the sense that it requires members of the armed forces to identify themselves in order to ensure the protection of their own civilian brethren.

In contrast, treaties regulating IHL barely address the rights enjoyed by one's own combatants. Putting prisoner of war status aside, the prohibition on the use of methods of warfare of a nature to cause superfluous injury or unnecessary suffering is a rare exception.[174] Unsurprisingly, however, the prohibition is interpreted as protecting enemy combatants (a causative concern) rather than one's own combatants (a reflexive concern).[175] Similarly, the law provides no clear answer on how to factor in harm caused to one's own soldiers—a reflexive dilemma known as force protection—or on whether war crimes can be committed by members of the armed forces against members of *the same* armed force. The Extraordinary Chambers in the Courts of Cambodia and the

---

[170] For a different view, see Eyal Benvenisti & Amichai Cohen, *War Is Governance: Explaining the Logic of the Laws of War from a Principal-Agent Perspective*, 112 MICH. L. REV. 1363, 1371 (2014) (noting that "IHL reflects domestic principals' attempts to create an effective means of monitoring and disciplining their agents").

[171] Richemond-Barak & Feinberg, *supra* note 168, at 477.

[172] Article 58 reads as follows: "The Parties to the conflict shall, to the maximum extent feasible: (a) without prejudice to Article 49 of the Fourth Geneva Convention, endeavor to remove the civilian population, individual civilians and civilian objects under their control from the vicinity of military objectives; (b) avoid locating military objectives within or near densely populated areas; (c) take the other necessary precautions to protect the civilian population, individual civilians and civilian objects under their control against the dangers resulting from military operations." AP I, *supra* note 48, at art. 58.

[173] *See* COMMENTARY TO AP I, *supra* note 45, ¶ 223.

[174] For a history of the provision, see YORAM DINSTEIN, THE CONDUCT OF HOSTILITIES 73–77 (3d ed., 2016).

[175] COMMENTARY TO AP I, *supra* note 45, ¶ 1416.

International Criminal Court have answered the latter question in the affirmative.[176] The outcome certainly upholds the values and objectives of IHL—though one might find it awkward that "an attack by a state or organization against its own armed forces" amounts to "an attack against a civilian population."[177] The acrobatic legal reasoning is the direct result of the law's primarily causative nature.

For similar reasons, the law has failed to address the circumstances in which a state may target its *own* nationals—except, as noted above, in the context of non-international armed conflict, when a state's governmental forces fight rebels within that state's territory. Take, for example, the dilemmas that arose over the targeting of U.S. national Anwar Al-Awlaqi in Yemen in 2011,[178] international law's helplessness in the face of a belligerent's use of its own civilians as human shields,[179] or the willful targeting of civilians by their own leaders—as in the case of the killing of Syrian citizens by President Bashar al-Assad.[180]

Unlike human rights law or international criminal law, international humanitarian law does not directly address a belligerent's responsibility for the harm intentionally caused to its own civilians. Human rights law may provide a partial solution. It imposes obligations on a state vis-à-vis its own civilians in peacetime, and continues to apply in cases of armed conflict alongside IHL. Human rights law arguably provides the better benchmark by which a state's obligations toward its own citizens should continue to be measured, even in times of war. That said, I can hardly see this body of law offering a broad-based solution for the increasingly challenging and common reflexive issues arising on the contemporary battlefield. The precise contents of a state's human rights obligations in time of war remains a matter of debate and interpretation, and imposing overly stringent obligations could undermine the delicate compromise between necessity and humanity achieved by IHL. The solution, in my view, is therefore best found in IHL itself.

---

[176] INTERNATIONAL CRIMINAL COURT, The Prosecutor v. Bosco Ntaganda, Case No. ICC-01/04-02/06 (January 4, 2017), https://www.icc-cpi.int/CourtRecords/CR2017_00011.PDF. See Ido Rosenzweig, *ICC's Ntaganda Decision on the Protection of Own Forces from Rape and Sexual Slavery* (July 3, 3017), https://armedgroups-internationallaw.org/2017/03/07/guest-post-by-ido-rosenzweig-iccs-ntaganda-decision-on-the-protection-of-own-forces-from-rape-and-sexual-slavery-much-ado-over-something/.

[177] Notification on the Interpretation of 'Attack against the Civilian Population' in the Context of Crimes against Humanity with Regard to a State's or Regime's Own Armed Forces, Case File No: 003/07-09-2009-ECCC-OCIJ, ¶ 69 (Extraordinary Chambers in the Courts of Cambodia, Feb. 7, 2017), https://www.eccc.gov.kh/sites/default/files/documents/courtdoc/2017-02-08%2013:53/D191_18_EN%20CAH%20.pdf.

[178] Mark Mazzetti, Eric Schmitt & Robert F. Worth, *Two-Year Manhunt Led to Killing of Awlaki in Yemen*, N.Y. TIMES (Sept. 30, 2011), http://www.nytimes.com/2011/10/01/world/middleeast/anwar-al-awlaki-is-killed-in-yemen.html.

[179] For a discussion, see Amnon Rubinstein & Yaniv Roznai, *Human Shields in Modern Armed Conflicts: The Need for a Proportionate Proportionality*, 22 STAN. L. & POL'Y REV. 93, 107 (2011) (claiming that "the relative lack of response—political or legal—to the use of civilians as human shields renders the prohibition merely theoretical.")

[180] Laurie Blank & Geoffrey Corn, *Losing the Forest for the Trees: Syria, Law, and the Pragmatics of Conflict Recognition*, 46 VAND. J. TRANSNAT'L L. 693, 694–95 (2013).

This is particularly true as reflexive dilemmas will continue to pop up in the context of asymmetric warfare. Waging war—as well as a growing conception of the law as imposing unilateral undertakings—is nowadays guided by states' *own* values and principles. States have made this clear.[181] In this context, issues surrounding a state's treatment of its own nationals, be they civilians or combatants, will only intensify. Though these dilemmas arise sporadically and in seemingly unrelated contexts, they share a common root: the regulations' marked emphasis on causative obligations.

Underground warfare brings to light many of these under-explored and under-theorized aspects of warfare. *First*, the party digging tunnels in urban areas, as noted above, intentionally places its population in danger. An underground munitions factory under a civilian building in Hebron, in the West Bank, puts all of the civilians living in its vicinity in direct, intentional, yet not always known danger. This danger, by virtue of its nature and span, exposes civilians to an unprecedented threat—raising questions as to the scope of a belligerent's (reflexive) obligations vis-à-vis its own civilians in time of war.

Second, the digging of tunnels in the midst of civilian populated areas complicates anti-tunnel operations. Although a ground operation might in some situations save civilian lives, it exposes one's armed forces to a very direct and pernicious threat. The issue of force protection has been the subject of heated debates; it re-emerges here in full force. To what extent can a belligerent fighting urban tunnels factor in foreseeable harm caused to its combatants in the planning of an anti-tunnel operation? This reflexive question has important ramifications for underground warfare waged in civilian populated areas.

Third, the reach of cross-border tunnels onto one's territory brings up the (reflexive) question of how anti-tunnel operations will affect one's own civilians and civilian infrastructure. As explained above, the effects of anti-tunnel operations targeting the section of a tunnel located on enemy territory can be felt on the other side of the border. What if—and the permutations are endless—Israel demolishes a tunnel and the destruction sparks a chain reaction that takes down a kindergarten in an Israeli kibbutz? Does the same proportionality calculus apply vis-à-vis a belligerent's own civilians as it applies to the enemy's civilians? Proportionality is typically understood as an assessment of the damage anticipated vis-à-vis *enemy* civilians. Nevertheless, in this case, an ex-ante risk assessment of the damage expected to result from the strike would also have to envisage one's own civilian losses (casualties, including mental harm in some cases,[182] as well as damage caused to civilian dwellings, roads, and agricultural lands.

Fourth, a state's duty of care toward its own people becomes relevant in a cross-border tunnel context. By not contending with the underground threat adequately, states could

---

[181] *See, e.g.,* Barack Obama, Nobel Lecture (Dec. 10, 2009), https://www.nobelprize.org/nobel_prizes/peace/laureates/2009/obama-lecture_en.html; Francois Hollande, Speech given in Bamako, Mali (Feb. 2, 2013), http://franceintheus.org/spip.php?article4310.

[182] *See* Lieblich, *supra* note 56, at 193.

be accused of endangering the civilian population.[183] This could include accusations that the state has underestimated the threat or, more specifically, that it has failed to protect civilians living in proximity to suspected areas or deploy adequate methods of detection. It also bears on the scope of a soldier's obligation to spare its own civilians,[184] and on the responsibility of a belligerent using its own nationals as human shields.

Fifth, reflexive issues arise in the context of non-international armed conflicts. Consider a group of rebels, pitted against governmental forces on that state's territory, digging tunnels against a variety of targets or using existing underground civilian infrastructure such as subway or sewage systems. The law governing non-international armed conflict, including but not limited to the concept of direct participation in hostilities, would provide an answer in these situations.

Conclusion

Historically tunnels had little to do with civilians. They were used to undermine fortifications and surprise the enemy in a variety of ways. Perhaps this explains why the law paid little attention to this tactic of war. Things have changed, however. The general trend is for civilians to come in increasingly closer contact with conflict, either because the conflict takes place in the midst of civilian populated areas, civilians are the designated targets of war, or civilians play a greater role in the military effort (for example as contractors). The growing use of the underground by nonstate actors—precisely those nonstate actors that have demonstrated a willingness to exploit civilians and civilian objects in war—suggests that civilian elements will increasingly be interwoven into underground warfare.

This relatively new take on underground warfare will intensify the challenges raised by urban warfare on one hand, and underground warfare on the other. Dilemmas so far unknown to military commanders and legal advisers will emerge, calling for an analysis that goes beyond the more traditional *in bello* questions examined in Chapter 6. With a focus on the interface between tunnels and civilians, this chapter has examined legal and operational issues arising out of the use of tunnels *near* civilians, *by* civilians, and *against* civilians.

Operationally, the unknown factor makes the treatment of urban tunnels a tantalizing task. Gathering intelligence on human presence inside a tunnel requires exceptional efforts—without any guaranteed success. Knowing whether civilians might have sought refuge inside a tunnel and, if so, how many, can prove as difficult as looking for a needle

---

[183] However, note that, in 2011, the Israeli Supreme Court discarded the position that the government had to ensure the protection, at all times, of all Israeli citizens from any security threat. *See* Richemond-Barak & Feinberg, *supra* note 168, at 480–81.

[184] *See* David Luban, *Risk Taking and Force Protection*, *in* READING WALZER (Yitzhak Benbaji & Naomi Sussmann eds., 2013).

in a haystack. Military commanders and state decision-makers face these difficult issues at all stages of an underground war: from the detection of tunnels up until their full elimination.

This is because the presence of civilians *near* tunnels affects the types of methods and measures that can be lawfully used: smoke for mapping, cement for neutralizing, or bulldozers for eliminating tunnels. Even when a tunnel constitutes a military objective—which I have generally assumed in this chapter—the question of the foreseeable harm caused to civilians, also known as the proportionality test, will ultimately determine the legality of the contemplated strike. The law does not "quantify" civilians in a uniform manner. Civilians who have contributed to the digging of a tunnel will not be counted as collateral damage, as they took a direct part in hostilities, thereby losing their immunity and turning into legitimate targets. Civilians who went underground for the specific purpose of shielding a tunnel from attack, assuming this can be proven, trigger fewer obligations on the part of the targeting state (in terms of the efforts necessary to ascertain their presence/number, or the taking of precautions in attack) than those who were coerced into doing so. The law does and should, as a matter of policy, continue to send the right signal regarding the use of tunnels *by* civilians and the dangers of underground civilian/combatant coexistence.

The use of tunnels *against* civilians, too, will likely witness a surge in coming years. The outcome could be devastating for civilians and civilian infrastructure. The versatility of tunnels makes for endless possibilities: the use of existing underground infrastructure to harm as many civilians as possible, the use of tunnels for tunnel mining against civilian targets, or their use, yet again, for kidnapping. The prospect of the use of cross-border tunnels in and out of residential areas and against civilian targets, which the 2014 use of tunnels by Hamas at the Gaza-Israel border embodies, uniquely threatens civilians on both sides of the conflict. This type of tunnel also raises a surprising array of reflexive issues, largely undeveloped under existing IHL.

The challenges abound for decision-makers, military planners, and legal advisers when underground warfare meets urban warfare. Nothing, however, compares to the hardships this up-and-coming reality springs upon civilians. Urban tunnels place civilians in highly precarious situations, leaving open the question of how the law can better deter, punish, and regulate the digging or use of tunnels near civilians or with the goal of hurting civilians. Acknowledging that the digging of tunnels in residential neighborhoods violates the principle of distinction and obligations owed by states to their civilians under the law of armed conflict, as well as the prohibitions on rendering military objectives immune from attack and spreading fear among civilians is a good place to start.

CONCLUSION

LT. GEN. BENNY GANTZ, formerly the IDF's Chief of Staff, is of the view that tunnels pose a strategic threat to Israel, but not an existential threat.[1] I subscribe to this assessment. This book does not seek to portray underground warfare as the most significant threat facing states. Advocating that greater attention be paid to underground threats does not mean placing such threats at the very top of a state's priority list. States should find a way to make resources available to increase awareness, cooperation, and prevention in the realm of underground warfare—without compromising their readiness on other fronts.

The experience of the United States on the Japanese islands during World War II and in Vietnam strengthens this conclusion. The highly aggressive use of tunnels by the Japanese and the Vietcong did not seriously threaten U.S. military superiority in either war. The tunnels inflicted heavy casualties, complicated the fight, and probably delayed victory. But victory was not truly endangered even by the most deceitful and deadly uses of the subterranean. One important caveat must be made, however. In both instances, the underground threats were met with a strong U.S. response—one that today would not be

---

[1] Dani Kushmaro, *Gantz in an Exclusive Interview: "Ministers Didn't Know? They Are Evading Responsibility"*, Mako.co.il (Mar. 1, 2017), http://www.mako.co.il/news-military/security-q1_2017/Article-cd9a5749c9a8a51004.htm (in Hebrew).

Underground Warfare. Daphné Richemond-Barak.
© Oxford University Press 2018. Published 2018 by Oxford University Press.

regarded as meeting the law's demands. A more muted response may not have allowed the United States to prevail in Iwo Jima and Cù Chi.

Although tunnels do not pose an existential threat, they present a quandary for states that is not easily resolved within the confines of the law. The challenge rises exponentially in situations where civilians are the designated victims of tunnel attacks, live near the tunnels, or are present inside them. In such situations, which will become more common in future conflicts, combatting underground threats will reach unprecedented levels of complexity. For this reason, at the normative level, I have resisted the temptation of imposing additional legal constraints on commanders. The existing legal framework is already very constraining. There is no need to heighten the level of scrutiny weighing on them. Even though the underground may hinder a commander's ability to take necessary precautions and gather information, it does not justify a tightening of the legal requirements. Given states' past practice, making the legal framework more stringent could prompt states to disregard the law in the highly threatening and challenging subterranean environment.

Urban tunnels will also subject civilians to the physical dangers, fear, and psychological trauma once experienced by tunnel rats and other veterans of tunnel warfare. In the case of cross-border tunnels, these will be felt by civilians on both sides of the conflict. Ironically, a tool designed to weaken the enemy on the other side of the tunnel can end up subjecting one's own population to the same hardships and a similar destiny.

This book takes a broad view of underground warfare and its ramifications—much broader than ever envisaged in any study. The focus is not on a single conflict or discipline. It is true that the law was the impetus behind this project and informs many of its conclusions. This is not surprising given my background. Early on in the process, however, I became aware that the law alone could not achieve this study's declared goals: to demonstrate that underground warfare has re-emerged as a global and rapidly diffusing threat of concern to all states, and that it raises unique operational and legal challenges. For this reason, I have structured the book around three axes: history, strategy, and law. The idea is to provide as complete a picture as possible of the reality of underground warfare, and to reconcile this reality with existing legal norms.

History reveals much about the versatility of tunnels and their perpetual appeal in war. Different actors have used the underground differently—from smuggling to hiding ammunition, seeking shelter, ambushing enemy forces, kidnapping, launching weapons, taking control of territory, or retaining such control in the face of enemy incursion. For a long time, the underground was used as an anti-personnel tool, that is, by combatants against other combatants, either on well-delineated battlefields or in remote mountainous regions. Using tunnels near or against civilians is a relatively recent trend. It is related to the rise of violent nonstate actors who manipulate the law to their benefit by weaving civilian elements into the conduct of hostilities. This can take many forms, including the use of human shields, disguising fighters as civilians, and launching attacks from civilian objects. That tunnel warfare has seen a similar trend is therefore not surprising.

These changes have had a tangible effect on underground warfare as stigma has come to attach to underground warfare, unlike in the past. of the tactic by violent nonstate actors and rogue states has worked as a of its perfidious nature. It has also increased the reputational costs of us more acceptable forms. The perceived lack of legitimacy cloaking the pra ...ans that states are less likely to resort to tunnel warfare than was once the case. Although Syria and North Korea continue to dig, it is difficult to imagine U.S., UK, or Australian forces making use of tunnels in a contemporary conflict.

Fewer states and more nonstate actors will make use of the subterranean going forward, and it will remain attractive as the capability gulf between guerrilla movements and technologically sophisticated states widens. As witnessed in Syria, nonstate actors will not only enhance their use of the subterranean, they will also innovate, learn to integrate the underground into broader operations, and combine them with other methods for maximum impact. Sporadic underground tactics will morph into long-term strategies. Underground warfare will become more advanced and widespread, and draw ever closer to the civilian world.

At the strategic level, the reality of underground warfare must be better understood. Tunnels too often have caught states unprepared. The time has come for states to take measure of the operational complexity that accompanies underground warfare. Ideally, states should devise long-term strategies to contend with underground threats. They should also initiate institutional dialogues on decision-making, military training, technological needs, and/or regional or international cooperation. Any of these would help enhance readiness in the face of the growing threat.

As states go through this process, they may be tempted to think that the key to the subterranean lies in technology. Technology, however, is no panacea. No single technology will succeed in mapping, detecting, or destroying tunnels. A combination of methods is required at each of these stages. It would be a mistake, for example, to believe that an underground barrier can, in and of itself, stop incursions. The case of Egypt demonstrates this well.

The frustration associated with tunnel detection can lead states to engage in an endless search for the right technology—a potential drain on a state's resources and energies. Consider Israel's efforts in this field:

> For fifteen years, Israel tried an array of seismologic, magnetic and radar systems to detect Hamas's tunnels, but without success. Because of the tunnels' depth—sometimes descending as far as 30 meters below the surface—the technologies used by U.S. agencies to find smuggling tunnels under the Mexican border were not applicable to the Israeli-Gaza border.
>
> Initially, Israel's political leadership sought to neutralize the tunnels through bombing. This proved ineffective, as it obscured the tunnel entrances and failed to destroy the tunnels' branches or the assault teams waiting underground. The

ability to detect these tunnels remotely and accurately ultimately required a major ground incursion by the IDF.

Even when the tunnel entrances were secured, other problems delayed and frustrated the operation to destroy the tunnels. A shortage of excavators and drillers meant the tunnels had to be dealt with sequentially rather than simultaneously, thereby prolonging the ground operation. Once on site, robots proved difficult to use, as they lost communications when they advanced 100 meters into the tunnel. Consequently, IDF engineers were sometimes only able to destroy the first or last 200 meters of a tunnel, which could easily be re-excavated by Hamas. Exploding the tunnels was also a challenge, as the air pressure at that depth reduced the effectiveness of various explosives. In certain cases up to 16 tons of Emulsion and sixty mines were needed to destroy a single kilometer of tunnel.[2]

This description encapsulates the difficulty of detecting and destroying tunnels, points to the need to diversify methods, and warns against focusing exclusively on technology as a matter of policy. Human and visual intelligence, monitoring, and information-sharing play equally important roles and should not be neglected. That underground warfare is characterized by a strong learning curve also cautions against placing too much emphasis on technology. Actors that use the underground for a specific purpose quickly learn of additional ways to maximize their strategic gains. As one belligerent puts in place mechanisms to better face the threat, the other improves its underground skills—a phenomenon well known to war scholars. In the context of underground warfare, it cautions against placing too much emphasis on technology.

Legally, I shy away from overly permissive or restrictive views of underground warfare. Underground warfare has been a feature of war for as long as war itself has existed. If states had objected to it, even for a moment, they would have attempted to regulate it (as they did with submarine warfare, for example). But they did not. It is therefore fair to conclude that states have tolerated underground warfare as a tactic of war. I refuse to interpret this, however, as affording belligerents a blank slate in all tunnel-related situations. The law of armed conflict should do more to prevent and condemn the use of urban tunnels, as well as those designed to harm civilians, immunize military targets, or spread terror among the civilian population. Tunnels may not be unlawful per se, but certain restrictions can and must apply. These restrictions cannot be based upon the purpose of a tunnel alone. A tunnel is a tunnel is a tunnel: it poses a security threat regardless of its purpose and should, at a minimum, be carefully monitored. An approach to underground warfare based solely on a tunnel's designation is not only too

---

[2] *2014 Gaza War Assessment: The New Face of Conflict: A Report by the JINSA-Commissioned Gaza Conflict Task Force* (2015), http://www.jinsa.org/files/2014GazaAssessmentReport.pdf, at 56.

simplistic, but it also fails to account for the versatility of tunnels. Until a tunnel is fully eliminated, it can be used, inherited or expanded by *any* actor for *any* purpose.

Underground warfare also challenges the law's theoretical foundations. The vast majority of norms governing war regulate the harm that belligerents may lawfully cause to the enemy—I refer to these norms as causative. By contrast, reflexive norms, that is, those that regulate a belligerent's duties vis-à-vis its own nationals in time of war, are few and far between. Tunnel warfare brings to light this underexplored and undertheorized side of humanitarian law in many ways. The party digging a tunnel in an urban area intentionally places its *own* population in danger. By undertaking anti-tunnel operations, its opponent exposes its *own* armed forces to a very direct and pernicious threat—raising the well-known and legally unsettled dilemma of force protection. Perhaps most remarkably, cross-border tunnels reaching onto one's territory bring up the (reflexive) question of how anti-tunnel operations affect one's *own* civilians and civilian infrastructure. The need to recognize and expand on a duty of care under the law of armed conflict challenges IHL's deeply rooted assumption that governments naturally spare and protect their own population. These are just some examples of how underground warfare exposes the weaknesses of IHL at the level of theory.

The law needs to adapt and stretch beyond its primarily causative focus in order to provide answers to important tunnel-related dilemmas. Beyond the law, contending with tomorrow's underground warfare requires greater awareness, more tools (technological and others) integrated into full-fledged strategies, and an enhanced dialogue among states. From a mere tool of war, underground warfare has evolved into a global security threat of concern to all states. From being confined to the military world (i.e., state-to-state, combatant-to-combatant use), it is constantly drawing closer to civilians. Our view of tunnel warfare therefore needs to change. Without going so far as to advocate the recognition of a new domain of war, underground warfare must be acknowledged as a subset of land warfare calling for tailored policies, skills, expertise, processes, and legal interpretations.

Index

Page numbers followed by *t* indicate tables

acoustic sensors, 95, 96
Additional Protocol I (AP I). *See* First Additional Protocol to the Conventions of 1977
adoption-capacity theory, 39–42. *See also* financial intensity
advance warning, xv, 162, 167, 193
aerial strikes/aerial bombing, 11, 16, 101–2, 106, 109, 212, 232, 237–40
  shelter and hiding from, 10, 30, 33, 34, 47
aerial surveillance, 161, 162
aerial warfare, 171
Afghani Karez tunnel, 47. *See also* irrigation canals
Afghanistan, xi. *See also* Soviet–Afghan War
  Allied War in, 15–17
aggression, acts of, 155
  definition and criteria for, 155, 155n222
Ago, Roberto, 150–51, 153
air law, 69–72

air warfare, 25, 37. *See also* aerial strikes/aerial bombing
Akande, Dapo, 131
Aleppo Earthquake Operation (2014 Aleppo bombing), xix, 31–32, 42, 240
al-Qaeda, xiv, 15–17, 47
al-Qaeda in the Islamic Maghreb (AQIM) entrenches in Mali, xi, 19–21, 114, 161
Al-Shifa Hospital, xxii, 209, 242
American Civil War, 4–5
Amidror, Yaakov, 90n63, 181n108
Anaconda, Operation, 17
animals, 90–91
Annan, Kofi, 154
Ansar Dine, 20, 21
Antarctic Treaty of 1961, 68
anticipatory (right to) self-defense, 126, 128, 132–35
anti-tunnel operations, xiv
  applicable law, 227–40
  how civilian presence affects, 226–31
    detection and mapping, 231–34

anti-tunnel operations (*Cont.*)
  neutralization and elimination, 234–40
  reasons for, 105
  state's need to understand detection and destruction methods before embarking on, xx
anti-tunnel strategy, components of a complete/full-fledged, xx, 87–88, 115–16
  cooperation, 114–16
  detection and mapping, 88–104
  neutralization and/or destruction, 104–11
  prevention and monitoring, 111–13, 115, 217.
  See also monitoring
Armed Activities on the Territory of the Congo, 61–62, 129, 130
armed attack
  defined, 127
  tunnel(s) as, 127–32
armed conflict. *See also* international armed conflicts; non-international armed conflicts
  defined, 78–79
armed conflict, law of. *See* international humanitarian law (IHL)/law of armed conflict/law(s) of war
Assad, Abu, xix
Assad, Bashar al-, 31–32, 75, 109, 211–12, 240, 246
attribution, 120–22, 153, 225–26
  of similarity, 39
autonomous weapons systems, 233–34
aviation law. *See* air law

B-52 bombers, 11, 15, 216
Bar Kokhba revolt, 3–4
Barton, Barry, 58
Bennett, Naftali, 101–2
Benvenisti, Eyal, 194
Bethlehem, Daniel, 130
biblical accounts of underground warfare, 3
bin Laden, Osama, xi, 15–16
Blumberg, Dan, 96, 101
Bocardo SA v Star Energy UK Onshore Ltd, 58
bomb shelters, 30, 125, 213. *See also* aerial strikes/aerial bombing: shelter and hiding from; shelters
  Al Firdos/Al Firdus, 176, 224
  caves used as, 30, 222–23

booby traps, 172, 200–201, 213
  defined, 200
Boothby, William "Bill" H., 92n81, 195n173, 198, 201n215
breaches of the peace, 155
Brownlie, Ian, 67
buffer zone, Gaza–Egypt, 24, 103, 111–12, 216–17, 231–32
bulldozers, 108–9, 238
bunker busters, 109–10, 204
bunkers, 13–14, 18–19, 26. *See also* command-and-control centers
  bombing, 9, 19n104, 47, 176–77, 224
  used for defensive purposes, xvi, 8
  in World War II, xvi, 8, 9, 19

Canadian Law of Armed Conflict Manual, 92
canine units, 91. *See also* dogs
Caroline incident, 132, 152n201
Cast Lead, Operation, 22, 27
causative nature of IHL, 244–46
causative norms, defined, 255
causative obligations, 247. *See also* reflexive vs. causative duties
cement, 105–8, 112, 217, 234, 236–38
chemical agents, 11, 92
Chemical Weapons Convention (CWC), 92
Chicago Convention on International Civil Aviation, 70
civilian infrastructure. *See also* underground civilian infrastructure
  anti-tunnel operations and, 231–40, 244, 247, 255
  destruction of, 109
  military underground structures must be kept separate from, 207
  tunnels dug in close proximity to, 49
civilian–military distinction. *See* distinction
civilian objects, protection of, 242–43
civilian populated areas
  proximity of tunnels to, 45
  spread of underground warfare to, 211–15
civilian population, spreading fear among, xxi, 49, 176, 207, 221, 222, 241, 249, 254
civilian protection. *See also* precautionary duties
  state practice and, 215–18
civilians. *See also* homes
  combatants and
    differentiating, inside tunnels, 224
  international law and, 167, 241

defined, 227
direct participation in hostilities, 227
impact of anti-tunnel measures
  on, 231–40
proximity of combatants to, 233. *See also
  under* Vietcong tunnels
targetable vs. non-targetable, 227–31
tunnels near, 210, 249. *See also* urban
  tunnels
  underground warfare meets urban
    warfare, 210–22
  use of tunnels against, 210, 240–43, 249
  use of tunnels by, 210, 222–40
    reasons for being in tunnels, 227
    taking shelter, 3, 4, 13, 17–18, 30, 33, 46, 210,
      211, 223n75, 227, 232
civilian world, extension of underground warfare
  to the, 38, 50, 51, 210, 226, 253
Clausewitz, Carl von, 184
command-and-control centers, 42, 79, 176, 178,
  224, 240
  also used as civilian shelters, 47, 177, 224
  Hamas, xxii, 209, 242
  tunnels used as, xxi, xxii, 48, 169, 176, 177, 184,
    209, 224, 228, 242
  in underground structures, xvi, 16, 52, 125,
    177, 224
*Congo v. Uganda. See Armed Activities on the
  Territory of the Congo*
Convention on Certain Conventional
  Weapons (CCW)
  Protocol I: Non-Detectable Fragments,
    197, 202, 203
  Protocol II: Mines, Booby Traps and
    Other Devices (1996), 84, 106,
    144, 200
  Protocol III: Incendiary Weapons, 193, 201
  Protocol IV: Blinding Laser Weapons, 197
  Protocol V: Explosive Remnants of War
    (2003), 84
Convention Relating to the Regulation of Aerial
  Navigation, 70
Corn, Geoffrey S., 67n27, 77n3, 187n129,
  188n139, 190n147, 198n198, 246n180
Corten, Olivier, 151
counterattacks, tunnels in urban areas immune
  to, 210
countermeasures, 143–47, 150
  defined, 144

Counter Tunnel Exploitation Robot
  (CTER), 233
Crater, Battle of the, 4–5
Crawford, James, 150–51
cross-border underground threats,
  assessing, 123t
cross-border vs. within-state tunnels, 44–45
Cù Chi, xiv, 10, 11, 47, 52, 97, 185, 211, 252
cuju est solum doctrine, 57–60, 65
cyberattacks, 120, 140, 144, 153, 176, 194, 225.
  See also cyberwarfare
  defined, 176
  tunnels contrasted with, 135, 225–26
cyber countermeasures, 144
cybervandalism, 225–26
cyberwarfare, 171, 176, 194, 226. *See also*
  cyberattacks; Tallinn Manual on the
  International Law Applicable to Cyber
  Warfare
  compared with underground warfare, xiii,
    126, 133–35, 144, 153, 168–71, 176, 190,
    194, 225–26
  international humanitarian law (IHL) and,
    168–71, 176
  lack of visibility, 225
  law acknowledging unique features of, 170,
    176, 194, 225

deceiving the enemy, 172, 173n61
deeply buried facilities, 125
  bunker busters and, 110
  construction of, xvii–xviii, 52
  detection of, xviii, 90, 99
  functions of, 52
  proliferation of, xviii
  tunnels and, xviii
deep underground, xx, 67
defensive use, xvi, 2, 8–10, 19, 30, 37, 52–53,
  125, 146
demilitarization of outer space and the
  seabed, 72
Demilitarized Zones, 137–38. *See also* Korean
  Demilitarized Zone
Democratic Republic of Congo (DRC), 61–62.
  *See also Armed Activities on the Territory
  of the Congo*
Department of Defense Law of War Manual, 189,
  191, 198, 239
Desert Storm, 176–77

destruction/elimination of tunnels (hard kill), xiv, 113
   methods of, 108, 234
   military advantage to be gained from, 178, 180–81
   vs. neutralization, 105, 116, 237
Detachment, Operation, 8–9
detection (of tunnels), xx, 90, 91, 231–34. *See also under* anti-tunnel strategy
   smoke used for, 14, 91–92, 234
   technology used for, 88, 92–104
detention facilities, underground, 33
detonation. *See* explosives
diffusion
   defined, 38–39
   direct vs. indirect, 39
   among social movements, 39, 42, 43
   of suicide terrorism, xix, 40, 43
   of tactics, 39, 114–16
   of underground warfare across battlefields, 39–43
Dinstein, Yoram, 127, 158, 179n99, 183, 191
direct participation in hostilities
   acts preparatory to combat, 228, 229
   civilian, 227
   criteria for determining whether an act constitutes, 228
disarmament, 83–84
disarmament, demobilization and reintegration (DDR) policies, 84
distinction, principle of, 167, 177, 190, 240, 243, 249
   Article 57 of Additional Protocol I and, 189, 192
   knowledge-based duties and, 187
   reason for, 182
   as reflexive obligation, 245
   tunnels intended for use against civilians and, 241, 249
dogs, sniffer, 90, 91. *See also* animals
domain (of war), 169–70
   cyberwarfare as a, 169–71
   underground warfare as a, 126, 163, 169–71, 255
Draft Articles on the Responsibility of States for Internationally Wrongful Acts (Draft Articles), 143, 144, 147, 148, 150–53
   Article 25, 150–53
drilling, 66, 104
   random, 102, 231–32

dual use objects, 180
due diligence, 76, 121, 122

Earthquake, Operation. *See* Aleppo Earthquake Operation
Egypt–Gaza barrier, 23
Egypt–Gaza buffer zone, 24, 103, 111–12, 216–17, 231–32
electrical resistivity, 98
electromagnetic induction, 98
elimination. *See* destruction/elimination of tunnels
emulsion, 110–11
escape tunnels, 89–90, 96–97
explosives, 240–41
   controlled, 35, 102–3, 109, 110, 163, 232–34
   detection of, 94

fear spreading among civilian population, xxi, 49, 176, 207, 221, 222, 241, 249, 254
financial intensity, 40. *See also* adoption-capacity theory; Horowitz, Michael
   defined, 40
First Additional Protocol to the Conventions of 1977 (AP I), 164–65, 169, 174, 176–80
   Article 36, 169, 199
   Article 40, 236
   Article 49, 176
   Article 51, 219, 221, 222, 227, 232
   Article 52, 177–80, 184, 186, 242
   Article 57, 188–89, 192–94
   Article 58, 174, 218, 245
   Article 86(2), 187
flags, false, 173. *See also* perfidy
flamethrowers, 14, 108, 109
flooding, 105–6, 235–36
fog of war, 186, 226. *See also* uncertainty; unknown factor
force, use of, 130, 139–43, 205. *See also* lethal force
   International Court of Justice (ICJ) on the, 140, 142, 147, 152, 158–59
   international law and the, 147, 151, 154
   prohibition on the, 147
   threat of the, 133, 141–43, 154, 158
Foster-Miller TALON, 94
Foster-Talon 4, 94
Fourth Geneva Convention (GCIV), 79–82, 164
   Article 49, 207, 245n172
   Common Article 3, 144, 165

fracking, 73
frontier incidents, 128, 140
functional kill. *See* neutralization of tunnels
Füsslein, Otto, 6–7

Gaddafi, Muammar, 2, 18–19, 213
Gantz, Benny, 240–41, 251
gas, use of, 106–7, 236–37
Gaza–Egypt border, 27, 216. *See also under* Hamas
Gaza–Egypt buffer zone, 24, 103, 111–12, 216–17, 231–32
Gaza–Israel border, 89, 232
Gaza Strip, 25
  Syria and, xvii, 2, 30, 32, 38, 39, 43n55
  underground complexes dug in, 52
Gaza Strip smuggling tunnels, 22–24, 53
Gaza War (2008-2009). *See* Cast Lead, Operation
Gaza War (2014). *See* Israel–Gaza conflict of 2014; Protective Edge, Operation
GBU-43/B Massive Ordnance Air Blast (MOAB), 110, 199
Geneva Convention relative to the Protection of Civilian Persons in Time of War. *See* Fourth Geneva Convention
Geneva Conventions, 165
  Common Article 2, 164
  Common Article 3, 155
Genghis Khan, 13
Goldin, Hadar, 29
gradiometry, 98–99
"grave and imminent peril," 148
gravity measurement technology, 98–99
Great Man-Made River, 18
grenades, 202
Gulf War, 18. *See also* Desert Storm
Guyana v. Suriname, 142

Hague Conventions of 1899 and 1907, 79–81, 173, 196–97. *See also* Martens Clause
Hamas, 29, 194
  command-and-control center, xxii, 209, 242
  tunnels at Gaza–Egypt border, 78, 216, 220
  from smuggling to terror, 22–24, 214–16
hard kill. *See* destruction/elimination of tunnels (hard kill)
Hezbollah, 26, 42–43
Higgins, Rosalyn, 130, 138–39, 198n199

high seas, 66, 67, 70–72, 170
Hirsch-Hoefler, Sivan, 218n43
Hitler, Adolf, 8, 19
Hollis, Duncan, 144
home demolitions and human rights law, 78, 231–32
homes, tunnel entrances located inside civilian, 181–82
Horowitz, Michael, 39–42
HPCR Manual on International Law Applicable to Air and Missile Warfare, 168–69
human rights law, 78, 83, 155
  applicability in times of war, 77, 78, 246
  home demolitions and, 78, 231–32
  international humanitarian law (IHL) and, 76, 78, 79, 83
  overview and nature of, 76–77
  tunnels and, 77, 78
  and use of lethal force, 45, 76–77
Human Rights Watch, 78, 239
human shields/human shielding, xv, 229–30, 246, 248, 252
  prohibition on, 219
  violation of the, 174, 219
  voluntary
    civilians who go underground to be, 227, 231, 249
    posing physical vs. legal obstacle to military operations, 230

IHL. *See* international humanitarian law (IHL)/law of armed conflict/law(s) of war
immediacy, 140–41, 143. *See also* imminent threat and imminent peril
imminence and imminent threats, 141
imminent threat and imminent peril, 105, 129–35, 143, 148, 153
imprisonment, underground, 241
improvised explosive devices (IEDs), 229
incendiary weapons, 201–2
  defined, 201
information, 187–89
  defined, 187
  vs. knowledge, 187
information-seeking obligations and proportionality, 190
infrastructure. *See* civilian infrastructure; underground civilian infrastructure

"inheritance" of tunnels, 43, 46, 105, 112, 113, 115, 215
  advantages of, 46, 113
  examples of, xiv, 10–11, 47, 53, 217. *See also under* al-Qaeda
  prevention of, 52, 112, 113, 115, 217
  risk of and threat posed by, xxii, 12
  and the need to eliminate tunnels, xiv, 105, 215, 217
  types of inherited tunnels, 46–47
innovations, military, 39–40
intelligence, surveillance, and reconnaissance (ISR) capabilities, xii, 187
intelligence gathering, 88–90
international armed conflicts (IAC), 164–65, 219
International Committee of the Red Cross (ICRC), 227–31
  on direct participation in hostilities, 227, 228
  Study on Customary International Humanitarian Law (Customary Law Study), 167n30, 194, 201, 202
  on targetable vs. non-targetable citizens, 227–31
International Court of Justice (ICJ), 82–84, 127–29, 149, 155, 167
  advisory opinion on "Legality of the Threat or Use of Nuclear Weapons," 130, 152
  necessity and, 82, 152, 153, 158–59
  on sovereign rights over natural resources, 61–62
  territorial integrity and, 136–38, 139n109, 156
  on the use of force, 140, 142, 147, 152, 158–59
  weapons and, 195, 198
International Criminal Court, 155, 245–46
  Rome Statute, 166, 197, 219
International Criminal Tribunal for the former Yugoslavia (ICTY), 78–79, 191, 200, 221
international humanitarian law (IHL)/law of armed conflict/law(s) of war (*jus in bello*), 163, 164, 206, 207, 209, 249. *See also specific topics*
  armed conflict and, 78–79
  duty of care under, 255
  ensuring respect for IHL and disseminating its knowledge, 188
  human rights law and, 76–79, 83
  impact, 254
  intentional harm and, 221
  international law and, 164, 244
  legality and status of tunnels under, 164, 175, 222
    the applicable legal framework: key principles, 164–68
    defining a tunnel under IHL, 168–72
    legality of digging and using tunnels in war, 172–77
    legal status of tunnels under IHL, 177–84
  overview and nature of, 78, 164
  proportionality and, 76, 167, 177, 182, 187
  psychological harm and, 220
  purposes and objectives, 144–45
  requires information and knowledge, 187
  terminology, xxi, 78
  tunnels and, xxi, 79
  tunnel warfare and, 53
  underground warfare and, 162
  and urban tunnels, 254
    legality of urban tunnels under IHL, 218–22
international law, 63, 64, 70, 72, 91, 122, 147, 163
  human shields and, 246
  international humanitarian law (IHL) and, 164, 244
  jus ad bellum and, xix, 122, 125
  nuclear weapons and, 152
  right of self-defense and, 45, 125
  rules in, 83–84, 141n124
  state-centric nature of, 125
  state/nonstate divide and, 125
  state sovereignty over water and, 65
  subfields, 60, 64. *See also* human rights law
  tunnels and, xiv, xix–xxi, 104, 113, 218, 241
  underground and, xiv, xix, 49, 56, 67, 69, 72, 73, 241. *See also* sovereignty over the underground: under international law
International Law Commission, 62, 142, 152. *See also* Draft Articles on the Responsibility of States for Internationally Wrongful Acts
international organizations, defined, 145n143
international vs. non-international armed conflict, 164–66. *See also* non-international armed conflicts
Iraq, 18, 176–77
  tunnels in, 212
    ISIS's, xiv, xvii, 33–35, 212–13, 217
i-Robot, 94, 233

irrigation canals, 13, 17–19, 35n204, 47, 213, 236, 241. *See also* afghani Karez tunnel
ISIS (Islamic State of Iraq and the Levant/Islamic State of Iraq and Syria), 33, 88, 110, 184, 212–13, 217
  smuggling tunnels, 211–12
  tunnel mining and, 33, 34
  tunnels in Iraq, xiv, xvii, 33–35, 212–13, 217
Israel, 156, 215
  cooperation and partnership between U.S. and, 114–15
  policy regarding tunnels, 26
  tunnels between Lebanon and, 43n33, 53, 89, 223
Israel–Gaza conflict of 2014, 194, 214. *See also* Gaza Strip; Protective Edge, Operation
Israeli border, Hamas's tunnels at the, 214, 215, 220. *See also* Gaza–Israel border
  underground warfare meets urban warfare, 24–30
Israeli Defense Forces (IDF), 24–30, 91, 110–11, 174n68, 254
Israeli Supreme Court, 81–83, 248n183
Israeli trauma and fear due to cross-border tunnels, 220
Ivan the Terrible, 4
Iwo Jima, Battle of, 8–9

Jachec-Neale, Agnieszka, 178, 179n97
Joint Direct Attack Munitions (JDAM) bombs, 102–3
jungle exception, 193
jus ad bellum (law governing the entry into war), 76, 120, 122, 166n27
  bellum proportionality, 129–31
  necessity and, 129–32, 151–53
  proportionality and, 129–31
  and right to self-defense, 126, 129, 130, 151
  strategic factors affecting, 123*t*, 123–26, 144, 152
jus cogens (peremptory norm), 65n53, 150, 151, 159
  countermeasures and, 146, 147, 150
jus in bello (law governing war). *See* international humanitarian law (IHL)/law of armed conflict/law(s) of war
jus post bellum, 76, 85
  law of occupation and, 79–85
  overview and nature of, 83

kibbutz
  cross-border tunnels exiting in or near, xii, 27–29
  Hamas operatives infiltrating, 29
kidnapping, 25–26, 28, 29, 124
knowledge, 187–88
  defined, 187
  vs. information, 187
knowledge-based duties imposed by international humanitarian law (IHL), 187–88
Korean Demilitarized Zone, xvii, xxi, 12, 13, 98, 102, 126, 231
Kurdish forces, 33–34, 51, 212

landmines
  anti-personnel, 10, 84
  tunnels compared and contrasted with, 113, 229
  detection of, 94
  removal after conflict, 84–85
land warfare, 37, 170
  underground warfare as a subset of, 171, 255
Law of War Manual. *See* Department of Defense *Law of War Manual*
League of Nations Covenant, Article 10 of, 136
learning curve, xvi, 50, 254
Lebanon
  tunnels between Israel and, 43n33, 53, 89, 223
  underground complexes dug in, 52
Lebanon War (2006), 26, 42
"Legality of the Threat or Use of Nuclear Weapons." *See Nuclear Weapons* advisory opinion
lethal autonomous weapons, 233–34
lethal force
  human rights law and use of, 45, 76–77
  military necessity and, 79, 243
  the right to use, 193–94
Liberation Tigers of the Tamil Eelam (LTTE), 42
Libya, 61, 213
  tunnels in, 2, 17–19, 213, 240
Libyan Civil War (2011), 20
Lieblich, Eliav, 194, 220
life, right to, 76–77, 243
lines of communication
  defined, 178
  tunnels as, 178–79

264 Index

liquid explosives, 110–11
London Agreement on Naval Armament, 175
long-term strategy, morphing of underground warfare from a war tactic into a, 52

magnetometers, 97–98
Mali, al-Qaeda in the Islamic Maghreb (AQIM) entrenches in, xi, 19–21, 114, 161
man-made tunnels, 46–47, 52. *See also specific topics*
Manual on International Law Applicable to Air and Missile Warfare. *See* HPCR Manual on International Law Applicable to Air and Missile Warfare
mapping, 231–34. *See also under* anti-tunnel strategy
  defined, 88
  technology used for, 88, 92–104
Mariana and Palau Islands campaign, 8
Martens Clause, 163
Massive Ordnance Air Blast (MOAB), 110, 199
Messines, Battle of, 5–6
metal detectors, 97–98
Mexico–United States border, 87, 89, 96, 112n208
  tunnels under, xv, 24, 95, 99, 104, 108, 119, 120, 126, 128, 166, 217, 253
military advantage(s), 82, 167, 177–81, 207
  assessment and calculation of, 180–81
  choosing between several, 193
  vs. damage to structure and civilians, 190–93, 198, 199, 229, 232, 237, 240, 243. *See also* proportionality
military necessity, 81, 151, 182n111. *See also jus ad bellum*: necessity and
  balance between damage and, 82
  balance between humanitarian concerns and, 188, 190, 230, 246
  human rights law and, 79, 246
  international humanitarian law (IHL) and, 188, 198, 230, 246
  lethal force and, 79, 243
  and measures undertaken during occupation, 82
  proportionality and, 76, 79, 82, 122, 129, 131, 243
  sewage water and, 235
  unnecessary suffering and, 196–205, 198n199. *See also* unnecessary suffering

  and violations of the right to life, 76–77
  voluntary human shields and, 230
  weapons and, 200, 203, 205, 206
military objective(s)
  defined, 177
  by location, 177–79
    defined, 179
  by nature, 177–79
  by purpose, 177–80
  tunnels as, 177–82
  by use, 177–80
Mines in the Battle of Messines (1917), 5–6
mining, tunnel, 25, 42, 50, 124, 125
  civilian infrastructure and, 51
  Gaza and, 25
  historical perspective on, xvii, 4–5, 50, 169
  ISIS and, 33, 34
  man-made tunnels used for, 46, 51
  military objectives and, 169, 176, 177, 179, 184
  nature of, 4
  state-to-state, during World War I, 5–8, 31n183
  in Syria, 2, 5, 32, 46. *See also* Aleppo Earthquake Operation
  used alongside long-term combat tunnels, 50
  used for cross-border smuggling tunnels, 51
monitoring, xx, 47, 89–90, 111–13, 115, 226
  benefits and advantages of, 112–13
  ongoing attacks, 193–94
  post-conflict, by a third party, 85
  tunnel-prone areas, 113, 115
Moon, 71
Morsi, Mohamad, 23, 105–6
MPLA (People's Movement for the Liberation of Awazad), 19, 20
Mubarak, Hosni, 22–23
Mujahedeen in Afghanistan, caves and tunnels used by, 13–15

Napoleon Bonaparte, 59
National Movement for Liberation of Azawad (MNLA), 20
Natonski, Richard F., 171n53
natural caves and tunnels, 47
natural resources and international law, 63–65
necessity, military. *See* military necessity
necessity, plea of. *See* plea of necessity
neutralization of tunnels (functional kill), 237
  vs. destruction/elimination, 105, 237
  methods of, 234

military advantage to be gained from, 178, 180–81
property damage resulting from, 80
Nicaragua v. United States, 83–84, 129, 130
no-mapping approach, 101–4
    measures undertaken in, 102–3
non-international armed conflicts (NIAC), 79, 164–66, 166n27, 219
nonintervention, 122
non-lethal weapons (NLWs), 205–6
    defined, 205
no quarter, 236
North Atlantic Treaty Organization (NATO), 18, 19, 115, 171
North Korean tunnels, xvii, 12–13, 52, 102, 104, 126, 225–26
Nuclear Weapons advisory opinion, 130, 152

occupation
    jus post bellum and the law of, 79–85
    proportionality and the destruction of property during, 82, 83
ocean floor/seabed/seafloor, xx, 63, 65n56, 66–69, 71, 72, 170
offensive use, xvi, xxii, 8–10, 31, 37, 50, 53, 125, 178, 242
Oil Platforms (Islamic Republic of Iran v. United States of America), 129, 146
Oketz Unit, 91
operational complexity, xv, 193, 210, 216, 253. *See also* unknown factor
organizational capital, 40
Outer Space Treaty of 1967, 68–69, 71, 72
Owada, Hisashi, 82

Palestine Liberation Organization (PLO), 156
Paris Convention Relating to the Regulation of Aerial Navigation (1919), 70
peace
    breaches of the, 155
    threats to the, 154–55
    tunnels dug in times of, 45
peremptory norm. *See jus cogens*
perfidy, 172, 175
    defined, 172
    legitimate ruses of war vs. forbidden acts of, 172–75
phosphorus, white, 202–3
Pillar of Defense, Operation, 27

plea of necessity, 147–54, 156, 158–59
poisoning agents, 11, 106–7, 216
Popular Movement for the Liberation of Azawad (MPLA), 19
precautionary duties, 162, 170, 174, 177, 180, 182, 187, 192–95
precautions, 177, 252
    attacks and, 192
    civilian homes and, 181–82
    civilians and, 180, 230, 240, 243, 245n172, 249
    dual use objects and, 180
    Geneva Convention and, 192
    human shields, targeting, and, 230, 249
    international humanitarian law (IHL) and, 187
    reduced ability to take, 193–95
    required under Article 57 of Additional Protocol I, 192–93
preemptive self-defense, 132–33, 135
preparatory acts, 228, 229
prisoner of war (POW) status, 166, 167n27, 227, 245
property, temporary requisition vs. permanent confiscation of, 81
property destruction during occupation, 82, 83
property law, 57–58. *See also* sovereignty over the underground
proportionality, 122, 162, 224, 229, 237, 240, 243
    ad bellum, 129–31
    Additional Protocol I and, 192–94, 232
    Article 53 of GCIV and, 82
    in bello, 131
    circumstantial factors and, 131
    definition and nature of, 190, 191, 247
    destruction of tunnels and, xiv
    dual use objects and, 180
    environmental concerns and, 168, 235
    human rights law and, 76
    human shields and, 229–30
    international humanitarian law (IHL) and, 76, 167, 177, 182, 187
    Israeli Supreme Court's three-pronged test of, 83
    and the meaning of civilian harm, 220
    and measures undertaken during occupation, 82, 83
    necessity and, 76, 79, 82, 122, 129, 131, 243
    non-deadly force and, 205
    and the objective of the use of force, 130

proportionality (*Cont.*)
  retorsion and, 158
  self-defense and, 129–31
  and size and scope of the armed attack, 130–31
  underground and, 192
  violation of right to life and, 76
  weapons and, 198, 199
proportionality assessment, 82, 129, 191, 224. *See also* proportionality calculus
  difficulties in, xiv, 129
  interconnected infrastructure as impeding, xiv
  invisibility of tunnels and, 231
proportionality calculus, 168, 181, 191, 229, 247. *See also* proportionality assessment
proportionality test, 249
proportionate defensive measures, 146. *See also* proportionality
Protective Edge, Operation, 1, 28, 30, 43n33, 91, 94, 115
  cross-border tunnels and, 28, 220
  escalation that began second phase of, 28–29
  goal of, 1
  in historical context, 1–2, 25, 28
  Israeli trauma and fear during, 220
Protocol I. *See* First Additional Protocol to the Conventions of 1977
psychological harm, 220
purpose
  analysis based on, 44, 180, 182, 226, 235
  defined, 179–80
  military objectives by, 177–80

radar, 99–100
rebel moles, 32
Red Cross. *See* International Committee of the Red Cross
reflexive dilemmas, 245, 247
reflexive issues, 246–49
reflexive norms, 245
  defined, 255
reflexive obligations and urban tunnels under IHL, 244–48
reflexive vs. causative concerns, 244, 245
reflexive vs. causative duties, 78n8. *See also* causative obligations
reflexive vs. causative norms, 255
Reisman, Michael, 132–33
religious and cultural sites, xiv, 215, 224, 232
remediation, cement, 108, 237. *See also* cement

remote sensing, 95–96
retorsion, 158
revolving door, 229
riot control agents, use of, 107
robots, 93–95, 233–34, 254
Rome Statute of the International Criminal Court, 166, 197, 219
Rosenzweig, Ido, 33n191, 181n109
ruses of war, 172
  forbidden acts of perfidy vs. legitimate, 172–75
Russo-Japanese War, 5

Saddam Hussein, 33, 47, 53
sample drilling. *See* drilling: random
Schachter, Oscar, 131, 153–54
Schmitt, Michael N., 179–80, 199
sea
  law of the, 71, 72. *See also* United Nations Convention on the Law of the Sea
    compared with law of the underground, 65–69
  sovereignty at, 170
Seabed Arms Control Treaty (Seabed Treaty), 68–69
seabed/seafloor. *See* ocean floor/seabed/seafloor
Second Lebanon War, 26, 42
seismic sensors, 95–96
self-defense
  interceptive, 127, 128, 158. *See also* Dinstein, Yoram
  necessity and, 129–32, 158
  preemptive and anticipatory, 126, 128, 132–35
  underground threats giving rise to a right of, 126–35
  underground threats not giving rise to a right of, 135
    illegal intervention in the affairs of another state, 138–39
    illegal threat or use of force, 139–43
    possible responses to, 143–56
    violation of sovereignty and territorial integrity, 135–38
self-determination, right to, 60–61, 147
sensors, 95–96
severity, 140
  defined, 140
sewage systems, 180, 242, 243

sewage water, 23, 106, 217, 235
Shahi-kot Valley, 17
Shalit, Gilad, 25–26, 124, 223n76
shelters, civilian, 48, 180, 184. *See also under* civilians
  designed for belligerent purposes, 47, 174
Shoval, Shraga, 95nn100–101
similarity, attribution of, 39
Simma, Bruno, 146
Sisi, Abdel Fattah el-, 24
Sloane, Robert, 152
smoke (used to detect and map tunnels), 14, 91–92, 234
smuggling tunnels, 24, 48, 104–8, 124
  economic impact, 139
  Hamas, 22, 23, 27, 50. *See also under* Hamas
  between Iraq and Syria, 35, 211–12
  military objectives and, 177
  tunnel mining and, 51
  as war-sustaining objects, 182–84
smuggling weapons, 169. *See also* smuggling tunnels
South Korea, xvii, 12, 13, 98, 102, 104, 126, 231
sovereignty over the underground
  under domestic law, 56–60
  under international law, 60–65. *See also* international law: underground and
Soviet–Afghan War, xiii, 15, 216, 236. *See also* Mujahedeen in Afghanistan
space law. *See also* Outer Space Treaty of 1967
  vs. air law, 71
  compared with law of the underground, 69–72
Special Tribunal for Lebanon, 221, 222
state/nonstate divide, 125
state responsibility. *See* Draft Articles on the Responsibility of States for Internationally Wrongful Acts
storage, use of tunnels for, 48
strategy, anti-tunnel. *See* anti-tunnel strategy
submarine warfare, 40
  compared with underground warfare, 168, 174–76, 225, 254
  lack of visibility, 225
  legal regulation of, 174–76
subterranean (SbT), xiii–xvi, xx, 33, 37, 195. *See also specific topics*

subterranean cities, 3
subterranean complexes, 3
subterranean tactics, 43, 50, 53, 86, 87, 162, 185, 193, 224
subterranean threats, 75, 86, 130, 133, 185
subterranean warfare, 83, 85–87, 95, 107, 114, 162, 171, 181, 192, 193, 205, 206, 210, 224, 251–53. *See also specific topics*
subway attacks, xxii, 242, 243
subways, 33, 212, 242
suffering. *See* unnecessary suffering
suicide terrorism
  compared with underground warfare, 40–43, 41*t*, 52
  diffusion of, xix, 40, 43
Sun Tzu, 161
superfluous injury, 168, 195–201, 245. *See also* unnecessary suffering
Supreme Court (Israel), 81–83, 248n183
surprise (in warfare), the element of, 224
Syria, 4, 204. *See also* Aleppo Earthquake Operation; ISIS
  civilian use of underground in, 222
  Gaza and, xvii, 2, 30, 32, 38, 39, 43n55
  Innovative use of underground warfare, xx, 30–33
  smuggling tunnels between Iraqi al-Anbar region and, 35
  tunnel mining in, xvii, 2, 5, 32, 46
  tunnels between Iraq and, 211–12
  tunnels in, xix, 33, 43, 50, 211
  widespread and innovative use of, xxii, 30–33, 50
  use of underground for offensive purposes, 30–31
Syrian Civil War, 30, 33, 36, 53, 223. *See also* Aleppo Earthquake Operation
Syrian–Turkish border, 89, 212, 222
  tunnels on, 51, 89, 212, 223

tactics, 52. *See also* anti-tunnel strategy; underground warfare strategy; *specific topics*
  diffusion of, 39, 114–16
  subterranean, 43, 50, 53, 86, 87, 162, 185, 193, 224
  Underground warfare as a tactic, xii, xiii, xix, 1, 2, 5, 7, 8, 32, 38, 52, 53, 168, 172, 206, 248, 253, 254

Tallinn Manual on the International Law
    Applicable to Cyber Warfare (Tallinn
    Manual), 129–30, 133–34, 140, 141, 143–44,
    153, 170, 176, 194
target of tunnel-based attacks, determining the,
    49–50, 126
tear gas, 106, 107, 236
technology, 233
    role of, xii, 85, 86, 88, 92–104, 112, 114–16,
        185, 253–54
    used for detecting and mapping tunnels,
        88, 92–104
terrain, xii, 89, 96, 109, 200. *See also*
    subterranean
    monitoring, 116, 117
territorial integrity
    defined, 135–36
    International Court of Justice (ICJ) and,
        136–38, 139n109, 156
    violation of, and right of self-defense, 135–38
terror among civilians. *See* fear spreading among
    civilian population
terrorism. *See also* Hamas; suicide terrorism;
    specific topics
    compared with underground warfare, 39–43,
        41*t*, 52, 221, 222
    defined, 221–22
    elements of, 221
    in times of peace, 221, 222
thermal imagery, 100–101
thermobaric bombs, 17, 200, 204. *See also* bunker
    busters
thermobaric weapons, 17, 108, 109, 204,
    216, 238–39
Third Tunnel of Aggression, 12–13
threats to the peace, 154–55
Tokyo subway sarin attack, xxii, 242, 243
Tora Bora, 15–17
Toronto and Region Conservation Authority
    (TRCA), 56–57
Toronto tunnel, 45, 55–57, 77
trenches, 4, 5, 21, 186
Tsagourias, Nicholas, 142n127
Tuareg, 19–20
tunnel bombs, 32–34. *See also* mining,
    tunnel
tunnel entrances located inside civilian
    homes, 181–82

tunnelers, 5–7
tunneling (tunnel digging), 55
    direct participation in, 229, 239
    legality, 55, 66–67, 217. *See also* sovereignty
        over the underground
tunnel neutralization courses, 14
tunnel rats, 10, 185, 252
tunnels. *See also* "inheritance" of tunnels; *See also*
    specific topics
    applicable law, 76–85. *See also specific
        areas of law*
    changes in the purposes of, xvii, 180, 241
    defining a tunnel under international
        humanitarian law (IHL), 168–72
    identity of tunnel-diggers and tunnel-users,
        48–49, 125–26
    inheritance of stages in clearing out, 14
    (legality of) the use vs. the digging of, 175
    threshold questions to be answered following
        discovery of, xx
tunnel typology, 37, 40–41, 44, 46–48
    what, 46–48
    when, 45–46
    where, 44–45
    who, 48–49
    against whom, 49–50
    why, 48
tunnel wars, historical perspective on, xiii–xiv
    tunnels as a feature of war from time
        immemorial, 3–5
Turkey. *See* Syrian–Turkish border

uncertainty, 148, 162, 172, 179, 180, 185, 186, 193.
    See also unknown factor
    cyberattacks and, 225
    of mapping, 101
    surrounding legal questions, xx, 55, 57, 77
underground, use of. *See also specific topics*
    intentionally directed at civilians, 210
underground civilian infrastructure, existing,
    53–54, 120, 141, 248
    monitoring, 47, 112. *See also* monitoring
    tunnel mining and, 51
    tunnels dug on the basis of, 17
    and use of tunnels against civilians, 242, 243,
        249
Underground Facilities Analysis Center
    (UFAC), 114

underground threats, strategic factors that affect a state's reaction to. *See also jus ad bellum*: strategic factors affecting
  what, 124
  when, 123
  where, 123–24
  against whom, 126
  by whom, 125–26
  why, 124–25
underground warfare. *See also specific topics*
  aspects of warfare brought to light by, 247–48
  compared with cyberwarfare, xiii, 126, 133–35, 144, 153, 168–71, 176, 190, 194, 225–26. *See also* Tallinn Manual on the International Law Applicable to Cyber Warfare
  compared with submarine warfare, 168, 174–76, 225, 254
  compared with terrorism, 39–43, 41*t*, 52, 221, 222
  defined, 76
  forms of, xvi
  tomorrow's, 50–53
  will become used almost exclusively by nonstate actors, 52
underground warfare strategy (and methods), 85–86. *See also* anti-tunnel strategy
  reasons for, 86–87
United Nations Charter, 139
  Article 2(4), 139–41, 143
  Article 19, 154
  Article 51, 125–27, 131–32, 155, 157
United Nations Convention on the Law of the Sea (UNCLOS), 55, 63, 65–67, 69, 72
  Article 85, 66
United Nations General Assembly, 61, 63, 64, 67, 155
United Nations Security Council, involvement of, 154–56
unknown factor. *See also* uncertainty
  anti-tunnel operations and, 185–86, 195, 237
  civilian presence and, 240, 242
  definition and nature of, xv, 184, 223–24
  explosives and, 238
  impact of, xv–xvi, 185–86, 192, 195, 207, 242
    difficulty assessing enemy capabilities, xv, 162, 172, 185–86

    difficulty assessing the level of the threat, 162
  implications for international humanitarian law (IHL), 186–95, 207
  and legal assessments, 231
  the right to use lethal force, the ability to take precautions, and, 193–94
  urban tunnels and, 223–26, 248–49
unnecessary suffering, 226n84. *See also* superfluous injury
  necessity and, 196–205, 198n199
  prohibition on means and methods causing, 168, 195–97, 199, 245
  terminology, 196, 198
  weapons and, 195, 197, 199–202, 205, 206
urban tunnels, 247
  legality under international humanitarian law (IHL), 218–22
  and reflexive obligations under IHL, 244–48
urban warfare, 53, 225, 248
  contrasted with underground warfare, 217
  the fog of war, the unknown, and, 186
  when underground warfare meets, 24–30, 186, 218, 249
  near civilians, 210–22
U.S. Law of War Manual. *See* Department of Defense Law of War Manual
U.S. War in Afghanistan. *See* War in Afghanistan

Vietcong tunnels, xvii, 216. *See also* tunnel rats
  civilians and combatants in, 9–12, 223
  insights from, 11–12
visit-and-search provision, 175

war
  law(s) of. *See* international humanitarian law (IHL)/law of armed conflict/law(s) of war
  tunnels dug in times of, 45
warfare. *See also specific topics*
  means and methods of, 168–69
War in Afghanistan (2001–present), 15–17
war-sustaining objects
  defined, 182
  tunnels as, 182–84
Watkin, Kenneth, 184

weapons. *See also* thermobaric weapons
    autonomous, 233–34
    military necessity and, 200, 203, 205, 206
    of a nature to cause superfluous injury, 197
    necessity and, 200, 203, 205, 206
    "new," 169
    nuclear, 130, 152
    principles governing the legality of, 195
    and unnecessary suffering, 195, 197, 199–202, 205, 206
weapons review, 169, 199–200, 205, 206
weapons underground, 195–206

Webster, Daniel, 132
white phosphorus, 202–3
World War I (WWI), tunnel mining in, 5–8, 31n183
World War II (WWII), xvi
    and the challenge of entrenched Japanese forces, 8–9
    diversified use of tunnels in, 8

Yadlin, Amos, 194
Yemen and Syria, tunnels between, 211

Zhawar Kili tunnel complex, xi, 16